D1055411

Critical Essays on
ELIZABETH BARRETT BROWNING

CRITICAL ESSAYS
ON
BRITISH LITERATURE

Zack Bowen, General Editor
University of Miami

Critical Essays on

ELIZABETH BARRETT
BROWNING

edited by

SANDRA DONALDSON

G. K. Hall & Co.
New York

G. K. Hall & Co.
1633 Broadway
New York, NY 10019

Library of Congress Cataloging-in-Publication Data

Critical essays on Elizabeth Barrett Browning / edited by Sandra
     Donaldson.
          p.   cm. — (Critical essays on British literature)
     Includes bibliographical references and index.
     ISBN 0-7838-8461-3 (alk. paper)
     1. Browning, Elizabeth Barrett, 1806–1861—Criticism and
interpretation.   2. Women and literature—England—History—19th
century.   I. Donaldson, Sandra.   II. Series.
PR4194.C75   1999
821'.8—dc21   99-18816
                                                                      CIP

This paper meets the requirements of ANSI/NISO Z3948-1992 (Permanence of Paper).

10 9 8 7 6 5 4 3 2 1

Printed in the United States of America

Contents

◆

General Editor's Note

◆

The Critical Essays on British Literature series provides a variety of approaches to both classical and contemporary writers of Britain and Ireland. The formats of the volumes in the series vary with the thematic designs of individual editors, and with the amount and nature of existing reviews and criticism, augmented, where appropriate, by original essays by recognized authorities. It is hoped that each volume will be unique in developing a new overall perspective on its particular subject.

In her introduction, Sandra Donaldson surveys the "mozaic of censure and adulation," as A. McKinley Terhune in 1956 characterized the century's worth of commentary that followed publication of *Sonnets from the Portuguese* and *Aurora Leigh.* Paradoxes have attended the growth of Barrett Browning's reputation as a poet—for example, despite the earlier availability of numerous letters as well as translations of the *Sonnets,* until recently little consideration of the methods and meanings of her poems has been offered. Such paradoxes are examined in a cultural context, both in the introduction and in many of the essays collected here. The introduction itself serves as a full bibliography, and the essays include studies of not only the *Sonnets* and *Aurora Leigh* but also *Casa Guidi Windows, A Drama of Exile,* the ballads, and other writings. We can see, too, that explorations of biographical matters, most notably Barrett Browning's relationship with Robert Browning, also have matured, coinciding with the development of feminist literary criticism.

Donaldson's selection of essays follows three lines of inquiry: the investigation of Barrett Browning's life; critical analyses of a work or works in terms of genre, style and comparison; and interpretations based on contemporary critical theory.

ZACK BOWEN
University of Miami

Publisher's Note

◆

Producing a volume that contains both newly commissioned and reprinted material presents the publisher with the challenge of balancing the desire to achieve stylistic consistency with the need to preserve the integrity of works first published elsewhere. In the Critical Essays series, essays commissioned especially for a particular volume are edited to be consistent with G. K. Hall's house style; reprinted essays appear in the style in which they were first published, with only typographical errors corrected. Consequently, shifts in style from one essay to another are the result of our efforts to be faithful to each text as it was originally published.

Introduction

SANDRA DONALDSON

Elizabeth Barrett Browning's writings are well documented, both privately and publicly. Wealthy families are keen record keepers, and in Barrett Browning's case, she was precociously literary and beloved by her parents and other relatives. As a result, the first volumes of *The Brownings' Correspondence,*[1] containing all available correspondence to and from both husband and wife arranged chronologically, are comprised of materials almost exclusively by her or relating to her. In addition, the editors of these volumes publish early reviews or excerpts, most notably those in journals now rare because of their fragility or ephemerality. Philip Kelley and Betty A. Coley in *The Browning Collections: A Reconstruction*[2] have described and recorded locations of all the Brownings' known manuscripts, books from their library, works of art they owned, portraits of them, and many other items. Barrett Browning's life is a bibliographer's and archivist's dream: she wrote a lot and much of it was saved.

Public notice of Barrett Browning's work began when she was 20 years old with the publication of *An Essay on Mind, with Other Poems* in 1826, which was reviewed briefly that year in *Eclectic Review* and also in *Literary Gazette.* Both reviewers noted her learnedness and suggested that philosophic or ethical poetry was difficult to write; the poems, the *Literary Gazette* said, have faults but they have many good qualities and presage future success.[3] Seven years later, she published *Prometheus Bound, and Miscellaneous Poems,* which also received two reviews. *Gentleman's Magazine* remarked with mock delight that the work is unique because the author is a learned young lady, urging more young ladies to learn Greek because they would then raise the standards of the other sex.[4] The *Athenaeum* was much harsher, warning anyone else against translating Aeschylus, using her version as an example of why not to.[5] Of the years after 1836, only one—1843—does not see any reviews, articles, reprints, or other significant mentions of her or her work. The number of entries in my annotated bibliography of the commentary on her work from 1826 to 1990 totals over 2,500.[6]

Although it is conventional to mention both strengths and weaknesses in reviews and notices of works, the difference between the two sets of reviews of Barrett Browning's first works is noteworthy. As the section on literary historiography and hagiography below shows, Barrett Browning and her work evoked responses that often came from one end or the other of the praise/censure continuum. In *A Room of One's Own,* Virginia Woolf observes about female literary characters that they have been either paragons of virtue or harridans of hate, citing, among others, Antigone and Rosalind at the one end and Clytemnestra and Lady Macbeth at the other, with few in between. Woolf suggests that these extreme portrayals are the result of women being viewed through the lens of passion rather than reason or knowledge.[7]

TWENTIETH-CENTURY SCHOLARSHIP: THE "PRINTING WOMAN" GAINS HER PLACE

The emotional motive for interest in Barrett Browning and her writings has influenced the nature of both the commentary written about her and the work in primary materials, sometimes for good and sometimes for ill. In the twentieth century, the era of scholarly publication, it is her letters that have generated the most activity. The first half of this century, continuing the activity of the nineteenth century, saw numerous printings of small groups of "finds" and those written to a single correspondent;[8] and presently, a multi-volume edition of the Brownings' correspondence edited by Philip Kelley, Ronald Hudson, and Scott Lewis is underway. Robert could not bring himself to destroy her letters as he did many of his own shortly before his death, another reason that up to the date of her death, 1861, the greatest number of letters in the correspondence volumes is by her. Fascination with the story of their courtship and marriage no doubt accounts for much of the continuing focus on her letters and the continuing production of biographies, as does interest in exploring ways to resolve the dilemma of loving both one's work and one's family.

No recent edition of the collected poems exists, however. An edition of the collected poems by Frederic G. Kenyon appeared in 1897; another, in six volumes, was edited and extensively annotated by Charlotte Porter and Helen A. Clarke in 1900; and a single-volume Cambridge edition was introduced by Harriet Waters Preston, also in 1900 (reintroduced by Ruth M. Adams, 1974).[9]

One important sign of Barrett Browning's reputation in some circles during the earlier half of this century, though for what reasons we can't be sure, is in bibliographical studies. Thomas J. Wise, once an admired collector and trusted bibliographer, published *A Bibliography of the Writings in Prose and Verse of Elizabeth Barrett Browning* (1918), which ran to 262 pages, and in 1929 he published *A Browning Library: A Catalogue of Printed Books, Manuscripts and Autograph Letters by Robert Browning and Elizabeth Barrett Browning,* which contained 50 items in a separate section on her work. Ehrsam, Deily, and Smith's *Bibliographies of Twelve Victorian Authors* includes a 20-page section on Barrett Browning. Published in 1936, it appeared shortly after the publication of a volume of letters to Barrett Browning's sister Henrietta (1929), which in turn was followed by Rudolf Besier's enormously popular play, *The Barretts of Wimpole Street* (1930).[10]

In the 1950s, Gardner B. Taplin regarded Barrett Browning as major, titling a piece in *Victorian Newsletter* "A Guide to Research Materials on the Major Victorians (Part II): Elizabeth Barrett Browning." A. McKinley Terhune's 1956 review essay on her[11] was updated by Michael Timko in 1968. Barrett Browning is one of the individual authors who is the subject of an annual review essay about criticism on her work in *Victorian Poetry,* which generally follows the style of Terhune and Timko (Frederic E. Faverty edited the two *Guides*); since 1983, this essay has been written by Dorothy Mermin.[12]

Another curious aspect of the history of interest in Barrett Browning's work has to do with its being the focus of a fascinating project of detective work in the 1930s, now a staple of literary research courses. A spurious edition of *Sonnets from the Portuguese,* said to have been published privately in Reading in 1847, attracted the attention of John Carter and Graham Pollard. They examined physical evidence and sought references to this edition in letters and other comments from the supposed time of printing. None of these investigations could authenticate the date of publication, and their inquiries implicated noted collector and bibliographer Thomas J. Wise in a much broader project of selling similarly forged copies of Victorian writers' works to mainly American purchasers. The story is told in a chapter of Richard Altick's *The Scholar Adventurers,* and the details of their research are in *An Enquiry Into the Nature of Certain Nineteenth Century Pamphlets,* which was reissued with a follow-up in 1983.[13] Barrett Browning's work thus became of importance to people working with primary materials, documenting manuscripts and published editions. A significant outcome was the publication in 1967 of a descriptive bibliography of her work by Warner Barnes.[14]

Modern scholarly work on the major poems began in earnest in 1950 with Fannie Ratchford's variorum edition of *Sonnets from the Portuguese.* In 1977 Julia Markus published a scholarly edition of *Casa Guidi Windows.* A critical edition of *Aurora Leigh* by Margaret Reynolds, a monumental project, was published in 1992, and Reynolds has drawn a paperback Norton Critical Edition from that work.[15] Barrett Browning's writings have now become the subject of numerous critical surveys and full-length studies, with Dorothy Mermin placing her in the main English tradition by viewing her as a precursor for male poets as well as female.[16] Not surprisingly, her work and influence form the centerpiece of studies of women writers and literary traditions.[17]

GONE MISSING: ELIZABETH BARRETT BROWNING
AND LITERARY HISTORIOGRAPHY

In Elizabeth Barrett Browning's case, a reception study and a survey of criticism are quite different enterprises, as Marjorie Stone rightly observes[18]—her writings affected many readers in unrecorded/unrecordable ways, although much has been written about Barrett Browning and her work. Until the 1970s, however, critical discourse about it is relatively rare, with a few notable exceptions. Most significant are Porter and Clarke's introductions to the volumes of their 1900 edition of the complete works, and Alethea Hayter's full-length study in 1962. Biographies abound and opinions flourish, but until recently there has been little critical analysis and interpretation and a small amount of scholarly work.[19]

"A bizarre mosaic of censure and adulation" is what Terhune calls the commentary on Barrett Browning's writings in the review essay cited previously. Two recent analyses of responses to her work look at the first and the second of those types respectively: the last chapter of Stone's full-length study of Barrett Browning's writings, "A Handmaid's Tale: The Critical Heritage," looks at the sources of censure, and Tricia Lootens's chapter in *Lost Saints,* "Canonization through Dispossession: Elizabeth Barrett Browning and the 'Pythian Shriek'," looks at the sources of adulation.[20]

Both Stone and Lootens conclude, as have many others, that in the nineteenth century, interest in Barrett Browning's work was submerged by interest in her life. She was transformed into an appendage of Robert, her husband, and set up as an exemplar of the womanly virtues of submission and support or, worse, as a wraith who haunted him even after death. It has always struck me as odd that people who sought to raise up Robert by devaluing or diminishing Barrett Browning couldn't recognize that by erasing her intellectual achievements they were diminishing Robert as well; in addition to their marital relationship, as poets they found each other intellectually stimulating.

In her analysis of Barrett Browning's erasure from literary history, Stone examines the obituaries first because "they prefigure many of the ideological strategies subsequently deployed to domesticate, diffuse or deny the subversive potential of Barrett Browning's example . . . [and] because the gender debate they reflect is so overt and so marked by internal contradictions and clashing perspectives." She lists several reasons Barrett Browning, like many Victorian poets, dropped from favor by the turn of the century: the early modernist preference for classical qualities excluded her work from consideration because she was "a Romantic writer fired by Promethean aspirations," and the aesthetic movement at the end of last century, too, "led to condemnations of Barrett Browning's politically or ethically engaged poetry."[21] Later critics with different political leanings also devalued her work, as did New Critics on formal grounds. Consistent throughout the rises and falls of critical fashion, however, are essays and reviews reviling her as an encroacher on male prerogative and as a foreordained failure, doomed by her sex. There were, however, a few critics not only in the United Kingdom but in the United States and in other European countries as well who did view her as a major poet, most notably French and Italian writers.[22]

First in her 1989 dissertation and now in *Lost Saints,* Lootens's analysis focuses on the nineteenth century: from the early enthusiastic reception of *Aurora Leigh* as the story of a woman's triumph to the subsequent appropriation and domestication of *Sonnets from the Portuguese* by the end of the century, Barrett Browning may be seen to have been silenced as a poet and canonized as a "secular saint." In both cases she was revered, Lootens observes, like many other literary artists; canonization, however, transformed her from a notable public poet into a "heroine of romance." Unlike Stone, Lootens emphasizes the mixed, complex, and ambiguous nature of the commentary on Barrett Browning's work. In her work on literary canonicity, Lootens charts the change in her own expectations about the reception of Barrett Browning's work: far from finding a clear divide between the hostility of male critics and acceptance by female writers, Lootens finds "profuse expressions of reverence . . . [and] not only strange alliances but deeply conflicted responses, both among and within critics. Sexual politics and gender mattered—but not in ways I could have predicted."[23]

Margaret Reynolds, too, analyzes the extremely different, seemingly opposed responses to Barrett Browning's work. In her critical introduction to *Aurora Leigh,* Reynolds observes:

> As poetry became, especially in the mid- and late-nineteenth-century, an increasingly marginalized cultural activity—dealing more exclusively with emotion, domesticity, and human interaction, and less obviously relevant than the productions of novelists dealing with social problems of industrialization— so poetry increasingly came to resemble the social status of the middle-class ideal of woman—small, pretty, personal, spiritual, and designed for private refreshment. . . . Because women were traditionally the raw material for poetry, when they themselves came to write they were supposed to be capable only of producing autobiography; because women were naturally private, feeling, and irrational, as was poetry itself, their writing of poetry was assumed to be doubly endowed with enthusiasm, artlessness, and self-revelation.

Reynolds argues that, at the same time that commentators undervalued and marginalized the subject matter and forms of many women poets' works, they made an exception for Barrett Browning. In Coventry Patmore's review of *Aurora Leigh,* he scoffs at her choice of a woman poet as the heroine of the poem because there are few such women and therefore they are of little interest. But Reynolds observes that Barrett Browning "worked within a double context: one, legitimate, created out of (male) traditions which informed her development but to which she could not belong," and the other, by women, which theorized about women and work and writing. This doubling is also seen in the argument of the poem, the "double vision" that Aurora says poets must possess. Using Browning's and Barrett Browning's categories of subjective and objective poets, Reynolds points out that she doesn't abandon "the subjective (and more recognizably feminine) inward view" but rather expands "seeing to include the objective faculties of mimesis, drama, and realism which reflected the contemporary scene and its urgent social concerns."[24] The poem both articulates and enacts her philosophy.

Lootens offers a somewhat different answer to the question of how and why serious consideration of Barrett Browning as a poet disappeared from literary history:

> The silence around Barrett Browning—and around other poets—turned out not to be an absence. It had and has a history, a "form". . . . [T]he ambitious, controversial author of *Aurora Leigh* and *Poems before Congress* did not merely fade out of literary historiography; rather, she entered it in the guise of a series of idealized—and standardized—heroines, as the center of a literary legend.
>
> In so doing, Barrett Browning served as an exemplar of female authorship throughout her century and well into our own [her biography a lurid cautionary tale, as Margaret Atwood called it]. . . . For the author of *Aurora Leigh,* that impassioned defense of women's desire to write, no fate could have been more ironic.[25]

Lootens takes Edmund Clarence Stedman as the type for the adulatory critic. His 1873 essay on Barrett Browning in *Scribner's Monthly* was published separately in 1875 and also incorporated as a chapter in his *Victorian Poets,* which was reprinted many times, stayed in print well into the next century, and was imitated and quoted by countless others. He calls her "a christian sibyl, priestess of the melody, heroism, and religion of the modern world." Seeking to overtop himself, he asserts that she "was the daughter that Milton should have had," then later suggests that she is less Shakespeare's daughter than Miranda to his Prospero.[26] For Lootens, he couldn't be a more perfect example of her argument: she cites Christopher Ricks, who cites the *Oxford English Dictionary* as giving the title of Stedman's book as the first instance of "Victorian" used as an adjective; she quotes the beginning of his essay as describing Barrett Browning as a "vanishing monument" ("Nothing is earthly, though all is human"); she lists the metaphors that he invokes to portray Barrett Browning's purity, including comparisons to Mary and Christ. Lootens astutely observes:

> Stedman's timing was crucial, both in terms of the developing institution of literary study and in terms of the institution of marriage. According to Raymond Williams, Terry Eagleton writes, "The only sure fact about the organic society

... is that it is always gone." There is probably another "sure fact": such a society is one in which women know, and are happy in, their places. . . . When "all the laws that governed sexual identity and behavior seemed to be breaking down," a number of anxious late-century critics turned to mid-Victorian England as such a lost society—and, somewhat ironically, to Barrett Browning as its heroine.

By this time Barrett Browning, who had died a decade and a half earlier, had become for Stedman "the apotheosis of womanhood," which she has remained for many people.[27]

Similarly, Stone takes Hugh Walker, the author of *The Literature of the Victorian Era* (1910), which was also often reprinted and cited, as the type of the censuring, censorious critic. Walker places Barrett Browning in the last subsection of the third chapter, "The Minor Poets," citing her as one of "The Poetesses." He calls her rhymes careless and claims that she attempts to be masculine and to imitate her husband's more successful verse. Walker said much the same in his 1897 study *The Age of Tennyson,* claiming that she is "not really a thinker; woman-like, she felt first, and the attempt to translate her feeling into thought was an error." He warned that the ease with which she wrote was "dangerous."[28]

In the first half of the twentieth century, Virginia Woolf was almost alone as a critic in seeing Barrett Browning as separate from her husband. Certainly Woolf is the most famous writer to have commented on *Aurora Leigh.* Woolf's remarks in the *Yale Review* of 1931 are mixed, acknowledging Barrett Browning's faults but describing the delights and deeps of her major work.[29]

Stone adds G. K. Chesterton as an insightful early twentieth-century commentator, citing a section of *The Victorian Age in Literature* (1913) in which it is Barrett Browning who is "by far the most European of all the English poets of that age." Lootens, too, cites Chesterton, but as the inventor of an incident about Barrett Browning deciding to accept Robert's proposal of marriage, calling the decision "possibly the best poem that she ever produced." Echoing Chesterton, Lootens says his invention "may be the most famous single paragraph he ever wrote," calling it ironic that "the overwhelming power of literary legend making" has overshadowed "a number of vivid, specific responses to Barrett Browning's verse" that he, Edmund Gosse, Stedman, and others published. Stone and Lootens agree that such specific responses are far more valuable than hagiography.[30]

By the time the canon of English literature had been established in the middle of this century by the compilers of anthologies and surveyers of the last century's literary scene, Barrett Browning's work was indeed banished to the servant's quarters, as Woolf so pointedly says it. Mentioned as minor poetry, her work was represented in anthologies and surveys, if at all, by one or more of the *Sonnets from the Portuguese* or, oddly, "A Musical Instrument."

Feminist Literary Criticism:
Elizabeth Becomes Barrett Browning

In the early 1970s, many literary critics, writers of poetry and fiction, and common readers found in Barrett Browning a foremother they had long been looking for. To say they discovered her work is not quite accurate because it was certainly available to anyone who knew to look for it, and several had, including besides Woolf and Hayter, Alice Meynell, J. M. S. Tompkins, and Martha Hale Shackford.[31] But there was little other academic writing to counter the image of her that had long been perpetuated in this century, of a sentimental love poet who wrote way too much.

This collection of essays presents some of the best of the work of critics over the past two-and-a-half decades. Once women had been admitted to take degrees at western universities late in the last century in the United States and in the United Kingdom, they learned well the techniques for literary analysis being taught in English departments. And since intellectual curiosity is a hallmark of good students, they and some of their male colleagues sought other materials to work with besides those taught in the received canon. When I was considering doctoral work in the mid-1970s and was looking ahead to writing a dissertation, I thought doubtfully "What on earth else is there to say about Shakespeare?" Somewhat later a member of my advisory committee suggested looking at Barrett Browning's work. This time I had two discouraging thoughts: "What on earth else is there to say about Mrs. Browning?" and "Humph, I'm a feminist; I'm not interested in sappy love poets." There were, however, people whose intellectual curiosity got the better of their politics and who were indeed looking at the writings and her life and finding much there to satisfy that curiosity.

For me as a student, then, it was both heartening and disheartening to learn that there was a great deal yet to be said about Barrett Browning. Why weren't there the frequently updated scholarly tools available for studying her work? Why weren't there the usual intriguing essays in scholarly journals and collections of criticism? The second question has been more quickly addressed than the first, and this volume itself is meant to fill a gap and acknowledge that work on Barrett Browning is now usual.

The explosion of criticism and scholarship on Barrett Browning that occurred with the advent of feminist literary criticism in the last quarter century includes the work of many who were instrumental in shaping that new field of criticism from a wider theoretical perspective: among them are Ellen Moers, Barbara Charlesworth Gelpi, Cora Kaplan, Michèle Barrett, Rachel Blau DuPlessis, and Sandra Gilbert.[32] Moers broke theoretical ground in 1976 with *Literary Women: The Great Writers,* outlining a tradition of various heroinisms and calling *Aurora Leigh* "*the* feminist poem."[33] The Women's Press of London broke access ground by bringing out the first edition of *Aurora Leigh* in more than a half century.

Not surprisingly the first essays of this period appeared, for the most part, in such nontraditional or ephemeral publications as *Mary Wollstonecraft Newsletter* and *Ideology and Consciousness*. A feminist reassessment of Barrett Browning's life and work for adolescent readers was published by the fledgling Feminist Press in 1972; its author, Mary Jane Lupton, had previously published a brief analysis of *Aurora Leigh* and its reception in *Women: A Journal of Liberation* (1970).[34] The Feminist Press recently celebrated its 25th anniversary, and the essays in *Mary Wollstonecraft Newsletter* have been collected in a volume published by a mainstream publishing house, Holmes and Meier (1981).

We like to tell stories about progress, how something early was simpler and later became more complex and revealing. But Lupton's work and the Marxist-Feminist Literature Collective's early essay on the Brontës and Barrett Browning charted areas that are still being explored. The Collective, whose members included Kaplan and Michèle Barrett, explores the determining force of economics and ideology in the construction of woman and examines the radical nature of Aurora as a desiring subject, linking gender and genre. Lupton's survey of the reception of Barrett Browning's writings in terms of her gender points readers toward aesthetic and intellectual questions in *Aurora Leigh* and calls for a revaluation of her political poetry and classical scholarship.[35]

Although some attention previously had been given to relating Barrett Browning's *Sonnets from the Portuguese* to the Petrarchan sonnet tradition, Susan Zimmerman in *Mary Wollstonecraft Newsletter* (1973) examines the sonnets with regard to the woman's role in the tradition, calling them epithalamia more in the tradition of *Song of Songs* than of Petrarch's sonnets. Though not explicitly feminist, Arline Golden's analysis of the sonnets in *Genre* in 1974 concludes that Barrett Browning modernized the amatory sonnet sequence by giving it a more psychological turn.[36]

The Case of *Aurora Leigh*

Fittingly, you won't find a miniaturized edition of *Aurora Leigh,* its cover all vines and scrollwork, displayed beside a cash register in a bookstore the way you will editions of *Sonnets from the Portuguese.* That does not mean, however, that there are not numerous and passionate readers of Barrett Browning's verse novel, a new generation that has brought this poem back from its long exile from the canon.

The questions about Barrett Browning and her work that tease critics are somewhat different from those about Robert. The previously unacceptable idea that various readers might see quite different meanings in a literary work was paradoxically considered to be incompatible with the concepts of irony and ambiguity, which were taken as the primary evidence of the intellectual suppleness of an author. "Quite bad," Harold Bloom pronounced *Sonnets from the Portuguese* in Oxford University Press's *Victorian Prose and Poetry*—and *Aurora Leigh* was "very bad," meaning that Bloom didn't much like the poems.[37] There is indeed irony and ambiguity, in, to take just two examples, "Lord Walter's Wife" and sonnet one of *Sonnets from the Portuguese*. Dislike, embarrassment, or limited perceptions and experience,[38] however, continue to blind some critics who overtly insist that the personal not be a part of the critical while, again paradoxically, using that standard to measure and condemn.

The story of a woman writer's quest to reconcile work and love fit exactly the interests of readers, once freedom movements spread throughout the West, starting in the mid-1960s. At first, the poem satisfied readers' need for a story that reflected lives they experienced or knew, but it quickly became the subject of a group of younger scholars exploring new modes of literary analysis, mainly from a feminist perspective. Most notably, psychoanalytic theory informs Barbara Charlesworth Gelpi's 1981 essay on sea imagery in *Aurora Leigh,* Virginia Steinmetz's 1981 study of patriarchal imagery and 1983 study of maternal imagery, and Dolores Rosenblum's 1983 essay on the development of self and language.[39] Increasingly, readings employ theories of deconstruction, discourse analysis, representation—Cixous, Bakhtin, and Foucault are regularly invoked.

I return to Reynolds's critical analysis, which ends with these observations about *Aurora Leigh* as a woman's book:

> [I]ts subjects and their treatment, its narrative and poetic form, are all dictated by that fact. Too frequently, however, that fact has been read not in relation to the historical context and cultural assumptions which produced the verse-novel but in the light of other, unexamined, ideological assumptions about what constitutes a woman's book. In these repeated, but diverse, erroneous readings lies the reason for the variety of critical reaction to *Aurora Leigh*. . . .
>
> *Aurora Leigh* has never been admitted to the canon of literature; women's texts are only permitted to appear there provided they are not read as women's texts. When *Aurora Leigh* can be included in the canon, recognized as of human and therefore generally significant interest *because* of its overriding address to the theoretical (and practical) questions of the cultural and literary formation, exclusion, and prohibition of women in writing, then its significance as a primary text of the nineteenth century might be acknowledged.[40]

As this collection of essays shows, scholarly work on Barrett Browning generally falls into one of three categories: re-viewing—as feminist critics use this term, "seeing again"—the story of Barrett Browning's life, her youth in Herefordshire and the years in London as well as her courtship and marriage with Robert and life in Italy, sometimes relating it to her literary works; analyzing one or more works in terms of genre or style (such as sonnet form, poetic diction, or the novel), other authors (especially Wordsworth and Milton, and also the Bible), or literary concepts (romanticism, especially sublimity) from the earlier canon; and interpreting her works using various theories (about alterity, by Bakhtin or Cixous, of readers' responses). In many cases, these authors explore what is new and liberatory about reading Barrett Browning's writing, both intellectually and spiritually.

Notes

1. Philip Kelley, Ronald Hudson, and Scott Lewis, eds., *The Brownings' Correspondence,* 14 vols. to date (Winfield, Kans.: Wedgestone Press, 1984–).

2. Philip Kelley and Betty A. Coley, *The Browning Collections: A Reconstruction with Other Memorabilia* (Waco, Tex.: Armstrong Browning Library, 1984).

3. *Eclectic Review,* July 1826, 78–82; *Literary Gazette,* July 15, 1826, 436 (both are excerpted in *The Brownings' Correspondence* 2: 122). The latter reviewer recommended that the author, a female, "address herself more to nature, and undress herself from the deep *blue* in which she is now attired," a reference to the low esteem in which women intellectuals—Bluestockings—were held; otherwise, the review is moderate and admiring.

4. *Gentleman's Magazine,* June 1833, 610–11.

5. *Athenaeum,* June 8, 1833, 362 (reprinted in *The Brownings' Correspondence* 3: 338).

6. Sandra Donaldson, *Elizabeth Barrett Browning: An Annotated Bibliography of the Commentary and Criticism, 1826–1990* (New York: G. K. Hall, 1993).

7. Virginia Woolf, *A Room of One's Own* (1929; reprint, New York: Harcourt Brace, 1957), 44–45, 86–87.

8. A widely read volume was *Letters of Robert Browning to Miss Isa Blagden,* collected and introduced by A. Joseph Armstrong (Waco, Tex.: Baylor University Press, 1923). These letters were reedited and supplemented by Edward McAleer, "New Letters from Mrs. Browning to Isa Blagden," *PMLA* 66 (1951): 594–612, and also *Dearest Isa: Robert Browning's Letters to Isabella Blagden* (Austin: University of Texas Press, 1951). Leonard Huxley's edition of the letters to Barrett Browning's sister Henrietta appeared in 1929 (London: John Murray). In 1954, Betty Miller edited *Elizabeth Barrett to Miss Mitford* (New Haven: Yale University Press); these letters were reedited and annotated by Meredith Raymond and Mary Rose Sullivan in *Letters of Elizabeth Barrett Browning to Mary Russell Mitford* (Waco, Tex.: Armstrong Browning Library, 1983). The first edition of her letters was a two-volume selection by Frederic G. Kenyon (London: Smith, Elder, 1897).

The love letters, first published by the Brownings' son, Pen, in 1899, were published in a scholarly edition in 1969 by Elvan Kintner (Cambridge: Harvard University Press). Daniel Karlin edited a selection titled *Robert Browning and Elizabeth Barrett: The Courtship Correspondence* (New York: Oxford University Press, 1989) to complement his study of them, *The Courtship of Robert Browning and Elizabeth Barrett* (Oxford: Clarendon Press, 1985).

9. Frederic G. Kenyon, ed., *The Poetical Works of Elizabeth Barrett Browning* (London: Smith, Elder, 1897); Charlotte Porter and Helen A. Clarke, eds., *The Complete Works of Elizabeth Barrett Browning,* 6 vols. (New York: Thomas Y. Crowell, 1900); Harriet Waters Preston, ed., *The Complete Poetical Works of Mrs. Browning* (Boston: Houghton, Mifflin, 1900; reprinted in 1974 as *The Poetical Works of Elizabeth Barrett Browning*). See Tricia Lootens's evaluation of the Preston/Adams volume's dismissive introductions in *Lost Saints: Silence, Gender, and Victorian Literary Canonization* (Charlottesville: University Press of Virginia, 1996), 157.

The Oxford Complete Editions are not introduced and appear to be reprints of Kenyon; the first appeared in 1904.

Selections from the poems appear more frequently, most recently a volume selected and introduced by Margaret Forster, 1988 (reintroduced by Colin Graham, 1996), and one by Meredith Raymond and Mary Rose Sullivan in 1993. Beginning in 1978, the first reprinted edition of *Aurora Leigh* (London: Women's Press) in over 50 years was introduced by Cora Kaplan (reprinted here); other editions have been edited or introduced by Gardner B. Taplin (Chicago: Academy Press, 1979), Kerry McSweeney (Oxford: Oxford University Press, 1993), and John Bolton and Julia Bolton Holloway (Harmondsworth: Penguin, 1995).

10.   Thomas J. Wise, *A Bibliography of the Writings in Prose and Verse of Elizabeth Barrett Browning* (London: Richard Clay, 1918); *A Browning Library: A Catalogue of Printed Books, Manuscripts and Autograph Letters by Robert Browning and Elizabeth Barrett Browning* (London: privately printed, 1929).

The bibliography in Theodore G. Ehrsam, Robert H. Deily, and Robert M. Smith, *Bibliographies of Twelve Victorian Authors* (New York: H. W. Wilson, 1936), 47–66, is not annotated but begins with the first reviews and notably does not include items primarily concerned with Robert. The other authors are Arnold, Clough, FitzGerald, Hardy, Kipling, Morris, Christina Rossetti, Dante Gabriel Rossetti, Stevenson, Swinburne, and Tennyson. Joseph Fucilla added 13 items to the list on Barrett Browning in *Modern Philology*, 1939.

Perhaps, too, the letters and then the play were the impetus for Jeannette Marks's thorough study, *The Family of the Barrett: A Colonial Romance* (New York: Macmillan, 1938).

11.   Alfred McKinley Terhune, *The Victorian Poets: A Guide to Research* (Cambridge: Harvard University Press, 1956), 84–92 (the quotation is on p. 90). The *Guide's* separate sections are on Tennyson, Robert Browning, Arnold, Swinburne, and Hopkins. Three group sections are on Barrett Browning, Edward FitzGerald, and Arthur Hugh Clough cited together; the Pre-Raphaelites; and the Later Poets. Interestingly, Terhune is a biographer of FitzGerald, famous for the remark at Barrett Browning's death, "No more 'Aurora Leighs,' thank God!" Likewise, the compiler of the citations on Barrett Browning in George Watson, ed., *New Cambridge Bibliography of English Literature,* vol. 3, *1800–1900* (1969) is Robert Pearsall, one of the composers of the bibliography on Robert (1953), rather than a Barrett Browning specialist. (The *CBEL* is currently being revised and will include Barrett Browning more prominently.)

12.   Gardner B. Taplin, "A Guide to Research Materials on the Major Victorians (Part II): Elizabeth Barrett Browning," *Victorian Newsletter* 13 (Spring 1959): 20–21; Michael Timko, "Elizabeth Barrett Browning," in *The Victorian Poets: A Guide to Research,* 2nd ed., ed. Frederic E. Faverty (Cambridge: Harvard University Press, 1968), 121–36.

13.   Richard D. Altick, "The Case of the Curious Bibliographers," *The Scholar Adventurers* (1950; reprinted, Columbus: Ohio State University Press, 1987), 37–64; John Carter and Graham Pollard, *An Enquiry Into the Nature of Certain Nineteenth Century Pamphlets* (London: Constable, 1934).

See subsequent work by Wilfred Partington, "A Revised Story About Mrs. Browning's Love Sonnets" and "The Exposure and Some Surprising Sequels," in *Forging Ahead: The True Story of the Upward Progress of Thomas James Wise* (New York: G. P. Putnam's, 1939), 246–68; and Nicolas Barker and John Collins's sequel, subtitled *The Forgeries of H. Buxton Forman and T. J. Wise Re-Examined* (London: Scolar Press, 1983), which accompanied a reissue of Carter and Pollard's *Enquiry.*

14.   Warner Barnes, *A Bibliography of Elizabeth Barrett Browning* (Austin: Humanities Research Center, University of Texas, 1967).

15.   Fannie Ratchford, ed., *Sonnets from the Portuguese, By Elizabeth Barrett Browning: Centennial Variorum Edition* (New York: Duschnes, 1950), and Julia Markus, ed., *Casa Guidi Windows* (New York: Browning Institute, 1977). Margaret Reynolds, ed., *Aurora Leigh* (Athens: Ohio University Press, 1992), and *Aurora Leigh,* Norton Critical Edition (New York: Norton, 1995).

16.   Gardner B. Taplin's biography of Barrett Browning contains some critical commentary (New Haven: Yale University Press, 1957), and in 1962 Alethea Hayter published a study of her poetry subtitled *A Poet's Work and Its Setting* (London: Faber and Faber), a chapter

of which is reprinted here. A volume in the Twayne English Authors series was written by Virginia L. Radley (1972). See also Kaplan's comprehensive introduction to the reissue of *Aurora Leigh.*

     In the 1980s and 1990s several full-length studies appeared: one by Angela Leighton (Bloomington: Indiana University Press, 1986); one by Helen Cooper (Chapel Hill: University of North Carolina Press, 1988); by Dorothy Mermin, subtitled *The Origins of a New Poetry* (Chicago: University of Chicago Press, 1989); and by Marjorie Stone, *Elizabeth Barrett Browning* (New York: St. Martin's Press, 1995).

     17. For example, Ellen Moers, *Literary Women: The Great Writers* (1976; New York: Oxford University Press, 1985); Sandra M. Gilbert and Susan Gubar, *Madwoman in the Attic: The Woman Writer and the Nineteenth-Century Literary Imagination* (New Haven: Yale University Press, 1979); Deirdre David, *Intellectual Women and Victorian Patriarchy* (Ithaca: Cornell University Press, 1987); Angela Leighton, *Victorian Women Poets: Writing Against the Heart* (Charlottesville: University Press of Virginia, 1992).

     18. Stone opens her study by noting that the reception history of Barrett Browning's works inevitably excludes "the transformations Barrett Browning's works produced in the minds and lives of those who did not write because they were immersed in action, or who spoke and wrote privately but were not heard or recorded." It is here, however, that "the seeds of historical change and the sites of historical struggle" are found (*Elizabeth Barrett Browning,* 189).

     19. Since Porter and Clarke's edition of nearly a century ago, several additional poems have been published and work has been done on attribution and authentication. See Frederic G. Kenyon, ed., *New Poems by Robert Browning and Elizabeth Barrett Browning* (London: Smith, Elder, 1914); H. Buxton Forman, ed., *Hitherto Unpublished Poems and Stories,* 2 vols. (Boston: Bibliophile Society, 1914); and Phillip D. Sharp's master's thesis, "Elizabeth Barrett Browning and The Wimpole Street Notebook" (Baylor University, 1981). See also Ratchford and Markus cited previously.

     20. Stone, *Elizabeth Barrett Browning,* 189–228. Lootens's book is an extension of her dissertation, "Elizabeth Barrett Browning: The Poet as Heroine of Literary History" (Indiana University, 1988). In *Lost Saints,* Lootens says about her own work: "[W]hat began as a reception study was transformed into a study of the formation of a literary legend. Now, that study has led further, into the investigation of nineteenth-century literary canonicity itself" (p. 3).

     21. Stone, *Elizabeth Barrett Browning,* 197, 194.

     22. For example, Germaine-Marie Merlette, *La vie et l'oeuvre d'Elizabeth Barrett Browning* (Paris: Librairie Armand Colin, 1905); Fernand Henry, introduction and notes to *Les Sonnets Portugais d'Elizabeth Barrett Browning* (Paris: E. Guilmoto, 1905); Fanny Zampini-Salazar, *La vita e le opere di Roberto Browning ed Elisabetta Barrett-Browning* (Turin: Societa Tipografico-editrice Nazionale, 1907); W. Nicati, *Femme et poete, Elizabeth Browning* (Paris: Perrin, 1912); Joseph Aynard, "Elizabeth Barrett Browning et le feminisme anglais," *Journal des debats,* 20 May 1913, p. 1.

     23. Lootens, *Lost Saints,* 141, 2.

     24. Reynolds, *Aurora Leigh,* 2–3, 5, 24.

     25. Lootens, *Lost Saints,* 2–3.

     26. Edmund Clarence Stedman, "Elizabeth Barrett Browning," *Scribner's Monthly Magazine* 7, no. 1 (November 1873): 101–14 (quotations are on pp. 102 and 113).

     27. Lootens, *Lost Saints,* 136–38.

     28. Stone, *Elizabeth Barrett Browning,* 209. Hugh Walker, *The Age of Tennyson* (London: George Bell, 1897), 234–36; the 1910 volume is an expanded revision of this volume.

     29. Virginia Woolf, "Aurora Leigh," *Yale Review* 20, no. 4 (June 1931): 677–90; reprinted in *Second Common Reader* (New York: Harcourt, Brace, 1932), 218–31.

     30. Stone, *Elizabeth Barrett Browning,* 212; Lootens, *Lost Saints,* 152.

     31. Alice Meynell wrote several introductions to editions of Barrett Browning's poems, in 1896, 1903, 1909, and 1916; J. M. S. Tompkins's *Aurora Leigh* was a Fawcett Lecture

(London: Bedford College, 1962); and Martha Hale Shackford's *E. B. Browning; R. H. Horne, Two Studies* was also originally a lecture (Wellesley: Wellesley Press, 1935).

32. Moers, *Literary Women;* Barbara Charlesworth Gelpi, *"Aurora Leigh:* The Vocation of the Woman Poet," *Victorian Poetry* 19, no. 1 (1981): 35–48; Rachel Blau DuPlessis, *Writing Beyond the Ending: Narrative Strategies of Twentieth-Century Women Writers* (Bloomington: Indiana University Press, 1985); Sandra M. Gilbert, "From *Patria* to *Matria:* Elizabeth Barrett Browning's Risorgimento," *PMLA* 99, no. 2 (1984): 194–211.

33. Moers, *Literary Women,* 40–41. Like Woolf, Moers also characterizes Barrett Browning as somewhat odd, saying about *Aurora Leigh* that it "appealed mainly to eccentric lady writers, like Emily Dickinson." In the context of celebrating such inventiveness and out-siderness, both Woolf and Moers are in fact changing the polarity of the negativity of their comments into a positive.

34. Mary Jane Lupton, *Elizabeth Barrett Browning* (Long Island: Feminist Press, 1972) (chapter 2 is reprinted here); Lupton, "The Printing Woman Who Lost Her Place: Elizabeth Barrett Browning," *Women: A Journal of Liberation* 2, no. 1 (1970): 2–5.

35. Marxist-Feminist Literature Collective, "Women's Writing: *Jane Eyre, Shirley, Villette, Aurora Leigh,*" *Ideology and Consciousness* 1, no. 3 (1978): 27–48 (reprinted in part here).
    For surveys of criticism, see Kay Moser, "The Victorian Critics' Dilemma: What to Do With a Talented Poetess?" *Victorians Institute Journal* 13 (1985): 59–66; Bina Freiwald, " 'The praise which men give women': Elizabeth Barrett Browning's *Aurora Leigh* and the Critics," *Dalhousie Review* 66 (1986): 311–36. See also Gardner B. Taplin, "Elizabeth Barrett Browning Scholarship: The Last Twelve Years," *Studies in Browning and His Circle* 7, no. 2 (1979): 34–54; and Deborah Byrd, "Recent Books on Elizabeth Barrett Browning," *Browning Institute Studies* 17 (1989): 115–27. For a survey of late nineteenth-century commentary, see Martha Foote Crow, "The Varying Fame of Mrs. Browning," *Methodist Review* (New York) 93 (January 1911): 82–100.

36. Susan Zimmerman, *"Sonnets from the Portuguese:* A Negative and a Positive Context," *Mary Wollstonecraft Newsletter* 2, no. 1 (1973): 7–20; reprinted in Janet Todd, ed., *Be Good Sweet Maid: An Anthology of Women and Literature* (New York: Holmes & Meier, 1981), 69–81. Arline Golden, "Victorian Renascence: The Revival of the Amatory Sonnet Sequence, 1850–1900," *Genre* 8 (1974): 133–47.

37. Lionel Trilling and Harold Bloom, eds., *The Oxford Anthology of English Literature,* vol. 2, *Victorian Prose and Poetry* (New York: Oxford University Press, 1973), 1475.

38. Dorothy Mermin titles one of her essays, "The Female Poet and the Embarrassed Reader: Elizabeth Barrett Browning's *Sonnets from the Portuguese,*" *ELH* 48 (1981): 351–67.

39. Gelpi, *"Aurora Leigh";* Virginia Steinmetz, "Beyond the Sun: Patriarchal Images in *Aurora Leigh,*" *Studies in Browning and His Circle* 9, no. 2 (1981): 18–41, and "Images of 'Mother-Want' in Elizabeth Barrett Browning's *Aurora Leigh,*" *Victorian Poetry* 21, no. 4 (1983): 351–67; Dolores Rosenblum, "Face to Face: Elizabeth Barrett Browning's *Aurora Leigh* and Nineteenth-Century Poetry," *Victorian Studies* 26, no. 3 (1983): 321–38.

40. Reynolds, *Aurora Leigh,* 53–54.

Experiments in Poetic Technique

Alethea Hayter

"I wonder to myself, in a climax of dissatisfaction, how I came to publish it," Mrs. Browning said of one of her earlier poems. If she herself wondered how she came to publish some of her past work, her readers must have the same wonder to a far greater degree, though not necessarily about the same poems. Any honest critique of her work must admit that she often wrote very bad poetry indeed—verses so flaccid, so clumsy, so sentimental, so banal, that it is astonishing that any poet of standing could have published such nonsense—and gone on publishing it; though she cut nine of the worst of her 1838 poems out of her first collected edition in 1850, she went on republishing others just as bad—"A Song against Singing," "To Bettine," "The Weakest Thing." It was not for want of re-examining and revising her work before and after publication. She did that constantly and in detail. She wrote her poetry on small slips of paper; she made a great many alterations when she transcribed it for the printer; and she filled all the margins of the proofs with further revisions. At each reprinting of her poems she revised them again, cutting out archaisms, tidying up rhymes, correcting metrical solecisms, but above all trying to heighten the effect for which she had originally aimed—sweetening the music, intensifying the colour, clearing the meaning. Unintended internal rhymes came out; ugly consonantal clashes were blunted; catarrhal sequences of M's and N's were softened into vowels. Sound and sense were more closely matched, ambiguities were clarified by moving commas or by inserting brackets, descriptions became less abstract and more specific, but the feverish search for exactly the right word, at any expense of oddness, which characterized her earlier style, changed to a less idiosyncratic and sometimes less vivid smoothness. Not only her revisions of her own poems, but the comments which she made on the MSS on which Browning and Horne sought her advice, showed what she aimed at most by such revisions: free flow of metre, perfectly fitting words, rightly placed emphases, the sinewy movement of natural speech. "Oh you inverter," she called Browning, pleading for "Natural sequency of words"; she found some of his catalectic

Reprinted from Alethea Hayter, *Mrs. Browning: A Poet's Work and Its Setting* (London: Faber & Faber, 1962), 37–57. Used by permission of the author.

lines "dragging," "clogged" or "willowy"; she urged him to use onomatopoeic effects—"make the water warble softly," "throw a wail into the line."[1]

Sometimes she would accept herself the suggestions about her metre, her diction and even her punctuation which her correspondents and her reviewers lavished on her. She conceded to Wordsworth that the construction of her sonnet to him was obscure; when Lockhart and Leigh Hunt criticized her use of the diaeresis to show that words like "callèd" were to be pronounced as two syllables, she abandoned the practice; when the *Quarterly* and *Blackwood* were ponderously ironical about the descriptions of the railway-lines across Lady Geraldine's property—

> the resonant steam-eagles
> Follow far on the directing of her floating dove-like hand

Mrs. Browning turned the resonant steam-eagles into "palpitating engines" and suppressed the floating dove-like hand altogether. But when Ruskin implored her to change the "Gehenna/and when a" rhyme in the first line of *A Drama of Exile* she rightly took no notice; those neighing amphibrachs were an entirely intentional effect and she would not change it.[2]

Her oddities of diction and rhyme were unquestionably deliberate. Some of her biographers have suggested in her excuse that her ear was not attuned to the rhythms and implications of ordinary speech; that her life had been so secluded that she did not realize which words were bookish and obsolete and which were current; that she had heard so few people speak that she did not know the ordinary pronunciation of words, and thought "patriotism" was pronounced with five syllables and "Berenice" with only three, that "Niagara" rhymed with "buy a car a," and "Goethe" with "duty."[3] Lady Ritchie says that Mrs. Browning "lisped her Rs," which I take to mean that she either addressed her husband as Wobert or used the French R. She probably dropped the final "g" of the present participle, as most of her upper-class contemporaries did; she certainly rhymed "Syon" with "dying," as Shelley rhymed "ruin" with "pursuing." And as if all these alleged peculiarities in her own speech were not enough, there is Miss Mitford's delightful conjecture that it was her cousin Kenyon's way of speaking, when he read Elizabeth Barrett Browning's own poetry aloud to her, that caused her not to notice the imperfections of her style.

John Kenyon, a distant connection of the Barretts and descended like them from a family of Jamaican planters, was a valued friend and critic of both the Brownings, as he was of many other nineteenth-century writers. Rich, philanthropic, a negligible poet himself but a generous and well-judging friend of other poets, he first told Robert Browning and Elizabeth Barrett about each other, and remained their friend and benefactor till his death. Here is Miss Mitford's lively picture of Kenyon reading Mrs. Browning's own poems to her. "Our dear friend, you are aware, never sees anybody but the members of her own family, and one or two others. She has a high opinion of the skill in *reading,* as well as the fine taste, of Mr. Kenyon, and she gets him to read her new poems aloud to her, and so tries them upon him (as well as herself). . . . So Mr. Kenyon stands upon the hearth-rug, and uplifts the MS, and his voice, while our dear friend lies folded up in Indian shawls upon her sofa, with her long black tresses streaming over her bent-down head, all attention. Now, dear Mr. Kenyon has lost a front tooth—not quite a front one but a side front one—and this, you see, causes a defective utterance . . . an amiable indistinctness, a vague softening of syllables into each other," which, thought Miss Mitford, blurred all the poetess's peculiarities of diction.

Mrs. Browning would not have accepted any of these defences for her poetry, had she admitted that a defence was needed. "The cultivated man or woman, however cut off from society and the acquisition through society of colloquial elegance, does not become *provincial* in the loss of it," she wrote to Miss Mitford, wondering how the Americans came by their "corruptions of speech."

There is no escape from the conclusion that Mrs. Browning, a laborious and thoughtful reviser of her work, published what we consider her mistakes and bad poems, not through carelessness but because she liked them like that. She always said so herself. "Can *you* call me careless? Remember all the altering of manuscript and proof," she wrote reproachfully to Kenyon. "That the books . . . are remarkable for defects and superfluities of evil, I can see quite as well as another; but then I won't admit that it comes of my careless- ness, and refusing to take pains. On the contrary, my belief is, that very few writers called 'correct' who have selected classical models to work from, pay more laborious attention than I do habitually to the forms of thought and expression. . . . If I write fast sometimes (and the historical fact is that what has been written fastest, has pleased most) I am not apt to print without con- sideration."

The chief charges brought against Mrs. Browning's technique are those of perverse and affected obscurity (her great crime in the eyes of her contem- porary critics) and careless cacophony in rhyming. The twentieth century has removed obscurity from the statute-book of poetical crime, but Mrs. Brown- ing is still held guilty of carelessness. She admitted to obscurity, though not to affectation as its cause; she always denied carelessness.

Several of the reviewers of her 1838 poems accused her of affectation and studying attitudes. Speaking of this to Miss Mitford, she showed gratitude for the praise she had otherwise received, and respect for the sincerity of her reviewers, but owned that "certainly it is not pleasant to be called 'affected' . . . or even to be charged with *attitudinising.* . . . *Indeed* I am not '*perverse*' as dear Mr. Kenyon calls it. I can understand what *he* means in his charge of unintelligibility, and often try tho' so often in vain, not to deserve it. But I do not understand how anyone who writes from the real natural impulse of feel- ing and thought,—and if I know myself, I *do*—can write affectedly, even in the manner of it. As to attitudes I never did study them. I never did take any thought as to forming a style—which formed itself by force of writing, and which (without perverseness) it will be a hard thing to form anew. . . . If I live I hope and believe that I shall write better—not more from natural impulse—I cannot do that—*I deny that charge of affectation*—but better."

There is a strangely faithful echo of this letter in another, written forty years later by another and very different poet, but one who was also accused of being perverse and unintelligible. "Obscurity I do and will try to avoid so far as is consistent with excellences higher than clearness at a first reading," wrote Gerard Manley Hopkins to Bridges in 1878. "As for affectation I do not believe I am guilty of it: you should point out instances, but as long as mere novelty and boldness strikes you as affectation your criticism strikes me as—as water of the Lower Isis."[4]

There was nothing assumed or deliberate about the obscurity of her poetry, Mrs. Browning insisted. Miss Mitford was implored not to believe Mr. Kenyon "when he says that I am *perversely* obscure. Unfortunately obscure, not perversely—that is quite a wrong word. . . . Because, *indeed,* I am not in the very least degree perverse in this fault of mine, which is my destiny rather than my choice, and comes upon me, I think, just where I would eschew it most. So little has perversity to do with its occurrence, that my fear of it makes me sometimes feel quite nervous and thought-tied in composition."

So she wrote in 1838. Seventeen years later she was still apologizing for the same thing. Ruskin had said he once thought her poems sickly, and with her usual candour she answered that no doubt her poems, like herself, had often been sickly, and that she had been called harder names than that—" 'affected,' for instance, a charge I have never deserved, for I do think, if I may say it of myself, that the desire of speaking or *spluttering* the real truth out broadly, may be a cause of a good deal of what is called in me careless and awkward expression. My friends took some trouble with me at one time; but though I am not self-willed naturally . . . I never could adopt the counsel urged upon me to keep in sight always the stupidest person of my acquaintance in order to clear and judicious forms of composition. . . . To say a thing faintly, because saying it strongly sounds odd or obscure or unattractive for some reason, to 'careless readers,' does appear to me bad policy as well as bad art." Like Hopkins in his letter to Bridges, she maintained that the reader as well as the writer must be expected to take some trouble.

"Thought-tied"—"spluttering the real truth out"; she often used these images to suggest the struggle, as with some physical impediment of speech, she went through in order to make her meaning clear.

> With stammering lips and insufficient sound
> I strive and struggle to deliver right
> That music of my nature.

In her own mind she heard clearly the meaning and the music, so clearly that it was essential to communicate it exactly, if she could only find words which perfectly corresponded with that meaning. Very early in her exchange of letters with Browning, they began to analyse the poetic process for each other, each knowing that the other could understand in a way that no layman could; and this question of meaning and expression was the first aspect of it that they touched. "What no mere critic sees, but what you, an artist, know," she wrote to him, "is the difference between the thing desired and the thing attained, between the idea in the writer's mind and the εἴδωλον cast off in his work. . . . The great chasm between the thing I say, and the thing I would say, would be quite dispiriting to me, in spite even of such kindnesses as yours, if the desire did not master the despondency. . . . I do not *say everything I think* (as has been said of me by master-critics) but *I take every means to say what I think.*"

The 'master critic' was Forster who had told her in 1844 that "she uses *all* her thoughts and feelings for whatever she does. The art of knowing what to keep and what to leave out she has not attained."[5] But her defence was a sound one. "I do not say everything I think . . . but I take every means to say what I think." She was a most laborious experimenter. Against every charge that she wrote carelessly, she maintained that she was a hard worker, scrupulous, meticulous, a professional and not an amateur. She told Browning that Kenyon had said she ought to write her poems twelve times over, but that it was the criticism of someone who did not really understand the creative process, in the way that she and Browning did. Laborious work may be done in the poet's head, before a line is written down; quickness in writing and insincerity do not necessarily go together; the creative process works at different rates on different days, and because a poet writes a hundred lines one day and only three the next, the three are not necessarily better than the hundred. The public is entitled to judge the result of a poet's effort, but they cannot judge how great the effort itself was. Only the poet himself can say how hard he tried, how close to his intention the final product is.

When even a man like Horne, himself a poet, asked her whether her painstaking experiments in rhyme were intentional, she good-temperedly told him he was naïf. "Know, then," she patiently explained, "that my rhymes *are* really meant for rhymes—and that I take them to be actual rhymes—as good rhymes as any used by rhymer and that in no spirit of carelessness or easy writing, or desire to escape difficulties, have I run into them,—but chosen them, selected them, on principle, and with the determinate purpose of doing my best, in and out of this poem" (i.e. *The Dead Pan*) "to have them received! . . . The double rhyming . . . has appeared to me employed with far less variety in our *serious* poetry than our language would admit of generally. . . . The single rhymes, as usually employed, are scarcely as various as they might be, but of the double rhymes the observation is still truer. A great deal of attention—far more than it would have taken to rhyme with conventional accuracy—have I given to the subject of rhymes, and have determined in cold blood to hazard some experiments. At the same time, I should tell you, that scarcely one of the 'Pan' rhymes might not separately be justified *by the analogy of received rhymes,* although they have not themselves been received. Perhaps (also) there is not so irregular a rhyme throughout the poem of 'Pan' as the 'fell*ow*' and 'prunell*a*' of Pope the infallible. I maintain that my 'islands' and 'silence' is a regular rhyme in comparison. Tennyson's 'tendons' and 'attendance' is more objectionable to my mind than either. You, who are a reader of Spanish poetry, must be aware how soon the ear may be satisfied even by a recurring vowel. I mean to try it. At any rate, there are so few regular double rhymes in the English language that we must either admit some such trial or eschew the double rhymes generally; and I, for one, am very fond of them, and believe them to have a power not yet drawn out to its length and capable development, in our lyrical poetry especially."

This long letter to Horne is very important to a consideration of Mrs. Browning's technique, because it establishes beyond doubt that her rhymes, which have been more criticized than any other feature of her poetry, were her deliberate cold-blooded choice. Saintsbury called her rhymes disgusting, atrocious, cacophonous, hideous. Oliver Elton declared that the effect of her rhymes was such that "no writer of any credit since Mrs. Browning has tried to imitate it." Her rhymes earned her so many hard names that Virginia Woolf, writing in 1932, could say, "The only place in the mansion of literature that is assigned to her is downstairs in the servants' quarters, where, in company with Mrs. Hemans, Eliza Cook, Jean Ingelow, Alexander Smith, Edwin Arnold and Robert Montgomery, she bangs the crockery about and eats vast handfuls of peas on the point of her knife."[6]

Certainly if Mrs. Browning's poetic manners are only fit for the servants' hall, it is not because she was badly brought up in poetry. She could eat like a lady when she wanted to. Few opinions on this question could be more expert than Tennyson's, and he told a friend of Mrs. Browning's that though the chief defect of her poetry was the want of harmony, "it might verily be retrieved, as I could fancy that she has an ear by nature." In fact, in her unpublished juvenilia and in *The Battle of Marathon* her rhymes are quite conventional and correct by the standards of Pope, including a few accepted sight-rhymes and rhymes of accented with unaccented syllables just as he did. But even these accepted variations are rare—in most of her early poems all the rhymes are full ones. She could always, when she wanted to, rhyme with the boring smoothness of the "Stanzas on the Death of Lord Byron," written in 1820, or with the musical intensity of "Bianca among the Nightingales," which dates from the last years of her life.

> The cypress stood up like a church
> That night we felt our love would hold,

And saintly moonlight seemed to search
And wash the whole world clean as gold;
The olives crystallized the vales'
Broad slopes until the hills grew strong:
The fireflies and the nightingales
Throbbed each to either, flame and song.
The nightingales, the nightingales.

So it is certain that when she used eccentric rhymes it was intentional experiment—it was her own "fresh strange music" as Browning called it in the first letter he ever wrote to her.

For her masculine, or monosyllabic, rhymes Mrs. Browning used all the accepted varieties and several others that were all her own, or derived from Spanish words. Of the accepted variations she used sight-rhymes—marble/warble, lover/over—and rhymed stressed with unstressed syllables. "*Prejudice* and *eyes* do make an imperfect rhyme—but I think that imperfect rhymes relieve the ear from a monotonous impression. They are sanctioned by the practice of the most uniformly correct poets—by the *frequent* practice of Pope himself," she wrote beseechingly to that inexorable traditionalist Boyd. She also used half-rhymes; as early as *The Battle of Marathon* she is rhyming "smoke" with "flock," and as late as "Little Mattie" (1862) she rhymes "off" with "enough." In one of her best poems she makes a very skilful use of the half-rhyme. "De Profundis" has an extremely simple basic pattern both of metre and rhyme, a four-foot iambic quatrain with a refrain, rhyming a a b b a. The refrain varies slightly from stanza to stanza; the first version of it is

And yet my days go on, go on,

and all versions of it end with the words "go on." The metre of the poem is very regular; there is no trisyllabic substitution, and very little trochaic. Such a prosodic scheme might easily be monotonous, and indeed part of the intentional effect is to create a cumulative impression of the monotony of grief—the very words of the refrain imply it. But she has introduced variety by means of the very device which conveys the dead level of grief; the unvarying "on" termination of the refrain is rhymed with a change-ring of "run," "stone," "tune," "down" in lines one and two of the different stanzas, and this is emphasized by the regularity of the "b" rhymes in lines three and four, which are nearly all full rhymes.

There are precedents for all these types of rhymes in the works of other poets, including some accounted particularly correct, as Mrs. Browning said. But a poem of hers such as "The Dead Pan" contains instances not only of all these kinds of rhymes, but of others which, as she said, Kenyon called "Barrettian"—her special note. "Most of the 'incorrectnesses' you speak of may be 'incorrectnesses,' but are not *negligences*. I have a theory about double rhymes for which I shall be attacked by the critics, but which I could justify perhaps on high authority, or at least analogy. In fact, these volumes of mine have more double rhymes than any two books of English poems that ever to my knowledge were printed; I mean of English poems *not comic*. Now, of double rhymes in use, which are perfect rhymes, you are aware how few there are, and yet you are also aware of what an admirable effect in making a rhythm various and vigorous, double rhyming is in English poetry. Therefore I have used a certain licence; and after much thoughtful study of the Elizabethan writers, have ventured it with the public. And do *you* tell me, *you* who object to the use of a different *vowel* in a double rhyme, why you rhyme (as everybody else does, without blame from anybody) 'given' to 'heaven,' when you object to my rhyming 'remember' and 'chamber'? The analogy is all on my side, and I *believe* that the spirit of the English language is also. . . . If I deal too much in licences, it is not because I am idle, but because I am speculative for freedom's sake."

Double rhymes had always pleased her ear; as early as 1826 she was rhyming "emotion" and "ocean," "taken" and "waken." She used a great many double rhymes such as the one Boyd attacked, full rhymes except for the vowel of the first syllable; such rhymes as "vesper/whisper" and "alters/welters." But these—the equivalent of the monosyllabic half-rhyme—had often been used in serious poetry by Byron and Shelley, Campbell and Hood, as well as by comic poets like Barham and Browning's eccentric ex-Jesuit friend Father Prout, and were to be used again by Wilfred Owen and Dylan Thomas. Mrs. Browning's real innovation was the assonantal double rhyme—such a rhyme as "benches/influences" or "flowings/poems." These do not strike so strangely on our ears as they did on those of Mrs. Browning's contemporaries. We have heard Mr. Auden rhyming "edges" with "benches" and "crisis" with "brightness"; and Mr. Eliot's person in the Spanish cape "overturns a coffee-cup" and "yawns and draws a stocking up" in assonantal languor of rhyme.

Mrs. Browning, it seems to me, sometimes brought off her assonantal double rhymes and sometimes offended. "Trident/silent," "enter/peradventure" and "honest/admonished" seem to me pleasant enough. But when she rhymes "glory" with "more thee," or "future" with "suitor" she is less happy. And she often goes even further than this, and uses such double rhymes as "know from/snow storm" or "angels/candles" or "panther/saunter" which are imperfect in both vowel and consonant. Most of these extreme variations are in "The Dead Pan," in which she pushed her experiments in double rhymes to the furthest point—perhaps beyond; but they are to be found also in "The Lost Bower," in "Catarina to Camoens," and in some of the late poems where, in spite of all the abuse her double rhymes had received, she is still intrepidly rhyming "Cascine" with "a green way."

Such rhymes will always tease some ears with the sense of something just off key, and please others with a feeling of freshness and fitness. Correct classicists like Landor will always write, "How is it possible that so serious a writer as Miss Barrett should not perceive that the two-word rhyme is only fit for ludicrous subjects:

> These rhymes appear to me but very so-so,
> And fit but for our Lady del Toboso.

But we are so much in the habit of seeing the common law of the land in poetry infringed and violated, that nothing shocks us."[7] But there can be no law of what can and cannot be done in serious English poetry; if any poet can use double or triple rhymes, assonance or *rime riche,* any old or new device, well enough so that the reader enjoys it without noticing it, that poet has got away with it. I do not think that Mrs. Browning quite did; her ear was just not fine enough, though it certainly was not as tone-deaf as her critics thought. But she introduced a freedom which has been of the greatest service to her successors—to Rossetti, to Hopkins, to half the poets of the twentieth century. She had, as Virginia Woolf said, "some complicity in the development of modern poetry."[8]

Mrs. Browning's determination to take every means to say what she thought caused her to draw on a very wide and eccentric vocabulary, and when even that was not wide enough, to make new words or new combinations of words. She did not restrict herself to the vocabulary of her own country in her own time. Many of her words, and especially her word-combinations, were based on Greek, Italian, French or Spanish forms, and she freely drew on archaic English—though less freely in her later poems. Up to 1844 she habitually used the second person singular and the old "-eth" termination for the third person; "do" as an auxiliary verb; "I wis" and "I ween," "yea" and "nay," "eftsoons" and "right daintily" and so on. She liked "yea" very much, she told Boyd, but only in the right place—"in poetry and in poetical prose,—anywhere where a warm and elevated diction is not out of place." The diction of poetry must be elevated—she did not care for dialect poems, she told Browning. But though elevated, it must not be artificial; it must call a spade a spade, with the exactest words that can be found to describe a spade, not with an elegant periphrasis. She criticized Barry Cornwall for having done a good deal to "emasculate the poetry of the passing age. To talk of 'fair things' when he had to speak of women, and of 'laughing flowers' when his business was with a full-blown daisy is the fashion of his school. His care has not been to use the most expressive, but the prettiest word." Her care was just the opposite; her words were often far from pretty, but they were crammed with expression.

Her favourite device was the use of compound words—honey-dream, spirit-index, bosom-swell, God-breath. Like almost every trick of her style, this was attributed to Tennyson's influence. "What vexed me a little in one or two of the journals," she told Cornelius Mathews when describing the critics' reaction to her 1844 poems, "was an attempt made to fix me in a school, and the calling me a follower of Tennyson for my habit of using compound words, noun-substantives, which I used to do before I knew a page of Tennyson, and adopted from a study of our old English writers, and Greeks and even Germans. The custom is so far from being peculiar to Tennyson, that Shelley and Keats and Leigh Hunt are all redolent of it, and no one can read our old poets without perceiving the leaning of our Saxon to that species of coalition." It was part of the common heritage of English poets, and she was no more influenced by Tennyson than, probably, Hopkins was directly influenced by her, though there is a curious coincidence in their taste for obsolete and archaic words, and above all for these compound words—her heaven-life, ransom-righteousness, sleep-smile, storm-pathos, God-orphaned, blood-bought, and his womb-life, seraph-arrival, foam-fleece, sea-romp, beam-blind, heart-fleshed. They both had the same purpose in using this device, though only Hopkins found a name for it—"inscaping." A favourite form of "inscaping" in Mrs. Browning's poetry is her habit of using prefixes to verbs, on the Greek model, to give a concentrated picture of movement or spatial relationship. The sea undersweeps the horizon; cheeks are overwept; the Duchess May upsprang to the horse's back; to "outbear," to "overlean," to "undershine" are verbs which she has coined to give movement and angle almost as the cinema gives them. She also went to Greek, just as doctors still do, for words to describe a precise condition—"nympholeptic," for instance. But she got into trouble with Ruskin for this. "I must try to coax you to send some of the long, compounded Greek words—which I, for one can't understand a syllable of—about their Greek business," he wrote to her in March 1855, and by way of coaxing her he broke out into verse himself three months later. "When you have succeeded in all your designs upon the English language, I might perhaps most graphically describe it as

> Tesseric, pentic, hectic, heptic,
> Phoenico-daemonic, and dyspeptic,
> Hipped-ic, Pipped-ic, East-Wind-nipped-ic,
> Stiffened like styptic, doubled in diptych,
> Possi-kephaly-chersecliptic,[9]

he wrote mockingly. Mrs. Browning was not to be teased out of her convictions. "I think you quite wrong in your objection to 'nympholept.' Nympholepsy is no more a Greek word than epilepsy, and no one would or could object to epilepsy or apoplexy as a Greek word. It's a word for a specific disease or mania among the ancients, that mystic passion for an invisible nymph common to a certain class of visionaries." And she went on to remind him that de Quincey and Byron had used the word—it was difficult to bowl her out in this kind of argument; she had read too much—and to say that "we are all nympholepts in running after our ideals—and none more than yourself, indeed." She can hardly have known how piercingly close to the bone she was getting in diagnosing this particular disease in Ruskin.

She was indeed a "huge coiner of words" as the *John Bull* reviewer said of her, and it would not be difficult to make up a poem, near enough to Ruskin's parody, out of words which she really did coin, some of them unjustifiably— audient, inscient, inly, oftly, sentiency, percipiency, vatic, fantasque, contrarious, humiliant. One of her favourite formations was to add "-ness" to an adjective formed from a noun, thus forming another noun. But she almost always did this to squeeze out an extra taste of meaning. When she wrote that the poet's

> long-subjected humanness
> Gave out its lion cry,

she obviously wanted to avoid the ambiguous meaning of the word "humanity"; in this context she meant simply the quality of being *human,* excluding all overtones of the quality of being *humane,* and she invented this back-formation to make the meaning absolutely clear. She calls one of her sonnets "Irreparableness"—an ugly word indeed, but how else would you express that meaning in a single word? When she is ironically describing the conventional ideal of womanhood, with its "particular worth and general missionariness," does not the last word conjure up a complete picture of the *jeune fille bien élevée* ageing into a busybody?

It was this search for concentration, for the most syntactically compressed possible way of saying a thing, which led her into her least amiable trick of word coinage—her use of adjectives as nouns. "The Dim," "the Created," "my mortal," "their tender I often felt holy, their bitter I sometimes called sweet," "Thy speech is of the Heavenlies." One such formation of which she was specially fond was "the possible"—"God's possible," "the possible of death," "through all that glorious possible." This trick almost never comes off.

> For God's possible is taught by His world's loving,
> And the children doubt of each,

she writes in "The Cry of the Children"; it is certainly a compressed way of saying that man's love shows other men what God's love can be, and children who have never experienced man's love doubt the existence of God's love; but it is compression by distortion, not by close enfolding and interlocking. "Bad English and bad taste" said the *Guardian* reviewer roundly of this stylistic trick, and the charge cannot be rebutted.

Mrs. Browning was a great admirer and a great practiser of imitative harmony, or onomatopoeia. It was one of the excellences of poetry which she often pointed out to Boyd in their early correspondence; she tells him, for instance, that she has been reading Saint Chrysostom out loud to herself, and that in his description of a battle the "imitative harmony is electrifying, stunning and overwhelming" as she puts it, going in for a little onomatopoeia herself in her description of onomatopoeia. Almost the only good line in the dreary *Battle of Marathon* is onomatopoeic—

> One long dull echo lengthening as it goes,

which is not bad for a fourteen-year-old. Later she became a master of this effect, as when she points her vivid image of the warm hand closing a pen-knife with a "click of the shutting" or imitates the whirr of a spinning-wheel or the drone and thump of factory looms. She was specially skilled in the management of the letter S in onomatopoeic effects. Tennyson, who hated this letter of the alphabet, was always removing it from his poetry, "kicking the geese out of the boat" as he called it; and Mr. Robert Graves has told us that "the art of poetry consists in knowing exactly how to manipulate the letter S."[10] Mrs. Browning was well aware of the power of this letter; in *Aurora Leigh* she tells how

> gradually a ripple of women's talk
> Arose and fell and tossed about a spray
> Of English S's, soft as a silent hush,
> And, not withstanding, quite as audible
> As louder phrases thrown out by the men.

In "A Romance of the Ganges" she alliterates insistently with the letter S, and by combining it with the liquid consonants, well suggests the lapse and rustle of a strong quiet river.

A good instance of her subtle imitative harmony is this image of a beautiful but treacherous woman:

> As a windmill seen at distance radiating
> Its delicate white vans against the sky,
> So soft and soundless, simply beautiful.
> Seen nearer—what a roar and tear it makes,
> How it grinds and bruises.

The second and third lines, describing the distant view of the windmill, are regular iambics in flowing alliterative polysyllables. The next two lines fling you forward under the noisy dangerous thing that looked so beautiful at a distance. Spondee and anapaest break up the iambic rhythm, and the last five accented words—all short, all but one monosyllabic—have five different and clashing vowel sounds.

She loved the musical echoes of a refrain, and some of hers are haunting: "It is in vain, it is in vain"; "Be pitiful, O God!"; "Sweetest eyes were ever seen"; this last the refrain of "Catarina to Camoens" which Browning loved so much that he called his wife "the Portuguese," and so provided the cover-name for her sonnets to him. Sometimes she overdid her refrains. "Toll slowly," which is effective in stanza one of "The Duchess May," has become too campanological by stanza ninety-five. Twenty-three repetitions of "The river floweth on" are more than enough even for such a mighty flood as the Ganges. And the last lines of the "Mask" stanzas, reiterating "And so you call me gay, she said," "The ending of my day, she said," "It were the happier way, she said," remind one of a conversation overheard on the top of a bus. But she excelled in the slightly varying refrain—in "A Valediction," in "Loved Once," in "De Profundis"; expressing an old woman's tender acquiescent fatigue— "At last we're tired, my heart and I," "What do we here, my heart and I?"; above all in the mounting physical passion and despair driving through that astonishing poem "Bianca among the Nightingales," where the reiterated bird song becomes intolerable anguish.

Mrs. Browning's metrical technique was not as eccentric and experimental as her rhymes. Saintsbury, who thought her "the worst rhymester in the English language," allowed that her ear for metre was often exquisite—a tribute perhaps partly due to her being on his side in the battle between accentual and quantitative theories of English metre. In her *Athenaeum* series of essays on English poetry, she attacked those who said that Chaucer's poetry was purely accentual, just because he did not write regular eighteenth-century iambic pentameters. All poets, whether Greek, German or English, whether Chaucer or Pope, write by quantity, she maintained. The antithesis between accent and quantity is false. "What is this accent but a stroke, an emphasis, with a successive pause to complete the time? And what is the difference between this accent and quantity but the difference between a harp-note and an organ-note?" Her readings in the English prosodists—Puttenham, Tyrwhitt, Guest—and in Porson and Bentley on Greek prosody, her correspondence with her friends Uvedale Price and Boyd, had convinced her that all English poetry could be scanned in feet, and she used the classical names for these feet, even maintaining that there are English pyrrhics, amphibrachs, choriambi. The examples of scansion given in her letters show that she admitted very free substitution, monosyllabic feet, a great deal of anacrusis and catalexis. If her own poetry is to be scanned on the same system, many of her more complicated metres would allow of several different possible scansions, and some of them (such as "The Cry of the Children" or "First News from Villafranca") are really far easier to treat accentually, not quantitatively—are virtually sprung rhythm, perhaps influenced by her favourite *Piers Plowman*. But since, to her, all poetry was divisible into recognized feet, of recognized though varying and interchangeable length, her poetry must, however cautiously, be scanned in this way. It is like watching a couple dancing a waltz on the deck of a rolling ship—it may be apparent to you that their motion is controlled by the roll of the ship rather than by the three-four rhythm of the band, but they think that they are dancing to the band, so you must judge their performance by that rhythm.

Mrs. Browning's ideas about metre can be tracked through her letters to her friends. A stirring trochaic war-song by the Greek poet Rhigas Pheraios has caught her ear, she writes to Boyd in 1828; and sixteen years later we meet it in "Hector in the Garden" and "The Lost Bower," to whose youthful memories and fancies its child-like garrulity suits very well, but less well to "The Dead Pan" whose great subject calls for some such stately metre as that of the "Hymn on the Morning of Christ's Nativity." A poem of Barry Cornwall's "used to thrill me through and through with the charm of lyric cadence and matchless pathos," she confided to Horne, and she used variations of its iambic stanza again and again—in "Loved Once," in "A Dead Rose," in "A Denial," all of them poems plaintive in feeling, as though she heard the broken effect of the three-foot line in a five-foot stanza as a sob or catch of the breath. But often the strange hurrying tunes came to her from nowhere, not as an echo from another poet; "the first stanza came into my head in a hurricane," she told Kenyon of "The Cry of the Children," with its panting third paeons. Sometimes she chose a stanza form for the beginning of a poem and found herself constricted by it afterwards. This is certainly true of the triplets of *A Vision of Poets,* for she admitted as much in a letter to Boyd;[11] it seems possible that she may also have regretted her committal to the stanza form of *Casa Guidi Windows,* which is not a true *terza rima,* since it has no *tornello,* and in cumulative effect is therefore rather clogged and uneasy.

Her correspondence with Boyd was a running battle, spread over twenty years, about her gradual abandonment of the smooth end-stopped unequivalenced rhythms of Pope to which the pre-Romantic Boyd was for ever devoted, and her increasing taste for enjambement and trisyllabic substitution. She began to feel more and more that rhythm should be harmonic, not simply melodic; to attack the influence of Pope on English versification, to defend elisions and "jumping lines," to experiment with new metres, new stanza forms—the lolloping dactyls of "King Victor Emmanuel Entering Florence"; the accomplished "Praed metre" of "Lord Walter's Wife"; the trochaic fourteeners of "The Duchess May," with an internal rhyme, a metre which does very well when Sir Guy and his Duchess are galloping through the rain—

> Steed on steed-track, dashing off—thickening, doubling, hoof
> on hoof

but would be intolerable in a poem of ninety-five stanzas if it were not broken up by shorter lines. Her long-lined poems owe much to Tennyson; "Lady

Geraldine's Courtship" certainly had "Locksley Hall" among its ancestors, and was long believed to have had an offspring almost as famous as its forebear—"The Raven." Poe was reported to have said that his poem was wholly suggested by the single line—

> With a murmurous stir uncertain, in the air the purple curtain

from "Lady Geraldine's Courtship"; but the dates do not fit, and Browning discredited the story.[12] One unusual metrical effect was certainly shared by Poe and Mrs. Browning—the use of amphibrachs; it is the most original of all her experiments. She used them in the opening of "The Brown Rosary"—

> Onora, Onora, her mother is calling.
> She sits at the lattice and hears the dew falling

but there it has no particular relevance to the content of the poetry, and incurs the great danger of all amphibrachic verse—from which even Poe's "The skies they were ashen and sober" is not exempt—of sounding like a limerick. Where Mrs. Browning really succeeded with this difficult metre was in the opening chorus spoken by Lucifer which she added in 1853 to *A Drama of Exile* and which Ruskin disliked so much.

> He saves not. Where's Adam? Can pardon
> Requicken the sod?
> Unkinged is the King of the Garden,
> The image of God.
> O her exiles are cast out of Eden—
> More curse has been hurled.
> Come up, O my locusts, and feed in
> The green of the world.

It is not harmonious, this combination of amphibrachs, anapaests and third paeons; it is not meant to be. It is a devil calling to devils, a harsh urgent shout of power.

Not all the metrical experiments of Mrs. Browning's middle years were successful, but they increased her skill in handling the conventional metres, so that when she wrote the blank verse of *Aurora Leigh*, she was master of at least two of the three chief excellences of this metre, as Saintsbury defines them—trisyllabic substitution, variation of the pause, and enjambement. She uses spondees, pyrrhics and anapaests at every place in the line; once, to give the sense of a sudden shock of recognition in the midst of a reverie, she follows a sequence of perfectly regular iambic lines by—

> What a face, what a look, what a likeness. Full on mine
> The sudden blow of it came,

three anapaests in a single line, jerking one awake just as Aurora, dreaming along the quais in Paris through the strolling crowds, was jerked to attention by the sight of the long-lost Marian's face.

How much she thought about the technique of the pause is shown by her comment on Chaucer's "sense of music in the pause"; on Marlowe's blank verse, revolving slowly and heavily like a wheel "with an orbicular grandeur of unbroken and unvaried music"; on Tennyson's "Oenone," in which she heard "a noble full orbicular wholeness in complete passages—which always struck me as the mystery of music and great peculiarity in Tennyson's versification, inasmuch as he attains to these complete effects without that shifting of the pause practised by the masters . . . Shelley and others. A 'linked music' in which there are no links!—*that,* you would take to be a contradiction— and yet something like that, my ear has always seemed to perceive; and I have wondered curiously again and again how there could be so much union and no fastening." She herself liked "playing at ball with the pause." She will put it at the end of the first foot in three successive lines, to imitate the toll of a bell:

> The duomo bell
> Strikes ten, as if it struck ten fathoms down,
> So deep; and twenty churches answer it
> The same, with twenty various instances

or she will toss it to and fro along the lines, to give the broken rhythm of speech.

Her wish to keep to the natural word order of speech also caused her to use enjambement very freely, though not always skilfully—there are too many weak endings in *Aurora Leigh*—and to shun inversion, which she always felt to be alien to the character of the English language. Where her syntax seems complicated, it is because she uses devices of compression such as ellipsis and enallage. The long paragraphs of her blank verse are not held together by loops of inversion but balanced by counterweights of antithesis, or enclosed in Chinese boxes of subordinate clauses. This is in her reflective passages; in the dialogue and narrative ones, she uses the straightforward pattern of natural speech, and sometimes almost destroys the rhythm altogether by weak endings and other licenses which would pass in dramatic blank verse but are anomalous in an epic. On the whole it is not in the colloquial dialogue, so much criticized by contemporary reviewers, that she becomes unpoetical; much of that has a nervous vitality in which the rhythm is all alive. It is the necessary passages of mechanical explanation that are sometimes so prosaic, but against these must be set the lively satirical passages, underlined by all the devices of epanaphora and "aside"; single lines of melting magic— "With spring's delicious trouble in the ground" or "I felt the wind soft from the land of souls"; and sustained passages as noble as the description of ancient Greek drama—

> Dies no more
> The sacrificial goat, for Bacchus slain,
> His filmed eyes fluttered by the whirling white
> Of choral vestures,—troubled in his blood,
> While tragic voices that clanged keen as swords
> Leapt high together with the altar-flame
> And made the blue air wink. The waxen mask,
> Which set the grand still front of Themis' son
> Upon the puckered visage of a player,—
> The buskin, which he rose upon and moved,
> As some tall ship first conscious of the wind
> Sweeps slowly past the piers,—the mouthpiece, where
> The mere man's voice with all its breaths and breaks
> Went sheathed in brass, and clashed on even heights
> Its phrased thunders,—these things are no more.

All the resources of alliteration and onomatopoeia have been used to heighten the intensity of this, and it quivers with excitement like the blue air above the altar.

Notes

1. *New Poems by Robert Browning and E. B. Browning,* edited by F. G. Kenyon, Smith Elder, 1914, pp. 139–73; *Letters of E. B. Browning addressed to R. H. Horne,* Bentley, 1877, vol. i, 111–14.

2. *Quarterly Review,* vol. ii, November 1845; "Bluestocking Revels," by Leigh Hunt, *Monthly Repository,* July 1837; *Blackwood,* vol. lvi, November 1844; *Horne,* i, 191; ii, 124; *Works of John Ruskin,* edited by Cook and Wedderburn, George Allen, 1909, vol. xxxvi, pp. 191–2.

3. But Goldsmith, in *The Traveller,* also made it "Niagára."

4. *Letters of Gerard Manley Hopkins to Robert Bridges,* edited by C. C. Abbott, Oxford University Press, 1935, p. 54. Letter of 30 May 1878.

5. *Examiner,* No. 1914, 5 October 1844.

6. *Historical Manual of English Prosody,* by G. Saintsbury, Macmillan, 1914; *The Brownings,* by Oliver Elton, Edward Arnold, 1934; *The Common Reader,* Second Series, Hogarth Press, 1932, p. 203.

7. *Walter Savage Landor,* by John Forster, Chapman and Hall, 1876.

8. *Flush,* Hogarth Press, 1933, p. 154.

9. *Works of John Ruskin,* vol. xxxvi, pp. 192, 215.

10. *Alfred Lord Tennyson, A Memoir,* by Hallam Tennyson, Macmillan, 1897, vol. ii, p. 14; *The Common Asphodel,* by Robert Graves, Hamish Hamilton, 1949.

11. Letter of 12 December 1843 quoted in *Bibliography of the Writings in Prose and Verse of E. B. Browning,* by T. J. Wise, London, 1918.

12. Letter of 11 February 1876 to W. H. Ingram, quoted in *Life and Letters of Edgar Allan Poe,* edited by Ingram, Hogg, 1880.

A Little Hemming and More Greek

MARY JANE LUPTON

> Put the broidery-frame away,
>   For my sewing is all done:
> The last thread is used to-day,
>   And I need not join it on.
> Though the clock stands at the noon
> I am weary. I have sewn,
> Sweet, for thee, a wedding-gown.
>   From *Bertha in the Lane* (1844)

Elizabeth Barrett was reading tales of wizards and magicians by the time she was four and one-half. At the age of twelve she had already been through Milton and Shakespeare, and she was passing on to philosophy. She read John Locke, Tom Paine, Voltaire, Rousseau and Mary Wollstonecraft (author of *A Vindication of the Rights of Woman,* 1792).

Equally precocious as a poet, Elizabeth had written by the age of ten several rhymed tragedies in English and French for her brothers and sisters to act out. A year or so later she composed *The Battle of Marathon,* an epic modelled on Alexander Pope's translation of *The Iliad.* The epic is imitative and tiresome, but it is not bad for a twelve-year-old, as the following lines should show:

> When from the briny deep, the orient morn
> Exalts her purple light, and beams unshorn;
> And when the flaming orb of infant day
> Glares o'er the earth, and re-illumes the sky;
> The twelve deceived, with souls on fire arose,
> While the false vision fresh in memory glows.[1]

At fifteen, she published in the *New Monthly Magazine* two poems on the loss of freedom in Greece. The Greek revolution had engaged other English poets

Reprinted from Mary Jane Lupton, *Elizabeth Barrett Browning* (New York: Feminist Press, 1971) 13–21. Used by permission of the author.

as well, most directly Lord Byron, whose death in Greece Elizabeth lamented in "Stanzas on the Death of Lord Byron" (1824). She was then eighteen.

Not all of Elizabeth's childhood and youth were spent writing and reading. She liked to play with dolls—and with frogs. She rode a pony. She studied (and neglected) the piano, grew white roses, did some needlework.

"I wish, Elizabeth, that you would spend more time on your hemming and less on all this Greek," complained her Grandmother Moulton.

The Greek which Grandmother Moulton found distasteful was to be Elizabeth's most remarkable intellectual achievement other than her poetry. At the age of twelve she received some second-hand help on the subject from Mr. MacSwiney, the tutor hired to prepare Edward Barrett (Bro) for Charterhouse School. There were no schools for young women at the time. It was not until 1848, when Elizabeth was forty-two years old and living in Italy, that Queen's College of London was established, primarily to provide an education for governesses, secondarily "to prepare future wives and mothers for a better performance of their traditional role." Other schools to open during Elizabeth's lifetime for the purpose of educating women were the North London Collegiate School (1850) and Cheltenham Ladies' College (1853). Generally, education for women during the early and mid-nineteenth century was considered "unladylike" and "bad for their health."[2] So Elizabeth learned her Greek essentially on her own, until in 1828 she made friends with the Greek scholar Hugh Stuart Boyd and began, with his help, an intensive study of the classics.

By the age of twenty-seven Elizabeth had earned a reputation as an intellectual, mainly because of her translation of the *Prometheus Bound* of Aeschylus. In the following years she also published translations of Anacreon, Sappho, Theocritus and others. Her major achievement in Greek studies was a critical survey of Greek Christian poetry from the fourth century of Constantine to the collapse of the Byzantine Empire in the fourteenth century. While she was at Torquay recuperating from her lung ailment, she read the complete works of Plato in Immanuel Bekker's eleven-volume Greek edition. Of her many favorite pieces of Greek literature, Euripides' *Hercules Furens* attracted her because, she said, "few things in real life are so affecting as to see a *man* shed tears."

Most of the tears in her own early ballads are shed by women. "The Romaunt of Margret," published when Elizabeth was thirty, is one of the poems Robert particularly admired. It is the lament of a lady whose brother has gone to war and left her with no one to serve, nothing to do.

> I fed his grey goshawk,
>   I kissed his fierce bloodhound,
> I sate at home when he might come
>   And caught his horn's far sound:
> I sang him hunter's songs,
>   I poured him the red wine,

He looked across the cup and said,
I love thee, sister mine.

Margret, Margret.
The Romaunt of Margret (1836)

The lady lies in the grass by the river and hears from the water that her brother is dead. Overcome with grief, Margret drowns herself. This poem, written four years before the death of Elizabeth's brother, presages her grief after Bro's drowning.

In another early poem, "Isobel's Child," a mother fears that her newborn infant will die. She thinks about her ailing child's future.

Wilt be a philosopher,
By whose voice the earth and skies
Shall speak to the unborn?
Or a poet, broadly spreading
The golden immortalities
Of thy soul on natures lorn
And poor of such, them all to guard
From their decay,—

As the poem continues, it becomes quite clear that the unnamed child is a male. Then, during the night, the baby dies. At first the mother is grief-stricken, but eventually she feels consoled when the child appears to her in a dream and tells of the wonders of heaven.

Mother, mother,
I tremble in thy close embrace,
I feel thy tears adown my face,
Thy prayers do keep me out of bliss—
O dreary earthly love!
Loose thy prayer and let me go
To the place which loving is
Yet not sad; and when is given
Escape to *thee* from this below,
Thou shalt behold me that I wait
For thee beside the happy Gate,
And silence shall be up in heaven
To hear our greeting kiss.
Isobel's Child (1838)

When the old nurse wakes in the morning and finds the child dead, Isobel, comforted by her dream, urges her to accept the infant's death as part of God's plan.

A calm, accepting attitude is characteristic of Elizabeth Browning's early heroines. Woman obeys the will of God. She bears and buries infants. Woman serves man. She waits on and for him. She is often tainted by sin ("The Lay of the Brown Rosary"). She dies of loneliness ("Bertha in the Lane"). She is humble ("The Virgin Mary to the Child Jesus"). In a poem written to celebrate Victoria's ascension to the throne of England, Elizabeth Barrett emphasizes the young queen's weakness and humility:

> The deathly scented crown
> Weighs her shining ringlets down;
> But calm she lifts her trusting face, and
> calleth upon God.
> *The Young Queen* (1837)

In a companion poem the young queen weeps from the weight of this very crown ("Victoria's Tears").

There are exceptions. In "Lady Geraldine's Courtship" the lady wears her crown well; at the end of the ballad she accepts the love of the poet: "Softened, quickened to adore her, on his knees he fell before her,/ And she whispered low in triumph." In "A Vision of Poets," the Moon-Lady both crowns the poets and initiates the poet-hero into worldly wisdom.

"A Vision of Poets," with its list of great writers, recalls the very early *An Essay on Mind*. This volume was Elizabeth's first to be read by a fairly wide audience. Edward Moulton Barrett helped to pay for the volume, printed in 1826, when Elizabeth was twenty. The title poem, like the juvenile *Battle of Marathon,* is written in heroic couplets. *An Essay* analyzes the nature of genius, the elements of mind, and the creations of mind (Philosophy, History, Science, and Metaphysics). The poem is not very interesting as poetry. It is, however, an impressive demonstration of the intellectual powers of a young woman who, except for the periods with MacSwiney and Boyd, was primarily self-educated.

Considering that this poem was written by a female intellectual, it contains a curious contradiction. Of the fifty or more figures of "genius" who populate *An Essay on Mind*—Milton, Homer, Bacon, Dante, Descartes, Paine, Byron, Berkeley, Horace, Shakespeare—only *one* woman is specifically mentioned, Eve, and then only in order to praise Shakespeare (ll. 964–79). Otherwise, all of the women except for the author are Muses—Genius, Reason, Knowledge, Mind, Poesy, Philosophy, Invention, Judgment, Truth. Of Mind Elizabeth writes:

> Thou thing of light! that warm'st the breasts of men,
> Breath'st from the lips, and tremblest from the pen!
> Thou, formed at once t'astonish, fire, beguile—
> With Bacon reason, and with Shakespeare smile!

Mind and other Muses in the poem are mythological goddesses whose function is to inspire and instruct men. According to literary tradition, men cannot write without the aid of the Muses. Yet the goddesses themselves produce no poetry, philosophy, or history on their own. Throughout *An Essay on Mind* Elizabeth accepts this conventional delineation. The female inspires, the male creates.

In one of the few sections of *An Essay on Mind* that might be called auto-biographical, Elizabeth describes the joy of learning which the school*boy* experiences when *he* begins to read the classics on *his* own.

> when, without a sigh,
> Swift hoop, and bounding ball, were first laid by,
> To clasp in joy, from school-room tyrant, free,
> The classic volume on the little knee,
> And con sweet sounds of dearest minstrelsy,
> Or words of sterner lore; thy young brow fraught
> With a calm brightness which might mimic thought,
> Leant on the boyish hand—

This description closely coincides with comments in her correspondence about her own childhood joys, her own preference for classic volumes rather than bounding balls. Yet she feels obliged to express the joy through a male character. (So too, in a later poem, "The Student," the hero-scholar who dies reading is a man, not a woman.) The lack of a single reference to a woman of genius in the twelve hundred and sixty-two lines of *An Essay on Mind* clearly indicates the absence of a feminist tradition in literature.

In a later, similar poem ("A Vision of Poets," 1843) she does include Sappho, a Greek woman poet of the seventh century B.C., in the company of male poet-heroes.

> And Sappho, with that gloriole
> Of ebon hair on calmèd brows—
> O poet-woman!
>
> (ll. 318–20)

Elizabeth Barrett Browning was often linked to Sappho of Lesbos, though she objected to the comparison. Elizabeth believed that her poetry should be judged "according to the common standards of human nature," *not* "according to a separate, peculiar, and womanly standard." She wanted to be recognized as a poet, not as a "female" poet or "poetess." Yet Elizabeth failed to realize, until much later in her career, that the "common standards of human nature" were in fact an illusion and that women, by virtue of rigid social conditioning, were not encouraged to express their full beings. Unwilling in her earlier poetry to view herself as a *woman* writer, Elizabeth invariably disguised her sex and wrote as a neutral person. This tendency, typical of her day, helps to explain why Aurore Dupin wrote under the pseudonym of George Sand, why Mary Ann Evans called herself George Eliot, why Emily Brontë published *Wuthering Heights* without revealing her sex. For women, even the most talented and articulate, were expected to attend to their men, not to their art. They were to be feminine, wifely, and maternal rather than creative. Elizabeth Barrett Browning accepted many of these male-determined standards, presenting in her earlier poetry conventional portraits of male or female behavior from a neutral point of view.

Notes

1.   This and all subsequent citations from the poetry of Elizabeth Barrett Browning are from *The Complete Poetical Works of Elizabeth Barrett Browning,* ed. Harriet Waters Preston (Cambridge, Mass.: Riverside Press, 1900).

2.   M. Jeanne Peterson, "The Victorian Governess: Status Incongruence in Family and Society," *Victorian Studies,* 14:1(September 1970), 7–26.

Elizabeth Barrett's Two Sonnets
to George Sand

SANDRA DONALDSON

Among Elizabeth Barrett Browning's early mature poems there appears the familiar stereotype of the powerless female who has only her self to sacrifice. In *Mrs. Browning,* Alethea Hayter notes, "The 1838 and 1844 volumes are haunted by a figure of sickening boredom—Mrs. Browning's Ideal Woman, noble, constant, self-sacrificing, and all blushes, tears and hair down to the ground."[1] Strong and capable women, however, do appear among these poems, presaging the appearance of Aurora Leigh, counteracting the image of the fainting female, and demonstrating that Barrett Browning was aware of the variety of women's experiences. In two sonnets to George Sand, Elizabeth Barrett exalts the union of the manly and the womanly in a "pure genius" ("To George Sand, A Desire," l. 12[2]).

Women who have the best characteristics of their own sex and gender plus those usually associated with "manliness" are considered androgynous in modern feminist criticism.[3] Only George Sand seems to have achieved in Barrett's eyes any balance between attributes conventionally called "manly" and "womanly."[4] As a person, Sand embodies the ideals Barrett, as a young girl, had described for herself: independence from the constraints of "feminine softness" and a display of "self-respect" that is not a "masculine prerogative."[5] After her marriage and upon meeting Sand, she wrote to John Kenyon that Sand

> seemed to be, in fact, *the man* in that company, and the profound respect with which she was listened to a good deal impressed me. . . . A scorn of pleasing she evidently had; there never could have been a colour of coquetry in that woman. Her very freedom from affectation and consciousness had a touch of disdain. But I liked her. I did not love her, but I felt the burning soul through all that quietness, and was not disappointed in George Sand.[6]

Reprinted from *Studies in Browning and His Circle* (Armstrong Browning Library, Baylor University, Waco, Tex.) 5, no. 1 (1977): 19–22. Used by permission of the publisher.

In the first sonnet on Sand, subtitled "A Desire" and published in *Poems* of 1844, Barrett points out how the polarized qualities usually called masculine and feminine are united in her, as well as in her two names, George Sand and Aurore Dupin Dudevant: "Thou large-brained woman and large-hearted man, / Self-called George Sand!" (ll. 1–2) She is a woman with a brain and a man with a heart, and thus she transcends being typed by gender. Then, as a genius and an angel, neither of which is ascribed any gender, she achieves perfection as other people do only in heaven:

> thou to woman's claim
> And man's, mightst join beside the angel's grace
> Of a pure genius sanctified from blame,
> Till child and maiden pressed to thine embrace
> To kiss upon thy lips a stainless fame.
>
> (ll. 10–14)

Patricia Thomson interprets the "desire" to be Elizabeth Barrett's wish that Sand "be freed from the downward pull of her passions and soar upward, stainless and sanctified from blame." Thomson also notes that concern for the blame that Sand has suffered reveals Barrett's own "consciousness of a censorious public"[7] that judges that certain topics are suitable or unsuitable for males and females, respectively, to read and that these topics should certainly not be written about by a woman—a judgment Barrett Browning would later fear about her own bold work, *Aurora Leigh*.

In the second sonnet, subtitled "A Recognition," Barrett reverses the process, using not the good qualities but the limitations conventionally associated with differences between men and women and showing how Sand overcame them. First, the man in Sand scorns any "womanly" weakness, particularly captivity as in love or marriage; then, the woman in her rebels against such "manly" scorn:

> True genius, but true woman! dost deny
> The woman's nature with a manly scorn,
> And break away the gauds and armlets worn
> By weaker women in captivity?
> Ah, vain denial! that revolted cry
> Is sobbed in by a woman's voice forlorn,—
> Thy woman's hair, my sister, all unshorn
> Floats back dishevelled strength in agony,
> Disproving thy man's name.
>
> (ll. 1–9)

The unshorn, floating hair, which signifies "dishevelled strength in agony" in lines eight and nine, is later echoed in *The Sonnets from the Portuguese*. Ellen

Moers, in *Literary Women,* chooses the image of feeling through one's hair—the "mystic Shape" of love holds the narrator of the *Sonnets* by the hair—as a specially female image.[8] In the sonnet to Sand, the hair, free and wild, indicates female emotion, but, contrary to convention, Barrett sees this passion as a strength, even a strength deriving from the agonies of love, in which a woman is most vulnerable, according to Barrett in her interpretation of Sand. There are a number of other poems among Elizabeth Barrett Browning's early works in which she turns conventional attitudes around, to show not only her understanding of a woman's perspective but her ability to find strength in what is regularly seen as a liability or, at best, a charming weakness. Tears, for example, in "Victoria's Tears" indicate that the young queen will be a humane ruler; in "A Drama of Exile," *Eve*'s being "first in the transgression"[9] shows her to be more human (perhaps more than Adam, but certainly more than she is traditionally given credit for being).

What Barrett concludes about Sand in the second sonnet is also true of herself:[10] like Barrett, Sand burns "in a poet-fire" (l. 10) while also revealing that her "woman-heart" beats "evermore / Through the large flame" (ll. 11–12). As in the first sonnet, the perfected poet approaches divinity and does not suffer any restrictions that might be associated with the one gender or the other:

> Beat purer, heart, and higher,
> Till God unsex thee on the heavenly shore
> Where unincarnate spirits purely aspire!
>
> (ll. 12–14)

Thus Sand combines traditionally masculine and feminine qualities and becomes for Barrett the ideal person, as Robert Browning was also to become.[11] And perhaps this is the appeal Barrett Browning herself held for Virginia Woolf, an early advocate of Barrett Browning's work and of the androgynous ideal in literature.

Notes

1. *Mrs. Browning, A Poet's Work and Its Setting* (New York: Barnes and Noble, 1963), p. 82.

2. Charlotte Porter and Helen A. Clarke, eds., *The Complete Works of Elizabeth Barrett Browning* (New York: Crowell, 1900; AMS Reprint, 1973); all citations are from this edition, and references are included in the text.

3. See especially Virginia Woolf's *A Room of One's Own* (New York: Harcourt, Brace and World, 1929), Carolyn Heilbrun's *Toward a Recognition of Androgyny* (New York: Knopf, 1973), and the second number of the second volume of *Women's Studies* (1974).

4. In her study "Elizabeth Barrett and George Sand," Patricia Thomson says Barrett "makes great play with the man-woman aspect of George Sand," but Thomson focuses on the

connection between Sand and Aurora Leigh drawn previously by Martha Hale Shackford and Alethea Hayter: Aurora "is all that Mrs. Browning had yearned that her idol might be—not only a great writer but a noble, chaste woman. Aurora is the George Sand of the 1844 sonnet, *A Desire.* after the 'miraculous thunder' has sounded and the transformation has taken place" (*Durham University Journal,* NS 33 [June 1972], 208 and 216).

5.   William S. Peterson, ed., "Two Autobiographical Essays by Elizabeth Barrett," *Browning Institute Studies,* 2 (1974), 131.

6.   Frederic G. Kenyon, ed., *The Letters of Elizabeth Barrett Browning* (New York: Macmillan, 1910; first published, 1897), II, 56–57.

7.   Thomson, p. 208.

8.   *Literary Women: The Great Writers* (New York; 1976), p. 169.

9.   From a letter to R. H. Horne quoted in *A Bibliography of the Writings in Prose and Verse of Elizabeth Barrett Browning* by Thomas J. Wise (London: Richard Clay, 1918), p. 54.

10.   Algernon Charles Swinburne uses the same image for Barrett Browning in his introduction to a new edition of *Aurora Leigh.* "No English contemporary poet by profession has left us work so full of living fire. Fire is the element in which her genius lives and breathes. . . ." *The Complete Works of Algernon Charles Swinburne,* ed. Sir Edmund Gosse and Thomas J. Wise (London: William Heinemann, 1926), vol. 16, p. 3.

11.   Mary Russell Mitford's opinion of Browning's androgynous appearance, however, is less than generous: "I saw Mr. Browning once and remember thinking how exactly he resembled a girl drest in boy's clothes . . . I met him once as I told you when he had long ringlets and no neckcloth—and when he seemed to me about the height and size of a boy of twelve years old—Femmelette—is a word made for him. A strange sort of person to carry such a woman as Elizabeth Barrett off her feet" (an extract from MS. letter, Yale University Library, quoted by Betty Miller, ed., *Elizabeth Barrett to Miss Mitford, The Unpublished Letters of Elizabeth Barrett Barrett to Mary Russell Mitford* (London: John Murray, 1954), p. xiii).

The Ring, the Rescue, and the Risorgimento: Reunifying the Brownings' Italy

FLAVIA ALAYA

I can't bear to think of any part of the whole mass of lies & intrigues,—I like no one man engaged in the matter, the King & the Emperor not a bit more than Garibaldi: well, it seems ordained that if you believe in heroes you will be sorry for it, sooner or later. I have of course heard other versions of the thing, different from yours,—don't know & hardly care *what* is the true, so bad is the best.[1]

Thus Robert Browning, lamenting the state of Italian liberation politics, and the failure of its heroes, in 1867—oddly enough, just when he was in the thick of composing *The Ring and the Book,* his richest tribute to the "belief in heroes," and his strongest statement of the need to care "what is the true" amid those "other versions of the thing." Watchful readers of both the letter and the poem will, of course, be cautious to register such inconsistencies against the rest of the biographical and literary record. They will not construe what Browning committed to the post in a despairing moment as either a final indictment of the Italian revolution or a final cynical judgment on the moral significance of what he committed to posterity.

But not all readers are equally or invariably watchful, and the ironic reflections this letter to Isa casts around itself are a reminder of the dangers that beset the unwary—or hobbyhorsical—biographical critic. Perhaps no poet since Shakespeare has been more alert than Robert Browning himself to the meaning of dramatic irony. Yet perhaps few have also been so tendentiously treated, in the service of a particular biographical gestalt, to the alienating of the moment's verbal gesture from its "seed of act." Nowhere has this

Reprinted from *Browning Institute Studies,* now *Victorian Literature and Culture,* 6 (1978): 1–41. Used by permission of the publisher.

been more true than in the area of his politics and, by extension, the relation-ship between his politics and his view of his role as a poet. I am convinced that the reasons for this have less, essentially, to do with political partisanship than with the anxieties of critics themselves about the relationship between literature and society or literature and life. And these anxieties have been made only more acute (if not necessarily more manifest) for their being inex-tricable from perceptions about the relationship between the two Brownings, who were not merely poet-contemporaries, but marital and sexual partners, bonded simultaneously in the private politics of marriage and the public poli-tics of the Italian revolution. Out of these interpenetrated sources of judg-ment a certain canonical critical posture has evolved: where criticism of Robert Browning touches his politics at all, it is usually to affirm his poetic "detachment" from them, and to allege that, apart from supporting the gen-eral principle of Italian unification, he discredited Elizabeth's political views before as well as after her death and was antagonistic to the poetic strategies by which she expressed them. The meticulous process of disentanglement these assumptions deserve is one that I can only begin to undertake here. Yet I hope it will suggest not merely how much remains to be said, but how much ought perhaps to be *un*said, to achieve a just assessment of the politics and poetics of both Brownings.

I

A signal instance of the kind of tendentious judgment I am referring to—and one, I think, that will illustrate how it has vitiated critical method as well as biassed critical conclusions—occurs in the case of Louis Napoleon (Napoleon III). Robert Browning's submission of the politics of the Emperor-President to the no-clothes treatment of *Prince Hohenstiel-Schwangau, Saviour of Society* (1871) is commonly read as his overview of a political career that had spanned more than two extraordinarily charged and changeful decades. It is also taken as his final declaration of a contempt he had always felt toward the Emperor, but (it is alleged) had repressed for several reasons, not least among them his fear of "wounding Elizabeth."[2] The roots of this interpretation are usually traced to a passage in one of Elizabeth's letters of early 1860, in which she reports on the domestic and political vicissitudes of the year just past. Among these had been Napoleon's startling military campaign against Austria in behalf of Italian nationalism, brilliantly successful until it was suddenly—and somewhat mysteriously—cut short before his armies could take Venice, and concluded with the treaty of Villafranca in July 1859. Elizabeth tells Sarianna Browning that this conflux of exciting events had inspired Robert and herself (at "Robert's own suggestion") to plan a common venture into political poetry. The passage runs thus:

> When I showed him my ode on Napoleon ["Napoleon III in Italy"] he observed that I was gentle to England in comparison to what he had been, but after Villafranca (the Palmerston Ministry having come in) he destroyed his poem and left me alone, and I determined to stand alone. What Robert had written no longer suited the moment. . . .[3]

An abundance of speculative possibilities might well emerge from this little hand-breadth of prose. Were both writing on Napoleon? Or were they composing their separate pleas for English intervention in Italy's behalf, which, in Elizabeth's case, celebrated the hopefulness of the French stand against Austria? Was Robert's renunciation of his own effort prompted by anger at Napoleon for the premature peace settlement at Villafranca? Or did he think, rather, that it was useless to chide a fallen British ministry for not accomplishing what it might well be the will of a new ministry to perform? And finally, was he dissatisfied with what he had written not merely because the moment had outlived it, but because he believed that no mere moment should be able to outlive a poem's general and timeless truth? Judging, however, by some typical modern extrapolations from the passage, the way through it is far from being so thorny: Robert was clearly outraged by Napoleon's conduct of the peace, which confirmed all his least flattering perceptions of the Emperor's dubious motives, began his poem not before the peace but after it, never really destroyed it at all but actually secreted it away, to resurrect it once again only when there was no longer any danger of "wounding" Elizabeth with it; and then, from the rankling sketch for that poem (really not a poem at all, but, like the passage in Elizabeth's letter, a completely unambiguous "hand-breadth of prose . . . yellow with age and Italian ink"),[4] breathed into full-blown life the same devastating portrait he would have composed in 1860, had he dared to outface his wife's silly adulation of a man whose only service after twenty years of public life had been to demonstrate that Robert's judgment on him had been timeless all along![5]

Speculation, of course, is always a mere cogency wandering among ambiguities. And we would be justified in alleging this in defense of such readings if we had been left with only this single ambiguous letter from which to determine the drift of Robert Browning's attitude toward Napoleon III before *Hohenstiel-Schwangau*. But that is far from the case, and there is ample testimony, emerging from an unprejudiced examination of others of Elizabeth's letters, of the difficulties *both* poets experienced in probing the character of this leader, whose relationship to the destiny of the Italian revolution was at once so pivotal and so problematical.[6]

Yet the instance might still lack the significance I am attributing to it were it not for the adequacy of Robert's own testimony. It is true, for the most part, that until Elizabeth died, he appears to have "left [her] alone" to speak for him on this subject. But once he had survived the emotional paralysis he experienced immediately following her death (during which time he felt the need to confess to friends that he could "read no newspapers" and knew "absolutely nothing of what has been going on"),[7] his revived spirits soon drew him back to politics, and particularly to the still-unsettled Italian question. Writing to W. W. Story from London in December 1861, he was already sufficiently gutsy to be able to condemn the "English judgment" on Napoleonic intervention in Italy. It had, he said, been "wrong from the beginning," in its complacency about the need for such intervention in the first place. And it was continuing wrong, in replacing that complacency with an equally unproductive despair of the whole enterprise of unification.[8] Two more years of pondering the issues were not fundamentally to alter his faith in the rightness of the French undertaking, as an 1863 letter, again to Story, demonstrates. The relevant passage is worth quoting whole:

> Oh, Napoleon! Do we really differ so thoroughly about him, after all? No understanding comes out of talk on such questions, because one presses to the support of the weaker points,—not necessarily untenable, but weak,—and the end is, *these* seem the argument. But I never answer for what any man *may* do, if I try and appreciate what he *has* done: my opinion of the solid good rendered years ago is unchanged. The subsequent deference to the clerical party in France, and support of brigandage [an allusion to Napoleon's protection of the Pope with French garrisons so that the nationalists could not penetrate Rome], is poor work—but it surely is doing little harm to the general good. . . . Austria is enormously strong just now, and if Italy attacks her without France to help, she will rue it, that's too likely.[9]

The subsequent retrospect of 1871, the year of composition of *Hohenstiel-Schwangau*, takes a different turn, but it reflects the mind of a man on the downside of a judgmental curve. He traces that curve quite vividly himself:

> I think in the main, he meant to do what I say, and, but for the weakness,— grown more apparent in these last years than formerly,—would have done what I say he did not. I thought badly of him at the beginning of his career [about 1849], *et pour cause;* better afterward, on the strength of promises he made, and gave indications of intending to redeem,—I think him very weak in the last miserable year.[10]

It is vital, I think, to remember that Isa Blagden, to whom Browning addressed this last letter, had been close enough to the Brownings in Italy to have experienced both poets' private struggles to arrive at a just estimate of this enigmatic man. A letter he had written to her a year earlier, as the Parisian debacle fulfilled itself, confirms, in the use of the first person plural, that same sense of *shared* disappointment and betrayal. In those early days, he observed, before "the mask fell," and a "lazy old and worn-out voluptuary" and "wretched impostor" was revealed, we all, in our various degrees, took the man on trust, believed in his will far too long after the deed was miserably inadequate to what we supposed the will. . . .[11]

Once this record has been scrutinized, the critical treatment it has normally received becomes remarkable. DeVane's influential *Browning Handbook,* for example, quotes many of the same letters (with the exception of those of 1861 and 1863 to Story). Yet, despite the focus of the letters to Isa on the judgment the poet is passing upon *himself,* DeVane calls no attention whatsoever to their character as a record of disenchantment. He refers instead to Browning's "essential conception" of Louis Napoleon, implying that the poet had never perceived him as anything but "a complete opportunist—radical and a member of the Carbonari in his youth, conservative and repressive when he had come into power."[12]

Our natural expectation that Browning's feelings would have had to undergo some evolution in the face of shifting political events is treated solely to the rationale of a "growing contempt" (p. 362). Browning's assertion, in still another letter to Isa, that "there has been no knavery" on Napoleon's part, "only decline & fall of the faculties corporeal & mental" (a judgment he considered vital enough to repeat to Edith Story in 1872),[13] is quoted entirely without comment. But his expostulation that "No human being could venture to approve the conduct of the Emperor—for what was ever more palpably indefensible?" is described by DeVane as "emphatic," and elevated to a position of high visibility alongside his own analytic observations (p. 362). There appears to be only one explanation of DeVane's reading—perhaps it would not be inappropriate to call it a misreading—of the evidence, and it emerges in DeVane's own words at the opening of this "Sources and Influences" section on *Hohenstiel-Schwangau:*

> The character of Napoleon III is one of the several subjects, like spiritualism, upon which Robert Browning and his wife could not agree. . . . To Mrs. Browning the man was justified in almost all his deeds, and she placed upon him all her hopes for the final freedom of Italy. To Browning he seemed a complete opportunist . . . [etc.]. (pp. 360–61)

It is, to put it very simply, the need to define Robert's politics by contrast with those of Elizabeth.

I have singled out DeVane's analysis here because of the traditional weight his readings have carried, and because that weight is usually justified by the scrupulous attentiveness he brings to his analysis. But he is far from alone in the tendency to mythologize the political contrast between the Brownings[14]—indeed in this respect he is probably among the more restrained of Robert's biographical critics, who have achieved something resembling an avalanche effect in their effort to portray the divinely "sane" husband as anchor and stay of the wife's (at best) overly "ardent" and (at worst) hysterically "unstable" personality. It would be difficult to date precisely the tremor powerful enough to have started the slide, for there were undoubtedly some who had long said privately what Henry James finally asserted publicly in 1903, shortly after the publication of Kenyon's edition of Elizabeth's letters, that she had obviously lost "the sacred and saving sense of proportion" which might have prevented her political convictions from becoming "a malady and a doom."[15] Since then, in any case, it has become a matter of simply filling out the myth with the sort of psychological realism that offers a challenge to the ingenuity of the twentieth-century biographer, and guessing at the devious course of Robert's gallant strategems for not letting his wife know what he really thought of her opinions. There was, for example, no point in "trying to show her that the whole situation was more complex than she conceived,"[16] or in advising her "how passionately and crudely she had projected on the complex realities of politics the pattern of romance."[17] Flashes of momentary reasonableness in her views, however, suggest that "under his loving surveillance" she showed promise of becoming "a less neurotic Italian patriot."[18]

But this tendency is not limited solely to Robert's biographers. Elizabeth's merely tend to give the contrast a more romantic air, as though to congratulate the wisdom of providence in providing a solid husbandly house in which the wing-beatings of an ineffectual angel-wife might be a little restrained. For didn't her continual expressions of "anti-patriotic feeling" exhibit unmistakable signs of her being "deranged"? Had she not persisted in blinding herself "to the real and solid friendship that had so long existed between England and Italy"? Unlike Robert, after all, "she did not really understand Italy or the Italians," and as a woman and recluse had found it difficult "to acquire anything like a clear grasp of English politics." Friends like Mrs. Jameson (she clearly had no need of enemies) must have "considered her fine intellect demented on the subject" of the revolution. But everyone could forgive her, for "she was tired; her nerves were on edge," her vivid imagination once having seized a single point of view, "her mind was no longer sufficiently well-balanced or poised for a fair judgment." And, in the end, "she was a poet."[19] Another friend, Eliza Ogilvy, who admitted deep disagreement with Elizabeth about Napoleon, was nevertheless surprised upon rereading her letters by the cool, dispassionate twilight of the century's close to find them "seething from end to end with passionate emotion," and to discover that Elizabeth was after all rather "a powerful torrent foaming against the rocks" than "a wide sea spreading over a hemisphere."[20] From a similar stand in hindsight, Kenyon had been likewise embarrassed to see the poet display so unstable a "mental tone" and such "hysterical" tendencies in the letters praising Napoleon and bewailing the English insensitivity to Italy. Subsequent events having so clearly proven her error on both counts, he too felt compelled to extenuate her "anti-patriotism" with her "precarious health."[21] The supposition throughout is that no one, least of all Robert, who had always had "a far deeper love for his country than had his wife," and had never displayed "an unpatriotic spirit,"[22] could possibly have perceived the Italian question in the same terms as she had perceived it.

I have tried to propose here that, judging at least from the instance of Louis Napoleon, the evidence does not sustain such a supposition. Robert's statement that "we all, in our various degrees, took the man on trust," remains still the most lucid summary of what their views had been during Elizabeth's lifetime. Critical opinion has nevertheless perverted that summary by distorting his own difference of "degree" into a difference of kind. It has also subtly manipulated arguments that merely demonstrate the *quantity* of emotion Elizabeth expended in the expression of her political views into judgments upon the *quality* of those views themselves.[23] Where Louis Napoleon is concerned, there can be no doubt arising from her *Poems Before Congress* about her assumption of his good intentions, nor from her letters about her commending that attitude to others. But this vocal position, carefully evolved out of long political analysis, even in its last admiring phase reflected keen political insight. For it was not so much the *man*, Louis Napoleon, who stood in the critical relation to Italy's survival she proposed, as the political *reputation* of the man—a reputation that enabled monarchist patriots to sustain among their followers the desperate faith that ultimate unification under the king of Piedmont was the sole and selfless ambition of Napoleonic intervention.[24] Certainly it required anything but a fever-heated nationalism to see (as Robert, judging from his 1861 letter to Story, clearly saw) that only the complicity of friendly powers in behalf of unification could possibly rescue Italy from the devastation wrought by centuries of their unfriendly complicity: that neither Garibaldi nor the Piedmontese army could have made a successful stand against Austria alone.

Napoleon's questionable peace with Austria at Villafranca was a confessed "blow on the heart" for Elizabeth. But if to have expressed herself in that way condemns her, it condemns equally all those who were sympathetic to Italy's hopes, among them the "calm scholastic Italian friend" who was "sad to think how the madhouses will fill after this."[25] Elizabeth sought rational remedy for her own disappointment in as much solid information as it was possible for her to gather from available sources. "I wish I could see clearly about Venetia. There are intelligent and thoughtful Italians who are hopeful. . . ."[26] If it was ultimately to these she gave assent, the choice had political no less than moral astuteness on its side. The equivocal evidence then circulating about Napoleon's real intentions often came from those observers (mainly English and Austrian) whose motives for discrediting him were themselves suspect. When it was rumored among his detractors that the Emperor had plans to grab Central Italy as a duchy for the young Prince, Elizabeth faced her friend Isa's anxieties with rueful resolve: "I should agree with you on Prince Napoleon," she wrote, "if it were not that I want the Emperor's disinterestedness to remain in its high place. We can't spare great men and great deeds out of the honour of the world. There are so few."[27] There is a moral risk in such propagandistic tactics, but the risk was calculated on Elizabeth's part: she knew precisely what she was doing, and was candid about it besides. One might conceivably condemn such politics as disingenuous, but one could hardly discredit them as either ingenuous or hysterical.

We might wonder rather at the disingenuousness of measuring emotional or intellectual instability by the tone of her poems or letters. Read with care, they reveal in fact several tones, several voices, each appropriate to its place, each under its own discipline. The style of much of her political poetry was a mainstay of Victorian hortatory verse, indebted variously to Shelley, to the cadences of the Biblical prophets, and to the odic tradition. As for her letters, some of them brilliantly evocative, all of them full of life, one can only marvel at the critical mischief done to our perceptions by unsympathetic readers. The hyperbolic rhetoric she frequently used in them represented another voice entirely, designed in part to sustain their element of pure suasion, but also to convey the spiritual immediacy of her presence to the English friends she wrote them for. "Not only the prestige, but the very respectability of England is utterly lost here"; "As to the Emperor, he is sublime"; "We shall have a free Italy at last for everything goes well here . . . ; the feeling of the people is magnificent"; "I have been living and dying for Italy lately."[28] Where the matter is less weighty, the hyperbolic manner presents no difficulties, as when she uses it for the weather: "We have been melting to nothing, like the lump of sugar in one's tea"; or for her health: "I am a mere rag of a Ba hung on a chair to be out of the way"; or vividly to express her affection: "Dearest Isa, . . . how perfect you are to me always";[29] or even, with disarming self-consciousness, to gush over her baby. But it was a voice less defined by the momentary subjects of the letters than by their communicative intention, particularly where they were written for other women, and evolving gradually into a characteristic domestic style. Clear mastery of voice enabled her to chasten or elevate that style to fulfill the hieratic office she defined for her poetry and her public prose.[30]

Meanwhile, her convictions remained the same whether infused with passion or bathed in serene resolve. Indeed, nothing emerges more clearly to the eye attempting to trace the underlying themes and arguments of her letters than their astonishing combination of candor and consistency—astonishing, since candor about our day-to-day responses to political events is just what normally traps us into inconsistencies. To Henrietta Barrett, Mary Russell Mitford, Anna Jameson, and a host of others, however, Elizabeth carried the heavy responsibility of being in every sense their Italian correspondent. Her letters amounted to monthly communiqués from the front—the club journalism of women to whom real clubs were closed—and were, like her poetry, fully aware of the changing assessments to which changing circumstances might compel her.[31] The simultaneous evidence this "journalism" provides of both her moral commitment to the Italian struggle and her profoundly responsible sense of her own influence with others, distinguishes it as much from mere political propaganda as from mere reportage, and lends it the power of true political literature.[32] The lapse of more than a century, and the horrors of more recent wars, may have given diminished perspective to "the dreadful struggle for national life . . . , the agony of a whole people with their house on fire," that represented to her the Italians' share in the revolutionary agonies of modern history. But they cannot entirely have destroyed our sympathy with her refusal "to dream and make a poem of it" out of preference for an art "which makes its way through beauty into use."[33]

Though they are deeply interfused, Elizabeth Browning's poetic practice is not of itself the measure of the wisdom or intelligence of her politics. Once proper distinctions are made between them, and due credit extended to both, the allegations of sharp differences between the political views of the Brownings collapse, and the critical tradition based on those differences collapses with them. The course of Robert's opinions on Louis Napoleon, as on the question of English intervention, seems plainly to have converged with Elizabeth's during those dark winters of 1859 and 1860, when much indeed had to be taken "on trust," and no unprejudiced spectator dared claim he could see his own political hand before his face. One might even make a claim that Elizabeth's Italian passion had by then become no more "a malady and a doom" for her than for Robert himself, who passed much of the winter of 1860 in Rome playing patriot, engaging in the bravado of secret and seditious meetings in sinister cafés, consorting with Sicilian patriots by night, and hunting down every scrap of political news by day *and* by night, until he had nearly become hysterical: "The Police have stopped my 'Nazione' . . .—what *am* I to do?"[34] Such activities were barred to Elizabeth, but they were the experience that partially underlay the development of her own views. Had she been able to spend her energies in the same way, we might have had fewer political statements but doubtless similar opinions. To use Robert's relative silence at this time as the ground of an argument that they fundamentally disagreed on political matters is simply illogical. But to have him derive an invidious gain in political sagacity from that silence is more than illogical—it is improper. Elizabeth's "Napoleon III in Italy" may have been overly sanguine. But from the standpoint of political courage it towers over Robert's *Hohenstiel-Schwangau* of 1871, and to celebrate Robert's as the politically wiser of the two poems is virtually to congratulate him for having outlived her. A reputation much less secure than Robert Browning's would hardly need so desperate a recourse to sustain it.

II

It can be said to Robert Browning's credit that he felt no such need to stand upon his advantages. Whatever fudging of the history of his feelings about Louis Napoleon he may have resorted to in retrospect,[35] he cannot be accused of ever passing invidious judgment on Elizabeth's political insight. Indeed, not having publicly revealed the extent of his own faith in the Napoleon of midcareer, as she had done hers, he would have had less reason to feel personally betrayed by the Emperor's "imposture" than to regard it as a rebuke to a trust they had held in common, but which he experienced the more sharply for her sake. Writing to Isa in July 1870, when he was first faced with Napoleon's exposure, and before he composed *Hohenstiel-Schwangau,* he gave utterance to feelings that mingled his own shame with what he was vicariously experiencing for Elizabeth: "Oh, oh, Ba—put not your trust in princes neither in the sons of men,—Emperors, Popes, Garibaldis, or Mazzinis,—the *plating* wears through, and out comes the copperhead of human nature & weakness and falseness too!" It would hardly be farfetched to suggest that the poem was intended to even up an old political score on her behalf.[36]

Whether or not such an act of gallantry qualifies as an authentic descent into political poetry very much depends, of course, on one's definition of political poetry. One way to confront (or, perhaps, avoid) the issue may be to read *Hohenstiel-Schwangau* as an exercise in anti-politics, so to speak, one that has as its sub-theme the ill-advisedness of writing political poetry at all, for is it not "ordained that if you believe in heroes you will be sorry for it sooner or later"? Such a reading at least serves the purpose of proving the accepted rule that Robert Browning would never let a transient political moment enter his poetry unless it might make its way (to reverse Elizabeth's credo) "from use into beauty," or at least into some transcendental equivalent for the non-utilitarian character of art. And it would preserve the conventional distinction between the Brownings, with Robert featured as "no poet of the hour" and Elizabeth slushed in "a weakness for causes."[37]

But it would also stand the obvious truth on its head—that Robert Browning's poetry is scattered with allusions to contemporary social and political problems and events, allusions clearly addressed to the experience of contemporary readers, and underscoring the relevance of the poetic task to the present conduct of life. His admiration for both Shelley and Euripides could have arisen only from a conviction that the poet at his best is far from "evasive" of the historical and personal moment he occupies, and to read the credo of "How It Strikes a Contemporary" in any other way would be to stretch the concept of esthetic distance to the breaking point. Finally, we cannot discredit his own professions of admiration for his wife's poetry, from which it is impossible to conclude that he patronized that alleged "weakness for causes" or merely tolerated her passionate excoriations of injustice. If anything, recent scholarship has accented the opposite view. It was Robert, for example, who advised Elizabeth to include the highly-charged "Curse for a Nation" among her *Poems Before Congress,* and who stood by in helpless frustration as it evoked a public outcry she was compelled to face alone.[38] Surely it is possible that, with their poetics as with their politics, we have tended to mythologize the either/or character of the Brownings. Perhaps, indeed, we have underestimated the complexity—even the ambivalence—of his definition of his own poetic strategy.

By the same token, we may also have exaggerated what appear to us to be the transient features of Elizabeth's political poetry, and thereby misconstrued their appearance to him. Certainly nothing in either Robert's character or his work offers evidence of his being closed to the permanent value of a poetry constructed upon what a recent writer has called "the *intimate* subject of the human being's relation to the state."[39] No academic self-interest would have prevented his seeing that such a poetry, remaining vigilant to the private realities embodied in public policy, could well mean "beyond the facts" and provide an essential moral vision through which to receive and organize the shattered spectacle of passing human events. He was also in a unique position to perceive that there was more than morbid insight in Elizabeth's saying that she was "living and dying for Italy," more than mere analogy in her jesting comparison of the state of her health to the state of the would-be nation and confessing to Anna Jameson that there were moments when she had "despaired of the republic."[40] They were statements rich with the poetic as well as the moral truth of her commitment to tell of a people's dignity and a people's suffering on the authority of her own body. The experience of sharing his wife's work-life at its most vital depths cannot be discounted as one among the many ways that Robert Browning came to know himself as a poet. To argue—as has been argued—that he would merely have judged as a crude "pattern of romance" the design she had "projected on the complex realities of politics," is to convey utter disregard for the imaginative sympathies that may have provided the most abiding source of the Brownings' compatibility.

What, in fact, *was* this "crude pattern" Elizabeth Browning is alleged to have projected upon contemporary events? As Honan and Irvine have defined it, it was the portrayal of Italy as "a beautiful woman weeping in chains, of an ogre applying the whip, and a knight riding up in shining armor and ideals to the rescue." Curiously enough, the theme, so expressed, becomes a clear version of the mythic archetype DeVane once characterized in Robert Browning's work as "the virgin and the dragon." It also represents a variation on the symbol of the "tragic woman" steeped in "the mud of calumny" that Mario Praz some time ago classified as the prevailing stereotype of nineteenth-century English poetry expressing its moral view of oppressed Italy.[41] The pattern is crude indeed, but where Elizabeth Browning is concerned its crudeness is more of the critics' making than the poet's. The image of the "weeping woman" enters her Italian poetry not because it has sprung spontaneously from the imagination of a "neurotic patriot," but out of her full awareness that it had become so stock a romantic device. A convention less insidious in English hands than among Italians themselves, it had permitted those "bewailers for their Italy enchained" to lend to their own humiliation the glamor of "Some personating image wherein woe / Was wrapt in beauty from offending much." Rather than reaffirming this literary tradition, so hypnotically perpetuated from Filicaja ("Had she been less fair, she were less wretched") to Mazzini ("A nation lies trembling under the brutal foot of Austria"), the revolutionary optimist in Elizabeth Browning vocally protests it. Unmistakably, she conveys her fear that such an image of feminine impotency, however poignant, is an image of despair—of an Italian spirit too enervated to face the demanding, masculine enterprise of revolution.[42] The present, she argues, needs its new mythos, for

> We hurry onward to extinguish hell
> With our fresh souls, our younger hope, and God's
> Maturity of purpose.
>
> (*C.G.W.*, I.240–42)

It was a new mythos she herself was prepared to provide by the time of *Poems Before Congress*. There, the "personating image" of Italy-as-woman has become her own, and, true to the emancipatory drive of her era, has emerged as a figure no longer abject but heroic, a new woman whose emergence into selfhood has transfigured the old role of victim. In "Napoleon III in Italy" the poet's choral persona sings out her triumph:

> —Can it be true, be true,
> That she lives anew?
>
>   . . .
>
> Italy, Italy—loosed at length
> From the tyrant's thrall,
> Pale and calm in her strength?
> (ll. 127–28, 164–66)

Once the "Juliet among nations," a figure of mere pathos and sentiment, Italy has here risen to become, like the "mystic woman" of Elizabeth's later dreams, a queen, "on her head the likeness of a crown."[43] Embodied in "A Court Lady," she is "Larger in judgment and instinct, prouder in manners and life," as she gloriously enters "the sunlight which gathered her up in flame" (ll. 6, 13).

To decode the myth's political reference, however, is also to discover that the liberation of this "woman" was, by 1860, no longer simply a mythic pattern for poetry. With the increasing attachment of sectors of the peninsula to the Kingdom of Italy, the myth had in fact begun to achieve the status of a political reality. Possibly Elizabeth Browning's vision was only a reflection of a cultural myth that had, by so deeply penetrating the European imagination, itself helped to *create* this political reality. In either case, it remains an insight that accentuates the poet's awareness of the organizing and inspiriting significance of such myths to nineteenth-century Europeans, struggling to come to political maturity amid the panic of the revolutionary nationalisms of their time. In perceiving Italy's deliverance as simultaneously rescue and rebirth—a mutual interplay of heroisms—she has revealed more than merely her sensitivity to the national egos embroiled in Italian liberation politics: she has substituted a true revolutionary archetype for the essentially colonialist one of rescued victim which she had inherited. She has also invested it with the primal force of all powerful archetypes, for she has envisioned Italy's new national being as mother and child at once, delivered out of her own flesh and baptized in her own blood.

Far then from being "crude," Elizabeth's Italian "romance" achieves both a richness and a subtlety lacking in the original myth of "the virgin and the dragon," without any sacrifice of its archetypal power—for it cannot be denied, least of all by critics of Robert Browning's poetry, that even the crude original might have its own kind of power. Whether referred to as the "St. George" or "Perseus-Andromeda" theme, or, after *The Ring and the Book,* as the "Pompilia-Caponsacchi" theme, or, after G. K. Chesterton's detective reading of that poem in the light of the Browning romance, as the "Browning-Mrs. Browning" theme (or, better still, as all of them at once, and thus as the single major unifying principle of his verse), that original has been characterized as magnificently simple, but never crude. DeVane has neatly summarized its incremental power:

> In Browning's Italian days, the Perseus-Andromeda pattern finds a more subtle expression—all the more obvious rescues have been accomplished—but after Mrs. Browning's death the pattern becomes prominent again in retrospect. This is especially true in *The Ring and the Book,* where Browning is trying to build his masterpiece on a huge scale, and to make it a masterpiece peculiarly his own. Here we see Pompilia-Mrs. Browning-Andromeda rescued from the dragon Guido by Caponsacchi-Browning-Perseus. . . .[44]

And so on. Yet what the exclusive focus of such archetypal reading on Robert's poetry overlooks is the mutuality of both poets' fascination with the rescue theme. For throughout those "Italian days," when for Robert Browning "all the obvious rescues have been accomplished," that same theme—though amplified as I have described into an archetype of mutual deliverance—was also developing into the master pattern of Elizabeth's imagination.

To restore the full process of that development, however, requires that we look outside the explicitly political poetry to *Aurora Leigh,* which stands chronologically between the cautious adumbration of the pattern in *Casa Guidi Windows* and its full vocalizing in the odic forms of *Poems Before Congress.*

There, within the narrative framework of her poem-novel, Elizabeth Browning has set her heroine upon an active quest for selfhood that is rendered authentic only by its share in the similar quests of others. Even the bizarre career of Marian Erle, drugged, raped, and thrown upon an indifferent world with an illegitimate child, is a parable of female victimization transfigured—not through male intervention but through the victim's own defiance—into an invulnerable core of personal autonomy. Aurora and Marian, outcasts from their own society but citizens of a frontier of social and moral regeneration, act as accomplices in their mutual liberation, as well as in the liberation of Romney, from the predatory tyrannies of a "protective" sexual code. The energy of their deliverance is emphatically their own, but it runs its circuit, through that complicity, into the deliverance of others.

But, interestingly, *Aurora Leigh* is also a poem that seizes the Italian theme Elizabeth Browning had first touched only spectatorially, and turns it inward. "From Casa Guidi Windows gazing," she had perceived the plight of Italy tenderly, angrily, but still cautiously, preserving its otherness to her as Englishwoman—or, more accurately, to the needs of a persona rhetorically addressing itself to the political sympathies of her English readers. Now, in *Aurora Leigh,* with its interweaving of geographical and human polarities, sexual and national identities, birth-realities and birth-metaphors, Italy and self have been dissolved into a unity that turns Aurora's odyssey of self-discovery into a psychobiography of the previous ten years of the poet's own life. She who had "written much . . . / For others' uses, will now write for mine,— / Will write my story for my better self . . ." (*Aurora Leigh,* I.2–4). Specifically, Aurora's personal quest is also a quest for the Italian mother who had given her spiritual as well as bodily birth:

> And now I come, my Italy,
> My own hills! Are you 'ware of me, my hills,
> How I burn toward you? do you feel tonight
> The urgency and yearning of my soul,
> As sleeping mothers feel the sucking babe
> And smile?
>
> (*A.L.,* V.1266–71)

For Elizabeth Browning, the personal parallel was far from merely fanciful, for if Aurora was Italian-born, her creator had been Italian-*re*born. During those first days in Pisa she had delighted in repeating Mrs. Jameson's description of her as "not improved, but *transformed.*" Her letters remembering the passage from England to Italy had been filled with images of rebirth. Out of their everlasting canticle of sunshine and springtime, of crystal days and tender evenings, of "thrushes and chianti" and "strawberries and cream," the Italy of sensuous joys emerges like a rediscovered pastoral of childhood. The fortunate woman-child knew the "father" of that transformation, and blessed him for it. But she had in a real sense been brought to birth by this woman-land, and could bless its mothering too, with an equally effortless and permanent love.[45] Here Henry James might have found the explanation of what seemed to him so strange, so *bodily,* a gratitude. Had Italy's "otherness" been less opaque to him, his sensitivity to the personal meanings realized in the confrontation of cultures might surely have alerted him to the country's peculiar resonance within Elizabeth Browning's psychic life. Her first return journey to England, like Aurora's, had been an awakening to the "otherness" of her own English self, embodied in her real father, and recounted in her poem:

> Could I find a home
> Among those mean red houses through the fog?
> And when I heard my father's language first
> From alien lips which had no kiss for mine
> I wept aloud. . . .
>
> (*A.L.,* I.252–56)

"Povera gente," as Elizabeth loved to quote her Italian servant exclaiming in London, "che devono vivere in questo posto!" One could *not,* after all, "live" there. Yet to reconcile that verbal, sequestered, scholarly, and poetic English-self with the maternal and life-celebrating Italian was the task of integration traced through her surrogate, Aurora Leigh.

It is hardly surprising, then, that as revolutionary activity in Italy quickened in the late 'fifties, this particular woman-poet should have identified its resurgent life with the bodily life restored to her there, or entangled the cultural myths of the nation's survival and rebirth with the personal myths of her own. An uncanny identification had already presented itself to her long before: the first glimmerings of Tuscan liberation, in the founding of the Civic Guard, had appeared on the first anniversary of her marriage, and her child, conceived during the revolutions of 1848, had been born within days of the popular uprising that led to the flight of Duke Leopold from Florence, when the people "boiled / and bubbled in the cauldron of the street" (*C.G.W.,* II.118–19). Liberation, both personal and political, infancy, maternity, and the shared and simultaneous vision of mother and child, coalesced thereafter. The poet's consciousness proposed that the "mystic woman . . . in white" who surfaced in the dreams of her last year "was Italy." For the more redundant imagination from which she sprang, that woman was also among the souls who are newborn and white-robed upon the opening of the seal, and thus Italy, mother, child, and self, in one. If another imagination as redundant as her own could have appreciated that flow of identities, then somewhere Robert Browning's spirit must have given assent to Elizabeth's myth, which could turn now Cavour, now Napoleon, now Garibaldi, and now Cavour again, into the Perseus of her less vulnerable Andromeda, the St. George of her pale but resolute princess—perhaps the Caponsacchi of her own transfigured Pompilia.

III

The year Robert Browning discovered the Old Yellow Book—1860—was the year of publication of *Poems Before Congress*. It was also the year of Italy's greatest tension, when the whole fate of the unification movement, which had already gathered such exciting momentum with Garibaldi's Sicilian expedition, seemed to turn finally upon the settlement of "the Roman question" and the disposition of the "problem" of the papacy. The Brownings spent most of that year, in fact, in Rome, where Robert's growing preoccupation with the "Roman murder story" of 1698 failed to drive out the stormy presence of the guerrilla revolution taking place around him, with what he himself described as its "every sort of conceivable horror, shootings, burnings & murderings."[46]

Perhaps there was no real problem of conflicted attention. His was a sensibility that had always tended to accumulate rather than to displace, a sensibility that would prove capable of many imaginative coalescences in the creative process that eventually gave such density to the ultimate shape of the raw "pure gold" of his trial document. That process was certainly long, and the part of it that occurred before the actual composition of *The Ring and the Book* has remained virtually impenetrable.[47] Yet in all the efforts to trace the poem's conception, very little has been said, beyond the rather simplistic Andromedizing of Elizabeth/Pompilia, of the possibility of its having deeper roots in the elegiac than in the dramatic mode—of the power, that is, of Elizabeth's memory to catalyze a creative act so explicitly defined as its monument and "guardian." Precisely because the private impulse is the one Robert himself would have been most likely to place under the protective shelter of silence, the search for "the seed of act" might better be directed toward the flux of daily acts of remembrance than fixed on the episodic—and confounding—trail of retrospect that Browning himself has left us. Elizabeth's death did not, after all, merely add an ironic personal poignancy to the story of Pompilia. It loaded with the near-religious freight of *witness* the gesture of using his poem to testify to his love. If it was a gesture Browning intended more seriously than sentimentally, as I believe he did, it must also have involved some concern for the larger meaning of Elizabeth's life, the life of a poet no less than of a woman, a wife, and a mother. Just such a concern had thrust itself upon him soon after her death, in the obligation of preparing her *Last Poems* for publication in 1862, and, not long thereafter, a selection of all her work for a memorial edition in 1866.

The abrupt severance from Italy might express, at first, a recoil from the vivid physical memory of the *person;* but it could not, under the circumstances, repress the personality as a recurring *presence*. Above all, it could not prevent Browning's recognition of the meaning of that personality as an embodiment of the morale of the Italian revolutionary enterprise. Such meaning was pressed upon him from without as well as from within. To the minds of her contemporaries, Italian as well as English, Elizabeth Browning's poetry and the Italian cause had become an identity. The memorial tablet composed in her honor by the distinguished nationalist poet, Niccolò Tommaseo, and affixed to the face of Casa Guidi, spoke with inevitable gallantry of one who "in cuore di donna conciliava scienza di dotto e spirito di poeta"—"in the heart of a woman reconciled the learning of the scholar and the spirit of the poet." But it rose to another kind of poetry in speaking of her having forged with her verse another kind of reconciliation: "aureo anello fra Italia e Inghilterra"—"a golden ring between Italy and England." For Italians in 1861 the political reference would not have been entirely elusive. Giving subtle expression to the new parity of the two nations, the phrase symbolically evoked the principle of Italian national dignity Elizabeth's poetry had sustained, and, in a sense, anticipated Italy's own self-reconciliation, the closing of the ring of Italian unity. It was clear that Robert would have to share the blessings of his *donna angelicata,* now almost an English patron saint of the Italian cause, and prophet of English supportive intervention in its favor. But this was not, perhaps, against his grain if, at about the same time, he could speak of the "spirit" of Italian unification in terms that almost precisely echo his later allusions to Elizabeth's spiritual presence—as "actively alive all the time," working "far above our heads, and rather near the heaven."[48]

Browning wrote these words to W. W. Story in late 1861, when he was seeing Elizabeth's *Last Poems* through the press, and shortly before assisting Story's *Roba di Roma* into its book publication in England. The service to Story, like the ritual effort of revisiting Elizabeth's poetic world, seems to have had its therapeutic side effects. It brought him close, with a scholarly and attentive closeness, to the Roman matrix of *The Ring and the Book;* it also awakened a nostalgia that began to dissolve the pain of inexpressible memories. By the spring of 1863, the recoil was virtually over. He was already writing regretfully of being unable to return immediately to Italy, where he now hoped "to end my life in the land I love best." By September he was promising that he should have "plenty of Italy yet."

> Oh you in Rome! The very words are music to my heart: if I live, in Italy I will finish living, and die to my content.[49]

The next four years neither repressed this hope nor the poet's unrelenting concern over the still-murky destiny of Italian unification. The ring of his book reconciled itself fairly smoothly during those years; the Italian ring was proving less tractable, and the efforts to work it into shape increasingly obsessive, to English and Italians alike. The London of the 'sixties had become the virtual epicenter of Latin political upheaval. Garibaldi's triumphal visit to England was nothing less than the major public event of 1864. Parliament and the press were preoccupied with the debate between Mazzinians and supporters of King Victor Emmanuel over the British diplomatic policy vis-à-vis Italy. The literary Browning hovered with scarcely-disguised personal interest over the publication of George Eliot's *Romola*—like his own poem an attempt to re-evoke a resonating moment in the Italian historical past—while the cannon-thunder of the present was brought home by George Meredith's 1866 war dispatches from the North Italian front. The socializing Browning, one lion among the pride of Chelsea, was taking his share of the vivid intellectual life that centered around Thomas Carlyle and included close ties with Mazzini. His social network was more than wide enough, in fact, to draw in the full range of Italianizers, from Swinburne, Morris, Meredith, and the Rossettis, to Morley, the Ashursts, the Russells, and the Trevelyans. It would be difficult indeed to overestimate the quantity of dinner-conversation London's cultural elite must have expended, during that Italy-fevered decade, upon the creative resolution of the Italian question.

The atmosphere was also heady with the intoxicant of hero-worship. On the basis of headcount alone, Elizabeth might no longer have been in a position to complain that "great men" were too few. Mazzini's eminence among those greats might even have persuaded her to a sympathetic reconsideration of "that man of unscrupulous theory" whom she and Robert both, in much earlier days, had admired extravagantly. Robert's views, in any case, were already sufficiently ambiguous to encourage the rumor among his acquaintances that he had become a Mazzini sympathizer.[50] They have remained sufficiently inexplicit to justify our own doubt that the romantic in him could have utterly withstood either the love-mysticism of Mazzini's thought or the luminosity of his presence. On one side, Carlyle's enduring friendship was proof that an English intellectual could reconcile respect for the man with distaste for his (then) radical visions for Italy and Europe. On the other, Meredith's depiction of "the Chief" in his novel *Vittoria* (1866) vividly dramatized the potency of those visions. But other imaginative influences were also at work. *Vittoria,* along with Meredith's earlier novel, *Emilia in England,* represented striking illustrations of the metaphorical control still exercised by the familiar image of Italy-as-woman. Via a process that paralleled her development in Elizabeth Browning's poetry from *Casa Guidi Windows* to *Poems Before Congress,* this "personating image" for transfiguring "woe" into freedom's rescue and rebirth had now, through both Meredith and Swinburne, emerged fully from the trembling shadows of Mazzini's early rhetoric and passed into the literary language of a new English generation. The "shamed sister" had finally yielded to the triumphant new woman. Chanting her rise in sunlit glory from the corpse of the old Eve, Swinburne's *Songs Before Sunrise* supplied vocal evidence that her symbolic power was far from exhausted. The debt of this new generation to the imagination of Elizabeth Browning, though it may have been made manifest by the reappearance of several of the *Poems Before Congress* in the 1866 memorial edition, did not have to be acknowledged to be real.

The same may be said of Robert Browning's debt, and of the impact of this historical and biographical context upon the crafting of *The Ring and the Book*. His apparent silence suggests a conscious acquiescence in the poet's status as "unacknowledged legislator," but it does not deprive Elizabeth's resurgent Italy of its force as an imaginative influence. That silence may even be more apparent than real. To those alert to its language, the relevant message confirms itself quietly throughout the poem, but with special distinctness in the powerful wish with which the last book concludes, that his "ring" might "succeed in guardianship" and justify its place "outside" her "rare gold ring of verse (the poet praised) / Linking our England to his Italy!"[51] Set off against the backdrop of the poem, it is a wish that is really an affirmation, made by a poet whose sense of personal loyalty is too deep to experience his obligation to the memory of another poet as mere sentimental duty, and whose sense of *Zeitgeist* is too perspicuous to regard contemporary Italian culture with indifference. As such, it carries a solemn, almost votive weight. With the exercise of a little sympathetic imagination, however, we may lighten that weight somewhat by taking a vicarious share in the naive delight Browning may have experienced when his fancy had played sufficiently around his documents to discover the tale those documents were telling. For there, caught in the magic of their web, was a rescue myth some time-warped cinquecento poet might have devised as an allegory of Risorgimento politics—or some wicked critic as a parody of Elizabeth's: a Roman girl of ambiguous lineage (the old Italy, "Juliet among nations") is forced into a repressive marriage with a foreign nobleman ambitious of shoring up his shaky dynasty (the Austrian Tyrant); but prompted finally by the stirring of new life within her (Young Italy), she seeks liberation through both her own (revolutionary) defiance of the accepted order and the sympathetic intervention of others (the foreign libertarian powers). Ah, the everlasting pattern of romance!

Yet the playfulness of fancy need not submerge the ultimate seriousness of the parable, once it is linked to a wish placed so earnestly within the power of the poem's controlling metaphor of the ring. To dominate that parable—to make it serve as both monument to Elizabeth and "guardian" to the cause she championed—requires, however, a higher degree of imaginative heat. We should need to feel some authentic guarantee that, against Pompilia's potentially tragic appeal for justice and autonomy for herself, solemnly resounds Elizabeth's appeal for justice and sovereignty for Italy. And we should be justified in listening for that resonance throughout the poem's symphonic structure of values—in demanding that, in some way, Elizabeth Browning's meaning deepen or enrich the meaning of the poem.

And that is far from difficult. One of the fundamental assertions of *The Ring and the Book,* that only the passion for justice can provide the seed of heroic act, was also the master-theme of Elizabeth's poetry. But the intelligence which in Elizabeth had acted as mainspring of that passion had also subjected it to an acute *caveat:* there could be no true heroism, finally, without the evocation of, and the acquiescence in, the heroism of others. Such an emphasis defines the most striking element of contrast between the "obvious rescues" of Robert Browning's earlier poetry and the rescues of *The Ring and the Book.* If we do not feel here (as we may with *Pippa Passes,* for example) any extravagance in the poet's optimism about heroes, or in his beamish confidence in amazing grace, it is precisely because they have been humanized by a convincing, unsentimental portrayal of individual acts of heroism within their spheres of dependency. Each resolute gesture, whether Pompilia's assertion of selfhood, Giuseppe's intercession, or the Pope's condemnation of Guido, dramatizes not merely an intuitive sense of justice but an insight into the reciprocity of courage. Indeed, without that reciprocity, each gesture is equally unimaginable, and we should be likely to see Pompilia and Caponsacchi without their faith in one another, and the Pope without his faith in both of them, condemned to the special hell Browning reserved for victims of their own ination. Nothing could be more alien to the primitive Perseus-fantasy of masculine heroism. The command to heroic action in *The Ring and the Book* emanates from the victim herself—not from the deficiency of her resources but from the sufficiency of her own will. Caponsacchi and the Pope are not merely saving, but being saved, and *The Ring and the Book* is a poem that celebrates Elizabeth by celebrating the heroism of mutual deliverance.

This sort of heroism was, as I have said, embodied in Elizabeth Browning's perception of her own life, as well as in her sense of poetic mission. But it was nowhere more fully reified for her than in the politics of Italian unification, where the courage of Italians could only be sustained by a simultaneous faith in themselves and in the compassionate courage of others. Viewed in this light, the naive Risorgimento parable embedded in the Old Yellow Book ceases to be quite so naive. Indeed it gains the dimension realized by Elizabeth Browning's later poetry, and becomes a layer of mythic history that, at Robert's hands, is simultaneously obscured and enriched by the realism of his sociological imagination. . . .

So resourceful a manipulation of his material into a welding of past and present represents the characteristic strength of Browning's poetry. One is tempted to say that it is the characteristic strength of all great Victorian art—the ability to capture, structurally, the archetypal permanence of human events, and texturally, their uniqueness, their historicity; and to do this in such a way that the historical texture itself—in this case the "old Roman murder story"—becomes a camouflage or subterfuge for the structure. By its very nature the archetype of rescue underlying that story contained multitudes. . . . And so it might not have seemed bizarre to him that Pope Innocent's conclusive role in relation to the ring of human judgment in the Book should so amazingly parallel Pius IX's potentially equivalent position in relation to the Italian "ring," the one element absolutely unique to Italy among all nineteenth-century movements of national liberation. Indeed, with a kind of joyful redundancy equalled only by Victorian architecture, Browning seems, in discerning this last coincidence, to have taken special delight in dramatizing every possible similarity. The Pope's monologue is at once temporally climactic, personally heroic, and institutionally prophetic, evolving a decision that simultaneously decides the case, defies convention, and defines the role of the papacy. Had the monologue been called "Pio Nono," and dramatized the putative self-communings of the man then occupying the papal seat, it could not have touched more deeply or explicitly every question about the relationship between spiritual and temporal judgment, justice, or responsibility in which the politics of the nineteenth century had embroiled the papacy of Pius IX. . . .[52]

Characterized by the British themselves as the greatest leader on the continent for the liberal reforms with which he had initiated his papacy, his turnabout after the 1848 revolution and the ill-starred Roman Republic had effectively killed all practical hope thereafter of his support for Italian unity. But surviving undaunted was the *im*practical hope that his earlier liberalism might contain the seed of future reconciliation. That hope continued to perpetuate itself through all the sickening deferrals of the 'sixties—indeed grew more intense, as military confrontation seemed the increasingly inevitable alternative. During these years of impasse, many watchers perceived that Italy's ultimate salvation, barring some political miracle, was likely to require a gratuitous act of heroic statesmanship on the part of the Pope, whether Pio Nono or his successor, and even the idea of a papal presidency (which at one point had even been promoted by Cavour) continued to be seriously proposed as a resolution. . . .[53]

That same hope would also have represented the resolution of the poem as elegy, for the problem of Italian sovereignty had succeeded in focusing the entire question of the survival of institutional religion in the face of modern liberalism, an issue with which both Brownings had always been profoundly concerned. . . . Simultaneously humanitarian and autocratic, progressive and reactionary, Pius IX was a man of whom it was rationally possible to expect anything—or nothing—an appropriate symbol of the possibilities for the Church in the nineteenth century. From that wider theological standpoint, the Pope's monologue is consistent with earlier sentiments the Brownings had expressed toward the potential for Christian leadership and Christian conscience among Catholic clerics.

But it may also be remembered that Elizabeth had used, in Part I of *Casa Guidi Windows,* a similar strategy of holding up the mirror of his best self to the Pope's nature, a fact which lends to Robert's portrait something of the character of a literary allusion *en famille.* For her, the promise of Pius's early years had awakened startling visions of papal political heroism. "A [hero]

pope? . . . / We fain would grant the possibility / For thy sake, Pio Nono!"
(*C.G.W.,* I. 864, 867–68):

> . . . If it can be true that he who rolls
> The Church's thunders, will reserve her fire
> For only light,—from eucharistic bowls
> Will pour new life for nations that expire,
> And rend the scarlet of his papal vest
> To gird the weak loins of his countrymen—
> I hold that he surpasses all the rest
> Of Romans, heroes, patriots. . . .
> (*C.G.W.,* I.850–57)

Although the rancor of Part II of her poem indicates that she had long since
dispelled such a prospect by the time of *Poems Before Congress,* some recurring
hope must have led her to include, in "Christmas Gifts," the plangent but
faithful cry of the Italian people among the "gifts of the time" presented to
the Pope at Christmas, 1859.

Robert's method is to stress the earlier, visionary hope, to give us a Pope
willing to transcend the limits and conventions of his experience in order to
live up to the symbolic charge of his office:

> I, who in this world act resolvedly,
> Dispose of men, the body and the soul.
> As they acknowledge or gainsay this light
> I show them,—shall I too lack courage?—leave
> I, too, the post of me, like those I blame?
> Refuse, with kindred inconsistency,
> Grapple with danger whereby souls grow strong?
> (ll. 1295–1301)

But this Pope is not a projection of mere fantasy. Elsewhere in his monologue,
his supposedly counter-reformation dilemma is couched in the language of an
anguished, Prufrockian modernism: "Shall I dare try the doubt now, or not
dare?" (l. 1306). When he congratulates Caponsacchi for having answered
the summons to "pity the oppressed" (l. 1557), or hears in Pompilia's "cry for
help" only an echo of the suffering of other women, he is giving expression
in modern terms—one could well add, in Elizabeth's terms—to the self-
consciously humanitarian values of the nineteenth century. He is a Pope who
has all the savor of the contemporary, but the contemporary as it had been
both perceived and idealized by Elizabeth. In fleshing out the reality, Robert
also redeems the ideal that the words of the dead poet could not infuse into
the acts of the living man, and accomplishes, as fellow-poet, the reverential
task that "Completes the incomplete and saves the thing" (I.735).

IV

In 1846, long before *The Ring and the Book,* and at a time when Robert Browning's politics were a more explicit if less integral part of his work, he had voiced, in *Luria,* an idea of charismatic nationalist leadership that confirmed his discipleship with Elizabeth in the Carlylean reverence for heroes. "A people," he wrote,

> is but the attempt of many
> To rise to the completer life of one,
> And those who live as models for the mass
> Are singly of more value than they all.
>   (V.299–302)

Prefiguring Elizabeth's own conviction that "this country-saving is a glorious thing" (*C.G.W.,* I.860), the lines establish another bond between the political visions of the two poets. But translated into terms that have significance for *The Ring and the Book,* they also suggest that, for Robert, the "rising" to national life was a form of life-completing creation very like all the other forms, from the creation of self to the creation of art, that so absorb our attention at the various levels of meaning attached to the metaphor of the making of the ring. They remind us, too, that in his lexicon of imagery, to be a people also meant to be a person—a "one"—and involved a power like that of personality itself to reconcile the tensions and oppositions of political or cultural identity. Either metaphor, of ring or personhood, evokes certain mystical connotations of national being: its nature as a oneness-out-of-many, its capacity to bind together seeming fragments and particularities into a common will, and centripetally to close the circle of conflicting and centrifugal individualities. Curiously enough, the credibility of this nationalist vision was, in the 1860s, being simultaneously tested on two political fronts—in the United States and in Italy. Both of these tests, in their different ways, painfully intensified the mystery of national union. The imaginative convergence of the two "revolutions" among English commentators was frequent, almost commonplace, at this time. But in Italy's case the mystery was especially manifest, revealing itself through the deeper historical fragmentation of the Italian cultural identity and the multiplicity of political and ideological counterstresses caught in the vortex of the revolutionary idea of unification. Elizabeth had captured this same perception, not with separate but with interpenetrated metaphors, in her appeal for a hero out of whose integrity might be born the national integrity—who might "insphere / These wills into a unity of will, / And make of Italy a nation" (*C.G.W.,* I.838–40).

Undeniably, the mystery of unity-in-diversity surrounds the making of *The Ring and the Book,* a poem conceived as a resolution of fragmented perceptions, an act of moral reconciliation. But if that act is explicitly reified outside of the poem's narrative content by the metaphor of the ring, introduced in the first book, it is also reified *within* the poem's narrative content by the metaphor of the person, also there in the first book, in the striking image of the dying Pompilia who, in her death, embodies the powerful and saintly force that brings together "helpful ministrants / As varied in their calling as their mind, / Temper and age":

> . . . from all of these,
> About the white bed under the arched roof,
> Is somehow, as it were, evolved a one,—
> Small separate sympathies combined and large,
> Nothings that were, grown something very much. . . .
> (I.1088–94)

Already heavy with the freight of so many prior associations, and gathering new ones as it makes its way through the poem's gradually unfolding allegory of mutual deliverance, the metaphor's political significance remains inalienable from the moral or artistic. Yet it is ultimately within the artistic sense of Pompilia's integrating power that such political significance seems to seek its greatest identity. To understand this fully we must respond as Browning himself might have responded to the very word *risorgimento*. An obvious parallel between the word's figurative meaning as a rising, resurgency, or resuscitation, and the creative power of the artist could scarcely have escaped a sensitivity so acute to the metaphorical vitality of language or to English and Italian linguistic equivalencies. Indeed, when the poet attempts to described in Book I his own act of "mimick[ing] creation" in restoring the fullness of interdependent life to so many independent, disembodied voices, he finally rejects the word "creation" for what he considers a regenerative act. The artist "creates, no, but resuscitates, perhaps."

> No less, man, bounded, yearning to be free,
> May so project his surplusage of soul
> In search of body, so add self to self
> By owning what lay ownerless before,—
> So find, so fill full, so appropriate forms,
> That, although nothing which had never life
> Shall get life from him, be, not having been,
> Yet something dead may get to live again. . . .

Such a man "Makes new beginning, starts the dead alive, / Completes the incomplete and saves the thing." His quickening breath relumes "Half-burned-out, all but quite-quenched wicks o' the lamp / Stationed for temple-service on this earth." His energy may "enter, spark-like, put old powers to play, / Push lines out to the limit" (I.719–56 *passim*).

The emotional and imaginative logic in Browning's conflation of Elizabeth/ Pompilia, Italy-as-woman, and the integrative and resuscitative power of national and artistic heroism, is not difficult to reconstruct within the context of a period in which his own political feelings had been so profoundly intensified by loss. Every event combined with every memory to nourish the piety normal to the survivor, and rededicate it to the service of the mission the dead poet had lived to see only partially fulfilled. On the testimony of Italians and English alike, Elizabeth's political poetry had subsumed the two heroisms, and performed just such an act of "galvanism to life" as he described. With the other political hero-saints of the Risorgimento, she shared, in Robert's view, that resuscitative creativity which penetrated the dead, disordered surface of a nation perceived as the derelict of history, and, "start[ing] the dead alive," attempted to call a new "person" into being. His act could reaffirm theirs—and hers.

During the 1860s it required a special heroism to make such a reaffirmation. The challenge that envisioned Elizabeth's, "newly created, / Beautiful Italy, calm, unhurried, / Rise heroic and renovated, / Rise to the final restitution," being still-unmet, it was not easy to preserve faith in Italy's also prefiguring "the grand solution / Of Earth's municipal, insular schisms." Perhaps only a Mazzinian mysticism (illustrated so beautifully by the patriot's favorite palindrome, "ROMA/AMOR") could continue to foresee in Italian unity the archetype of human solidarity itself, of "Love's one center devour[ing] these centres / Of many self-loves" ("Italy and the World," VII, VIIII, XIV). Yet for all the cryptic character of its politics, *The Ring and the Book* preserves that faith, the conviction of which one is tempted to hear in Pompilia's dying words, "I rise."

But the subtlety of Browning's gesture was, in another sense, only an equivalent for the subtlety of his material: Pompilia, like the old Italy, rises to no earthly inheritance of her own. Rather, she dies to this world, leaving it as the task of other social soldier-saints and ringmakers to insure that inheritance for her son. The poet-speaker, at the close of the poem, is not past teasing us with the boy's future prospects:

> Did the babe live or die. . . .
> Was he proud,—a true scion of the stock . . .
> Or did he love his mother, the base-born,
> And fight i' the ranks, unnoticed by the world?
> (XII.814–22)

There is more than a hint of irony in these lines, an irony no less justified for the new Italy, whose joyful self-realization was still unforeseeable in 1869, and even then was no warrant of a national future, than for the young Gaetano—the joyful one—named by Pompilia for "a new saint, to begin anew" (XII.103). Until the surprising events of 1870, the possibility remained that the full closing of Italy's ring through the symbolic reconciliation of Rome might endure only as the wishful fantasy of a few imaginations, and thus commend the "wonder" and the "wild desire" but not the wisdom or vision of a poet like Elizabeth Browning. Such circumstances might have made it necessary for the tendering of this particular ring of his book to retain its character as a private symbolic gesture, a privileged communication. But it was a communication that, like so much of the poetry Robert Browning was to write thereafter, renewed a contract, in this case between two poets who had once been—quite literally—political bedfellows. And it was a mode of simultaneously assuring both the participant here and the observer hereafter the undisturbed serenity of having fulfilled a mutual obligation to history.

Notes

1. *Dearest Isa: Robert Browning's Letters to Isa Blagden,* ed. Edward C. McAleer (Austin: Univ. of Texas Press, 1951), p. 284 (19 Nov. [1867]).

2. See especially volume I of Maisie Ward's *Robert Browning and His World* (New York: Holt, Rinehart and Winston, 1967), where the arguments about Robert's self-repression run for several pages (pp. 285–87), and all turn in one way or another on the decisive role of his sensitivity to Elizabeth's feelings and reputation, or his desire to avoid her characteristic poetic strategies.

3. *Letters of Elizabeth Barrett Browning,* ed. Frederic G. Kenyon (New York: Macmillan, 1899), II, 368–69.

4. *Letters of Robert Browning, Collected by Thomas J. Wise,* ed. Thurman L. Hood (New Haven: Yale Univ. Press, 1933), p. 152.

5. This is a composite of standard views (DeVane, Honan and Irvine, Ward, Miller) which, I am afraid, when taken together, cannot help but parody themselves. Only Honan and Irvine put sufficient weight upon the reference in the passage to the ministry to conclude that the poem was more likely to have been destroyed than preserved. Their discussion nevertheless imputes to Robert Browning a completely undivided mind on the subject of the Emperor "from Villafranca to 1871": William Irvine and Park Honan, *The Book, the Ring, and the Poet* (New York: McGraw-Hill, 1974), p. 373.

6. Other readers, troubled by the critical inconsistency that grants general trustworthiness to Elizabeth's letters but will not extend it to their comments on political perceptions she and Robert held in common, will note with pleasure the appearance of an essay by Leo A. Hetzler in *Victorian Poetry,* 15 (Winter, 1977), as I was preparing my own for publication. In the context of a study of "The Case of Prince Hohenstiel-Schwangau: Browning and Napoleon III," Hetzler carefully traces through Elizabeth's letters the similar (if not precisely parallel) evolution of both poets' views (pp. 338–39), commenting by the way that those letters "reveal her to be a well-informed observer of the political scene and gifted with an unEnglish empathy for the inner workings of the French mind and spirit" (p. 338). It seems worth highlighting (since Hetzler does not explicitly do so himself) that, in both content and tone, his comments represent a marked departure from prevailing critical conventions on this subject.

7. *Browning to His American Friends,* ed. Gertrude Reese Hudson (London: Bowes and Bowes, 1965), p. 79 (30 Aug. 1861).

8. *Ibid.,* p. 88 (17 Dec. 1861).

9. *Ibid.,* p. 129 (5 Sept. 1863).

10. McAleer, p. 371.

11. *Ibid.,* p. 356.

12. William Clyde DeVane, *A Browning Handbook,* 2nd ed. (New York: Appleton-Century-Crofts, 1955), p. 361. Further page references to this work will appear in the text.

13. McAleer, p. 347; Hood, p. 152.

14. Hetzler's essay, already cited, is the significant exception. Alluding to DeVane among several others (pp. 335–37), he openly breaks from the "traditional" critical view of the Emperor "as a figure with whom Browning could have little political sympathy" (p. 337), and not only elicits the genuine complexities of the Browning letters quoted here but provides a fuller accounting of this and other evidence (see especially pp. 339–42).

15. Henry James, *William Wetmore Story and His Friends* (Edinburgh: Blackwood and Sons, 1903), II, 53–54. Among other things, James' judgment was hopelessly biased by his antipathy toward progressivist Italian politics, making it difficult for him to forgive anyone responsible for what he described as "punch[ing] a hole" in the "vast, rich canvas" of pre-unification Italy (I, 94).

16. Ward, I, 286.

17. Honan and Irvine, p. 364.

18. *Ibid.,* p. 367.

19. Isabel Clarke, *EBB: A Portrait* (1929; rpt. Port Washington, N.Y.: Kennikat Press, 1970), pp. 258–59.

20. Eliza M. Ogilvy, "Recollections," in *Elizabeth Barrett Browning's Letters to Mrs. David Ogilvy,* ed. Peter N. Heydon and Philip Kelley (New York: Quadrangle Press and the Browning Institute, 1973), pp. xxxiv–xxxv. The recollections were originally published as a memoir to accompany an 1893 edition of Elizabeth Browning's poems.

21. Kenyon, II, 306.

22. Clarke, p. 258. One is inclined to infer the political bias of such remarks from their originating largely with earlier British biographers or commentators. Time and post-World War II politics have had a moderating influence. Alethea Hayter's relatively recent *Elizabeth Barrett Browning* (New York: British Book Center, 1965), for example, presents a more balanced account of the political issues: nevertheless, even she patronizingly stresses the poet's "ardor" and "passion," along with her inability to "grasp" the historical or political process (pp. 134–35). It is instructive to contrast the appreciation of Italian critics, e.g., Francesco Viglione, who described her as Italy's "only English friend . . . without ulterior motives" regarding the Risorgimento: *L'Italia nel pensiero degli scrittori inglesi* (Milano: Bocca, 1946), p. 473 (my translation). M. L. Giartosio de Courten stays with the "ardor," but enthusiastically grants Elizabeth "the clear eyes of the seer poet": "Elizabeth Barrett Browning e il Risorgimento," *Il Risorgimento,* 2 (settembre 1950), 146 (my translation). See also the sympathetic observations of Giuliana Artom-Trèves in *The Golden Ring: the Anglo-Florentines, 1847–1862,* trans. Sylvia Sprigge (London: Longmans, Green, 1956), pp. 90–92, and esp. 90n.

23. The past need to disparage Elizabeth among some Robert Browning devotees seems so profound as to be a disorder. Not satisfied to characterize her as unpatriotic, they attribute her success to a vulgar and topical popular appeal that was guaranteed to obscure the greater genius of her husband. Most deeply misogynist has been the view that her illness and dependency drew off Robert's vital energies and deprived him of a nurturing matrix for his own creativity: here, see esp. William Clyde DeVane, "The Virgin and the Dragon," *Yale Review,* NS 37 (September 1947), 33–38. Feminist and historical re-readings have begun to cut through such biases, e.g., Julia Markus's recent critical edition of *Casa Guidi Windows* (New York: Browning Institute, 1977), and Hetzler, who observes that "the emotion with which [EBB] often voiced her opinions may cause one to overlook the discerning reasoning that underlies them" (p. 339).

24. The emphasis on monarchist supporters of unification is important since the anti-monarchist Mazzinists were also anti-Napoleon. The two camps represented moderate (Cavour/monarchist) and radical (Mazzini/republican) approaches to unification. Both poets,

though they had been early personal admirers of Mazzini, grew increasingly disenchanted with what they saw as the counterproductive politics of his opposition to Cavour diplomacy.

25. Kenyon, II, 382.

26. *Ibid.*, p. 331.

27. *Ibid.*, p. 341.

28. *Ibid.*, pp. 314, 316–17, 334.

29. *Ibid.*, pp. 318, 322.

30. Julia Markus corroborates this argument with her observations on the poet's choice of the subjective persona for *Casa Guidi Windows:* "Once we learn to trust her voice again, we will be able to uncover the significance of the very intimate 'I' narration of the poem. For the daring subjectivity of voice is a conscious and confident assertion of the moral and social role of the poet in her times" (p. xix).

31. She openly recanted her support for Grand Duke Leopold of Tuscany in Part II of *Casa Guidi Windows* (ll. 40–65), partly, it would seem, to dramatize just how much honest and concerned observers were at the mercy of changing events. Cf. Giartosio de Courten, who characterizes the "discrepancy" as a deliberate "guarantee of sincerity" (p. 135, my translation).

32. On the strength of EBB's poetry as political literature, see Markus, pp. xxxiv–xl. See also Hayter, who commends the "disinterestedness" of her politics (p. 135). She thus makes a virtue of the very quality Henry James had condemned when he characterized her expense of "so much disinterested passion" upon the cause of "a people not her own" as "a possession, by the subject, riding her to death, that almost prompts us at times to ask wherein it so greatly concerned her" (II, 54).

33. Kenyon, II, 382–83. The letter containing these words was addressed to Henry Chorley, unsympathetic reviewer of *Poems Before Congress* for the *Athenaeum,* and author of a nastily jingoistic novel about Italian politics, *Roccabella,* which he impudently dedicated to Elizabeth Browning. The letter bears comparison with the forceful statements in Book V of *Aurora Leigh* on commitment and contemporaneity in art, views that were to become incompatible with the modernist esthetic that featured the artist as "observer" and art as transcending the present moment. Cf. Henry James's description of EBB as a poet whose "sense of the general had all run to the strained and the strenuous," and whose spirit had failed "to keep above" (II, 54–55).

34. McAleer, p. 67.

35. Compare, for instance, the letters to the Storys already cited with his comments on the genesis of the poem to Robert Buchanan in early 1871: "I wrote, myself, a monologue in his [Louis Napoleon's] name twelve years ago, and never could bring the printing to my mind as yet. One day perhaps" (Hood, p. 145). This, of course, to a fellow-poet who had just published a poem on the same theme; the "one day" was later that year.

36. McAleer, p. 341 (19 July 1870). The vindication idea becomes even more convincing in the light of Hetzler's reading of the poem as in some sense a defense of Napoleon's underlying sincerity, for that strategy would have avoided the implication that Elizabeth's trust had been misguided.

37. The exemplary phrases come from Edward Dowden, *Robert Browning* (London: Dent, 1904), p. 120, and Barbara Melchiori, "Browning and Italy," *Writers and Their Backgrounds: Robert Browning,* ed. Isobel Armstrong (Athens: Ohio Univ. Press, 1975). p. 170, respectively. Melchiori insists on Robert's tendency toward "evasion" of contemporary issues as part of a deliberate strategy for "maintain[ing] his position as observer" (pp. 172, 181). "The Italy that really mattered to Browning was the Italy that he found in the library, the Italy of the past. . . ." (p. 171).

38. Valuable insight into Browning's emotional and moral dilemma over this episode is provided by Robert Gladish, "Mrs. Browning's 'A Curse for a Nation': Some Further Comments," *Victorian Poetry,* 7 (Autumn, 1969), 275–80.

39. E. L. Doctorow, "The New Poetry," *Matchbox* (a publication of Amnesty International), Summer, 1977, p. 1.

40. Kenyon, II, 346.

41. Honan and Irvine, p. 364; DeVane, "The Virgin and the Dragon," *passim;* Mario Praz, *Studi e svaghi inglesi* (Firenze: Sansoni, 1937), pp. 27–75.

42. *Casa Guidi Windows,* I, 1–216. The phrase from Filicaja appears as a leitmotif throughout this passage. Mazzini's phrase comes from his address to the newly-created Friends of Italy in February, 1851, reported in Italy among the *Raccolta di atti e documenti della democrazia italiana* (Genova: Moretti, 1852), pp. 216–48. The poet may also have recalled the wounded, bleeding, "formosissima donna" of Leopardi's "All'Italia" (1818). In introducing her edition of *Casa Guidi Windows,* Markus also stresses EBB's rejection of the victim tradition. Further line references to this poem will be to this edition; citations for other poems come from *The Poetical Works of Elizabeth Barrett Browning,* ed. Harriet W. Preston, Cambridge Edition (Boston: Houghton Mifflin, 1974).

43. Kenyon, II, 321.

44. DeVane, "The Virgin and the Dragon," p. 37.

45. Critics psychoanalyzing EBB's devotion to heroes as part of a quest for a "father-substitute" (Hayter p. 239) have diverted readers from the woman-orientedness of even her political poetry and the role of a mother-quest in her psychic life. Repeated use of the pomegranate throughout her work as a life-omen and quest symbol is indicative.

46. McAleer, p. 63.

47. See Paul Cundiff, *Browning's Ring Metaphor and Truth* (Metuchen, NJ: Scarecrow Press, 1972).

48. Hudson, p. 89.

49. *Ibid.,* pp. 126, 130, 133.

50. Contemporary accounts of the London cultural ambience in relation to Browning and Mazzini may be found in William Michael Rossetti, *Rossetti Papers, 1862–1870* (New York: Scribner's, 1903) pp. 225–31; and Moncure Daniel Conway, *Autobiography: Memories and Experiences* (1904; rpt. New York: Da Capo, 1970), II, 60–66. See also Harry Rudman, *Italian Nationalism and English Letters* (London: Allen and Unwin, 1940), esp. pp. 25–32. For Mazzini perceived as rescuer-saint of the Risorgimento within an elaborated version of the virgin-dragon myth, see Richard Garnett, *History of Italian Literature* (New York: Appleton, 1928), p. 374.

51. Quotations from *The Ring and the Book* are taken from Richard Altick's edition (Harmondsworth, Middlesex: Penguin, 1971).

52. I am not aware of any exploration of Browning's Pope (even by Browning's contemporaries) that takes the issues out of the historical context of Pope Innocent and develops them in relation to Pius IX. An unconscious association may have led Melchiori to refer inadvertently to the Pope of the poem as "Pius X" (p. 174).

53. The idea was first associated with Italian political philosopher Giovanni Gioberti and implied for some by Cavour's "free Church in a free State." It gained currency in England, however, through a widely-circulated translation of Charles de Montalembert's *Pius IX and France in 1849 and 1859* (London: W. Jeffs, 1859), an eloquent defense of Pio Nono by a respected conservative intellectual. Edward Dicey, a friend of the Brownings and author of *Rome in 1860* (Cambridge: Macmillan, 1861), also stressed the popular expediency of the new state's political accommodation with the papacy (pp. 269–70).

Introduction

CORA KAPLAN

> Never flinch,
> But still, unscrupulously epic, catch
> Upon the burning lava of a song
> The full-veined, heaving, double breasted Age:

With this "woman's figure" the doubled female voice of *Aurora Leigh,* its woman-poet-author and woman-poet-heroine, defines the poet's task. The age is Victoria's, but Elizabeth Barrett Browning calls back a looser Elizabethan speech to extend her image from matriarch to nursing mother, "the paps from which we all have sucked." Milk and Lava pour from the poem in twin streams; *Aurora Leigh* (1857) produces the fullest and most violent exposition of the "woman question" in mid-Victorian literature. In her discussion about self-determination Barrett Browning remembers and revises the work of other great women writers from Mme de Staël to George Sand and integrates the debate on gender relations, into which most eminent Victorians were drawn in the forties and fifties, with other political and cultural issues of those years. *Aurora Leigh* is a collage of Romantic and Victorian texts reworked from a woman's perspective. Gender difference, class warfare, the relation of art to politics: these three subjects as they were argued by the English and Continental intelligentsia are all engaged as intersecting issues in the poem. The longest poem of the decade, it is, to use another "woman's figure," a vast quilt, made up of other garments, the pattern dazzling because, not in spite, of its irregularities.

"Fate has not been kind to Mrs. Browning as a writer. Nobody reads her, nobody discusses her, nobody troubles to put her in her place." Virginia Woolf's comment is almost as true today as in 1932. Elizabeth Barrett Browning's "place" among eminent Victorians was so well assured in her lifetime that she was a prominent candidate for poet laureate when Wordsworth died at mid-century. It is empty today. The chairs have been moved up to

Reprinted from *Elizabeth Barrett Browning:* Aurora Leigh *and Other Poems* (London: Women's Press, 1978), 5–36. ©Cora Kaplan; used by permission of the author.

hide her absence from that otherwise meticulously reconstructed feast Victorian studies have served up to us in the past twenty years. Her excision from the retrospective canon of great Victorian poets began relatively recently with the twentieth-century revision of literary taste, although women writers like Woolf never cut her out of *their* list. *Aurora Leigh,* Barrett Browning's "art-novel" or "novel-poem," was widely noticed and enjoyed an immediate and continuing popularity for at least a generation following its publication in 1857. It ran through thirteen editions in England by 1873 and was still read and republished up until the turn of the century. Conceived as early as 1845, just at the point of her meeting with Robert Browning, she saw it ambitiously if somewhat vaguely as a "sort of novel-poem . . . running into the midst of our conventions, and rushing into drawing rooms and the like 'where angels fear to tread'; and so, meeting face to face and without mask the Humanity of the age and speaking the truth of it out plainly. That is my intention." The intention lay fallow during the intense and artistically productive years of her early married life, but in 1853 she started to write it in great bursts—towards the end, some three years later, at the rate of thirty or forty lines a day—writing, revising and producing fair copy, sometimes simultaneously. Her dedication of the poem to her loved and admired friend John Kenyon shows how much she staked on "the most mature of my works, and the one into which my highest convictions upon Life and Art have entered." To a correspondent in 1856 she wrote, "I mean that when you have read my new book, you put away all my other poems . . . and know me only by the new." The hectic composition and self-assurance are reflected in the finished poem whose "Speed, energy, forthrightness and complete self-confidence," says Woolf, make us "read to the end enthralled."

Aurora Leigh comes between two very explicitly political books: *Casa Guidi Windows* (1851) and *Poems Before Congress* (1860), verse which deals much more directly than *Aurora Leigh* with the revolutionary issues of 1848 and after. Elizabeth Barrett was a lyric poet with an interest in political and social questions; Elizabeth Barrett Browning was primarily a political poet whose subjects were slavery, suppressed nationality (Italy), the plight of the poor and the position of women.

Aurora Leigh is Barrett Browning's fullest exploration of this last subject. In 1845, when the poem was forming in her mind, she did not directly relate it to the woman question, but saw the success of an earlier poem, "Lady Geraldine's Courtship," about the love of a titled woman for a poor poet, as encouragement "to go on, and touch this real everyday life of our age, and hold it with my two hands. I want to write a poem of a new class, in a measure—a Don Juan, without the mockery and impurity. . . ." "Lady Geraldine" touched on a subject central to most women novelists of the time: the ability of women to choose their own partners without the approval of kin or society. *Aurora Leigh* includes this as a sub-theme only; its more modern preoccupation is whether marriage itself is a good thing, especially for women with a vocation. Elizabeth Barrett Browning, justifying her elopement to Mary Russell Mitford, explains, "It never was high up in my ideal, even before my illness brought myself so far down. A happy marriage was the happiest condition, I believed vaguely—but *where were the happy marriages?*" Novels which concerned themselves only with happy marriages, Jane Austen's for example, struck her with their "narrowness—the want of all aspiration towards, or instinct of the possibility of *enlargement* of any kind. . . ." Yet she was equally dubious about the political implications of the woman question. Again to Miss Mitford she wrote, "I am *not,* as you are perhaps aware, a very strong partisan of the Rights-of-woman-side of the argument—at least I have not been, since I was twelve years old. I believe that, considering men and women in the mass, there *is* an *inequality* of intellect, and that is proved by the very state of things of which gifted women complain; and more than proved by the manner in which their complaint is received by their own sisterhood." She thought the feminist views of her friends Anna Jameson or Harriet Martineau too advanced for ordinary middle-class women to take in, and this prejudice "proved" female inferiority. The conscious snobbery of this view is mitigated by her contradictory belief that "the difference between men and women arose from the inferiority of education of the latter," and her strong defence of women as writers and reformers. But her chief sympathies were reserved for women who wrote: "*You,* who are a woman and man in one, judge if it isn't a hard and difficult process for a woman to get forgiven for her strength by her grace . . . every woman of letters knows it is hard."

Aurora Leigh expresses this equivocal view of the woman question. The story of a young poet, the daughter of an English father and Italian mother, it is about the development of a woman writer. Aurora is brought up alone in Italy by her widower father. He dies when she is thirteen and she is sent back to England to live with his sister, a maiden lady, in the English countryside. The aunt tries to educate her as a perfect English lady, but the young woman resists and secretly constructs a syllabus of her own from her father's stored library. At twenty she receives a proposal from her cousin Romney, heir to the Leigh fortunes, who asks her to abandon poetry and join him in a life given over to social and political reform. She refuses, eloquently defending poetry and women's right to determine their own careers. Her aunt is furious; the marriage was blessed, even arranged, so that Aurora would inherit her share of the family fortune. The aunt dies with an unopened bequest from Romney in her hands. Aurora is left only £300 (she refuses Romney's money) and heads for London and a garrett where she slowly builds herself a reputation as a writer. Romney pursues his own career, rescuing, in the course of his good works, a poor girl, Marian Erle, who has run away from her brutal and drunken parents. He sets her up as a sempstress in London and eventually decides to marry her, not for love but as a gesture towards the breakdown of class barriers. Aurora, who has seen little of her cousin in her years in London, is informed of this imminent marriage by Lady Waldemar, an aristocrat passionately in love with Romney. Lady Waldemar wishes Aurora to intervene in the marriage, but after meeting Marian, Aurora gives it her blessing. On the wedding day rich and poor gather for the ceremony. Marian stands her bridegroom up, explaining in a letter that she does not really love him. Distressed, Romney returns to his utopian projects. Aurora finishes a major book and goes to the continent to rest. There she glimpses and pursues Marian, whom she discovers with an illegitimate son. It appears that Marian had been persuaded against the marriage by Lady Waldemar, betrayed by her servant and raped and abandoned in France. Aurora persuades Marian to accompany her to Italy. In Florence the two women live in relative happiness and self-sufficiency with the child. Through a series of rather clumsy plot manipulations Aurora learns that Romney has been ill and is convinced he is married to Lady Waldemar to whom she has written an outraged letter. He arrives soon after, unwed, and ready to atone for Marian's misfortunes by marrying her. Marian will have none of it! She sees her early love for Romney as an unequal infatuation and her commitment to her child as excluding marriage which might produce legitimate siblings. Aurora learns that Romney has been blinded during a riot where local peasants and his London down-and-outs combine in the sacking and burning of Leigh Hall. He has given up his socialism and philanthropic schemes. There is a mutual confession of love. Romney accepts Aurora's "art" as a higher good than politics and asks her to speak for them both in the future. Aurora, Marian and Lady Waldemar form the triptych through which Barrett Browning speaks her views on the woman question.

In the opening of Book V of *Aurora Leigh* there is a long discursive section on the poet's vocation where the author dismisses the lyric mode—ballad, pastoral and Barrett Browning's own favourite, the sonnet—as static forms: the poet "can stand/Like Atlas in the sonnet and support/His own heavens pregnant with dynastic stars;/But then he must stand still, nor take a step." The move into epic poetry chipped at her reputation in establishment circles, but enhanced her popularity. It was a venture into a male stronghold; epic and dramatic verse are associated with the Classicists and with Shakespeare, Milton, Shelley and Tennyson, and later, Browning. In 1893 the influential critic Edmund Gosse wrote that women have achieved nothing "in the great solid branches of poetry in epic, in tragedy, in didactic and philosophical verse. . . . The reason is apparently that the artistic nature is not strongly developed in her." This typical retrospective judgment may be a clue to *Aurora Leigh*'s modern oblivion, and one reason why such an important and diverse poet as Barrett Browning is now known almost exclusively as the author of *Sonnets from the Portuguese* (1850), her brilliant series of love lyrics to her husband. Twentieth-century male poet-critics echo Gosse's belief that women's voice in poetry, as in life, should be confined to the lyric. How can one account then for a sustained narrative poem that is both didactic and philosophical as well as passionate and female, an unmannerly intervention in the "high" patriarchal discourse of bourgeois culture? *Aurora Leigh* makes few apologies for this rude eruption into the after-dinner subjects that go with the port and cigars. Barrett Browning knew less about "this live throbbing age,/That brawls, cheats, maddens, calculates, aspires," than Mrs Gaskell. But it is the latter, in *Mary Barton,* who intervenes with the authorial voice to offer a timid sop to male expertise: "I am not sure if I can express myself in the technical terms of either masters or workmen. . . ."

The taboo, it is stronger than prejudice, against women's entry into public discourse as speakers or writers, was in grave danger of being definitively broken in the mid-nineteenth century as more and more educated, literate women entered the arena as imaginative writers, social critics and reformers. The oppression of women within the dominant class was in no way as materially brutal as the oppression of women of the working class, but it had its own rationale and articulation. The mid-century saw the development of a liberal "separate but equal" argument which sometimes tangled with, sometimes included the definition of women's sphere and the development of the cult of true womanhood. The publicity given on the woman question hardly dented the continued elaboration of mores and manners which ensured that daughters were marriageable, i.e. virgins. Patriarchal dominance involved the suppression of women's speech outside the home and a rigorous censorship of what she could read or write. All the major women writers were both vulnerable to and sensitive about charges of "coarseness." The Brontë sisters, Sand and Barrett Browning were labelled coarse by their critics, and, occasionally, by other women. Sexual impurity, even in thought, was *the* unforgivable sin, the social lever through which Victorian culture controlled its females, and kept them from an alliance with their looser lived working-class sisters.

The debates on the woman question which took up so many pages of leading British periodicals between 1830 and 1860 should not be seen as marginal to a male-dominated ruling class, increasingly threatened from below by an organising proletariat. Caught between this and the need to accommodate a limited demand for equity from informed women of their own class, they were equally committed to the absolute necessity of maintaining social control over females, and its corollary, the sexual division of labour. To get a sense of the space and importance given to the issue, one only has to leaf through the major quarterlies for a given year. The winter 1857 issue of the *North British Review* had both a substantial review of *Aurora Leigh* and a long review article dealing with eight books, titled "The Employment of Women," which ranges from an abrupt dismissal of Margaret Fuller's *Woman in the Nineteenth Century* for its romantic obscurity, to a serious discussion of Anna Jameson's *The Communion of Labour,* a work which argued that middle-class women should be "employed" in ameliorating the condition of the female poor. In support of Mrs Jameson the article quotes both Tennyson's *The Princess* and *Aurora Leigh.*

The right to write was closely connected with every wider choice that women might wish to make. In an age characterised by the importance of the popular press as the place of ideological production and the spread of female literacy, it was of prime importance to warn women off questioning traditional sexual morality. Public writing and public speech, closely allied, were both real and symbolic acts of self-determination for women. Barrett Browning uses the phrase "I write" four times in the first two stanzas of Book I, emphasising the connection between the first person narrative and the "act" of women's speech; between the expression of woman's feelings and thoughts and the legitimate professional exercise of that expression. Barrett Browning makes the link between women's intervention into political debate and her role as imaginative writer quite clear in her defence of Harriet Beecher Stowe's *Uncle Tom's Cabin*. She rejoices in Stowe's success as "a woman and a human being" and pushes the message home to her timid female correspondent:

> Oh, and is it possible that you think a woman has no business with questions like the question of slavery? Then she had better use a pen no more. She had better subside into slavery and concubinage herself I think as in the times of old, shut herself up with the Penelopes in the "women's apartment," and take no rank among thinkers and speakers.

Writing is a skilled task learnt at the expense of "Long green days/Worn bare of grass and sunshine,—long calm nights/From which the silken sleeps were fretted out . . . with no amateur's/Irreverent haste and busy idleness/I set myself to art!" *Aurora Leigh* enters, however, tentatively, into debates on *all* the forbidden subjects. In the first person epic voice of a major poet, it breaks a very specific silence, almost a gentlemen's agreement between women authors and the arbiters of high culture in Victorian England, that allowed women to write if only they would shut up about it.

Barrett Browning makes the condition of the poem's very existence the fact that its protagonist is a woman and a poet. Aurora's biography is a detailed account both of the socialisation of women and the making of a poet. Her rejection of her cousin's proposal is directly related to her sense of her own vocation. Books III and IV are full of the trivia of a young writer's daily life. Book V, the poem's centrepiece, begins as a long digression on the poet's task. Having established Aurora as artist so firmly in the first half of the poem, she can afford to let Books VI to IX take up the narrative line and extend the discussion of female autonomy to her working-class character, Marian Erle, and Marian's scheming opposite, Lady Waldemar. Aurora has a vocation and a recognised status and can be identified by more than her sexual or emotional relationships within the poem. The female voice, simultaneously the author's and Aurora's, speaks with authority on just those questions about politics and high culture from which women were generally excluded. *Aurora Leigh*'s other subject, the relationship between art and political change, is reformulated by the fact that, in the poem, the poet is female and the political reformer male. The poetic and all it stands for in *Aurora Leigh*—inspiration, Christian love, individual expression—becomes feminised as a consequence. The mechanical dogmas of utopian socialism, Romney's "formulas," are straw theories with little chance against this warm wind. Abstract political discourse yields, at the end of the work, to poetry.

So much we can find in *Aurora Leigh* without situating the poem too precisely in the historical moment of its production. Read in the 1970s, it does at first seem to be, as Ellen Moers has said, "*the* feminist poem" radical in its celebration of the centrality of female experience. In spite of its conventional happy ending it is possible to see it as contributing to a feminist theory of art which argues that women's language, precisely because it has been suppressed by patriarchal societies, re-enters discourse with a shattering revolutionary force, speaking all that is repressed and forbidden in human experience. Certainly Elizabeth Barrett Browning saw herself as part of a submerged literary tradition of female writers. Physically she compared herself to Sappho, "little and black"; Mme de Staël was her romantic precursor, George Sand her contemporary idol. No woman poet in English after Emily Dickinson and before Sylvia Plath rang such extreme changes on the "woman's figure," but women's writing, both prose and poetry, is now a rich cultural resource. Its relation to political change in the situation of women is no less problematic for us than it was for Barrett Browning and her contemporaries. We have only to look at the sections of the poem which are crude and alienating, the vicious picture of the rural and urban poor, to see that there are painful contradictions in a liberal feminist position on art or politics.

Both liberal and radical feminism insist that patriarchal domination is *the* problem of human cultures. It tends to ignore or diminish the importance of class conflict, race and the operations of capital, and to make small distinction between the oppressions of middle-class women and working-class or Third World women. The strains in *Aurora Leigh* which prefigure modern radical feminism are not only the heroine's relation to art, but also the way in which Barrett Browning manipulates her working-class figure, Marian Erle. Marian is given the most brutal early history of any figure in the poem—drunken ignorant parents, a mother who "sells" her to the first male buyer—but she enters the world of our genteel protagonists literate and unsullied. Taken up by Romney as a symbolic cause—his marriage to her is intended as a sort of virtuous miscegenation between the classes—she is betrayed, raped and abandoned in a series of villainies which suggest that sisterhood is a frail concept at best. When Aurora finds and rescues her in Book VII, a genuine alliance of female sympathy is formed between women of different classes who have the added complication of loving the same man.

But this sisterhood is bought in the narrative at the expense of a representation of the poor as a lumpen motley of thieves, drunkards, rapists and childbeaters, except for Marian, whose embourgeoisement in terms of language and understanding occurs at embarrassing speed. Only children (innocents) and prostitutes (exploited by men) escape with full sympathy. What is really missing is any adequate attempt at analysis of the intersecting oppressions of capitalism and patriarchy. Elizabeth Barrett Browning has as her particular political target in the poem the Christian Socialism adapted from Fourier and Owen and practised by F. D. Maurice, Charles Kingsley and others, but since she has no answer to the misery of the poor except her own brand of Christian love—and poetry—her solutions to class conflict are even less adequate than theirs. Inevitably a theory which identifies the radical practice of art with the achievement of radical social change, or asserts the unity of female experience without examining the forms taken by that experience in different social groups, will emerge with a theory of art and politics unconnected with material reality and deeply élitist. This is true of the book read in her time and ours.

Aurora Leigh is more than a single text. It is different as it is read and understood at each separate point in history, as it is inserted into historically particular ideological structures. There is a danger in either blaming the poem for its political incoherence by relegating those debates to history or in praising it only for the euphoria with which it ruptures and transforms female language. Works of art should not be attacked because they do not conform to notions of political correctness, but they must be understood in relation to the seductive ideologies and political possibilities both of the times in which they were written and the times in which they are read. Otherwise Barrett Browning's belief that the "artist's part is both to do and to be" stands in place of, not on behalf of, political transformation.

When *Aurora Leigh* was published in 1857, its author was one of the leading literary figures in England, her reputation ensuring extended notices in the periodical and newspaper press. Ruskin called it "the first perfect poetical expression of the Age," and there were delighted responses from Swinburne, D. G. and William Rossetti, Walter Savage Landor and many other writers, critics and artists. Reviews in the major quarterlies were considerably less favourable. Most could not cope with the transitions from high to common language, "wilfully alternated passages of sorry prose with bursts of splendid poetry," the ambitious scope of the subject matter and the obscure and violent imagery. The overriding technique of the reviewers was to quote passages "of great beauty" next to lines they disliked. They wanted the plot to be either more realistic or more allegorical—either *Jane Eyre* or Tennyson's *Princess,* not both at once. A few radical critics, especially the *Westminster Review,* objected to her castration of Romney's socialist projects; a few conservative reviewers thought that the conventions "which are society's unwritten laws, are condemned in too sweeping and unexamining a style." The *National Review* found the imagery "savage":

Burning lava and a woman's breast! and concentrated in the latter the fullest
ideas of life. It is absolute pain to read it. No man could have written it; for
independently of its cruelty, there is a tinge in it of a sort of forward familiarity,
with which Mrs. Browning sometimes, and never without uneasiness to her
readers, touches upon things which the instinct of the other sex prevents them,
when undebased, from approaching without reverence and tenderness.

Several reviewers object to Aurora as being "not a genuine woman," alternately cold and intellectual, and morbidly preoccupied with the "misappreci-
ation of woman by man." *Blackwoods'* declared, "We must maintain that
woman was created to be dependent on the man, and not in the primary
sense his lady and his mistress. The extreme independence of Aurora detracts
from the feminine charm, and mars the interest which we otherwise might
have felt in so intellectual a heroine." The *Dublin University Review* is even
more explicit:

Indeed in the effort to stand, not only on a pedestal beside man, but actually to
occupy his place, we see Mrs. Browning commit grave errors. . . . She is occasionally coarse in expression and unfeminine in thought; and utters what, if
they be even truths, are so conveyed that we would hesitate to present them to
the eye of the readers of her own sex. . . . The days when such a woman as
Aphra Behn can hope to be palatable to the female sex are gone forever.

The *North American Review* was more enlightened about the poem's feminism:

When we transfer Mrs. Browning from the ranks of female poets to those of
the poets of England, we would not be understood to separate her from the
first class. Mrs. Browning's poems are, in all respects, the utterance of a
woman—of a woman of great learning, rich experience, and powerful genius,
uniting to her woman's nature the strength which is sometimes thought peculiar to a man. She is like the Amazon in the midst of battle . . . [and has] . . .
attained to such a height of poetic excellence, not in spite of her woman's
nature, but by means of it.

What is remarkable about even the most negative and chauvinist reviews is
that they acknowledge the great power of the poem, recognise its importance
in contemporary literature and place its author in the first rank of poets.

While the greatest part of these long reviews is given over to summary
of the plot interspersed by quotation, there are occasional acute analyses of
what it means to be a woman writer. *The National Review* said:

She gives no voice to the world around her. It is herself she is pressed to utter.
And this is not only the unconscious but the direct and conscious aim of her
striving. . . . She is never the passive subject of that sort of inspiration by which
some *men* [my italics] almost unconsciously render back the impressions of
things around them; what comes from her is part of her. It is the song of her

own soul she "struggles to outbear" and she grasps the outer world to make it yield her a language.

In this respect the critic may be confusing what is characteristically female in Barrett Browning's verse—the need to transform a metaphorical tradition and political perspective formed and dominated by the male voice—with the personal or individual elements in the poem. The critic who notes her popularity with women is close to the mark when writing that she "speaks what is struggling for utterance in their own hearts and they find in her poems the revelation of themselves."

What the critical reception indicates is how fully the poem, with all its dissonant and outrageous elements, was taken to the heart of Victorian culture. Everybody in polite society read it, even the Queen and Barrett Browning was delighted by reports that it had corrupted women of sixty and been banned by horrified parents. The ways in which the poem is challenged and embraced is a comment on the contradictory presence of women writers on the woman question in mid-Victorian culture. It is as if they appear so prominently in the discourses of the ruling class in direct relation to their continued powerlessness in its social and political structures.

Aurora Leigh is a dense and complex text. Deliberately discursive and philosophical, the reflective sections of the poem state very clearly Barrett Browning's position on women's relation to self-determination, art, love, politics. The self-conscious didacticism of the poem includes some of its best "poetic" passages: Aurora's description of her aunt; her bitter diatribe on female education; her definition of modern poetry. But these sections are complemented by a less visible polemic built into the poem's structure and narrative. The plot borrows elements from so many other literary sources, and reworks them in a semi-parodic and sometimes semi-conscious fashion, that one can find a cutting commentary on the literary and political culture through an analysis of the "sources" of the plot alone. The narrative, often criticised for its lack of realism or simple credibility, is an elaborate collage of typical themes and motifs of the novels and long poems of the 1840s and 1850s. Years of ill-health, during which Elizabeth Barrett saw few people outside the Barrett household, had reinforced an early indiscriminate addiction to print, a habit that persisted through her married life. Characterising her life as secluded even before her illness, she thought that living less in society than in books and poetry was "a disadvantage to her art." She compared herself in her late thirties to a "blind poet" who would willingly exchange "some of this lumbering, ponderous, helpless knowledge of books, for some experience of life and man." She lived with peculiar intensity through the written word, her own and other people's. Books substituted for the variety and pattern of social experience which make a novelist. Many social events in *Aurora Leigh,* as well as many of the social types, are drawn more from fiction than from life, but released through poetic licence from the demands of a realistic mode of representation. In the bed-sitting-room at Wimpole Street, and in the sequence of apartments in France and Italy after 1846, the Victorian world as represented in the social novel is reduced to a sort of essence and reconstituted in *Aurora Leigh* as a different brew altogether. Several times removed from the "real," it is neither a distorted reflection of Victorian life nor a lifeless imitation of other literature, but a living critical commentary on both, full of its own ideological idiosyncrasies.

Victorian readers already familiar with Tennyson, Clough, Kingsley, the Brontës, Gaskell and Sand would have caught echoes that we are too far away to hear. Barrett Browning played very self-consciously too on earlier, romantic sources. The growth of the poet in Books I and II takes us very naturally back to Wordsworth, and large parts of the poem play with themes and characters from a novel that every literate lady of Elizabeth Barrett's generation loved, Mme de Staël's *Corinne, or Italy* (1807). The narrative of *Aurora Leigh* is a critical revaluation of its multiple sources in which didactic asides are interleaved with the story, much as de Staël leavened her romance with long sections on Italian manners, culture and art.

Crucially, the seemingly fragmented, discursive poem (two thousand lines longer than *Paradise Lost* as one reviewer noted sourly) is tightened and held by a rope of female imagery. One reviewer at least appreciated the "command of imagery" which gave a "vital continuity, through the whole of this immensely long work." Approved and taboo subjects are slyly intertwined so that menstruation, childbirth, suckling, child-rearing, rape and prostitution, are all braided together in the metaphorical language. The mother-child relationship—Aurora and her mother, Aurora and her father, Marian and her son—receives special emphasis. Suckling becomes a multi-purpose symbol of nurturing and growth. It links the narrative themes of Aurora's development as a poet and Marian's rehabilitation, to the philosophical and aesthetic themes: the relationship of art to its "age." Mothering and writing are identified as the process of "stringing pretty words that make no sense/And kissing full sense into empty words."

The force of the "woman's figure" is an argument for the genre Barrett Browning has chosen. The social and domestic novel that operated under the constraints of realism, as realism was defined in the middle of the nineteenth century, had little room for the rhetorical excesses acceptable in the female gothic novel written half a century earlier, and in the romance *Corinne*. After Jane Austen's reaction against the emotional and romantic in women's writing, heightened language became a dangerous tool for women novelists. Sneaked in as explosive interjections in Charlotte Brontë's novels, they immediately brought upon her the accusation of coarseness. More liberty was given to poets. Felicia Hemans, one of the most popular women poets in England before Elizabeth Barrett replaced her in the public eye, was rarely criticised for her passionate expression. Her love-crossed heroines could weep or commit suicide with impunity, while Brontë's Lucy Snow or Jane Eyre were reproved for a private howl at bedtime.

Most of the charges of coarseness are directed at any indication that women had a self-centred, independent sexuality. In Charlotte Brontë's novels, women are characteristically made to repress these feelings. Elizabeth Barrett's inhibitions are reflected in her comment on Sand's "disgusting tendency . . . towards representing the passion of love under its physical aspects." Even Aurora resists and denies her passion for Romney lest he suppress or divert her sense of vocation. As a result, Aurora's sexuality is displaced into her poetry, projected onto landscapes, the Age, art, through the "woman's figure." Love denied is rerouted through language. Comparing England, where her mind and spirit mature, to Italy which represents the body and passion, she describes England as a series of negations of the sexualised Italian panorama:

> . . . Not my headlong leaps
> Of waters that cry out for joy or fear . . .
> Not indeed
> My multitudinous mountains, sitting in
> The magic circle with the mutual touch
> Electric panting from their full deep hearts
> Beneath the influent heavens and waiting for
> Communion and commission. Italy
> Is one thing, England one.

This is straight out of *Corinne,* protected from censure by being suggestive, half-completed metaphor. Breasts, one is tempted to add, are one thing in verse, another in prose.

Aurora Leigh should be read as an overlapping sequence of dialogues with other texts, other writers. None of these debates are finished, some pursue contradictory arguments. The poem tries to make an overarching ideological statement by enlarging the personal to encompass the political, but the individual history interior to the poem—its "novel"—cannot answer the questions which the work as a whole puts to discourses outside it. What is true of *Aurora Leigh* is, of course, true of all writing. The pauses and awkward jumps in the text, the sense that the speaker has turned abruptly from one discussion to another, has omitted some vital point or has clammed up just as the argument gets interesting—those moments should claim our attention as powerfully as the seeming integration of structure and symbol. The text's unity is that adult voice that does not permit interruption as it tells us how things should be: its unintegrated remarks and pointed silences remind us that the "knowledge" of any one age is constantly open to rupture and revision. If we follow Elizabeth Barrett Browning through a select few of the debates in which she engaged we can understand the ways she could and could not meet "face to face and without mask the Humanity of the age," and speak "the truth of it out plainly."

Corinne, or Italy was published in 1807, a year after Elizabeth Barrett's birth, when Mme de Staël was forty-one. Set between her already famous study of literature and society (*De la litterature* etc. 1800), and her equally well known work on Germany in 1810, it enjoyed an immediate and dramatic popularity. Two English translations vied for popular favour and for literary women of several generations it was a traumatic, even catalytic, experience. Elizabeth Barrett at twenty-six called it "an immortal book" that deserved to be read "once every year in the age of man." Corinne is an idealised heroine. Ellen Moers calls her the "fantasy-transposition of Mme de Staël's own speciality as woman of genius," a poly-artist, "poet, improvisatrice, dancer, actress, translator, musician, painter, singer, lecturer." Born in Italy of an English father and Italian mother, she is orphaned at ten when her mother dies, and left by her father in the care of her Florentine aunt until she is fifteen when "my talents, my taste, even my character, were formed." Sent back reluctantly to England to live in Northumberland with her father, Lord Edgermond, and his cold, correct second wife, she finds her manners and education improper by English standards. At a dinner party she quotes some "pure" Italian verses on love and is roundly ticked off by her stepmother, who tells her "that it was not the custom for young ladies to speak in company, and that above all they ought never to cite verses which contained the word love." Her father too reproaches her: "Women amongst us, have no other vocation than domestic duties; the talents which you possess will serve to relieve the irksomeness of solitude," or entertain a husband. Lord Edgermond looks back on his first marriage as a youthful indulgence, although Corinne sees his transformation into a pompous English country gentleman as his "bending beneath that leaden cloak which Dante describes in the infernal regions." She compares the attitude towards her talents in Italy where they are regarded as "celestial endowments" with their reception in England as a kind of deformation. De Staël takes revenge on her own dreary year in England by describing with savage minuteness the dulling and crippling effect of English ideas of female education and socialisation. Corinne's stepmother monitors her thought as well as her behaviour, and de Staël makes the damp, cold climate a projected corollary of a world where "Birth, marriage, and death" composed the whole history of society.

Although Corinne spends some pleasant hours educating her young half-sister, she eventually defeats her own chance of happiness in England by displaying her talents too brilliantly to the father of a prospective suitor, Oswald, Lord Nelville. He decides against her on the grounds that she does not conform to an English idea of womanhood. Her own father dies, leaving her at the mercy of Lady Edgermond. Eventually, after refusing a proper marriage, she returns to her native Italy to pursue her career, promising to adopt a pseudonym rather than bring disgrace to the family. In Rome Oswald meets her, acknowledged now as the first lady of Italian arts. Travelling to dispel depression following his father's death, he falls in love with Corinne's beauty and genius. Much of the novel is taken up with their passionate but uncon-summated courtship which gives de Staël her excuse for long asides on Italian culture. Corinne knows that Oswald was to have been her husband but puts off telling him her story for two-thirds of the tale. He is shaken to discover that his father may have disapproved the marriage and rushes back to En-gland, promising fidelity, but in fact to discover how full and explicit was his father's interdiction. At first he remains faithful to Corinne but eventually yields to the attractions of her young half-sister, a conventional English vir-gin, and marries her. Corinne follows him to England and witnesses his betrayal. Back in Italy, she falls ill and gradually declines, hanging on for an improbable but somehow moving encounter with Oswald who, discontented with his marriage, returns in search of "Italy" with his wife and little daugh-ter. Corinne tutors the daughter in music and gives lessons to her half-sister in the art of becoming an adequate wife for the demanding Oswald. She dies and is mourned by all of Italy. De Staël leaves us considering the appropriate-ness of Oswald's choice.

Ellen Moers suggests that the first books of *Aurora Leigh* are a "return to Corinne" because Barrett Browning borrows heavily from the earlier work for her conception of her poet-heroine, her description of Aurora's genealogy and early life, and above all, her indictment of the socialisation of English women. It could be nearer the truth to say that *Aurora Leigh* carries on an extended debate with Corinne about all these matters. There is no single plot element that Barrett Browning uses that she does not change in some significant way. What Moers calls the "myth of Corinne" became the private fantasy of two generations of genteel women readers. The primal scenes of the myth are its belief in the possibility of female genius and the rejection of the woman who embodies it by her chosen lover. It is powerful and painful. The most signifi-cant alteration made by Barrett Browning is the most vulgar one. Corinne dies of disappointed love; Barrett Browning makes damned sure that Aurora, her modern Corinne, survives.

Like Corinne, Aurora is the daughter of an "austere Englishman" and a beautiful Florentine, but her father comes to England when "no longer young" to study that subject of perennial interest to the English bourgeoisie, the "secret of Da Vinci's drains." Italy itself does not move him; rather it is Italy embodied in a beautiful young woman in a Catholic procession which "shook with silent clangour brain and heart,/Transfiguring him to music." As in *Corinne,* and in so much Protestant writing about Italy, classical architec-ture, Catholicism and warm weather come to represent a blurred sensuality, missing in England, which opens the self to its permitted corollary love. Aurora, like Corinne, is orphaned, but with a crucial difference in timing. Aurora's mother dies when she is four not ten, leaving her unreconciled and unfraternised to "the new order." "As it was . . . I felt a mother-want about the world,/And still went seeking, like a bleating lamb/Left out at night in shutting up the fold,—/As restless as a nest-deserted bird." There is no woman to socialise Aurora, no mother to be cuddled by or imitate. Her loss is, however, a tragedy mixed with blessing. Although she forgoes an early and desirable experience of love and loving, to make her "unafraid of Love" she also avoids, if we adopt a Freudian schema for the socialisation of children, the full conflict of the Oedipal crisis which occurs at about four or five since she does not have to "give up" her father to her mother and identify with the weaker sex. Aurora's "mother-lack" makes her less conventionally feminine, perhaps less spontaneously affectionate, but also inclines her to identify with Marian, another semi-orphan, to protect and defend at all costs the maternal experience. Aurora is raised not by a Florentine aunt, but by her bereaved father "Whom love had unmade from a common man/But not completed to an uncommon man." This unfinished man, seduced from an absorption of patriarchal duties, "law and parish matters," teaches Aurora "all the ignorance of men,/And how God laughs in heaven when any man/Says 'Here I'm learned; this, I understand;/In that I am never caught at fault or doubt'." Unlike Corinne, Aurora does not display any precocious talents except a fine intelligence. As if to prove that Barrett Browning had read Freud she conveniently kills off Aurora's father at the onset of puberty:

> I was just thirteen,
> Still growing like the plants from unseen roots
> In tongue-tied Springs,—and suddenly awoke
> To full life and life's needs and agonies
> With an intense, strong, struggling heart beside
> A stone-dead father. Life, struck sharp on death,
> Makes awful lightning.

Discreet as this passage may now sound, it is probably the closest any English woman writer had come to an explicit reference to menstruation and the stirrings of sexual desire. What is even more important is that this awakening is not provoked by a romantic encounter with a male object (except of course the forbidden one, the father). "Life's needs and agonies" are assumed to be part of the natural development of female personality, not a set of feelings inspired by a marriageable male. In this subversive assertion of the autonomy of female sexuality Barrett Browning follows the spirit of Corinne. Her version of orphaning is one of the most interesting narrative inventions in the poem. The deaths of Corinne's parents deprive her of certain essential protection; she is allowed to stay in Italy until her character and talents are fully formed. De Staël makes the point that in a world where women's only option is to marry, the absence of the appropriate kinship structures makes women seriously vulnerable. Corinne goes back to Italy where her genius gives her a protective immunity, and where, in any case, manners and morals are more relaxed. Elizabeth Barrett Browning is making a slightly different statement.

Aurora's eccentric education in anti-patriarchal attitudes equips her more fully for the life she will eventually lead than a traditional upbringing. Her mother's picture becomes the glassed image of the representation of women in western culture "mixed, confused, unconsciously" with "Whatever I last read or heard or dreamed/Abhorrent, admirable, beautiful,/Pathetical, or ghastly, or grotesque." Her father's rejection of the conventional wisdom of patriarchal discourse mingled with her "restless," "seeking" "mother-want" is precisely the proper education for a poet who will take over the mother function of "stringing pretty words that makes no sense,/And kissing full sense into empty words." De Staël was interested in describing the evolution of natural genius in women, in refuting Rousseau's claim that women could not express the thoughts they inspired. Barrett Browning adds to that point a whole psychological dimension about the making of a woman writer, rejecting a romantic view of the evolution of genius and emphasising instead through a negative example, the role of family and early education in woman's development. Corinne's genius is nurtured in Italy, thrives only on Italian soil. Barrett Browning, loyal to her native England, does not allow Italy to take the credit for Aurora's poetic gifts. These are drawn out in green England which she comes to love. Elizabeth Barrett's country childhood at Hope End is preserved in her description of the Leigh's estate. England's "sweet familiar nature" provided a substitute for loving family "presence and affection" for the growth of the spirit. England nurtured the spirit and the mind; Italy the passions. Barrett Browning was a faithful English romantic, bred on Wordsworth and Keats. Accordingly *Aurora Leigh* is *Corinne* anglicised, the radical opposition between feminine poetic Italy and masculine England modified. Corinne finds no asylum in England; her two sojourns there are disastrous. Aurora finds her vocation in England and is recognised *there* (though without the exotic fanfare accorded Corinne) as a major poet. Italy remains the "magic circle" where love can be expressed and experienced.

Even in what seem direct steals from de Staël, important changes have been made. Aurora's spinster aunt who "liked a woman to be womanly" is a fair copy of Lady Edgermond; the ridiculous education she imposes on Aurora is an updated version of the tasks given to Corinne. Aurora is taught a jumble of useless facts and dates and a set of accomplishments: to play and draw, dance, spin glass, stuff birds and model flowers. No Corinne, Aurora does it all badly; she has only one gift which she develops herself, helped by her father's early instruction in the classics, "He wrapt his little daughter in his large/Man's doublet, careless did it fit or not," and her own secret borrowing from the remains of his library. The savage passage on female education jumps out at us from the poem; the aunt who, caged herself, kept that wild bird Aurora caged, owes something to Elizabeth Barrett's maternal maiden aunt "Bummy." She is, however, an older generation of Englishwoman, and Barrett Browning's critique of female education is not sustained throughout the poem, nor is an alternative system described. The point of that critique, like de Staël's, is that all female training, whether adequate or hopelessly faulty, is directed at making women better wives so that they may assert "their right of comprehending husband's talk . . . their, in brief,/Potential faculty in everything/Of abdicating power in it. . . ." Self-realisation is the issue here, not only for women of genius but for all women. Barrett Browning is engaging with quite another set of adversaries than those de Staël routed in *Corinne.* Corinne was an unacceptable wife because she was an artist. Aurora, initially, wants no part of a marriage which will not accept her aspirations as valuable and give them space; but she is not unmarriageable in the same sense. Contemporary male enlightenment allowed women of Elizabeth Barrett Browning's generation any amount of literary talent and intelligence (though the stage and the platform were still forbidden arenas), but clever wives were seen as an asset to a man's career, which naturally took precedence. Aurora and Marian are capable of surviving as Corinne is not without marriage or love, although in the end Aurora triumphs over her rivals and has her career *and* her man.

Aurora Leigh is superficially more "realistic" than *Corinne* but the reconstructed ending suggests a desire to repair, through rewriting, a tragic story that bit deep into the consciousness of the young Elizabeth Barrett. There is an evangelical note in her revision reinforced by the fact, known to her readers, that her personal history suggested a happy ending was possible. *Corinne,* as inspiration, myth and prophecy, was tangled up in so many ways in Elizabeth Barrett Browning's life and work and more subtle points in the text of *Aurora Leigh* reflect its influence. In both works Italy is the social landscape for "light" amours. In *Aurora Leigh* the passions released by the Italian setting are enduring, sanctified, while Oswald's early history included a sordid affair with a French aristocrat. Unscrupulous and scheming, she provides the model for *Aurora Leigh*'s Lady Waldemar. De Staël's version of English patriarchal puritanism comes dangerously near parody. The alterations Barrett Browning incorporates show how the patriarch-ungrateful-child theme cut. On one level she accepts de Staël's version of a desexualised England. Sexuality, even in the brutal instance of Marian's rape, occurs across the channel. The Brownings' own marriage took place in England but was consummated abroad. But consciously Barrett Browning rejects the sort of national stereotyping indulged in by de Staël. Lady Waldemar is a light *English* aristocrat. Romney's father is a shadowy figure who positively wants the cousins to marry. There is also transposition of the close relationship between Oswald and *his* father to that between Aurora and her father. The portrait of the elder Lord Nelville as a kind but autocratic patriarch who directs his children's marital choices from the grave was too close to the reality of Edward Barrett Moulton Barrett who barred his ailing daughter's passage to Italy, that land of health and passion, and never forgave her for marrying Browning. In the world of the poem things are otherwise and better. Aurora's father is constituted as an anti-type to the figure of a patriarchal tyrant. At his death he explicitly frees his daughter from the constraints of the Oedipal tie with the injunction that rings through the body of the poem: ". . . His last word was 'Love—'/'Love, my child, love, love'!"

The most bizarre echo of the novel occurred after Barrett Browning's death in Florence in 1861, which occasioned a day of mourning throughout her adopted city. Robert Browning described it in a letter to Elizabeth's brother George:

> She was buried yesterday, with the shops in the streets shut, a crowd of people following sobbing, another crowd of Italians, Americans, and English crying like children at the cemetery, for they knew who she was, the "greatest English poet of the Day, writer of the sublimest poems ever penned by woman, and Italy's truest and dearest of friends," as the morning and evening papers told them.

"The love-affair of Elizabeth Barrett with George Sand is much less celebrated than her romance with Browning, but in its own way it was as intense, as liberating and as clearly, if not as fully, documented." Patricia Thomson's excellent account of that relationship leaves so little out that it is almost enough to summarise her essay. Sand's life and work represented for Barrett Browning an excursion into the forbidden world of "immortal improprieties." Hugo, Sand, Balzac were her "triumvirate" of French writers, but she also read Sue, Soulie, de Queilhe and came away exhilarated and disappointed with *home* for being "so neutral tinted and dull and cold by comparison." Her sonnets on Sand reflect her wish that the Frenchwoman could be passionate and pure "true genius and true woman." Elizabeth Barrett was fascinated and repelled by the androgyny involved in Sand's masculine charade; much more important, she found in Sand, only three years her senior, an emotional, intellectual and political affinity and a passionate literary style missing in her English contemporaries. As Thomson points out, both "were warm, impulsive, emotional; both were Romantics, Byron-worshippers in their youth, radicals, moderate feminists; both were genuinely and effortlessly creative, enthusiastic reformers—but for both, literary creation came first." No single Sand novel can be produced as a source for *Aurora Leigh;* rather the whole Sand oeuvre, her philosophy and a modified version of her life, play into Barrett Browning's conception of her poet heroine. Aurora as a name was chosen after some debate—she hovered between Laura and Aurora—with her friend Harriet Hosmer throwing in her vote for the name with more "backbone." Aurore Dudevant was the "woman" in George Sand, the woman that Barrett Browning wanted Sand to acknowledge. Aurora's garrett in London is modelled on Sand's attic in the quai St Michel and her unequivocal equality with her male contemporaries mimics Sand. But Aurora is "a woman of repute;" just as Barrett Browning has given *Corinne* a new ending, so she has restored her living idol's lost reputation. When Barrett Browning chose to evoke specific references to contemporary works, she kept her audience and its reading habits carefully in mind. *Corinne* was an old favourite with the English reading public. George Sand might have been thought a subversive taste. Her novel *Consuelo* provoked Robert Browning to label Sand insultingly "la femme qui parle." Elizabeth Barrett rejected this judgment but incorporates it in a curious way in *Aurora Leigh,* transferring it from the woman writer whom she most admired to the feminist polemicists, like her friends Anna Jameson or Margaret Fuller, and placing the accusation "A woman's function plainly is— to talk" in Aurora's mouth, not Romney's. Finally, it is in the sexual metaphor, as Thomson shows, that Sand's liberating effect on Barrett Browning is most apparent. Although Aurora's love must be sanctified, the poet Aurora can speak freely of . . . "Spring's delicious trouble in the ground,/ Tormented by the quickened blood of roots,/And softly pricked by golden crocus-sheaves . . . ," a passage that anticipates in its boldness and modernity both T. S. Eliot and Dylan Thomas and matches the erotic eloquence of Barrett Browning's unknown contemporary, Walt Whitman.

In her celebration of "sexual passion" and woman's right to feel it, Barrett Browning is clearly on the side of Sand and the Brontës, "coarse" to the bone. While the Brontës emphasise society's demand that women suppress their expression of passion, Sand and Barrett Browning insist that women could and should have passion and vocation. Barrett Browning thought *Villette* a "strong" book, better than *Shirley,* possibly better than *Jane Eyre* which she had liked, but conveniently forgotten when writing *Aurora Leigh,* forgotten so thoroughly that when a friend challenged her for making Romney's accident a repeat of Rochester's she had to send for *Jane Eyre* from the lending library to refresh her memory. Romney is merely blinded, she points out, *not* disfigured. "As far as I recall the facts, the hero was monstrously disfigured and blinded in a fire the particulars of which escape me, and the circumstance of his being hideously scarred is the thing impressed chiefly on the reader's mind certainly it remains innermost in mine." Romney is painlessly "mulcted in his natural sight," like Milton, though his own words in the poem "mulcted as a man" make Elizabeth Barrett Browning's denial of the castration image less convincing. Nonetheless Romney's blindness has a multiple set of determinants. Elizabeth Barrett's earliest teacher and life-long friend Hugh Stuart Boyd, the classical scholar, was blind. Boyd played the role of mentor to the talented young classicist, and his critical attitude towards her early poetry is partly reflected in Romney's slighting remarks in Book II. The image of the "blind poet" shut out from life but with an intense inner life is one which Elizabeth Barrett used about herself. Thomson suggests that Sir Ralph in Sand's *Indiana* is a closer model for Romney than Rochester as he plays the same protective role towards Indiana, his orphaned cousin, as Romney does to Aurora, and their final confession of love has a setting much like the last scene of Book IX. Romney's blinding simultaneously robs him of his "manly" image and his masculine, mechanical projects for social improvement. His blindness brings spiritual enlightenment and forces Aurora's love out into the open. His helplessness gives the cousins a parity they did not have before, but it also symbolises the exchange of insight and merging of sexual identity in sexual passion. Romney is made a sort of poet through the loss of his natural sight. Aurora's speech must now substitute for his vision. Contemporary critics complained of the fashion women writers were falling into of disfiguring their heroes. The fashion was not casual, for in the imaginary world of fiction and poetry, disfigurement was the punitive equaliser which insured that the male partners would not easily reassert their dominant functions. The analogy to *Jane Eyre* stands, but with the added meanings which resolve the man of action into the enlightened lover, and allow the speaker of the poem to become the only doer. All the oppositions which Romney and Aurora separately represent—male and female, poet and reformer, speaker and actor—are dispersed and merged through the light, dark, sight, sound imagery of the final pages of the poem.

In 1853 Elizabeth Barrett Browning read Mrs Gaskell's latest novel *Ruth,* the story of an unmarried mother, with much greater enthusiasm than she had shown for *Mary Barton* (1848). Of the earlier book she said, "There is power and truth—she can shake and she can pierce—but I wish half the book away, it is so tedious every now and then; and besides I want more beauty, more air from the universal world—these class-books must always be defective as work of art." The style was "slovenly" and later, reading *Ruth,* she thought it "a great advance on *Mary Barton,*" an opinion which shows Barrett Browning's élitism as well as her weakness as a critic. This preference tallies with her resistance to books which dealt intimately and sympathetically with working-class characters. She thought *Ruth* "strong and healthy at once, teaching a moral frightfully wanted in English society," a moral so important she incorporated it into *Aurora Leigh* through the second part of Marian's history. Ruth's passage to unmarried motherhood is very different from Marian's. The beautiful daughter of a respectable farmer, she is sent, after her parent's death, to an establishment which trains sempstresses. Seduced by a young gentleman who whisks her to Wales and heartlessly abandons her, she is taken up and protected by a kind, dissenting clergyman. She moves in with him and his sister in their northern manufacturing town where they pass her off as a young widow. Eventually she is discovered. Disgraced in the eyes of the town, she becomes its saviour by turning to nursing. After heroic service in a typhoid epidemic she dies, and is canonised by the community. Mrs Gaskell is at pains to defend the unmarried mother against permanent stigma; her Ruth must atone for her sin through service, rather like Hester in Nathaniel Hawthorne's *The Scarlet Letter* (1852), a book also known to Barrett Browning. The question of innocence and atonement for sexual deviation is a vexed one for women authors. Marian has to be raped while unconscious in order to free her from any responsibility for her loss of virginity. A "pure" victim of male violence, her case is less complicated than Ruth's. However in order for the author to absolve her she must be denied the self-generated sexuality which is permitted to upper-class women in *Aurora Leigh* but which taints all working-class women except Marian. Barrett Browning was no more liberated about expressed female sexuality outside marriage than most of her readers, and the right to a passionate consummation within marriage is seemingly reserved for the well born. Through the trauma of her rape Marian becomes a virtuous untouchable, at once transformed from a good child into a self-determining woman (like Ruth), but an unmarriageable one. The instinctive horror of the defiled woman evoked in *Aurora Leigh,* as it is in *Ruth* and in most Victorian fiction, suggests how deeply internalised were the rules of sexual conduct. Barrett Browning's aversion to realistic portrayals of working-class women is apparent in her idealisation of Marian, and the equally heroicised slave mother in "The Runaway Slave at Pilgrim's Point" (1848). The conflict and contradiction in her position on female sexuality and class is poignantly suggested by her use of the *Ruth* theme in *Aurora Leigh*.

Corinne and the romantic feminism it represents provided the palette from which Elizabeth Barrett Browning worked in creating *Aurora Leigh*. The composition, the style and the subject are altered, but the colours are unmistakable. George Sand and Barrett Browning herself are superimposed on each other and the composite portrait placed on the faded outlines of Corinne to produce Aurora. Its deliberate double exposure reflects the identification of the English poet with the French novelist. Yet the subject of *Aurora Leigh* is larger than the mere recreation of a poet-heroine.

At the beginning of 1846 she told Browning she had heard Tennyson was "Writing a new poem—he has finished the second book of it—and it is in blank verse and a fairy tale, and called *The University,* the university-members being all females . . . I don't know what to think—it makes me open my eyes. Now isn't the world too old and fond of steam for blank verse poems, in ever so many books to be written on the fairies?" Tennyson's poem, renamed *The Princess,* appeared on Christmas Day, 1847, one of the two major poetic works of the decade before *Aurora Leigh* which deal centrally with the woman question. The other is Arthur Hugh Clough's *The Bothie of Tober-Na-Vuolich* published in the revolutionary year, 1848.

Both Tennyson and Clough, in rather different ways, were influenced by contemporary debates on feminism and women's place. *The Princess* vacillates between burlesque and high-seriousness. Tennyson in later years was highly critical of its unevenness, but the absence of his usual coherent manner is part of its pleasures. Large sections of *The Princess* read like an Asterix cartoon version of the war of the sexes. Modern Tennyson critics argue plausibly that his conscious intention was serious and sympathetic to feminism. He wanted to write a poem that dealt with modern problems. *The Princess* throws up a spectre of a doomed feminist separatism, symbolised by the motto of the University which threatens death to any man who enters its grounds. The all-female university cannot of course be allowed to survive, since it constitutes a serious challenge to patriarchal power and discourse. Princess Ida tries in vain to defend her heroic experiment, but women's nature, their maternal instinct, natural jealousy of each other and desire for the opposite sex all contribute to the downfall of the project. Once the men have penetrated the sacred ground the end is near; the threat dissolves in liberal compromise. Happy couples, the Princess and her Prince, will work together to improve the condition of women. The surface burlesque which involves the infiltration of the University by the young prince and his followers, all in drag, is funny but never titillating. Much more eroticised is Tennyson's fascinated horror at the very idea of a female bonding strong enough to survive without men while stealing and making use of Promethean knowledge.

Elizabeth Barrett Browning knew the poem well and was directing her work at the same audience. The dialogue between *The Princess* and *Aurora Leigh* is both more inhibited and more oblique than that between *Corinne* and *Aurora Leigh;* there are many points of agreement between Tennyson's and Barrett Browning's view of Victorian feminism. Barrett Browning rejects the "mapping out of masses to be saved/By nations or by sexes." Neither poet had any time for militant or separatist feminism; both offer similar resolutions to gender antagonism. Ida and Aurora are two formidable women, educated and autonomous, who reject marriages arranged by their male kin. Each has an individually developed philosophy, Ida on feminism and Aurora on art, which they are unwilling to compromise to please a suitor. Each assumes, mistakenly, that since they cannot find male approval for their vocations they will live without love. In the end both discover they have been loved as much for their independence as in spite of it. Their enlightened lovers, the Prince and Romney, are converted to their cause. Most important, the political resolution of both poems transforms the private marriage into the public act. The Prince promises Ida: "Henceforth thou has a helper, me, that know/The woman's cause is man's: . . . We two will serve them both in aiding her . . . /Will leave her space to burgeon out of all/Within her." Aurora echoes this worthy sentiment in Book II when she argues with Romney "That every creature, female as the male,/Stands single in responsible act and thought/As also in birth and death." Where Barrett Browning quarrels with Tennyson is over the concept of ideal marriage as gender complementarity. "You misconceive the question like a man,/Who sees a woman as the complement/Of his sex merely," Aurora says to Romney, answering Tennyson's formulation in the words of the Prince: "Either sex alone/Is half itself and in true marriage lies/Nor equal nor unequal: each fulfills/Defects in each. . . ." Romney's symbolisation of married love resists the two-halves-make-a-whole imagery. Instead he concentrates on the special quality of "the love of wedded souls," a concept which does not depend on oppositional images of sexual identity.

He calls it the ". . . human, vital fructuous rose/Whose calyx holds the multitude of leaves,/Loves filial, loves fraternal, neighbour-loves/And civic." *Aurora Leigh* avoids a discussion which locates and fixes social biological definitions of the feminine or the masculine, a subject which Tennyson dwells on at dismaying length. His feminism stops this side of redefining gender difference. Woman may change only:

> All that not harms distinctive womanhood . . .
> Yet in the long years liker must they grow;
> The man be more of woman she of man;
> He gain in sweetness and in moral height
> Nor lose the wrestling thews that throw the world;
> She mental breadth nor fail in childward care
> Nor lose the childlike in the larger mind;
> Till at the last she set herself to man
> Like perfect music unto noble words.

Romney, on the other hand, yields the speaker's role to Aurora: "Now press the clarion on thy woman's lip . . . And breathe thy fine keen breath along the brass." Tennyson's attachment to woman's traditional role is clear. His wife of the future still minds the kids and hums the tunes without the words.

The love scene between Aurora and Romney in Book IX owes something to the final pages of *The Princess.* Having brought the shadow text into consciousness, Barrett Browning criticises some of its arguments. The "fairy story" frame was not what she was looking for. Poets should "represent the age,/Their age, not Charlemagne's . . . To flinch from modern varnish, coat of flounce,/Cry out for togas and the picturesque/Is fatal,—foolish too." As wary of political feminism as she was of socialism, her silence about the central polemic in *The Princess,* the recuperation of an autonomous women's movement into a liberalised version of kinship and marriage structures, can be reckoned as a kind of agreement.

Arthur Hugh Clough's *The Bothie of Tober-Na-Vuolich,* using a modern scenario, also takes as its subject the radical revision of bourgeois marriage, without reference to contemporary feminism. Clough identified himself very fully with the European revolutionary movements of 1848, calling himself a socialist, and falling into deep depression at the failure of the popular cause: "Liberty, Equality, Fraternity driven back by shopkeeping bayonets . . ." he wrote disconsolately from Paris in 1848. *The Bothie* however was written earlier, in a mood of revolutionary optimism. A party of undergraduates go on a summer holiday to Scotland with their tutor. One, Philip Hewson, is the poet radical of the circle; his views include eccentric ideas about male-female relations.

> Never believe me, I knew of the feelings between men and women
> Till in some village fields . . .

> Chanced it my eye fell aside on a capless, bonnetless maiden,
> Bending with three-pronged fork in a garden uprooting potatoes.
>
> . . . longing delicious possessed me,
> Longing to take her and lift her and put her away from her slaving.
> Was it embracing or aiding was most in my mind: hard question!
> But a new thing was in me . . .
>   in part 'twas the charm of the labour.

Philip argues that the artificial intercourse between the sexes in polite society is a "dull farce." Women who are "not dolls" will "feel the sap of existence/Circulate up through their roots." He wants his women "Comely in gracefullest act, one arm uplifted to stay it/Home from the river or pump moving stately and calm to the laundry." Some of this description, if leeched of its bathetic seriousness, is reminiscent of the cameos in Whitman's *Song of Myself* (1855). Clough, like Whitman, romanticises domestic labour and eroticises the women who do it.

Philip eventually courts and marries a superior farmer's daughter, and the couple emigrate to New Zealand, but not before he completes university and acquires a first. His sexual preference for working girls must have struck a sympathetic chord with the fantasies and illicit sexual practice of middle-class Victorian men. In *The Bothie* this passion is presented as both respectable and politically correct. Clough offers us the cross-class marriage between Philip and Elspie as the ideal union, though it is Philip, not Elspie, who is presumably liberated by this connection. When Elspie asks Philip to leave her some of his books when he goes back to university, he resists the idea. Clough's poem highlights the contradiction involved both in the glorification of manual labour and the idealisation of the working girl. Both attitudes may have ruptured the complacent pieties of genteel society, simultaneously attacking its class values and its kinship rules. For women, however, it was a retrograde movement that took them out of the ballroom and boudoir, back to the kitchen and the nursery. The ennobling and arousing effect of this transition seems largely to be in the eye of the male beholder.

The Bothie, and its callow philosophy of modern marriage, is one of the targets in *Aurora Leigh*. The cross-class marriage is parodied in Romney's determination to wed Marian. There is cruel and direct send-up of Clough's sensual obsession with women at work in Book V, where a radical student at Lord Howe's party declares his determination to do away with "Prejudice of Sex/And marriage-law." The student reports that Lady Waldemar is so taken with Romney's schemes that she goes to help him at the phalanstery. He offers the conservative Sir Blaise a fully pornographic vision of that elegant lady: "Round glittering arms, plunged elbow-deep in suds/Like wild swans hid in lillies all a-shake." These lines stand out in the poem as the only ones where corrupt sensuality is vividly evoked as a by-product of utopian socialism. Clough's voyeurism and chauvinism are unmasked along with his phony politics.

Barrett Browning's critique of Tennyson and Clough reflects her refusal to accept male versions of female experience and the co-option by liberal men of the women's issue. But the male writer who engaged her critical attention most completely during the writing of *Aurora Leigh* was Charles Kingsley; the utopian socialist to whose novel *Alton Locke, Tailor and Poet* (1850), *Aurora Leigh* is a sort of counter-text.

Alton Locke was greeted by a critical reception that was both noisy and scathing. Because it dealt sympathetically with Chartism and had a working-class hero it was an easy target for establishment periodicals. Kingsley was thirty-one at the time of its publication, a Church of England parson already well-known as one of a band of liberals who called themselves Christian Socialists and had been influenced by the utopian socialism of Fourier and Owen. Their brief to "Christianise socialism, and socialise Christianity" was deliciously vague, but the projects in which they involved themselves were more concrete. In the mid-forties the group, whose leading theorist was F. D. Maurice, was involved in the setting up of Queens College, London, the first institution of higher learning for women. Kingsley was an effective muckraking journalist who wrote an excellent pamphlet for their series "Politics for the People" on the immiseration of artisans in the garment trade, *Cheap Clothes and Nasty*.

Elizabeth Barrett Browning had read *Alton Locke* and Kingsley's earlier novel *Yeast*. In 1852 she met Kingsley and wrote:

> Few men have impressed me more agreeably than Mr. Kingsley. He is original and earnest and full of a genial and almost tender kindliness which is delightful to me. Wild and theoretical in many ways he is of course, but I believe he could not be otherwise than good and noble let him say or dream what he will.

A year later, to Miss Mitford, she enlarged on her praise:

> I am glad he spoke kindly of us because really I like him and admire him. Few people have struck me as much as he did last year in England. "Manly," do you say? But I am not very fond of praising men by calling them *manly*. I hate and detest a masculine man. *Humanly* bold, brave, true, direct, Mr. Kingsley is—a moral cordiality and an original intellect uniting in him.

This passage is written in the year she began work on *Aurora Leigh*, so much of which is given over to a refutation of the politics Kingsley espoused in his life and work. A comparison of Aurora's description of Romney in Book II and her assessment of him in Book V shows how Kingsley figures in the poem.

One man—and he my cousin and he my friend
And he born tender made intelligent
Inclined to ponder the precipitous sides
Of crippling questions . . .
With kindness, with a tolerant gentleness.

Romney, like Aurora, is a synthesis of real-life and literary models. The quoted passage reminds us too of Barrett Browning's honorary cousin and life-long friend John Kenyon to whom the poem is dedicated.

However, her liking for Kingsley and her hostility to his ideas make him a perfect pattern for her "wild and theoretical" hero who must be converted from socialism to Art.

Kingsley was the richest contemporary resource for Barrett Browning because his reformist programme included attention to the woman question, explicitly treated in *Yeast* and dealt with marginally but seriously in *Alton Locke, Tailor and Poet*. The latter book forms the ideal foil for *Aurora Leigh*. The problems of social identity and self-determination for both working-class men and middle-class women were temptingly parallel. Charlotte Brontë had touched on the subject in *Shirley,* Mrs Gaskell in *North and South,* but Kingsley's creation of a working-class *poet* was a gift to Barrett Browning. *Aurora Leigh* might well be subtitled *Woman and Poet* and a later poem, *Mother and Poet,* picks up on the dissonance between the two descriptions. The self-taught hero of *Alton Locke* shares the same initials with our heroine. In his evolution as a poet he meets similar prejudice and encounters similar difficulties in finding an individual voice.

Alton Locke is the story of a clever working-class boy brought up by his mother in a rigid, dissenting household where imaginative literature was regarded as corrupting. The boy is apprenticed to a master tailor, in whose workshop he is exposed to worldly vulgarity and the realities of artisan poverty. He falls in with some radical workmates, one of whom introduces him to an old Scots bookseller, Sandy Mackaye, an impish but loving caricature of Kingsley's friend Thomas Carlyle. Eventually the conflict with his mother becomes so strong he leaves home. An upwardly mobile cousin at university introduces him to some aristocratic intellectuals. Locke accepts one man's patronage and falls in love with his pretty empty-headed daughter. Patronage and his hopeless love for Lillian contribute to a decision to take the political sting out of the poetry he is soon to have published. As the crisis of the forties ripens, Locke is drawn into Chartist politics through his tailor friends. At a country meeting he speaks feelingly about the condition of the rural poor. A riot ensues in which he tries unsuccessfully to stop the destruction and looting of property. Jailed for three years, he emerges with his health broken in time to witness the downfall of the Chartist movement at Kennington Common. He is nursed by Lillian's cousin Eleanor, Lord Lynedale's widow, who has anonymously intervened on his behalf throughout his career.

Eleanor converts Locke and his comrade Crossthwaite to Christian Socialism and the two men emigrate to Texas, to start a new life. Locke, alas, dies during the crossing. The high points of the novel aesthetically and politically are the scenes among the poor. The description of St Giles is genuinely harrowing, and worth quoting since it is these scenes that Barrett Browning cannibalises for *her* picture of the London poor. Mackaye calls it the mouth of hell and points Locke at the gin shop where he can see an "Irishwoman pouring the gin down the babbie's throat . . . Drunkards frae the breats!—harlots frae the cradle!" Mackaye drags him to "a phalanstery of all fiends . . . Up stair after stair . . . while wails of children and curses of men steamed out upon the hot stifling rush of air from every doorway, till at the topmost story, we knocked at a garret door." There Mackaye introduces Locke to a family of girls who keep themselves and a sick sister alive by sewing and whoring alternately. Kingsley's inferno is drawn to evoke pity, horror and indignation. If a cause and a solution are not offered at least Kingsley does not suggest that it lies in the original sin of the poor. When Elizabeth Barrett Browning picks up and imitates this scene, compassion and any pretence at social analysis have dropped out of it. Aurora notes "a woman rouged/Upon the angular cheekbones, kerchief torn/Thin dangling locks, and flat lascivious mouth/Cursed at the window both ways, in and out/By turns some bed-red creature and myself—/Lie still there mother! like the dead dog/You'll be tomorrow. . . ." This description is typical of Barrett Browning's portrait of the poor. Kingsley concentrates on poverty and ignorance; Barrett Browning prefers a close-up which emphasises an almost racial distinction between whore and lady and the total absence of affectionate bonds of kinship, particularly between mothers and daughters. Kingsley highlights the sympathy and solidarity among the poor in much the same way as Mrs Gaskell. He does not moralise about prostitution, but has his tubercular sempstress say bitterly "it's no merit o' mine Mr. Mackaye that the Lord's kept me pure through it all. I should have been just as bad as any of them if the Lord had not kept me out of temptation in His great mercy by making me the poor, ill-favoured creature I am." In contrast Barrett Browning makes Marian's purity, even after her rape, entirely the result of individual merit and "natural" virtue.

Barrett Browning also uses *Alton Locke* for her description of the riot at Leigh Hall. In Kingsley's novel Lord Lynedale gives his estate over to socialist experiment. Barrett Browning makes Romney's phalanstery the scene of social disorder, cleverly transferring the description of the riot in which Alton gets arrested to the incident at Leigh Hall. It is a reactionary running together of two very different episodes in Kingsley's novel in order to drive home the point that utopian socialism cannot alter the natural depravity of the lower orders.

Kingsley's panaceas for the class conflict he describes are particularly wet and weak and *Alton Locke* has passages of ugly racism and anti-semitism of which Barrett Browning could never be guilty. Nevertheless, Barrett

Browning's handling of the working class suggests just how her lack of first-hand knowledge of the world had damaged her political sensibility. Her only excursion into the London slums was made to redeem her dog Flush from dog thieves. Yet she was interested in social questions and wrote several compassionate poems, *The Cry of The Human, The Cry of the Children, A Plea for the Ragged Schools of London*. She saw herself as a "democrat," but her response to the failure of the 1848 revolutions suggest this veneer of democracy was easily scratched. The years between '48 and '56 had left her deeply cynical about the ability of the working classes to transform themselves into good bourgeois republicans. Her faith in leaders of Italian nationalist movements became directly in proportion to their aristocratic position and élitist aims. The picture of natural depravity set against natural virtue in *Aurora Leigh* confirms this disillusionment.

Also taken up and argued in *Aurora Leigh* are the role of the poet and the proper vocation for intelligent women. Kingsley was committed to the idea that Locke should remain loyal to his class as a "People's Poet" rather than enter the bourgeoisie. When Locke discovers Tennyson he describes him as a model of the democratic poet, not in his political opinions "but in his handling of the trivial everyday sights and sounds of nature." Aurora's version is identical. "For poets . . . half poets even are still whole democrats—." Both descriptions take poetic licence with the meaning of "democrat," the sentiment is straight out of Carlyle.

Kingsley rejects class mobility for Locke—and Barrett Browning's Aurora rejects androgyny as a masque or aspiration for women writers. She refuses all current definitions of women's roles and rejects the notion that there is a creative limitation on women as artists. Women should tackle epic as naturally as the ballad. One of Elizabeth Barrett Browning's closest friends was the American sculptor, Harriet Hosmer, whose giant figures were also epic attempts. However Barrett Browning did see women as constrained by their mediated relation to patriarchal power. Self-determination about work was more important than the right to choose one's own mate, and was always a struggle. This argument appears at various points in the poem and has a particular relation to Kingsley's view of the liberated woman represented by Eleanor, who explains that she was an only child and an heiress, "highly educated."

> Every circumstance of humanity which could pamper pride was mine. . . . I painted, I sang, I wrote in prose and verse—they told me, not without success. Men said that I was beautiful . . . I worshipped all that was pleasurable to the intellect and the taste. The beautiful was my God. I lived in deliberate intoxication, on poetry, music, painting and every antitype of them which I could find in the world around. At last I met with one whom you once saw. He first awoke in me the sense of the vast duties and responsibilities of my station—his example first taught me to care for the many rather than the few.

Proud of her intellect she delves into Bentham, Malthus, Fourier and Proudhon and helps her husband with his social experiments. When Lynedale died the "blow came. My idol— . . . To please him I had begun—To please myself in pleasing him I was trying to become great. . . ." Eleanor ends up living with a household of ex-prostitutes where the women work for each other and the workrooms "were not a machinery but a family." Here, in brief, is Corinne converted into a female reformer. Eleanor's history is replied to in *Aurora Leigh* through the angry disagreement between Romney and Aurora in Book II. Romney suggests that art is an inappropriate and vaguely unworthy occupation for a woman. Aurora replies. "Whoever says/To a loyal woman, 'Love and work with me,'/Will get fair answers if the work and love/Being good themselves, are good for her—the best/She was born for."

Kingsley's attack on women's art in *Alton Locke* stung. It is precisely his notion of higher good for Eleanor that is rejected and eroded throughout *Aurora Leigh* so that Romney finally accepts Aurora's art and love as the combined forces which will "blow all class-walls level as Jericho's."

There are nastier digs at Kingsley's ambitions for aristocratic ladies and the criticism is levelled not only at Kingsley but at Elizabeth Barrett Browning's feminist friends, Anna Jameson and Harriet Martineau. Mrs Jameson's book on women and labour which recommends projects similar to Eleanor's for idle rich women receives a sideways blow from Barrett Browning. A point that Barrett Browning accepts, reluctantly, is the notion that women cannot do without male approval for their work or rely on their own assessment of their talents or deal with material outside of the personal. Some of the most acute and enduring passages in *Aurora Leigh* are given over to discussing this problem.

> We women are too apt to look to one,
> Which proves a certain impotence in art.
> We strain our natures at doing something great
> Far less because it's something great to do,
> Than haply that we, so, commend ourselves
> As being not small and more appreciable
> To some one friend. We must have mediators
> Betwixt our highest conscience and the judge:
> Some sweet saint's blood must quicken in our palms
> Or all the life in heaven seems slow and cold.

Women's achievement in art is hindered by this seeming inability to perceive "Good only . . . as the end of good." The manifesto of liberation is placed in the very centre of the poem and is the heart of its plea for women to attempt emotional and intellectual autonomy.

> Yet so I will not.—This vile woman's way
> Of trailing garments shall not trip me up:

> I'll have no traffic with the personal thought
> In Art's pure temple. *Must I work in vain*
> *Without the approbation of a man?*
> *It cannot be; it shall not.* [my italics]
> We'll keep our aims sublime, our eyes erect,
> Although our woman-hands should shake and fail;

No woman engaged in work traditionally defined as male can read this passage without being touched by it. "Love" is quite pointedly not mentioned in these lines for Barrett Browning is distinguishing between Corinne's disease, the loss of genius through the loss of a lover, and the more general anxiety about male approval in patriarchal culture.

The feminism of *Aurora Leigh* is produced as a complex of objections to a liberal male response to the "woman question" as well as a revaluation of the concepts of self-determination as they were dealt with by contemporary women writers and feminists. The rejection of male left politics, "Fourier's void, And Comte absurd,—and Cabet puerile./Subsist no rules of life outside of life" is marked by Romney's failure and his capitulation to a new trinity: Art, a very feminised Christianity and Love. A male discourse denying female experience and wisdom, which attempts to co-opt women into a male-designed version of utopia, must fail as certainly as Ida's University. However there is a congruence between Barrett Browning's feminist perspective and that of the utopian socialists for both deny to the working classes any self-generating consciousness. Marx notes the latter in the Communist Manifesto. Nowhere in the literature of the mid-century is the bourgeois rejection of working-class consciousness more glaring than in *Aurora Leigh,* though it is certainly present in Charlotte Brontë, Gaskell and Stowe, among others. *Aurora Leigh* reminds us that there is a female as well as a male version of liberal bourgeois ideology. The feminist analysis in the poem is in some ways so advanced and so piercing that we forget it is central partly because the political analysis of the poem is so weak, so over-dependent on the vacillations of Barrett Browning's favourite thinker, Carlyle. It exists by creating a vacuum around it which whirls away problems of class oppression. Centred is the woman as speaker-poet. In the text she has virtually replaced all male prophets. The "woman's figure" dominates the symbolic language of the poem just as women's experience dominates its narrative. Yet for all its difficulties the poem remains radical and rupturing, a major confrontation of patriarchal attitudes unique in the imaginative literature of its day.

When we reach for later texts to compare it to we can look at Emily Dickinson's lyrics about love and art, lyrics which were so directly influenced by all Barrett Browning's work, and *Aurora Leigh* in particular, that Ellen Moers has suggested they be read as parallel texts. After Dickinson there are scores of feminist poets who celebrate women's experience with the "woman's figure." That most difficult venture for women, writing about women writing, is still rarely attempted in imaginative literature. Doris Lessing's *The Golden Notebook* (1962) and Kate Millet's *Flying* (1975) are major attempts to discuss the relationship between women's experience, politics and creativity. *Aurora Leigh* stands behind them as the first and most powerfully sustained literary effort to engage these issues.

Returning to the frame of the Victorian world we should remember that the description of Aurora as an independent author living and working in London was possibly the most "revolutionary" assertion in the poem, the item more likely to corrupt the daughters of the gentry than Barrett Browning's sympathetic reference to the plight of prostitutes, for it affected the real possibilities and conditions of the lives of middle-class women. She does not suggest that the literary life lived single is romantic or exciting. More subversively and seductively she indicates that it is possible, interesting and productive, a fact that was beginning to be true for the generation of women who came after the mid-century.

Elizabeth Barrett Browning saw the representation of her age of steam as a kind of duty to the future. Her sense of the "age" is both wider and narrower than that of the contemporary social novel. *Aurora Leigh* combines the pleasures of the Victorian novel with those of the Victorian poem. Our obsession is with the Victorian and Edwardian worlds themselves. They are our middle-ages. There, in fancy dress, the still-present hierarchies of class and gender are displayed without shame, unsuppressed by the rhetoric of equality which glosses our own situation. Class conflict and the inequality between sexes were the spoken subjects of much of that literature and sexual transactions across class lines the erotic subtext of many popular works. In modern fiction sexuality is the spoken subject, power relations the subtext which must wear a fig leaf. Consequently our literary appetite for the Victorians is easily explained. They give us two kinds of coarseness: a coarse drama of class against class and men against women, picked out in strong colours, and even coarser interpretations of these conflicts. They offer solutions which swing between the compassionate and cowardly, the needle often poised at silly. They are our fairy-tales; the Brontës, Mrs Gaskell, George Eliot, Christina Rossetti, Emily Dickinson, Elizabeth Barrett Browning our sisters Grimm.

Women's Writing:
Jane Eyre, Shirley, Villette, Aurora Leigh
[excerpt]

THE MARXIST-FEMINIST LITERATURE COLLECTIVE

WHO ARE WE?

This paper arises from the work of a group which has been meeting in London for one and a half years (though some of its members joined more recently). It was presented at the Essex Literature Conference in July 1977, by the whole Collective, whose members at the time were Cheris Kramer, Cora Kaplan, Helen Taylor, Jean Radford, Jennifer Joseph, Margaret Williamson, Maud Ellmann, Mary Jacobus, Michèle Barrett and Rebecca O'Rourke.

The cumbersome title—Marxist-Feminist Literature Collective—covers (or perhaps conceals), on one side of the hyphen—in the adjective "Marxist"—a diversity of positions in relation to Marxism. On the other side of the hyphen, the adjective "feminist" points, among other things, to an important aspect of our practice. A major contribution of the women's movement has been the organisational principle of collective work; for all of us, the method of work within the group has been a departure from and a challenge to the isolated, individualistic ways in which we operate in academic spheres. Our paper, in its polylogic structure and presentation, draws on the continuing play of ideas and debate from within which we speak, and challenges the monologic discourse of patriarchal literary criticism.

THEORETICAL INTRODUCTION

A Marxist-feminist critical practice proposes to account for the inadequacies of a standard Marxist approach to literature and ultimately to transform this approach. In this paper we discuss the articulation of class and gender in

Reprinted from *Ideology and Consciousness* 1, no. 3 (Spring 1978): 27–48. Used by permission of Cora Kaplan for the Collective.

terms both of the historical conjuncture of 1848 and of the problems of a Marxist-feminist method in theorising literature. Literary texts are assumed to be ideological in the sense that they cannot give us a knowledge of the social formation; but they do give us something of equal importance in analysing culture, an imaginary representation of real relations.

A Marxist-feminist approach, by focussing on gender as a crucial determinant of literary production, can provide a better understanding of literature as a gender differentiated signifying practice. This is not to privilege gender over class, but to challenge the tradition in which women's writing has often been hived off from the mainstream of male writing and criticism.

Both Marxism and Feminism have rightly taken considerable interest recently in the possibility of an integration between Marxist and psychoanalytic thought. Both Marxism and psychoanalysis propose their methods as exhaustive; but we argue that it is only through a synthesis of these two, problematic though that is, that we can unfold the crucial interdependence between class structure and patriarchy.

Lukàcs argued that coherent literary works could only be produced by a unified, ascending social class, and in this context he stressed 1848 as the date at which the bourgeoisie as a class and realism as a literary form began to decline. The limitations of this approach are notorious, and too numerous to list here. What we shall do is not only, using the ideas of Jacques Lacan, Pierre Macherey and others,[1] analyse the incoherences and contradictions in the texts we discuss, but also relate these precisely to the marginal position of female literary practice in this period.

Central to our analysis of these texts is a recognition of the marginality of their authors to the public discourse of mid-nineteenth century society. The partial exclusion of women from the public literary world is one aspect of the general marginality of women in this period, as instanced by their exclusion from the exercise of political power and their separation from production. This congruence between the marginality of women writers and the general position of women in society is represented in the situation of many female characters in the texts.

The period of protest which culminated in the political events of the 1840s marked the transition from a manufacturing economy to the industrial capitalist mode of production—developments which had serious consequences for women and the family. Working-class women were drafted into production as a source of cheap labour; bourgeois women remained in the home and were separated from production. In both cases women were excluded from ownership of the means of production, distribution and exchange.

However, the inadequacy of a solely economic mode of analysis is shown by Engels' optimistic claim in 1884 that, because of working-class women's entry into the industrial labour process, ". . . the last remnants of male domination in the proletarian home have lost all foundation."[2] It is clearly necessary also to analyse the contemporary ideological formation in terms of the hegemony of patriarchal attitudes. Such attitudes are represented for example in the double standard of sexual morality, whereby women were either madonnas or whores, and middle-class women in particular were subject to the constraints of the ideology of domesticity and the angel in the house. The ideology of romantic love, while masking the economic basis of bourgeois marriage in this period as the exchange of women, shows by its persistence that it exists autonomously, independent of its specific economic functions in a given historical conjuncture.

The four texts under consideration foreground these questions. *Jane Eyre* (1847), *Shirley* (1849), *Villette* (1853), and *Aurora Leigh* (1857), can be read as a discussion of gender definition, kinship structures, and to some extent the relation between these and social class. The texts of Charlotte Bronte and Elizabeth Barrett Browning refuse to reproduce contemporary economic and ideological determinations; instead they represent a systematic evasion or interrogation of the Law of these determinations. Althusser has stressed its inescapability: "The Law cannot be 'ignored' by anyone, least of all by those ignorant of it, but may be evaded or violated by everyone. . . . ."3

We argue that this "evasion" of the law occurs in the texts in the interrelated areas of social class, kinship and Oedipal socialisation. The necessary connections between these three areas are represented in the texts' presentation of two key points of articulation—the institution of marriage and the role of the *pater familias*.

All the major female characters of the texts have an extremely marginal and unstable class position, and all display an obvious discrepancy between their class position and their alleged rightful status; their status is bourgeois, but they are all orphans and most of them are without financial independence. Comparing these texts with those of Jane Austen, the lack of determinacy of class background is striking.

The bourgeois kinship structure of the period, predicated on the exchange of women, is similarly evaded. None of the heroines have fathers present to give them away in marriage. More importantly, we can analyse marriage itself as the crucial point of articulation between class and kinship structures. This can be seen in two ways: on one hand, the only women in the texts who are free to exercise choice in marrying—Jane Eyre, Aurora Leigh, Shirley and Polly de Bassompierre—have, or miraculously acquire, some degree of financial independence.

On the other hand, the example of Caroline Helstone demonstrates with great force the law which Charlotte Bronte otherwise evades, in that her marriage to Robert Moore can only take place when the repeal of the Orders in Council has enabled him to be a successful capitalist. Without this repeal, he would have emigrated to Canada and she would have been an Old Maid!

The evasion of Oedipal determination, so crucial to gender definition in this period, will be discussed in more detail in its most striking manifestation, in *Aurora Leigh*. But in all these texts the devised absence of the father represents a triple evasion of all the areas we have so far mentioned—class structure, kinship structure and Oedipal socialisation. Its consequences are that there is no father from whom the bourgeois woman can inherit property, no father to exchange her in marriage, and no father to create the conditions for typical Oedipal socialisation.

The subversiveness of this evasion was recognised by contemporary reviewers, for in 1848 Lady Eastlake wrote in the *Quarterly Review:*

> We do not hesitate to say that the tone of mind and thought which has over-thrown authority and violated every code human and divine abroad, and fostered chartism and rebellion at home, is the same which has also written *Jane Eyre*.[4]

In discussing literary texts, it is important to look at the way women's access to language is ideologically determined. One of the effects of the lack of access to education of which women writers complain is to exclude them from the discourses of institutions such as universities, law, politics and finance which structure their oppression. Women, who are speaking subjects but partially excluded from culture, find modes of expression which the hegemonic discourse cannot integrate. Whereas the eruptive word cannot make the culturally inaccessible accessible, it can surely speak its absence. Kristeva has classified these modes of expression as "semiotic" as opposed to "symbolic."

Inevitably, the work of Kristeva has been considered for its obvious bearing on our analysis. Her notion of the semiotic comprised the repressed, pre-linguistic elements which are located in the tonal, rhythmic, expressive and gestural qualities of poetic discourse. In our view, her association of these qualities with the feminine is fallacious; she has used a cultural ascription of feminity to describe pre-linguistic elements which are in fact universal, and she thus risks privileging and feminising the irrational. But as we all know, intuition is still the short-change given women by the patriarchy. Not only are there limitations from a feminist perspective, but by calling the feminine, or the semiotic, subversive, she formulates an anarchic revolutionary poetics which is politically unsatisfactory. Her argument, seductive as it is, idealises and romanticises the discursive ruptures of the avant-garde. Her failure to locate these notions historically also tends to eternalise the social exaggeration of biological difference. Nevertheless, her suggestive writings have polyphonic resonances in our work, which alludes to, sometimes even dwells on, the explosive and temporarily liberating dissonance within the texts.

INTRODUCTION TO THE TEXTS: GENDER AND GENRE

In 1859, Charlotte Brontë made a final, impatient plea to Lewes:

> I wish you did not think me a woman. I wish all reviewers believed "Currer Bell" to be a man; they would be more just to him. . . . . I cannot, when I

write, think always of myself and what you consider elegant and charming in femininity. . . .[5]

Criticism of women writers is in general divided between the extremes of gender-disavowal and gender-obsession. The second tendency, which Brontë struggles against in Lewes, patronises women writers as outsiders to literary history, without justifying this apartheid. The Brontës are considered important "women novelists," not simply novelists. This kind of "gender criticism" subsumes the text into the sexually-defined personality of its author, and thereby obliterates its literarity. To pass over the ideology of gender, on the other hand, ignores the fact that the conditions of literary production and consumption are articulated, in the Victorian period, in crucially different ways for women and men. Any rigorous Machereyan analysis must account for the ideology of gender as it is written into or out of texts by either sex. Women writers, moreover, in response to their cultural exclusion, have developed a relatively autonomous, clandestine tradition of their own.

Gender and genre come from the same root, and their connection in literary history is almost as intimate as their etymology. The tradition into which the women novelist entered in the mid-19th century could be polarised as at once that of Mary Wollstonecraft and of Jane Austen, with the attendant polarisation of politics—between revolutionary feminism and conservatism—and of genre—between romanticism and social realism. Wollstonecraft and Austen between them pose the central question of access to male education and discourse on the one hand, on the other the annexing of women's writing to a special sphere, domestic and emotional.

Austen's refusal to write about anything she didn't know is as undermining to the patriarchal hegemony as Wollstonecraft's demand for a widening of women's choices: the very "narrowness" of her novels gave them a subversive dimension of which she herself was unaware, and which has been registered in critics' bewilderment at what status to accord them.

Bourgeois criticism should be read symptomatically: most of its so-called "evaluation" is a reinforcement of ideological barriers. Wollstonecraft's, and later Brontë's, ambivalent relation to Romanticism, usually described as clumsy Gothicism, is bound up with their feminism. Romanticism becomes a problem for women writers because of its assumptions about the "nature of femininity." The tidal rhythms of menstruation, the outrageous visibility of pregnancy, lead, by a non-sequitur common to all sexual analogy, to the notion that women exist in a state of unreflective bios, the victims of instincts, intuitions, and the mysterious pulsations of the natural world. Intuition is held to be a prelapsarian form of knowledge, associated especially with angels, children, idiots, "rustics" and women. These excluded, or fabulous, groups act for the patriarchy as a mirror onto which it nostalgically projects the exclusions of its discourse. As a glorified, but pre-linguistic communion with nature, intuition lowers women's status while appearing to raise it.

While Wollstonecraft and Brontë are attracted to Romanticism because reluctant to sacrifice, as women writers, their privileged access to feeling, both are aware that full participation in society requires suppression of this attraction. The drive to female emancipation, while fuelled by the revolutionary energy at the origins of Romanticism, has an ultimately conservative aim—successful integration into existing social structures. Romanticism, after the disappointments of the French Revolution, was gradually depoliticised, and it is only in the mid-nineteenth century, in a period of renewed revolutionary conflict, that it once again becomes a nexus of ideological tension where gender, genre, politics and feminism converge. . . .

AURORA LEIGH: CURSE AND WRITE

Villette was published in the year Elizabeth Barrett Browning began work on her "intensely modern . . poetic art-novel," *Aurora Leigh.* Most of Barrett Browning's mature work has overt, traditional political content, and expresses a fiery Romantic individualism mixed with passionate concern for the oppressed poor, suppressed nationality (Italy), the slave and women. Romantic individualism is not suppressed or mediated by the author's gender or by gender concerns in Barrett Browning's poetry. Speaking directly from the female position, she proposes political syntheses which include demands for the reconstruction of social and political relations in forms other than those offered by reformist or conservative patriarchal ideologies. Unlike most other women writers in England, Barrett Browning expressed her consciousness of 1848 as a revolutionary moment which was an appropriate subject for art. Her disillusionment with the political resolutions of 1848 is articulated in *Aurora Leigh* (1857) through a mode of discourse which is only intermittently homologous with the political feminism of the day, but consistently hostile to existing patriarchal discourses and institutions.

The most significant way in which *Aurora Leigh* takes up the issue of gender difference in bourgeois culture is through its focus on the woman as poet. Barrett Browning argued that Victorian feminists privileged the ideological over the practical: "By speaking we prove only that we can speak." She attempts to resolve the contradiction implicit in her own speech by seeing poetry as action: "The artist's part is both to be and do. . . . turning outward, with a sudden wrench . . . the thing [s/he] feels inmost. . . . . ." On this Möbius strip we too as Marxist-feminist critics and writers inscribe ourselves.

The unrepressed Romanticism of Barrett Browning's politics and aesthetic theory throws into relief the question of women's access to full subjectivity in culture in *Aurora Leigh.* Marriage as a way of finding a vocation through a man's work, as an attempt to annul class difference, as a means of class mobility, as a way for women to gain protection, as a repair for male violence, as *anything* but the union of two desiring subjects, is attacked in the poem. The conflicts about kinship and marriage, and the oppressive rules of femininity, which dominate Austen's and Brontë's work are produced with a difference in *Aurora Leigh.* Romney and Aurora are second cousins, and their union is a partial defiance both of Victorian prescriptions about sex roles and of the rules of exogamy. By making marriage the resolution of problems about neither women's place in culture nor their place in class, *Aurora Leigh* projects those problems back on to the independent activity of women themselves. The first and most central activity is that of writing itself.

Thus the question posed in *Aurora Leigh,* openly, discursively, rather than invisibly stitched into the design of the poem, is this: can woman be at once the speaker/writer of her own discourse and a desiring, choosing subject in her own right? In any text written by a woman the author has tacitly assumed the role of speaker. Female literary production breaks the cultural taboo against women as public speakers, a taboo felt by almost all women who defined themselves as writers in the nineteenth century. Instead of weeping Barrett Browning urged women: "Curse and write." Yet the social and public silence of women after puberty was central to the construction of femininity, a term Elizabeth Barrett Browning hated. The central contradiction for female authors as producers of their own speech is suppressed or displaced in the work of Austen and Brontë. By making her heroine a poet Barrett Browning breaks what is virtually a gentlemen's agreement between women writers and the arbiters of high culture in Victorian England that stated that women could write if they would only shut up about it.

In *Aurora Leigh* the contradiction of women speaking and women silent is partially dissolved in the first lines of the poem:

> Of writing many books there is no end;
> And I who have written much in prose and verse
> For others' uses, will write now for mine. . . . .

Writing as a creative expression of the self for a public audience is here asserted as the "given" of the protagonist's history. In *Villette* the writing even of letters is a problem, in *Shirley* writing is an unfulfilled talent. Speaker and woman are conventionally joined at the beginning of the poem. At the end this unity is queried; and the dissonance and lack hinted at throughout is exposed as the suppression of Aurora's love for Romney and the error of her youthful passion "to exalt/The artist's instinct in me at the cost/of putting down the woman's." Both lives have been distorted through denial of love, but Aurora does not now reject her art; on the contrary, love completes her original presentation of self. The condition for Aurora's marriage which Barrett Browning sets in the narrative is that she retain her position as speaking subject. A woman poet is the speaker throughout the poem even when it is the authorial voice and not Aurora who seems to be speaking. This doubled female voice is strengthened too by the choice of genre. The lyricisation of blank verse in Romanticism demands a first person singular speaker.

The verse form, its constantly reflexive quality and the irresistible congruence between the female poet/producer and female poet/speaker make the Romantic mode dominant, bringing with it feminised organic metaphors of nourishing and succouring:

> I drew the elemental nutriment and heat
> From nature as earth feels the sun at nights
> Or as a babe sucks surely in the dark.

There is a new force here in the equation between creativity and the mother-child relationship.

Crucial to Aurora's installation in the poem as a poet is the way in which Barrett Browning revises the experience of orphaning. Aurora loses her mother at the Oedipal moment—age four—and her father as she attains the menarch. ("I was just thirteen, . . . and suddenly awoke/to full life and life's needs and agonies . . . beside/A stone-dead father.") Aurora thus avoids the usual social experience of Oedipalisation—she does not have to realise her mother as a rival or come to terms with her own lack of masculine power; instead she projects on to her mother's portrait a composite and shifting image of women as they are glassed in Western culture. Meanwhile her father has taught her that male discourse is to be challenged ("He taught me all the ignorance of men. . . ."). Conveniently he dies before the intense father-daughter relationship becomes sexually dangerous. Aurora's socialisation is presented as an alternative to, or circumvention of, Victorian childhood. Aurora remains female but not feminine. Her early education equips her to enter and criticise patriarchal discourse: orphaned, she is uniquely placed to rebel, and as an adult she takes over and professionalises her mother's function of "kissing full speech into empty words."

Barrett Browning thought *Villette* a strong book, better than *Shirley,* possibly better than *Jane Eyre.* In correspondence with a friend about the parallels between Rochester and Romney's blinding she comments: "The hero was monstrously disfigured and blinded in a fire the particulars of which escape me." Romney is merely "mulcted in his natural sight." The semi-suppressed source and the significance of the revision are both obvious. The mulcting of Romney's sight leads to a clear-sighted abandonment of his misguided social projects—"mapping out of masses to be saved"—and leaves room for Love and Art, Aurora's project. In a democratic marriage work and love become shared activities involving no sexual division of labour, "Art," the poem itself in its real and fictional existence, making the synthesis possible. The blinding of Romney removes him as an independent actor, weakens his alignment with the dominant male culture, increases his dependence on Aurora and makes it impossible for him to see her as a sexual object.

The conclusion of the poem produces all the contradictions endemic to feminist reformism within an essentially bourgeois and "romantic" problematic. Barrett Browning has instituted companionate marriage in place of the traditional Victorian family. However she goes further than this, suggesting that Marian and Aurora could support each other without men if necessary, and making Marian refuse Romney at the end of the poem not because she thinks herself defiled by rape but because she no longer loves him, and because she prefers to claim her child for the mother-child dyad rather than accept a surrogate paternity. Paradoxically, male violence in its most brutal form—the unknown rapist—has made her independent. Thus the poem's conclusion asserts a new definition of reform: the restructuring of male-female relations as an alternative to male political discourse and theory: "Fourier's void,/And Comte absurd—and Cabet puerile." (Shades of the Webbs, and the utopian sexual politics of 1968.) We may call this resolution ideological and/or utopian but there is no doubt that it constitutes a significant revision of social and gender relations. Throughout Bronte's work the basic need of women is to make a love-match. By excluding the importance of the self-expression of which her novels are themselves the practice, Bronte also excludes her own solution, that of being a professional woman writer. Only Barrett Browning is able to inscribe this radical alternative within the text itself, and to centre it in the structure of her narrative.

Writing for women represents a kind of repair. For Elizabeth Barrett Browning it was an act of imagination which expanded the stunted and fragmented image of self demanded by conventional sexual and social relations; she speaks of her poetry as the "Escape from pangs of heart and bodily weakness—when you throw off *yourself*—what you feel to be *yourself*—into another atmosphere and into other relations where your life may spread its wings out new." The androgynous Romantic bird image effects the transformation of woman into poet. *Aurora Leigh* itself is one of the first great works by a woman to insist on a reading that privileges gender and asserts women's right to the pen. The silk handkerchief of gender cannot be pulled out of the text by the critic as the kicking phallic rabbit of class.

THE OPEN END

Our aim here has not been to rescue these works, nor to celebrate them. It has been to take issue with a selective literary tradition in which certain works have been installed in the canon and others excluded. A tradition out of which some works have been misread and some not read at all. This is a matter not solely of critical, but also of material reproduction. *Aurora Leigh,* for instance, has been virtually unavailable since 1897. Only recently has a feminist press decided to reprint it.

In dealing with the texts we had necessary recourse to the wider theoretical debate in Marxism, feminism and psychoanalysis. Our reading of the texts was predicated upon our insistence that class, kinship, gender and socialisation are related in both material and ideological terms, and that these relations must be theorised and historicised.

We do not wish to see the inscription of psychoanalysis within historical materialism without the transformation of both by feminist theory. Historical materialism has obscured the specific social relations of reproduction and kinship in its analysis of the general mode of production, whereas the problem with Lacanian psychoanalysis is that the concept of the symbolic order consolidates as it theorises patriarchal structures. Thus Althusser, in the "ISA's" essay and in "Freud and Lacan," develops the category of an ungendered human subject. We would argue that Marxist critics must confront the proposition that all subjects are gendered and that all literary discourse is gender specific. In this paper we have signalled the silence of women within public discourse. What has enabled us to break that silence is the political practice of the Women's Movement.

Notes

1. Relevant works by Lacan, Macherey and others are listed in the bibliography.

2. Engels, F. *The Origins of the Family, Private Property and the State* Pathfinder, New York, 1972, p. 80.

3. Althusser, L. "Freud and Lacan" in *Lenin and Philosophy and Other Essays* New Left Books, London, 1975, p. 195.

4. Lady Eastlake, review of *Jane Eyre, Quarterly Review,* Vol LXXXIV December 1848, p. 174. (Quoted in Stern, J. "Women and the Novel" in *Women's Liberation Review,* No. 1, October 1972.)

5. Wise, T. J. and Symington, J.A. (eds): *The Brontës: Their Lives, Friendships and Correspondence,* 4 Vols, Shakespeare Head, London, 1932. Vol iii, p. 31.

Bibliography

Althusser, L. (1971) "Ideology and Ideological State apparatuses" in *Lenin and Philosophy and Other Essays,* London: New Left Books.

Eagleton, T. (1975), *Myths of Power: a Marxist Study of the Brontës,* London: Macmillan.

Kristeva, J. (1976), *La Revolution du Langage Poetique,* Collections Tel Quel, Paris: Seuil.

Kristeva, J. (1976), "Signifying Practice and Mode of Production" translated and introduced by G. Nowell-Smith, *Edinburgh Film Festival Magazine,* 1.

Lacan, J. (1977) *Ecrits,* translated by Alan Sheridan, London: Tavistock.

Macherey, P. (1970) *Pour une Theorie de la Production Litteraire* Paris: Maspéro.

Macherey, P. (1977) Interview translated and introduced by Jean Radford and Colin Mercer, *Red Letters,* 5.

Working into Light:
Elizabeth Barrett Browning

Helen Cooper

A year after the publication of Elizabeth Barrett Browning's *Poems of 1844*, which established her as Britain's foremost woman poet, she was painfully aware of the absence of foremothers:[1]

> . . . England has had many learned women, not merely readers but writers of the learned languages, in Elizabeth's time and afterwards—women of deeper acquirements than are common now in the greater diffusion of letters; and yet where were the poetesses? The divine breath . . . why did it never pass, even in the lyrical form, over the lips of a woman? How strange! And can we deny that it was so? I look everywhere for grandmothers and see none. It is not in the filial spirit I am deficient, I do assure you—witness my reverent love of the grandfathers![2]

Chaucer, Spenser, Shakespeare, Milton, Pope, Wordsworth: British poetry embodied four hundred years of male practice of the art. Unlike Arthur Quiller-Couch, who describes how Britain nurtured the men who became its major poets—claiming a university education as a virtual prerequisite for "poetical genius"—Barrett Browning never formulated a penetrating political or social analysis of the factors contributing to the absence of great women poets.[3] However, in letters of 1845 she demonstrates some ambivalence over this issue. To Robert Browning she confesses:

> . . . let us say & do what we please & can . . there *is* a natural inferiority of mind in women—of the intellect . . not by any means, of the moral nature—& that the history of Art . . & of genius testifies to this fact openly. . . .

Seeming "to justify for a moment an opposite opinion," her admiration for George Sand undercuts this:

Reprinted from Sandra M. Gilbert and Susan Gubar, eds., *Shakespeare's Sisters: Feminist Essays on Women Poets* (Bloomington: Indiana University Press, 1979), 65–81. Used by permission of the publisher.

Such a colossal nature in every way—with all that breadth & scope of faculty which women want—magnanimous, & loving the truth & loving the people—and with that "hate of hate" too. . . .[4]

In the same year she admits to a Miss Thomson, who had solicited some classical translations for an anthology:

Perhaps I do not . . . partake quite your "divine fury" for converting our sex into Greek scholarship. . . . You . . . know that the Greek language . . . swallows up year after year of studious life. Now I have a "doxy" . . . that there is no exercise of the mind so little profitable to the mind as the study of languages. It is the nearest thing to a passive recipiency—is it not?—as a mental action, though it leaves one as weary as ennui itself. Women want to be made to *think actively:* their apprehension is quicker than that of men, but their defect lies for the most part in the logical faculty and in the higher mental activities.[5]

It is not women's "natural inferiority of mind" that hinders them, but their training into a "passive recipiency." Such a mental state is incompatible with the active thinking necessary for a poet.

Deprived of "grandmothers," Barrett Browning energetically explored what it meant to be a woman poet writing out of a male tradition, in which she was thoroughly self-educated. In 1857 she formulated a clear statement of the material appropriate to the woman poet when she challenged the critical reception to her discussion of prostitutes in *Aurora Leigh:*

What has given most offence in the book . . . has been the reference to the condition of women in our cities, which a woman oughtn't to refer to . . . says the conventional tradition. Now I have thought deeply otherwise. If a woman ignores these wrongs, then may women as a sex continue to suffer them; there is no help for any of us—let us be dumb and die.[6]

The "conventional tradition" allowed to early nineteenth-century women poets is exemplified by the works of two of the most popular of them, Felicia Hemans (1793–1835) and Letitia Landon (1802–1838). In the preface to *The Venetian Bracelet* (1829), Landon justifies "Love as my source of song":

I can only say, that for a woman, whose influence and whose sphere must be in the affections, what subject can be more fitting than one which it is her peculiar province to refine, spiritualise, and exalt? I have always sought to paint it self-denying, devoted, and making an almost religion of its truth. . . .[7]

Hemans's rage at the condition of women's lives is carefully controlled. Writing on "Evening Prayer at a Girls' School," she encourages the girls to enjoy the present, for

> Her lot is on you—silent tears to weep,
>   And patient smiles to wear through suffering's hour,
> And sumless riches, from affection's deep,
>   To pour on broken reeds—a wasted shower!
> And to make idols, and to find them clay,
> And to bewail that worship,—therefore pray!
>   . . . . .
> Meekly to bear with wrong, to cheer decay,
> And oh! to love through all things,—therefore pray!

Hemans's advice bristles with ambivalence. The contempt surfacing for "broken reeds" and "clay idols" that waste women's energy is undercut by the resignation of the last two lines. Landon and Hemans see self-denial and suffering, a woman's natural duty, as their subject matter. Barrett Browning grew to realize the abuse of women as her material, believing that the world may be made finer for women through their unflinching concern for one another. Refusing to be contained within boundaries prescribed as "woman's sphere," she interpreted the woman poet's special subject matter as being anything and everything which honestly illuminates her life.

Not only did Barrett Browning reject any limitation on the content of women's poetry, she also insisted on a rigorous assessment of women's work:

> The divineness of poetry is far more to me than either pride of sex or personal pride. . . . And though I in turn suffer for this myself—though I too . . . may be turned out of "Arcadia," and told that I am not a poet, still, I should be content, I hope, that the divineness of poetry be proved in my humanness, rather than lowered to my uses.[8]

This standard is revolutionary, for the "poetesses" had always been judged by very different criteria from their male counterparts. H. T. Tucker aptly demonstrates this:

> The spirit of Mrs. Hemans in all she has written is essentially feminine. . . . She has thrown over all her effusions, not so much the drapery of knowledge or the light of extensive observation, as the warm and shifting hues of the heart.[9]

Tucker exemplifies a criticism purporting to speak highly of women's work while in fact condemning it. To avoid recognizing her language as overly sentimental and vague as he would that of a male poet, he praises the "warm and shifting hues of the heart" and exonerates her from lacking "the drapery of knowledge or the light of extensive observation."

To realize her aesthetic Barrett Browning took the idea of excellence from, yet resisted the domination of, the male poetic tradition. Increasingly she absorbed a woman's culture: her letters are peppered with references to Hemans, Landon, and other women poets, to Jane Austen, Charlotte Brontë,

George Eliot, George Sand, Mrs. Gaskell, and Harriet Beecher Stowe, to Harriet Martineau and Margaret Fuller, and to the young American sculptor Harriet Hosmer. She probes their work, their assessment of themselves, their strengths and weaknesses, creating for herself a network of support while systematically breaking through the limiting proprieties ascribed to women poets.

Informing this sense of community was the memory of the love between herself and her mother, who died suddenly away from home in 1828 when Barrett Browning was twenty-two. Three years later she records in her diary:

> How I thought of those words *"You will never find another person who will love you as I love you"*—And how I felt that to hear again the sound of those beloved, those ever ever beloved lips, I wd barter all other sounds & sights—that I wd in joy & gratitude lay down before her my tastes & feelings each & all, in sacrifice for the love, the exceeding love which I never, in truth, can find again.[10]

The relationship between Barrett Browning and Edward Moulton Barrett, her father, has become legend, but the love between the poet and Mary Graham-Clarke, her mother, has been ignored by critics. Certainly her father educated her from the full bookcases in his study and was intensely a part of her adult life. However, the education the young poet received from her mother about the nurturing power of love between women also needs exploration and documentation, for it is this that resonates through such poems as her sonnets to George Sand and *Aurora Leigh*.

By the age of twelve Barrett Browning had read Mary Wollstonecraft's *A Vindication of the Rights of Woman.* Taplin, her biographer, records her reading in 1828 in *The Literary Souvenir:*

> . . . a sentimental poem by Miss Landon called "The Forsaken," which represented the lament of a country girl whose lover had left her to look for city pleasures. Elizabeth thought the verses were "beautiful and pathetic." She was also much affected by a poem by Mrs Hemans—it "goes to the heart," she wrote—describing the death of a mother and her baby in a shipwreck.[11]

Yet her second book, *An Essay on Mind,* privately published in the same year, bears the unmistakable imprint of Pope's style:

> Since Spirit first inspir'd, pervaded all,
> And Mind met Matter, at th' Eternal call—
> Since dust weigh'd Genius down, or Genius gave
> Th' immortal halo to the mortal's grave;

and so on for more than a thousand lines.

The Seraphim and Other Poems (1838) and *Poems of 1844* were Barrett Browning's first widely published volumes and the first in which a new sense of herself as a woman poet emerged. The latter especially brought good reviews:

> Mr. Chorley, in the "Athenaeum," described the volume as "extraordinary," adding that "between her poems and the slighter lyrics of the sisterhood, there is all the difference which exists between the putting-on of 'singing robes' for altar service, and the taking up lute or harp to enchant an indulgent circle of friends and kindred."[12]

"The Seraphim" (1838) and "The Drama of Exile" (1844) are both long dramatic poems, influenced by Milton's work. "A Vision of Poets" (1844) and "Lady Geraldine's Courtship" (1844), both about poets, seem traditional because the writers are male. In each case, however, the writer's vision is clarified through interaction with a strong and intelligent woman. In the former the woman specifically instructs the poet as to his true function. Although the poet is not yet identified as a woman, as she will be ten years later in *Aurora Leigh* (1856), this is a radical departure from male tradition, where the woman's function is not to know about poetry but to "inspire" the poet from afar through her beauty or to seduce him away from his work.

Barrett Browning was certain of her dedication to poetry:

> I cannot remember the time when I did not love it—with a lying-awake sort of passion at nine years old, and with a more powerful feeling since. . . . At this moment I love it more than ever—and am more bent than ever, if possible, to work into light . . not into popularity but into expression . . whatever faculty I have. This is the object of the intellectual part of me—and if I live it shall be done. . . . for poetry's own sake . . . for the sake of my love of it. Love is the safest and most unwearied moving principle in all things—it is an heroic worker.[13]

To this poet love is not self-denial and resignation, but a powerful energy source for the transformation of vision into poetry. Sloughing off the male mask in "The Soul's Expression" (1844), she describes forcefully her own creative process:

> With stammering lips and insufficient sound
> I strive and struggle to deliver right
> That music of my nature, day and night
> With dream and thought and feeling interwound,
> And inly answering all the senses round
> With octaves of a mystic depth and height
> Which step out grandly to the infinite
> From the dark edges of the sensual ground.
> This song of soul I struggle to outbear
> Through portals of the sense, sublime and whole,
> And utter all myself into the air:

> But if I did it,—as the thunder-roll
> Breaks its own cloud, my flesh would perish there,
> Before that dread apocalypse of soul.

Her determination to "work into light" necessitates the "stammering lips and insufficient sound" with which she struggles to "deliver right / That music of my nature." Her vision comes through her senses, as she seeks transcendence to "step out grandly to the infinite / From the dark edges of the sensual ground." As a woman trained to a "passive recipiency," she experiences the active energy of creativity as potentially destructive. Compelled to deliver the "music of my nature," she fears to give herself totally to her imagination "and utter all myself into the air," fears "my flesh would perish there, / Before that dread apocalypse of soul." And yet it was through the power of her imagination that she created her identity and her ability to deal with her eight-year "captivity" as a Victorian female invalid, as "The Prisoner" (1844) reveals:

> ... Nature's lute
> Sounds on, behind this door so closely shut,
> A strange wild music to the prisoner's ears,
> Dilated by the distance, till the brain
> Grows dim with fancies which it feels too fine:

"Behind this door" she responded passionately to George Sand's novels, and her sonnet "To George Sand: A Recognition" (1844) contains a clear statement about the special nature of a woman's voice writing of women's concerns:

> True genius, but true woman! dost deny
> Thy woman's nature with a manly scorn,
> And break away the gauds and armlets worn
> By weaker women in captivity?
> Ah, vain denial! that revolted cry
> Is sobbed in by a woman's voice forlorn,—
> Thy woman's hair, my sister, all unshorn
> Floats back dishevelled strength in agony,
> Disproving thy man's name: and while before
> The world thou burnest in a poet-fire,
> We see thy woman-heart beat evermore
> Through the large flame. Beat purer, heart, and higher,
> Till God unsex thee on the heavenly shore
> Where unincarnate spirits purely aspire!

The male mask can never hide the "revolted cry . . . sobbed in by a woman's voice forlorn." She implies no woman can "break away the gauds and armlets worn / By weaker women in captivity." Barrett Browning recognized that if women generally are exploited and oppressed, then all women as a class suffer, no matter any individual woman's apparent privilege. She identifies herself here as part of a community of women, "we," as opposed to "the world" of men.

In *Poems of 1844* there is a strongly evolving consciousness of herself as a woman poet and of her belief that the "sole work" of the poet "is to represent the age," as "The Cry of the Children"—about child factory-workers—shows.[14] But this new voice and subject matter were not supported by nor obvious to all of her old friends. In September 1843 she articulates to an early mentor, Hugh Boyd, her belief in this new poetry:

> Will you see the "Cry of the (Children)" or not? It will not please you, probably. It wants melody. The versification is eccentric to the ear, and the subject (the factory miseries) is scarcely an agreeable one to the fancy. Perhaps altogether you had better not see it, because I know you think me to be deteriorating, and I don't want you to have further hypothetical evidence of so false an opinion. Frankly, if not humbly, I believe myself to have gained power since . . . the "Seraphim." . . . I differ with you, the longer I live, on the ground of what you call the "jumping lines" . . . and the tenacity of my judgement (arises) . . . from the deeper study of the old master-poets—English poets—those of the Elizabeth and James ages, before the corruption of French rhythms stole in with Waller and Denham, and was acclimated into a national inodorousness by Dryden and Pope.[15]

Barrett Browning asserts her "power," the "tenacity of her judgement," and her defiance of both her critics and the established poetic tradition. In the following year, August 1844, she explains to John Kenyon:

> I wish I could persuade you of the rightness of my view about "Essays on Mind" and such things, and how the difference between them and my present poems is not merely the difference between two schools, . . . nor even the difference between immaturity and maturity; but that it is the difference between the dead and the living, between a copy and an individuality, between what is myself and what is not myself.[16]

She grew increasingly convinced that women writers should actively concern themselves with social conditions. In 1853 she exhorts the art critic and her life-long correspondent, Mrs. Jameson:

> Not read Mrs. Stowe's book! But you *must*. Her book is quite a sign of the times, and has otherwise and intrinsically considerable power. For myself, I rejoice in the success, both as a woman and a human being. Oh, and is it possible that you think a woman has no business with questions like the question of slavery? Then she had better use a pen no more. She had better subside into slavery and concubinage herself, I think, as in the times of old, shut herself up with the Penelopes in the "women's apartment," and take no rank among thinkers and speakers.[17]

"A Curse for a Nation" confirms Barrett Browning's refusal to "subside into slavery and concubinage." Written for the abolitionist movement in America and published in *Poems Before Congress* (1860), the poem incurred the wrath of critics disturbed by her interference in politics. Tough poetry results from her conviction that this is precisely her role:

> "Therefore," the voice said, "shalt thou write
>   My curse to-night.
> Because thou hast strength to see and hate
> A foul thing done *within* thy gate."
>
> "Not so," I answered once again.
>   "To curse, choose men.
> For I, a woman, have only known
> How the heart melts and tears run down."
>
> "Therefore," the voice said, "shalt thou write
>   My curse to-night.
> Some women weep and curse, I say
> (And no one marvels), night and day."
>
> "And thou shalt take their part to-night,
>   Weep and write.
> A curse from the depths of womanhood
> Is very salt, and bitter, and good."

Barrett Browning specifically repudiates her assigned role as "lady" who knows only "How the heart melts and tears run down." She designates herself as spokesperson for those less-privileged women who "weep and curse, I say / (And no one marvels), night and day," thereby defying patriarchy's division of "ladies" from working-class women.

Her anger against critics who disavowed her right to step beyond the limits laid down for "lady poets" had been revealed some years earlier in a fascinating discussion of Florence Nightingale, whom she came to see as performing an age-old role, that of angel on the battlefield:

> I know Florence Nightingale slightly. . . . I honour her from my heart. . . .
> At the same time, I confess to be at a loss to see any new position for the sex, or the most imperfect solution of the "woman's question," in this step of hers. . . . Since the seige of Troy and earlier, we have had princesses binding wounds with their hands; it's strictly the woman's part, and men understand it so. . . . Every man is on his knees before ladies carrying lint, calling them "angelic she's," whereas, if they stir an inch as thinkers or artists from the beaten line (involving more good to general humanity than is involved in lint), the very same men would curse the impudence of the very same women and stop there. . . . For my own part (and apart from the exceptional miseries of the

war), I acknowledge to you that I do not consider the best use to which we can put a gifted and accomplished woman is to *make her a hospital nurse.* If it is, why then woe to us all who are artists![18]

Barrett Browning wants to start healing the wounds of women by naming them. She writes of the Crimean War:

War, war! It is terrible certainly. But there are worse plagues, deeper griefs, dreader wounds than the physical. What of the forty thousand wretched women in this city? The silent writhing of them is to me more appalling than the roar of the cannons.[19]

The "homely domestic ballad" which Chorley sees as being purified on "passing into female hands" is subverted by Barrett Browning to condemn men's seduction and exploitation of women.[20] "The Rhyme of the Duchess May" (1844), a long ballad-poem set in the Middle Ages, tells of an orphaned girl betrothed by her guardian at twelve to his son. Grown into womanhood, she refuses this marriage, having chosen her own lover. The viewing of women as a commercial commodity is pointed up by her guardian's response to her decision:

> Good my niece, that hand withal looketh
> somewhat soft and small
> For so large a will, in sooth.

To which the niece astutely replies:

> Little hand clasps muckle gold, or it were
> not worth the hold
> Of thy son, good uncle mine!

The duchess secretly marries her lover. When her uncle's soldiers try to reclaim his "property," even her husband intends to kill himself on the assumption that his wife will be forgiven. She refuses to see herself as property and dies with her chosen husband to avoid life with a man she detests.

The finely honed ballad "Amy's Cruelty" (1862) hinges on the ironic observation that what seems to be a woman's cruelty to her lover is in fact her only defense against exploitation:

> Fair Amy of the terraced house,
>   Assist me to discover
> Why you who would not hurt a mouse
>   Can torture so your lover.
>   . . . . .
> But when *he* haunts your door . . . the town
>   Marks coming and marks going . . .

> You seem to have stitched your eyelids down
> To that long piece of sewing!

Amy's life is circumscribed. She sits daily in the "terraced house" fulfilling her sewing duties. Yet she has the power to protect herself and the insight to know the dangers of love:

> He wants my world, my sun, my heaven,
> Soul, body, whole existence.
>
> . . . . .
>
> I only know my mother's love
> Which gives all and asks nothing;
> And this new loving sets the groove
> Too much the way of loathing.
> Unless he gives me all in change,
> I forfeit all things by him:
> The risk is terrible and strange—
> I tremble, doubt, . . . deny him.

The "risk is terrible": in "Void in Law" (1862) a court finds a marriage void because only one witness was competent. The husband can now marry another woman, approved by society, one whose:

> . . . throat has the antelope curve,
> And her cheek just the color and line
> Which fade not before him nor swerve.

The first wife and child are legally abandoned.

"Bianca Among the Nightingales" (1862), one of Barrett Browning's most technically exciting ballad-poems, opens with a frank celebration of sexuality. Bianca remembers embracing her lover in the Italian moonlight:

> And *we,* too! from such soul-height went
> Such leaps of blood, so blindly driven,
>
> . . . . .
>
> The nightingales, the nightingales!
> We paled with love, we shook with love,
> We kissed so close we could not vow. . . .

The nightingales, whose singing "throbbed" in Italy with the passion of their love, haunt Bianca in "gloomy England," where she follows her lover who has abandoned her to pursue a woman of great beauty: "These nightingales will sing me mad." Bianca delineates the difference between his love for her and for the other woman:

> He says to her what moves her most.
> He would not name his soul within

> Her hearing, —rather pays the cost
> With praises to her lips and chin.

She is physically to be praised as ritualistically as any sonneteer's mistress. She has a "fine tongue" and "loose gold ringlets," but to Bianca she is "mere cold clay / As all false things are." The only person who will know this woman's soul is Bianca: "She lied and stole, / And spat into my love's pure pyx / The rank saliva of her soul." Barrett Browning explores the reality that a woman who truly wishes to be herself, to experience her sexuality and some kind of fruitful relationship with the male world will be challenged by the more acceptable norm of the woman who has learned to remain all beautiful surface, hidden both from herself and from the men she must please. The refrain "The nightingales, the nightingales" moves relentlessly from an affirmation of love to a taunting that drives Bianca to madness. In the last stanza the extended refrain and repetition enact her frenzy:

> —Oh, owl-like birds! They sing for spite,
> They sing for hate, they sing for doom,
> They'll sing through death who sing through night,
> They'll sing and stun me in the tomb—
> The nightingales, the nightingales!

Bianca knows she can never be like the other woman, but neither can she bear the ostracism attendant on being different.

The woman who is not abandoned is just as easily prey to exploitation. "Lord Walter's Wife" (1862) sets her husband's friend straight when he is horror-stricken at her suggestion of an affair—the logical conclusion to his flirtatious innuendoes:

> A moment,—I pray your attention!—I
> have a poor word in my head
> I must utter, though womanly custom
> would set it down better unsaid.
> . . . . .
> You did me the honour, perhaps to be
> moved at my side now and then
> In the senses—a vice, I have heard, which
> is common to beasts and some men.
> . . . . .
> And since, when all's said, you're too
> noble to stoop to the frivolous cant
> About crimes irresistible, virtues that swin-
> dle, betray, and supplant,
>
> I determined to prove to yourself that,
> whate'er you might dream or avow

> By illusion, you wanted precisely no more
> of me than you have now.

This poem caused Thackeray much embarrassment when it was submitted to him for publication in the *Cornhill Magazine* in 1861:

> . . . one of the best wives, mothers, women in the world writes some verses which I feel certain would be objected to by many of our readers. . . . In your poem, you know, there is an account of unlawful passion, felt by a man for a woman, and though you write pure doctrine, and real modesty, and pure ethics, I am sure our readers would make an outcry, and so I have not published this poem.[21]

Barrett Browning replies in no uncertain terms:

> I am not a "fast woman." I don't like coarse subjects, or the coarse treatment of any subject. But I am deeply convinced that the corruption of our society requires not shut doors and windows, but light and air: and that it is exactly because pure and prosperous women choose to *ignore* vice, that miserable women suffer wrong by it everywhere. Has paterfamilias, with his Oriental traditions and veiled female faces, very successfully dealt with a certain class of evil? What if materfamilias, with her quick sure instincts and honest innocent eyes, do more towards their expulsion by simply looking at them and calling them by their names?[22]

This strong conviction in the last year of her life that the responsibility of the woman poet was to confront and name the condition of women had manifested itself in her poetry from the *Seraphim* on, as she sought to delineate the complexity of female experience. She wrote powerfully about the institution of motherhood in patriarchy, and the experience of biological motherhood. "The Virgin Mary to the Child Jesus" (1838) is a meditation in Mary's voice. She begins poignantly, unsure what name she can call this child who is both of her flesh and also her Lord. She watches Jesus sleeping, imagines he dreams of God his father, whereas the best she can give him is a mother's kiss. Patriarchal Christian tradition exalts Mary as most honored; a woman writes of the pain Mary would experience mothering a child simultaneously hers and not hers:

> Then, I think aloud
> The words "despised,"—"rejected,"—every word
> Recoiling into darkness as I view
>   The DARLING on my knee.
> Bright angels,—move not—lest ye stir the cloud
> Betwixt my soul and his futurity!
> I must not die, with mother's work to do,
>   And could not live—and see.

The implications of the poem point beyond the immediate meditation to a consideration of how patriarchy always destines its sons for a life beyond their mothers. Another early poem, "Victoria's Tears" (1838), explores how the young woman is jolted from her childhood into mothering her country as its queen (when women were not even enfranchised). Barrett Browning contrasts the grandiose coronation with her sense of what the young woman has lost:

> She saw no purples shine,
>   For tears had dimmed her eyes;
> She only knew her childhood's flowers
>   Were happier pageantries!
> And while her heralds played the part,
>   For million shouts to drown—
> "God save the Queen" from hill to mart,—
> She heard through all her beating heart,
>   And turned and wept—
> She wept, to wear a crown!

Both poems pinpoint the isolation of the "token woman," whose position of supposed privilege is actually one of loneliness and confusion.

In "The Cry of the Children" (1844), she exposes how hopeless it is for the child factory workers to cry to mothers powerless to alleviate their suffering:

> Do ye hear the children weeping, O my brothers,
>   Ere the sorrow comes with years?
> They are leaning their young heads against their mothers,
>   And *that* cannot stop their tears.
>   . . . . .
> But the young, young children, O my brothers,
>   Do you ask them why they stand
> Weeping sore before the bosom of their mothers,
>   In our happy Fatherland?

The capitalization of "Fatherland" but not of "mothers" underlines the power structure: the natural flesh bond between the child and mother is helpless before the demands of patriarchy. The children mourn Alice, who died from the brutal working conditions: "Could we see her face, be sure we should not know her, / For the smile has time for growing in her eyes. . . ." That it is a girl who dies from such work in a society that draped its middle-class women with prudery, passivity and sentimentality should not go unnoticed. Repetition creates the delirium of these children's exhaustion, pulling us into their experience:

For all day the wheels are droning, turning;
    Their wind comes in our faces,
Till our hearts turn, our heads with pulses burning,
    And the walls turn in their places:
Turns the sky in the high window, blank and reeling,
    Turns the long light that drops adown the wall,
Turn the black flies that crawl along the ceiling:
    All are turning, all the day, and we with all.
And all day the iron wheels are droning,
    And sometimes we could pray,
"O ye wheels" (breaking out in a mad moaning),
    "Stop! be silent for to-day!"

Victimization is again exposed in "The Runaway Slave at Pilgrim's Point" (1850), spoken in the voice of a young black woman slave being flogged to death where the pilgrims landed. On the plantation she had loved a black male slave. The white overseers, learning of this love, beat the man to death and, seeing her grief, her owner rapes her. Her initial response to the child born of this rape is love:

Thus we went moaning, child and mother,
One to another, one to another,

but

. . . the babe who lay on my bosom so,
    Was far too white, too white for me;
As white as the ladies who scorned to pray
Beside me at church but yesterday.

Soon she cannot look at her son and strains a handkerchief over his face. He struggles against this, wanting his freedom: "For the white child wanted his liberty— / Ha, Ha! he wanted the master-right." The dichotomies her son represents overwhelm her. She loves him but hates that, being male and white, he will grow up with the right to violate a woman as her rapist, his father, did. She loves him but:

Why, in that single glance I had
    Of my child's face, . . . I tell you all,
I saw a look that made me mad!
    The *master's* look, that used to fall
On my soul like his lash . . . or worse!
And so, to save it from my curse,
    I twisted it round in my shawl.

She strangles her son so she will neither have to repudiate him later, nor experience her rape reenacted every time she looks into his face. She runs from the plantation holding the child to her for many days before burying him. Her owner catches her and flogs her to death. Taplin's dismissal of the poem as "too blunt and shocking" only underscores the poem's explosive exposure of racism and sexism.[23]

Barrett Browning had four pregnancies in the four years after her marriage. Only the third ended with a birth, that of her son, Robert Wiedeman ("Penini") in 1849. The experience of childbirth and biological motherhood informs "Only a Curl" (1862), written on receiving a lock of hair from the parents of a dead child unknown to the poet. In language movingly reminiscent of "The Soul's Expression," written twenty years earlier about the creative process, Barrett Browning comforts by saying how once a mother has known her power in childbirth her child is always in some way part of the mother's experience:

> . . . I appeal
> To all who bear babes—in the hour
> When the veil of the body we feel
> Rent round us, —while torments reveal
> The motherhood's advent in power,
>
> And the babe cries!—has each of us known
> By apocalypse (God being there
> Full in nature) the child is our own,
> Life of life, love of love, moan of moan,
> Through all changes, all times, everywhere.

She records in her letters what a powerful and health-giving experience childbirth was. Even today, forty-three is considered "late" for giving birth to a first child. For Barrett Browning, almost given up as dead three years earlier, to have that much physical power was exhilarating.

One of her last poems, "Mother and Poet" (1862), confronts, like "The Virgin Mary to the Child Jesus," the conflict between a mother's relationship with her sons and their destiny within patriarchy. It is spoken in the voice of Laura Savio, an Italian poet and patriot dedicated, as was Barrett Browning, to the unification of Italy. Savio's two sons were killed fighting for "freedom." The poet reconsiders the meaning of both motherhood and patriotism after their deaths:

> To teach them . . . It stings there! I made them indeed
>   Speak plain the word *country*. I taught them, no doubt,
> That a country's a thing men should die for at need.
>   *I* prated of liberty, rights, and about
>   The tyrant cast out.

She imagines the victory celebrations:

> Forgive me. Some women bear children in strength,
>   And bite back the cry of their pain in self-scorn;
> But the birth-pangs of nations will wring us at length
>   Into wail such as this—and we sit on forlorn
>   When the man-child is born.
>
> Dead! One of them shot by the sea in the east,
>   And one of them shot in the west by the sea.
> Both! both my boys! If in keeping the feast
>   You want a great song for your Italy free,
>   Let none look at *me!*

To Barrett Browning, whose son had grown up listening to her passionate political talk and at twelve spoke eagerly of his own desire to fight for freedom, this is an assessment of great integrity about her own complicity in patriarchy. She understands that the energetic womanhood manifest in the bearing of children is undermined by mothers, like herself, who incorporate patriarchal values into their own consciousness and become breeders of cannon fodder. Taplin brushes the poem off as "devoid of inspiration," quite missing the poet's sophisticated insight into women's contribution to their own oppression.[24]

"Mother and Poet" fuses three of Barrett Browning's preoccupations in her writing—art, politics, and motherhood—as a manifestation of powerful womanhood. "What art's for a woman?" she has Laura Savio ask. In her own career she was increasingly convinced that women as "artists and thinkers" must be concerned with social interaction, social conditions, and political events. Realizing that the "personal is the political," she used her physical and emotional experiences as a woman to illuminate the public sphere. In doing so she created a voice and vision for herself as a woman poet and became truly our "grandmother." Like many grandmothers, she has been unjustly ignored; like many grandmothers, she has healing wisdom to share. As early as 1845 she believed:

> . . . we should all be ready to say that if the secrets of our daily lives & inner souls may instruct other surviving souls, let them be open to men hereafter, even as they are to God now. Dust to dust, & soul-secrets to humanity—there are natural heirs to all things.[25]

Notes

1.   Christened Elizabeth Barrett Moulton Barrett, the poet shortened her maiden name to Elizabeth Barrett Barrett—E.B.B. These initials remained unchanged when she took her husband's name in 1846. Half her work was published under the name Elizabeth Barrett

Barrett, half under Elizabeth Barrett Browning. I have decided to use the latter name throughout this discussion of her work, as it is the one she herself adopted.

2. *The Letters of Elizabeth Barrett Browning*, ed. Frederic G. Kenyon. (New York: Macmillan, 1897), I, 231–32.

3. Sir Arthur Quiller-Couch, *The Art of Writing*. Quoted in Virginia Woolf, *A Room of One's Own* (New York: Harcourt, Brace and World, 1929), pp. 111–12.

4. *The Letters of Robert Browning and Elizabeth Barrett Barrett*, 1845–1846, ed. Elvan Kintner (Cambridge, Mass.: Harvard University Press, 1969), I, 113–14.

5. *Letters of EBB*, I, 260–61.

6. Ibid., II, 254.

7. Quoted in *Poetical Works of Letitia Elizabeth Landon* (London: Longman, Brown, Green, and Longman, 1850), I, xiv.

8. *Letters of EBB*, I, 232.

9. *Poems by Felicia Hemans*, ed. Rufus Griswold (Philadelphia: John Ball, 1850), p. x.

10. *Diary by E.B.B.*, ed. Philip Kelley and Ronald Hudson (Athens, Ohio: Ohio University Press, 1969), p. 88.

11. Gardner B. Taplin, *The Life of Elizabeth Barrett Browning* (New Haven: Yale University Press, 1957), p. 21.

12. *Letters of EBB*, I, 180. Editor's note.

13. *Elizabeth Barrett to Miss Mitford*, ed. Betty Miller (London: John Murray, 1954), p. 102.

14. *Aurora Leigh*, Fifth Book, 202.

15. *Letters of EBB*, I, 153–56.

16. Ibid., I, 187.

17. Ibid., II, 110–11.

18. Ibid., 189.

19. Ibid., 213.

20. Henry F. Chorley, *Memorials of Mrs. Hemans* (Philadelphia: Carey, Lea & Blanchard, 1836), p. 56.

21. *Letters of EBB*, II, 444.

22. Ibid., 445.

23. Taplin, p. 194.

24. Ibid., p. 397.

25. *Letters of RB and EBB*, I, 469.

"New Yet Orthodox"—The Female Characters in *Aurora Leigh*

KATHLEEN HICKOK

I

Interest in *Aurora Leigh,* by Elizabeth Barrett Browning, has revived during the last few years, chiefly because of the feminist perspective from which this remarkable "verse novel" examines nineteenth-century England. In turn, renewed interest in *Aurora Leigh* has led to re-evaluation of Barrett Browning's[1] other poems, especially those depicting female figures, a process rewarded with rediscoveries of numerous of her poems long ago allowed to disappear from the literary canon of Victorian poetry.[2] We must not forget, however, that just as *Aurora Leigh* exists in the context of Barrett Browning's other poetry, her other poetry itself exists in the context of the nineteenth-century feminine poetic tradition in England—a tradition exemplified by such poets as Felicia Hemans, Letitia Landon, Mary Howitt, and Caroline Norton; a tradition with which Elizabeth Barrett Browning was demonstrably familiar.[3]

Under this microscope, her poems appear not as *sui generis,* but as part of a field of established poetic figures, themes, and purposes shared by her feminine peers. To name several, these included, first, stereotypical female figures such as the lovelorn pining maiden, the fallen woman, the self-sacrificing wife, and the bereaved mother; second, critical examination of the Victorian ideology of love and marriage—especially criticism of the marriage ideal, of the presumed differences between woman's love and man's, and of the tension in gifted women's lives between love and fame; and, finally, the aim of social protest—concerning English seamstresses, child labor, prostitution, the American slave trade, and the miserable condition of the British poor. For each of these traditions there were established poetic norms of imagery, plot, theme, point of view, and tone.

Reprinted from *International Journal of Women's Studies* 3 (1980): 479–89. Used by permission of the author.

Of course, it is true that an imaginative difference, a twist of plot, or a mastery of imagery usually saved Barrett Browning's poems from the tedium of most giftbook verse. In Book III of *Aurora Leigh,* Aurora remarks upon the difficulty of simultaneously observing and transcending conventionality in her work:

> My critic Belfair wants another book
> Entirely different, which will sell (and live?)
> A striking book, yet not a startling book,
> The public blames originalities. . . .
> Good things, not subtle, new yet orthodox,
> As easy reading as the dog-eared page
> That's fingered by said public fifty years,
> Since first taught spelling by its grandmother,
> And yet a revelation in some sort:
> That's hard, my critic Belfair.[4]

Barrett Browning accomplished this task to some extent in popular poems like "The Poet's Vow" (1836), "The Romaunt of the Page" (1839), and "Lady Geraldine's Courtship" (1844). By and large, however (as I have shown elsewhere[5]), her early poetry fell well within conventional expectations and traditional forms.

However, *Aurora Leigh* is another matter entirely. In *Aurora Leigh,* Barrett Browning departed from the feminine traditions of the century with sufficient force to impress many, alarm some, and startle nearly all of her readers.[6] Years later Swinburne remembered, "The advent of 'Aurora Leigh' [in 1856] can never be forgotten by any lover of poetry who was old enough at the time to read it . . . they never had read, and never would read anything in any way comparable with that unique work of audaciously feminine and ambitiously impulsive genius."[7] Swinburne was right: *Aurora Leigh* was a courageous, thorough-going exposition of feminist beliefs about nineteenth-century women. Yet Barrett Browning conveyed her socially advanced ideas in a vehicle which—despite its claim to singularity as a verse novel—represented well known female characters involved in specifically female predicaments, all of which were already quite familiar to the reading public. The audacity and the achievement of *Aurora Leigh* resided in its confrontation all at once of so many social and personal facts of nineteenth-century English life and in its challenge to the validity of the conventions which customarily concealed those facts.

Barrett Browning realized, of course, just what she had dared to do; consequently, she was astonished by the poem's sensational popular success. She had fully expected, she said, "to be put in the stocks" for it "as a disorderly woman and free-thinking poet."[8] Yet she also believed it to be "nearer the mark . . . fuller, stronger, more sustained" than any of her previous poems.[9] Apparently, the technique of presenting radical ideas within a familiar context—"new yet orthodox"—constituted a camouflage sufficient to get the poem past the reading public's barricades of self-defensive disapprobation.

Of course, there *were* objections from some quarters to the immorality and impurity of the situations and the shamelessness and coarseness of the language in the poem. Furthermore, *Aurora Leigh* was not, finally, a critical success. In addition to their other reservations, reviewers were nearly unanimous in finding the poem's characterizations weak and its major figures unattractive. Since, with the exceptions of Romney Leigh and Aurora's father, all these characters are female, it is most illuminating to approach the poem's relationship to its social and literary context by examining Barrett Browning's various representations of English womanhood within it.

II

In *Aurora Leigh,* Barrett Browning focuses on female characters in each of the three social classes in England. Lady Waldemar, of course, represents the upper class. She is an idle aristocratic lady, who dabbles somewhat carelessly in philanthropy and affairs of the heart. Aurora Leigh, despite an aristocratic heritage from her father, is essentially a middle-class professional woman, who depends upon her own earnings as a writer for support. Marian Erle comes from the lower class. The daughter of a "tramp," she has become (with the help of Romney Leigh) a seamstress, in order to avoid a life of prostitution. Until she and her illegitimate child are rescued by Aurora, she lives a life of abject poverty which constantly borders upon outright destitution. From the poem's glorification of Marian Erle and vilification of Lady Waldemar, we might conclude that Barrett Browning's sympathies lay with the oppressed lower classes of England.

However, that would be an oversimplification. Marian's father is an unsavory character who drinks, beats his wife, and evades employment; in turn, her mother abuses Marian and tries to barter her virginity for favors from a neighboring squire. Lady Waldemar's servant later succeeds where Marian's mother failed, by selling Marian into sexual slavery. Furthermore, the throngs of angry poor people who threaten and finally maim the generous, if misguided, aristocrat Romney Leigh are nasty, brutish, and ungrateful mobs. Romney himself is a gentleman in the best sense of the word, and though his social peers are sometimes snobbish and hypocritical, they also include admirable men like Vincent Carrington, the painter, and Lord Howe, Aurora's faithful friend and correspondent. Despite the novelistic way in which characters of diverse social classes are made to rub elbows throughout the poem, class consciousness does not supply its unity of perspective. Feminist consciousness does.[10]

In *Aurora Leigh,* Elizabeth Barrett Browning explored virtually all the women's roles with which the public was familiar in mid-nineteenth-century

England. By considering the poem's female characters in terms of their social roles and in light of the continual feminist commentary upon women in general which Aurora provides, we can discover the full force of the poem: *Aurora Leigh* rejects the conventional wisdom about women at virtually every point.

The interaction between Aurora and the three women who were significant figures in her childhood immediately illustrates some of the poem's departures from tradition. To begin with, Aurora's mother was not an Englishwoman at all, but a foreigner, a Florentine, whose southern charms won the heart of Aurora's austere English father "after a dry lifetime spent at home / In college-learning, law, and parish talk" (I. 66–67). Through love of her, he "had suddenly / Thrown off the old conventions, broken loose / From chin-bands of the soul . . ." (I. 176–178). Unfortunately, this woman was so weakened by the birth of Aurora that she died when the child was only four years old. Aurora's recollection of her sense of loss owes something, perhaps, to many popular women poets' descriptions of maternal death, as well as to Barrett Browning's own bereavement at age twenty-two.

> I felt a mother-want about the world,
> And still went seeking, like a bleating lamb
> Left out at night in shutting up the fold,—
> As restless as a nest-deserted bird . . .
> (I. 40–43)

Yet her dead mother's portrait on the wall stirs the child not simply to adoration but also to terror.

> And as I grew
> In years, I mixed, confused, unconsciously,
> Whatever I last read or heard or dreamed,
> Abhorrent, admirable, beautiful,
> Pathetical, or ghastly, or grotesque,
> With that still face . . .
> (I. 146–151)

The mother figure becomes for Aurora a kind of Lamia, alternately benign and malignant, according to the child's own fantasies and fears. This unsentimental depiction of childhood bereavement is much more psychologically sound than the treatment of the subject in most popular women's poetry.

In her natural mother's stead, Aurora has Assunta, an Italian servant whose devotion to the child is quite touching. Assunta cares for Aurora until she is thirteen, when the English father suddenly dies and his relatives send for Aurora to come to England. Once again, Aurora is separated from maternal love; both she and the faithful servant are devastated with grief.

> I do remember clearly how there came
> A stranger with authority, not right
> (I thought not), who commanded, caught me up
> From old Assunta's neck; how, with a shriek,
> She let me go,—while I, with ears too full
> Of my father's silence to shriek back a word,
> In all a child's astonishment at grief
> Stared at the wharf-edge where she stood and moaned . . .
> (I. 223–230)

The demands of English laws and customs separate the child and her surrogate mother—who is, after all, only a servant and thus beyond consideration; we feel both the injustice and the inevitability of this outcome. By the time Aurora, as a grown woman, returns to Italy, her beloved Assunta is dead. The longlasting affection between Barrett Browning and her own maid-servant Wilson may have contributed to the representation of this female servant in *Aurora Leigh*. In any case, its sympathetic depiction of Assunta is extraordinary, considering that women's poetry in the nineteenth century generally failed to characterize female domestics at all; and the recognition of a genuine love between mistress and servant shows unusual sensitivity on Barrett Browning's part to the humanity of the serving class.

Reaching England, Aurora is turned over to the care and tutelage of her maiden aunt, whom Barrett Browning approached with neither of the prevailing attitudes—sentimentality or ridicule—but with a degree of individuality which distinguishes this particular spinster from the current poetical stereotype.

> She stood straight and calm,
> Her somewhat narrow forehead braided tight
> As if for taming accidental thoughts
> From possible pulses; brown hair pricked with grey
> By frigid use of life . . .
> Eyes of no colour,—once they might have smiled,
> But never, never have forgot themselves
> In smiling; cheeks, in which was yet a rose
> Of perished summers, like a rose in a book,
> Kept more for ruth than pleasure,—if past bloom,
> Past fading also.
> (I. 272–276, 282–287)

This physical description of Aunt Leigh emphasizes the repression and rigidity of a single woman who found herself consigned to "A harmless life, she called a virtuous life, / A quiet life, which was not life at all" (I. 288–289). She fills her days with the poor-club, the book-club, obligatory calls from the neighbors, and hatred for her brother's wife, Aurora's mother. When she dies, some seven years after Aurora's arrival in England, she is found sitting "Bolt upright in the chair beside her bed" (II. 925) with blank open eyes and an unbudging posture that aptly reflect her living personality.

Looking back, Aurora recognizes the essential difference between her aunt and herself, and expresses this difference in a classic image from women's poetry—that of the caged bird.

> She had lived
> A sort of caged-bird life, born in a cage,
> Accounting that to leap from perch to perch
> Was act and joy enough for any bird.
> . . . I, alas,
> A wild bird scarcely fledged, was brought to her cage,
> And she was there to meet me. Very kind.
> Bring the clean water, give out the fresh seed.
> (I. 304–307, 309–312)

Aurora was not an ideal English girl when she came to Aunt Leigh, but a natural, undisciplined, Italian child, and the spinster determined to take her in hand and mold her into the courtesy-book ideal of English maidenhood. Consequently, Aurora, who had been tutored by her father from his own store of genuine knowledge, is now set to the task of absorbing the English girl's customary mix of trivial information, accomplishment, and conventionality. Only her communings with nature and her clandestine reading from her father's library enable her spirit to survive. The long passage in which Aurora describes the struggle (I. 372–481) is classic in its denunciation of both the process and the product of women's education. Aunt Leigh fails in her attempts to quench the spark of independence and intellectuality which Aurora brought within herself from her Italian girlhood. "Certain of your feebler souls," Aurora conceded, "Go out in such a process; many pine / To a sick inodorous light" of English womanhood. "My own," she thanks God, "endured" (I. 470–472).

The character of Aurora is the most fully delineated in the poem, which traces her growth and maturation, the cultivation of her talents, and the education of her heart. After her successful defiance of the conventional demands of English girlhood, Aurora continues to reject current social ideas which pertain to her own situation and to the condition of women in general. She refuses to marry her cousin Romney and subordinate or abandon her artistic pursuits in order to participate in his own vocation of social work. "You want a helpmate, not a mistress, sir," she accuses, "A wife to help your ends,—in her no end" (II. 402–403). Mistakenly, she believes their match would be loveless, utilitarian, and she chooses instead to award her devotion to her art. "You'll grant that even a woman may love art, / Seeing that to waste true love on anything / Is womanly, past question" (II. 495–497). Aurora's objections to marriage are undeniably feminist and, in light of English law and custom, justifiable. Yet she misunderstands her own emotional needs, and we the readers recognize from the beginning what it takes Aurora many lonely years to perceive: her own need for intimacy and her love for her cousin Romney.

So deep are these emotions that Aurora, in absence of any other opportunity, acts them out by playing husband and father to Romney's affianced Marian Erle and her illegitimate child. All through Book VII of the poem, Aurora takes on an androgyny of character,[11] dismissing her feminine tears and fears and letting the man inside her (VII. 212, 230) predominate over the woman. "It is very good for strength," she learns, "To know that someone needs you to be strong" (VII. 414–415). She takes full responsibility for Marian and her baby, conveying them to Italy and safety in her own dead father's house, where the three form a tight little family group. Aurora soon discovers, through putting on the masculine role, that male-female personality distinctions are artificial, and that there is no magic in masculinity after all:

> Note men!—They are but women after all,
> As women are but Auroras!—there are men
> Born tender, apt to pale at a trodden worm . . .
> (VII. 1017–1019)

This new-found sympathy with men as human beings like herself is part of what softens Aurora toward Romney and enables her in the poem's conclusion to recognize and declare her love for him. Of course, the fact of his blindness is significant also. His handicap finally equalizes them, in a way, and allows Aurora to exercise both her sympathy and her strength. The marriage they now contemplate will be passionate, mystical, mature—a union of separate souls each bringing its own capacities to the joint endeavor humbly to do God's work. If this is an idealized version of marriage, it is at least more egalitarian than the conventional marriage ideal of complementary male-female roles. Furthermore, Barrett Browning manages here to do something that even the most critical of her contemporary women poets failed to do: she not only criticizes the existing structure of marriage, but she boldly envisions a joyful alternative.

In thus viewing Aurora in relationship to her man, we must not neglect her other great passion: her art. Ellen Moers has rightly called *Aurora Leigh* the "epic of the literary woman."[12] Despite Swinburne's protest that Aurora's life as a professional writer was "too eccentric" to be believed,[13] it is quite convincingly presented. We see her struggling with the double standard of literary criticism which frustrated so many women writers (II. 232–243), opening her fan mail (III. 210–232), and experiencing doubts about the quality of her work (I. 881–895). Aurora is constantly aware of financial pressures, writing for cyclopedias, magazines, and weekly papers, just to buy a little time to pursue her poetry (III. 306–328). She is her own most severe critic, always unsatisfied with her completed work and striving to make the next poem better than the last. Barrett Browning does not shrink from admitting the diligent work and punishing schedule Aurora's artist's life requires:

> I worked on, on.
> Through all the bristling fence of nights and days
> Which hedges time in from the eternities,
> I struggled,—never stopped to note the stakes
> Which hurt me in my course. The midnight oil
> Would stink sometimes; there came some vulgar needs;
> I had to live that therefore I might work,
> And, being poor, I was constrained, for life,
> To work with one hand for the booksellers
> While working with the other for myself
> And art.
>
> (III. 295–305)

Aurora has a high conception of her calling and a determination to maintain her integrity as a poet. When, in the story's conclusion, she tells Romney, "Art is much, but Love is more" (IX. 656), it is not as a repudiation of Art but as a greater testimony to the joy of love. "O Art, my Art, thou'rt much," she continues, "but love is more! / Art symbolises heaven, but Love is God / And makes heaven" (IX. 657–659). The pursuit of artistic excellence and public fame is not wrong in itself, but only insofar as it necessitates the sacrifice of human love. Elizabeth Barrett Browning was herself living proof that this sacrifice was avoidable, even in nineteenth-century England.

Lady Waldemar, the villain of the poem, twits Aurora on their first meeting with the contemporary stereotype of the literary woman:

> You stand outside,
> You artist women, of the common sex;
> You share not with us, and exceed us so
> Perhaps by what you're mulcted in, your hearts
> Being starved to make your heads: so run the old
> Traditions of you.
>
> (III. 406–411)

Yet in her arrogance of speech, she reveals not a truth about women artists, but rather a hint of her own potential for cruelty. Some critics have felt that Lady Waldemar is made to appear worse than she actually is, by being presented only through the eyes of the jealous Aurora, and that judged impartially, she would seem less a *femme fatale*.[14] Others have dismissed her as a mere adventuress,[15] a stereotypical "Wicked Lady of Quality."[16] Certainly there is something of the *femme fatale* in Lady Waldemar's deceptiveness and her sexual appetite, but she can perhaps be judged most accurately by observing in her the dilemma of the post-Regency aristocrat, the bored lady of leisure. Both her coarseness of language and her sophistication of manner can be seen as attributes of Regency society. Now that a different era is upon her, she attempts to take on the colors of the "modest women" (III. 580) of the present day, but succeeds only in achieving hypocrisy. In this result, she resembles Lady Howe, whose air of condescension is her most natural attitude (V. 582–607).[17]

Lady Waldemar's chief crime is that she does not take life as seriously as a proper Victorian woman ought to do. She unintentionally mocks Romney's attempts to do good by playing at philanthropy as a sort of lovers' game, and she offends Aurora Leigh by the frankness and physicality of her feelings for Romney.

> Am I coarse?
> Well, love's coarse, nature's coarse—ah, there's the rub.
> We fair fine ladies, who park out our lives,
> From common sheep-paths, cannot help the crows
> From flying over,—we're as natural still
> As Blowsalinda.
>
> (III. 454–459)

Outrageous though she may be, Lady Waldemar's earthiness and cynicism are attractive in their own colorful way—to the modern reader, at least, if not to the likes of Romney, Aurora, and their peers. The callous way in which she dispatches Marian Erle to the colonies is reprehensible, of course. But the blame for Marian's abduction and rape lies with the unscrupulous servant, not with Lady Waldermar directly. Probably she is sincere when she expresses her regrets about the incident and writes to "thank" Aurora Leigh "For proving to myself that there are things / I would not do—not for my life, nor him" (IX. 19–20). She is not merely a conventional villain, nor yet a careless aristocrat. She seems rather to be an anachronism, a vital, energetic woman vexed by the century's continuing encroachments upon her freedom to express those qualities. Her attachment to Romney Leigh, invested though it is with pride, represents a genuine attempt to find a niche. "I cannot choose but think," she writes Aurora, "That, with him, I were virtuouser than you / Without him" (IX. 167–169), and the statement has a ring of truth.

The well known case of Marian Erle must be considered in light of both existing social conditions and the mid-century literary tradition of the fallen woman. The primitive lifestyles among the lowest classes of England were definitely conducive to the type of casual immorality epitomized in Marian's mother's attempt to sell her daughter to a local squire. Marian's frantic flight into the city, the hopelessness of her life as a seamstress (like Lucy Gresham), and the squalor of her living quarters are accurately presented. Furthermore, the horrifying circumstances of her abduction, rape, and imprisonment in a

Paris brothel were not unrealistic, as W.T. Stead's series of articles on the white slave trade would later attest.[18] Neither is Marian's reintegration into society unlikely; had she married a respectable man and settled into a bland domesticity, it would not have violated probability, but only literary and social conventions.

In "A Year's Spinning" (1846), Barrett Browning had depicted the fallen woman in an entirely conventional manner: seduction, abandonment, illegitimate motherhood, infant death, and the grave. In *Aurora Leigh,* Marian's childhood friend Rose Bell, who apparently has become a prostitute of the sort later interviewed by sociologist Bracebridge Hemyng,[19] seems to be irrevocably lost to sin. Even Marian pities Rose: "I heard her laugh last night in Oxford Street, / I'd pour out half my blood to stop that laugh, / Poor Rose, poor Rose!" (III. 927–929). Barrett Browning, of course, knew, and on occasion adhered to, the literary stereotype of the harlot's inevitable progress to the grave or to perdition.

In depicting Marian Erle, however, she rejected those familiar patterns entirely. Marian's story is in consonance with the reality, not the myth, of the "great social evil" of England. She is not seduced, but raped; she is not abandoned by a faithless lover, but flees from sexual captivity. Her devotion to her illegitimate infant son is rewarded by smiles and affection, not by bereavement. The child cannot even be properly said to "redeem" his mother, for, though despoiled, she has never sinned. When Marian is offered the incredible option of honorable marriage, she refuses; nor does she then sink into a premature grave, but lives peacefully on, for the sake of her son. It is only as a mother, and not as a ruined woman, that Marian approaches conventionality. In declining Romney's offer of marriage, she replies, "Here's a hand shall keep / For ever clean without a marriage-ring, / To tend my boy ..." (IX. 431–433). No doubt the story of Marian Erle owed something to Mrs. Gaskell's *Ruth* (1853), but Barrett Browning's fallen heroine's fate far exceeds Mrs. Gaskell's for social realism and for sheer audacity. Furthermore, the astonishing facts are that *Aurora Leigh* appeared one year before William Acton's groundbreaking study *Prostitution,*[20] six years before Henry Mayhew's *London Labour and the London Poor,*[21] and almost thirty years before Stead's "The Maiden Tribute of Modern Babylon." Her literary representation of Marian Erle was far ahead of its time.

Contemporary critics who disliked the characters of Aurora Leigh and Lady Waldemar adored Marian Erle, although they found her idealistic beliefs and elegant language to be out of synchrony with her lower-class background.[22] The sentimental appeal of the guiltless sexual victim was perhaps irresistible. However, the unrelenting realism with which Barrett Browning articulated Marian's wrongs and alluded to the extent and horrors of English prostitution raised eyebrows among most conservative English readers. In describing these tabooed subjects in the most explicit language, Barrett Browning purposely defied both literary and social conventions. In her own defense, she explained, "If a woman ignores these wrongs, then may women as a sex continue to suffer them; there is no help for any of us—let us be dumb and die."[23]

III

Aurora Leigh believed in performance, rather than argument, as the way to prove the validity of women's God-given abilities and prerogatives (VIII. 813–846). Elizabeth Barrett Browning obviously shared this opinion, for *Aurora Leigh* was an incredibly wide-ranging and intense poetical production, for a poet of either sex. After *Aurora Leigh,* no subsequent poem of hers ever "caught the crowd"[24] in quite the same way. The poetry she published between 1856 and her death in 1861 reached a certain level of sophistication appropriate to her age and experience, but by and large, it also lapsed back into tradition and conventionality in its characterization of women. With the achievement of *Aurora Leigh,* however, the continuing significance of her contribution to the literature of women was assured. The risk she had dared to take in defense of nineteenth-century womanhood was justified by the popular impact, if not by the critical reception, of her longest poem. Today, without even a hint of condescension, we may pronounce *Aurora Leigh* the nineteenth-century masterpiece among English poems written by and about women.

Notes

1. "Barrett Browning" seems to be the most respectful shorthand version of Elizabeth Barrett Browning's name which will at the same time distinguish her from her husband.

2. See, for example, Helen Cooper, "Working into Light: Elizabeth Barrett Browning," in *Shakespeare's Sisters: Feminist Essays on Women Poets,* ed. Sandra M. Gilbert and Susan Gubar (Bloomington: Indiana University Press, 1979), pp. 65–81.

3. Barrett Browning published poetry in various ladies' giftbooks and annuals, as did most popular women writers of her day. Among these were *Findens' Tableaux, Keepsake, The Amaranth,* and *The English Bijou Almanack.* She wrote thoughtful poems upon the deaths of Felicia Hemans and Letitia Landon. In his biography of Barrett Browning, Gardner B. Taplin notes that she knew the writings of Mary Howitt and Caroline Norton; he also records an instance of her satisfaction with a copy of the *Literary Souvenir,* in 1826. See Gardner B. Taplin, *The Life of Elizabeth Barrett Browning* (New Haven: Yale University Press, 1957), pp. 128, 237, 411.

4. Elizabeth Barrett Browning, *The Complete Works,* ed. Charlotte Porter and Helen A. Clarke (New York: Thomas Y. Crowell, 1900), IV, 80–81, Book III, lines 68–79. Further citations from the poem will be from this edition and will be referred to by book and line number.

5. See my doctoral dissertation, "Representations of Women in the Work of Nineteenth-Century British Women Poets," Chapter X (University of Maryland, 1977).

6. See Taplin, pp. 310–13, 337–47, on the reception of *Aurora Leigh.*

7. Algernon C. Swinburne, "Introduction," *Aurora Leigh* (London, 1898), p. ix, quoted in Taplin, p. 310.

8. *The Letters of Elizabeth Barrett Browning,* ed. Frederic G. Kenyon (New York: Macmillan, 1898), II, 252.

9. Ibid., II, 253.

10. For a provocative Marxist-Feminist analysis of the poem, see Marxist-Feminist Literature Collective, "Women's Writing: 'Jane Eyre,' 'Shirley,' 'Villette,' 'Aurora Leigh'," in *Eighteen-Forty-Eight: The Sociology of Literature,* ed. Francis Barker, John Coombes, et al., Proceedings of the Essex Conference on the Sociology of Literature, July 1977, pp. 185–206.

11. Barrett Browning had recognized and, to some extent, applauded this aspect of the character of George Sand, whom she very much admired. See the 1844 sonnets, "To George Sand: A Desire" and "To George Sand: A Recognition." The former opens, "Thou large-brained woman and large-hearted man, / Self-called George Sand!" (II, 239). George Sand's novels are generally acknowledged as sources for *Aurora Leigh.*

12. Ellen Moers, *Literary Women: The Great Writers* (New York: Doubleday, 1977), p. 60.

13. Quoted in Moers, p. 310.

14. J.M.S. Tompkins, *"Aurora Leigh,"* The Fawcett Lecture, 1961–62 (London: Bedford College, 1961); reviewed in *Modern Language Review,* 58 (October, 1963), 625–26.

15. Taplin, p. 320.

16. Alethea Hayter, *Mrs. Browning: A Poet's Work and Its Setting* (New York: Barnes and Noble, 1963), p. 171.

17. For this observation on Lady Howe, I am indebted to Elaine Ruth Harrington, "A Study of the Poetry of Elizabeth Barrett Browning," doctoral dissertation, New York University, 1977, p. 338.

18. W.T. Stead, "The Maiden Tribute of Modern Babylon," a series of articles in the *Pall Mall Gazette* during July, 1885.

19. For *London Labour and the London Poor,* Vol. IV (see note 21 below).

20. William Acton, *Prostitution* (1857), ed. Peter Fryer (New York: Praeger, 1969).

21. Henry Mayhew, *London Labour and the London Poor* (1862); Vol. IV rpt. as *London's Underworld,* ed. Peter Quennell (London: Spring Books, 1957).

22. See Taplin, p. 341.

23. Barrett Browning, *Letters,* II, 254.

24. Ibid., II, 242.

The Domestic Economy of Art:
Elizabeth Barrett and Robert Browning

Dorothy Mermin

When Robert Browning and Elizabeth Barrett secretly married and eloped to Italy in 1846, he was thirty-four years old and she was forty. She was famous and widely respected as a poet and an unusually learned woman; he had achieved a more circumscribed but substantial literary success. Both were still living in their parents' homes and had always had the ordinary needs of daily life taken care of for them by others. Neither had ever earned a living or taken any responsibility for the management of a household. Elizabeth had only recently begun to recover strength after seven years of illness (probably pulmonary tuberculosis, then dormant) and to move outside of the one dusty, airless room in Wimpole Street to which illness had confined her. The elopement was an act of high courage for them both, since they thought that the unaccustomed exertion might prove fatal. When they reached Paris, Elizabeth was very happy but dangerously exhausted, and they immediately threw themselves on the maternal care of Mrs. Anna Jameson, a writer and friend of them both, who was also on her way to Italy and agreed to travel with them. Mrs. Jameson was astonished, delighted, but fearful. "I have . . . here," she wrote, "a poet and a poetess. . . . Both excellent; but God help them! for I know not how the two poet heads and poet hearts will get on through this prosaic world."[1]

In fact, they got on very well. They not only took very good care of each other, they took extravagant pleasure in doing so. Robert's anxious attention to his wife's health was entirely justified, but it often manifested itself in behavior strikingly like that of a parent to a very small child. They first set up housekeeping in Pisa, and Elizabeth's letters tell in joyous detail how he cajoles her to eat, lulls her to sleep, and gives her claret at dinner, "pouring it into the glass when I am looking another way, and entreating me by ever so much invocation when I look and refuse! and then I never being famous for resisting his invocations, am at the end of the dinner too giddy to see his face and am laid down at full length on the arm chair and told to go to sleep and profit by the whole." Her tasks as she describes them a month after their marriage seem strangely childish:

> Even the pouring out of the coffee is a divided labour, and the ordering of the dinner is quite out of my hands. As for me, when I am so good as to let myself be carried upstairs, and so angelical as to sit still on the sofa, and so considerate, moreover, as *not* to put my foot into a puddle, why *my* duty is considered done to a perfection which is worthy of all adoration.

Her appreciation is often faintly tempered, as it is here, by her sense of the ridiculous; some women, she notes, "might not like *the excess*." She tells him not to talk so much of how she walks about, "as if a wife with a pair of feet was a miracle of nature." He was particularly insistent on carrying her: in and out of coaches and inns, and from room to room at home. "I am taken such care of; so pillowed by arms and knees . . . so carried up and down stairs against my will. . . ." She fears he will injure himself carrying her, and is "quite seriously angry"; "sins of this sort are his only sins against me." His quasi-parental protectiveness diminished as she became stronger, but it never disappeared and sprang back into life at her every illness. He was always watchful of her health, tried to protect her from overstimulation, scolded her for tiring herself. She could not visit her friend Mary Russell Mitford from London in 1852: Robert "would as soon trust me to travel to Reading alone as *I* trust Peninni [their son] to be alone here. I believe he thinks I should drop off my head and leave it under the seat of the rail-carriage if he didn't take care of it."[2] He nursed her through all her illnesses, and just before she died—in 1861, after fifteen years of marriage—she ate a little jelly to please him.

Browning's tender attentiveness to his wife was fairly matched by hers to him. She made less show of it than he did, but then there was less need for her to take care of him. When Robert returned from telling Mrs. Jameson of their arrival in Paris, Elizabeth characteristically thought of his exhaustion rather than hers and insisted that he lie down. Before they married, she fretted about his headaches and urged him to take care of himself so strongly and so often that one is sometimes in danger of forgetting, reading their correspondence, who was really the invalid. Love, gratitude, maternal impulse, the fearfulness generated in her by the death of her most beloved brother, could all account for her excessive solicitude, but it is probably also a matter of her resistance to Robert's parental behavior toward her. Marriage was her escape from an unnatural and unnaturally prolonged dependency on her father, and one suspects that she felt ambivalent at best about Robert's invitation to sink back into childishness. Her father was a tyrant to his nine children, benevolent when they bent to his will, but exacting absolute obedience. He allowed neither sons nor daughters to marry. Elizabeth explained that she had once said in jest:

"If a Prince of Eldorado should come, with a pedigree of lineal descent from some signory in the moon in one hand, & a ticket of good-behaviour from the nearest Independent chapel, in the other"—?—

"Why even *then*," said my sister Arabel, "it would not *do*." And she was right, & we all agreed that she was right.[3]

She loved her father with intense, unembarrassed devotion, but she knew that his behavior was neither right nor sane. When he would not make it possible for her to go to Italy, although her health and even her life seemed to depend on it, she ceased to believe in his love for her, and his hold on her was broken. She married and left. She still trembled at his wrath, hoped for his forgiveness, wrote him many letters (which were eventually returned to her unopened), and grieved at his death; but she never regretted her marriage, and she gloried in her freedom.

For Robert too, however, marriage marked the abrupt and very painful end to a prolonged dependency. His parents had loved, admired, and supported him, and although he said that they acknowledged his independence and "have never been used to interfere with, or act for me," he relied on them in many ways.

There was always a great delight to me in this prolonged relation of childhood almost . . . nay altogether—with all here. My father and I have not one taste in common, one artistic taste. . . . what I mean is, that the sympathy has not been an intellectual one—I hope if you want to please me especially, Ba, you will always remember I have been accustomed, by pure choice, to have another will lead mine in the little daily matters of life. If there are two walks to take (to put the thing at simplest) you must say, "*This* one" and not "either." . . .

As this curious passage suggests, the deeper tie was to his mother. She was a devout, cultivated, strong-minded, and agreeable woman, fond of music and gardening, the center of a pleasant, peaceful household. Robert says little about her in the letters to Elizabeth, except that they had headaches at the same time—a "superstition," Elizabeth called it, but he insisted it was fact. He never saw his mother again after he went off with his wife, although Elizabeth said that he spoke of her every day, and his grief when she died in 1849 was prolonged and terrible. Elizabeth's explanation of his reluctance to revisit England in 1851 is suggestive: "The idea of taking his wife & child to New Cross [his parents' home] & putting them into the place of his mother, was haunting him day & night."[4]

When they married, each was eager to take care of the other, but neither wanted to make any assertion of will or power. Perhaps it was hard at first to break old patterns of behavior. Furthermore, they were both scornful of conventional marriages that functioned in terms of tyranny, submission, worldly values, and emotional emptiness, and were determined that their own would be different. But it took them a while to find their own way. When Robert admired Elizabeth for standing up to him in arguments, she admired his admiration. She had lived all her life under a preposterous domestic tyranny, and his refusal to exert any power over her, except in the form of loving persuasion—which generally succeeded—at first made her uncomfortable. "I am not very fond of praising men by calling them *manly*," she said in 1853; "I hate and detest a masculine man."[5] But such things are sometimes easier said than totally believed, and when she calls Robert "unmasculine" or tells him that he takes "the woman's part" one hears discomfort as well as pleasure and surprise. Eventually they did find their own way, however, in a combination of equal freedom, equal respect, and mutual nurturing.

Their manner of life made this relatively easy. They began housekeeping in idyllic simplicity, living in furnished rooms in Pisa, eating whatever the restaurant below chose to send them. Elizabeth's maid, Wilson, took care of her—when Wilson fell ill and Elizabeth had to dress herself, it was a notable event—and of routine household affairs. Elizabeth's early descriptions of their life in Pisa breathe forth delight and wonder, as if she were playing house. She never took responsibility for the household, then or later. "What would become of me (& of the house) I wonder," she wrote in 1858, "if I had a house to manage! It's a privilege on my part & an advantage on my husband's, that I have never ordered dinner once since my marriage."[6] Robert's part was harder: finding places to live in the many cities they stayed in (Pisa, Florence, Paris, Rome, Bagni di Lucca, Siena), arranging travel, keeping accounts, paying the bills. Choosing houses or apartments seems to have been particularly trying, since they often turned out to be unsatisfactory for his delicate wife, and he would frantically search for new ones; more than once they had to pay for lodgings that Elizabeth refused to occupy. (Her tendency to regret decisions once they were made—if not the choice of house, then the length of the lease—must often have made him uncomfortable.) But many of the responsibilities as well as all the actual work of the household were taken care of by servants. These made problems occasionally: one manservant proved smelly and unattractive, and in 1855 Elizabeth's maid, Wilson, married his replacement and caused some inconvenience by having a child three months later. But the Brownings were always taken care of. " 'The kitchen' is an unknown horror to me,"[7] Robert had written feelingly before their marriage; neither he nor Elizabeth ever had to have anything to do with it.

The emotional focus of their lives and the balance of maternal solicitude shifted decisively when Elizabeth gave birth to a son in March 1849, after two and a half years of marriage. Thereafter their lives were much more complicated. Elizabeth was delighted—she had assumed that her age and ill health would make it impossible for her to have children—and took a much more active role. Her new maternal cares extended to her husband, too, for his mother died right after the child was born, and he plummeted from joy into extreme grief and months of depression. Elizabeth explained in a letter how she cajoled him back to health by appealing to his solicitude for her:

My husband has been suffering beyond what one could shut one's eyes to in consequence of the great mental shock of last March—loss of appetite, loss of sleep, looks quite worn and altered. . . . I had the greatest difficulty in persuading him to leave Florence for a month or two. . . . I had to say and swear that baby and I couldn't bear the heat, and that we must and would go away.[8]

One feels some reluctance here—did she want to shut her eyes? She would have scorned such dissimulation earlier.

Robert eventually recovered his spirits and appetite, however, and then she could concentrate on her baby. She had disliked and avoided most conventional feminine pursuits since childhood, but for the baby's sake she bought a thimble; her own clothes never interested her much (her husband cared more for such things and sometimes insisted that she make herself more fashionable), but Pen, as the child came to be called, was lavishly clad in velvet and lace and feathers. On the way to Paris in 1855 they lost a box containing among other things some "ms. notes" for *Aurora Leigh,* but Elizabeth's chief anxiety was for Pen's clothes.[9] The note of excess recurs: Elizabeth adored her son, and Robert fussed and worried about him during his long widowerhood. The parents did little of the actual physical work of caring for the child—the doctors even insisted on a wet nurse, though Elizabeth wanted to nurse him herself—but they spent a great deal of time and thought on him. Elizabeth's letters are filled with beautifully drawn scenes of a childhood surrounded by love. One anecdote illustrates the new relationships in the household:

Robert is very fond of him [the baby], and threw me into a fit of hilarity the other day by springing away from his newspaper in an indignation against me because he hit his head against the floor rolling over and over. "Oh, Ba, I really can't trust you!" Down Robert was on the carpet in a moment, to protect the precious head. He takes it to be made of Venetian glass, I am certain.[10]

They were gently parental toward the baby and toward each other, each evidently feeling like the only really responsible adult, the only fit mother.

As Pen grew older, his mother took the main responsibility for him: his clothes, his schedule, his social arrangements. But he never went to school, and both parents spent a lot of time teaching him. Instruction was sometimes difficult, since although he was always charming, he did not always apply himself to work, and they could not be severe. In 1859 they were each spending two hours a day, Elizabeth instructing him in language, Robert in music, and finding it burdensome. "We mean to have a master for him presently," Elizabeth wrote. "It won't do to give up our art for teaching—it is not good even for Peni." Teachers, when they came, did not relieve her entirely: "He doesn't work for his Abbé with his heart in it," she reports, "unless I sit by him." The drawback to being a mother, she found, was that it interfered with writing. In Paris in 1855, they were in a particularly bad apartment and it was hard for her to work, but the child came first. "I don't know how my poem [*Aurora Leigh*] is ever to be finished. It's as much as I can do, to get through Peni's lessons"—and then she cheerfully praises Pen's learning and his velvet hat. But such complaints are rare, and she did finish *Aurora Leigh*. Robert said later: "My wife used to write it, and lay it down to hear our child spell, or when a visitor came—it was thrust under the cushion then."[11] Robert usually had a room of his own for writing, but Elizabeth worked wherever she was.

They had time to devote themselves to their child, their art, and each other because they had essentially no other obligations. Neither worked for money, and living in Italy freed them from the social responsibilities they would have faced in England. Their social circles were casual and unrestricting: expatriate English and Americans, travelers, artists, single and quite emancipated women, and varied eccentrics. They were certainly not Bohemian, but they did not care to spend time upholding social forms or protecting their social status. Robert was the more conventional and sociable of the two, with time and energy to spare; he would have liked to live in Paris or London, but Elizabeth was never happy for very long except in the comparative isolation of Florence and the quiet towns nearby, where they sometimes spent their summers. Their letters are full of affectionate yearning and urgent invitations to relatives and dear friends to visit them, but they were happier alone; none of their sisters and brothers ever came to Florence, but once when numerous relations stayed with them in Le Havre, in the summer of 1858, they were both miserable. Elizabeth was always weary and depressed in London, where social obligations pressed heavily on them. On the whole, epistolary relations served her well enough. All her life she had jealously guarded the time she needed to read and write from the demands that society makes of women, just as Robert had refused to expend his powers in money-making or a career.

Money, however, was a serious problem both practically and emotionally for several years. Robert gave his wife more care and devotion than the world expected of husbands, but he could not give her the financial support that the world did expect. His father lent him a hundred pounds for their elopement but could give no more, and his writings earned nothing at all. They lived on Elizabeth's inheritance from her uncle, an allowance from her cousin, John Kenyon, and the income from her poetry. Life in Italy was marvelously cheap compared to London, but they were never financially easy until 1856, when John Kenyon died and left a substantial sum to each of them. Before they married, Robert offered to get a job, but she refused to let him sacrifice his genius to the world's opinion. She could never believe that money was really important, and her husband's carefulness in paying bills and avoiding debt amused and sometimes annoyed her. "There never was anyone who looked round a corner with a more imaginative obliquity, when the idea of money-difficulty is suggested in any form, than Robert does. It is we who remind our creditors of their claim on us. . . ."[12] Once they ran almost completely out of money while traveling with Pen and Wilson, and Elizabeth reported unsympathetically that "Robert [was] in a horrible fright all the way—he lets his imagination master him indeed."[13] His anxious and clearly necessary cares in this respect seemed to her honorable but superfluous, even unpoetical. She was inclined to believe that genius carried with it freedom from many social forms—from judgments on men's careers and restrictive notions of women's roles and powers—and liked to joke about the common notion that poetry and prudence are incompatible. Robert, however, thought that poets should behave like other people and managed their worldly business as properly and conventionally as he could.

At first they tried to live without the world, except by correspondence, and only slowly widened their social circle. Although they did not like to acknowledge it, they were reluctant to let each other go. In the early months of their marriage Robert insisted that they wanted no one to disturb their solitude, while Elizabeth urged him to go about and see things. The first time they *almost* spent a night apart was in July 1850, when Robert went to Siena to find a place to rent and could not get an early train back. "Such a day I passed, feeling as if I had lost my head—or something," Elizabeth reported with a nice ambiguity—but at three in the morning he returned after all. She did not in fact like him to leave her, despite her protestations, and her least attractive side appears in her petulant indignation whenever someone tries to call him from her: when his sister summons him to his cousin's funeral (he did not go) or their friends the Storys, distracted at the death of one child and the illness of another, ask for his company for a few days. Increasingly, however, their solitude was broken, especially in livelier cities than Florence. In Rome in 1859, Elizabeth was not well enough to go out much, and Robert "began by refusing all invitations to dinner—and he never dines out now—*except when he does.*" She was clearly more displeased than she liked to admit. "As to Robert he is lost to me and himself. If once a fortnight we have an evening together, we call it a holiday, both of us. . . . It pleases me that he should be amused just now (not but that he denies being amused very often); and I think it's good for him—in an occasional winter like this." "I believe I get some good for future lonely or quiet hours to digest," Robert explained glumly.[14] He for his part objected to many of his wife's visitors, either because they might tire her, or—especially when they shared her interest in spiritualism—because he thought they were taking advantage of her. They had many friends, but they both were wary and resentful of friendships that threatened to separate them or seemed to make inordinate demands.

Each was inclined to think the other too good-natured, too generous, too susceptible and solicitous of others. The mothering qualities that upheld their marriage seemed less attractive when others were the object of them. Elizabeth professed astonishment that Robert's sister asked him to come from Paris to London for his cousin's funeral: "she understands nothing about Robert's susceptibilities"—"why, he would have had to go to the very cemetery, of course, where his mother's remains lie. . . . He is always a thousand times too good and tender."[15] Robert did not go, frightened by his wife's distress; but a few days later Elizabeth had a new complaint: He went to nurse an old lady, gave her medicine, was prepared to spend the night. Elizabeth, not unreasonably, thought this excessive.[16] Usually, though, it was Robert who tried to protect his wife from her own sensibility. When bad news was expected he intercepted her mail and dealt it out to her gently. He thought her much too trusting and generous and was particularly annoyed by her misplaced confidence in various practitioners of spiritualism, the one matter on which she refused to let him protect her.

The justification for all this anxious mutual solicitude, this selfishness à deux, was not just love, but also art. The Brownings protected themselves from distraction, closed themselves up in their own world, and left their families, friends, and country behind them, so that they could work. The pattern of their lives together is reflected—sometimes with a strange obliquity—in their sense of themselves as poets and in some of the poems they wrote while they were married.

They admired each other's poems before they met, in terms that augured well for their meeting. When Elizabeth defended Browning's poetry to her skeptical friend Mary Russell Mitford, she always stressed maleness, passion, power. He is "very masculine," "eminently masculine and downright," "a true soul-piercing poet"; a scene "pants" with "power"; she feels "clenched passion . . . concentrated passion . . . burning through." Browning, reciprocally, chiefly praised and quoted her plangent ballads of love and longing. After reading her 1844 *Poems* he wrote the letter that began their correspondence: "I love your verses with all my heart, dear Miss Barrett," he began, ". . . the fresh strange music, the affluent language, the exquisite pathos and true new brave thought . . . and I love you too."[17]

They found in each other what they missed in themselves. Browning felt that his life had been dangerously happy and easy: "For when did I once fail to get whatever I had set my heart upon?—as I ask myself sometimes, with a strange fear." But everything he had so far set his heart upon had not been enough. He needed something else to want. He had ceased expecting to fall in love and declared himself tired of society, tired even of books. In her situation, her poems, and her letters he read a knowledge of suffering that was outside his own experience and is in fact rather conspicuously absent from his early poetry. For a long time she was afraid to let him meet her, marked as she was by age, illness, and sorrow. Then she distrusted his love and felt that she would be ungenerous to return it. She could teach him "nothing" she said, "except grief," and the suspicion that grief was what he wanted to learn made her uneasy. "I have sometimes felt jealous of myself . . . of my own infirmities, . . . and thought that you cared for me only because your chivalry touched them with a silver sound." Once he explained, rather awkwardly, how glad he was that the state of her health required her to go to Italy (and thus in effect to marry him): "Nor am I so selfish, I hope, as that (because my uttermost pride & privilege and glory above all glories would be to live in your sick-room and serve you,)—as that, on that account, I would not rather see you in a condition to need none of my service. . . ." The parenthetical assertion buried in this convoluted syntax is extravagant, but his behavior bore it out. He saw in her poems, moreover, not only deep feelings but also the ability to express them. In his second letter he compared his poetry to hers: "You *do* what I always wanted, hoped to do, and only seem now likely to do for the first time. You speak out, *you,*—I only make men & women speak. . . ."[18] He had already produced a substantial body of remarkable poetry, his reputation and his powers were alike increasing, and he had every reason to be sanguine. All that he seemed to lack was what Elizabeth Barrett had in abundance: dark experience of the inner life, and the ability to express it. Through his marriage, furthermore, he enacted the recurrent central myth of his poetry, Perseus' rescue of Andromeda.

And Elizabeth Barrett was ready to be rescued. Although she did not realize it, her illness was no longer active and her strength was returning. She was sick of isolation and did not cherish sorrow; she was ashamed of her nervousness, easy tears, and morbid terrors. Her early poetry expresses yearning, grief, and the pain of renunciation, but she had always tried to cultivate intellect in herself, not feeling. She had written at age fourteen: "My feelings are acute in the extreme but as nothing is so odious in my eyes as a damsel famed in story for a superabundance of sensibility they are carefully restrained!"[19] She had resisted in many ways the tedious demands that society made on upper-middle-class women, but now, she said, she had learned to value cheerfulness and society. She was desperately restless, longing to travel and know the world. Visitors wearied her, but she knew that solitude made her morbid and deprived her of the materials she needed for her writing. Browning coveted the knowledge she had drawn from introspection and inner experience, but she wanted to write about the world and valued his energy, strength, freedom, and knowledge of life. He wanted to be able to speak from his own subjectivity, and she hoped that he would; but for herself, she wanted to write something more impersonal, a novel-poem of modern times. She saw no attraction in illness, no heroism in caring for the ill. When all England honored Florence Nightingale in 1855, she resented the implication that "the best use to which we can put a gifted and accomplished woman is to *make her a hospital nurse.* If it is, why then woe to us all who are artists!"[20] One of her late poems, "A Court Lady," tells of a noblewoman who dressed herself up in court attire to visit soldiers in a hospital, praising their courage and exalting their patriotism and helping them by her majestic presence to die nobly. That was Elizabeth Barrett Browning's idea of an artist's proper role in a sickroom.

So it is not surprising that his attentiveness always quickened when she was sad or ill, and that her response to this was ambivalent. One sometimes feels something working a little against his overt will to make her strong and free; he carried her, nursed her, mothered her, tried to protect her from the world's folly and evil. She in turn sent him off to enjoy the sights of Pisa and Florence, the dinner parties of Rome, even when he said he wanted to stay alone with her. One does not want to stress this—he certainly did not want to keep her an invalid and was particularly eager to help her free herself from the opium to which medical advice had addicted her, while she was not pleased when he did start dining out. But the original basis remained: He was drawn to her weakness, she to his strength.

As writers, despite the differences that drew them together they were enough alike to help each other. They both wrote poems that were learned, innovative, difficult. They found in each other the sympathetic yet discriminating audience that Browning especially, whose works had met mostly with incomprehension, needed. The early part of their epistolary courtship was much taken up with her comments on his poetry, earnestly solicited and modestly offered. Her praise—subtle, just, accurate, unstinting—probably helped him more than her criticisms did. Her suggested emendations are mostly in the direction of clarity and smoothness, for she was anxious for his public success; an ear attuned to Browning's mature voice and to twentieth-century poetry will reject most of them.[21] She asked him to tell her in turn the faults in her poems, but although she was genuinely receptive to criticism and would not have taken offense, he put her off with lavish, rather awkward praise. He refused to be her teacher in poetry, although he helped her translate Greek. He must have helped her most, however, simply by taking her work seriously. Her father had been extremely proud of her precocious talents, but he always laughed, she said, "like Jove," at the idea that people could be "busy" with poetry.[22] Doctors tried to cure her nervousness by denying her the use of pen and paper (it is amusing to see her more than once offering Robert the same advice). Still, although he praises her genius and quotes her poems, it is *his* poetry, not hers, that the letters discuss.

Before they married she frequently urged him not to write unless he was feeling quite well, while he was occasionally seized with compunction and asked her not to neglect her own work for the sake of his. The terms of their solicitude changed after their marriage, when it became evident that she wrote much more fluently and happily, and moreover with greater public success, than he did. Her letters often return, lightly but insistently, to her worries about his work, reporting on Robert's application to his poetry and Pen's to his lessons in similar tones. She writes from Bagni di Lucca in the summer of 1853: "We are going to work hard . . . if Robert does not make good use of that cheerful little blue room with two windows, I shall give him up, I say." He did work hard then, but four years later, after the failure of *Men and Women* had discouraged him, she reports from the same place on a somewhat sharper note: "Robert has no models for his drawing, and no studio. Well—

now poetry must have its turn, and I shall not be sorry for that. He has taken a passion for drawing, and . . . devotes himself to it too much, perhaps, neglecting his own art."[23] This comment is as near as she ever comes to criticizing him; it suggests that she is really worried.

Criticism might have been uncomfortable, since Browning did not become successful with the public until after his wife's death, although he was highly esteemed by those whose opinions really mattered. She was much more famous, and her work actually made money. When Wordsworth died in 1850, her name was mentioned for the laureateship; Robert's was not. In their Florentine circle she was the great writer, he the husband who graciously rejoiced in her success. Sometimes she seemed to feel some friendly rivalry, reporting to correspondents on their relative progress in writing. She was a little unhappy when she saw *Men and Women* reaching completion before *Aurora Leigh:* "It may be better not to bring out the two works together," she says, solacing herself, but adds, "If mine were ready I might not say so perhaps." The failure of *Men and Women,* which was not only the best book Browning ever published but also the one most likely to be liked and understood, was a terrible disappointment. *Aurora Leigh* got mixed responses from the critics, but it went into many editions. Robert's bitterness bursts forth in a letter to their publisher authorizing him to bring out the second edition of *Aurora Leigh;* he speaks of "we" and "us" and then catches himself up: "(*Us*—I am the church-organ-bellows' blower that talked about *our* playing, but you know what I do in the looking after commas and dots to i's)." But despite the errant judgments of the world, each believed absolutely in the other's greatness as a poet. Elizabeth understood with fine discrimination the consummate power of his work, while Robert asserted in 1871 that "*she* was the poet, and I the clever person by comparison." But she, it is clear, knew otherwise, and perhaps he did too, for he goes on to explain that one must "remember her limited experience of all kinds, and what she made of it."[24] In any case, his faith in her as a poet enhanced the value of her appreciation, and in the psychological economy of their marriage his genius must have balanced her success.

The effect of their marriage on the actual poems they wrote was, in general, to open up for each of them the territory represented by the other. His poems move from the monstrous psychological world of fanatics and murderers into realms of normal human feeling, exploring with particular zest and acuity various shades of love. Hers move from inwardness, literary themes, and legend to social and political scenes and subjects. The changes begin in the first poems they wrote after their marriage—poems in which they seem to go, in effect, too far, half assuming the other's identity and speaking as if in the other's voice. These early poems are in large part, curiously enough, about mothering.

Barrett Browning's "The Runaway Slave at Pilgrim's Point" is a contribution to the battle against slavery in America, a dramatic monologue spoken by a slave woman who has killed her infant because it had had "a look" like its white father's: "The *master's* look, that used to fall/On my soul like his lash . . . or worse!"[25] She tells her dreadful tale of oppression and murder with the hallucinatory vividness, swinging energy, and crazily self-justifying logic of Johannes Agricola or Porphyria's lover, Browning's earliest dramatic monologuists. For Barrett Browning the poem had manifold personal relevance. Her family had been slaveholders in Jamaica and produced many children of mixed blood, including another Elizabeth Barrett;[26] her father, the family remarked, treated his children like slaves; she herself was dark; and in the eyes of her father and brothers she was a "runaway." Escape from her father into marriage with a man who explicitly refused to be "master" probably freed some long-repressed feelings and allowed her to write this cry of self-assertion against the tyranny of men and infants, the tyranny that is built into the structure of the family and disguises itself as love.

The first poem Browning wrote after their marriage was probably "The Guardian-Angel: A Picture at Fano." By a strange reciprocity with "The Runaway Slave," it expresses an infantile yearning for a protective maternal figure. The speaker addresses the angel, who is pictured with a praying child, and asks to take the child's place:

> And wilt thou bend me low
> Like him, and lay, like his, my hands together,
> And lift them up to pray, and gently tether
> Me, as thy lamb there, with thy garment's spread?[27]

Whereas "The Runaway Slave" is a dramatic monologue that resembles the poems Browning wrote, "The Guardian Angel" is explicitly personal, mentioning Browning's wife, their excursions, and his friend with accurate particularity. He seems finally to be doing what they had agreed that he should do: speak out in his own voice. But the voice sounds more like Elizabeth Barrett's at its worst than his own, with its paraphernalia of angels, wings, and children, the thinness, the stiff archaisms, the near-bathos of the diction, and the depressed and inhibited tone. Later Browning was to remark that his wife, unlike himself, took no "scientific interest in evil."[28] "The Runaway Slave" confronts evil, however, whereas Browning's speaker asks the angel to cover his eyes and make him see the world, "earth and skies / And sea," with "different eyes" (30–32).

> O world, as God has made it! All is beauty:
> And knowing this, is love, and love is duty.
> What further may be sought for or declared?
> (33–35)

This is not his wife's view of the world, but it is a view that he sometimes hopes his love for her will help him discover.

The same excessive identification appears in *Christmas-Eve and Easter-Day* (1850), Browning's first important work after his marriage. Here he sets forth ideas on various religious topics, again apparently speaking quite openly, again yearning for a protective maternal figure. A vision of Christ appears to him in "a sweepy garment, vast and white" (*Christmas-Eve,* 438), to which he clings as he travels from one form of worship to another, and which saves him at the end, when he is "lapped again•in its folds full-fraught / With warmth and wonder and delight" (1231–32), like the happy baby of a full-skirted Victorian mother. Elizabeth is usually blamed for the poem's form and doctrine, which resembles her own, but she had reservations about it; she "complained of the *asceticism,*" and Robert replied that "it was 'one side of the question.' "[29] Still, the poem is tougher and more astringent in tone than "The Guardian Angel"; it marks the end of Browning's overt poetical dependency on his wife, as it marks his last show of yearning to be caught up and protected by maternal love.

Strong and ambivalent feelings about motherhood recur prominently, however, in Barrett Browning's later work. In *Aurora Leigh* all young women yearn for mothers. " 'When mothers fail us, can we help ourselves?' " (VI, 1229). The maternal breast repeatedly appears, often in very strange images, as the ultimate object of desire; Aurora turns to the hills of Italy, for instance, like a "sucking babe" to its sleeping mother (V, 1267 ff.). Throughout *Aurora Leigh,* however, mothers sometimes nurture but more often betray or destroy their children, while children both sanctify and consume their mothers. Marian Erle's mother had beaten and abused her, and Lady Waldemar's arrangements for taking care of her end in her being raped—a betrayal that Marian bitterly recognizes as " 'A motherly, right damnable good turn' " (VII, 10). Love for the child engendered by the rape saves Marian's life and spirit, but at the cost of everything else: " 'I'm nothing more / But just a mother' " (VI, 823–24). Aurora's story shows a similar doubling of love and hostility. Her mother died early—"She could not bear the joy of giving life, / The mother's rapture slew her" (I, 34–35)—and Aurora as a child is haunted by her dead mother's portrait, which seemed "by turns/ Ghost, fiend, and angel, fairy, witch, and sprite," Muse, Psyche, Medusa, "Our Lady of the Passion, stabbed with swords / Where the Babe sucked," Lamia . . . (I, 153 ff.). When Aurora becomes a successful writer, she imagines married life with similar though less lurid ambivalence, describing herself ironically as " 'a printing woman who has lost her place/ (The sweet safe corner of the household fire / Behind the heads of children)' " (V, 806–808), and thinking in a gloomy moment that she might have been happier with "chubby children hanging on my neck / To keep me low and wise" (II, 516–517). To love a child is to lose one's own life; this is the unspoken assumption behind the maternal cruelty that everywhere haunts the poem.

The poem tacitly insists, furthermore, that only women can nurture, protect, and feed, even though most refuse to do so. Marian, Aurora, and the structure of plot and imagery reject with astonishing violence Romney's repeated efforts to be, in effect, a mother. Near the end of the poem Romney recapitulates his disastrous career as a social reformer through a series of perverse maternal images. He had imagined the poor, he says, as prisoners inside the "Phalarian bull, society" (VIII, 388), which simultaneously holds them in its male womb and tramples them with its hoofs (VIII, 385 ff.). Then he saw them as the "great famishing•carnivorous mouth" of a "huge, deserted, callow, blind bird Thing," which he tried to feed with worms (VIII, 395 ff.). The consequence of this misguided maternalism is that its ungrateful objects destroy his ancestral home, which he describes in terms—covered floors, "Carved wainscots, panelled walls, the favorite slide / For draining off a martyr (or a rogue) . . . stairs . . . slippery darkness" (VIII, 967 ff.)—that again suggest a womb. Aurora agrees to marry him only when he comes to her blind, defeated, humble, "like a punished child" (VIII, 362). Stripped of both masculine and maternal attributes, he accepts the role that Aurora had rejected for herself. "Work for two," he tells her, "As I, though thus restrained, for two shall love" (IX, 911–12). The general rebellion in *Aurora Leigh* against Romney's loving domination seems to amplify Elizabeth's strain of resistance against Robert and may suggest that although she did not consciously encourage his dependency on her, she did in some way desire it. The poem's insistence on the dark side of motherhood probably reflects the pain and fear of her pregnancies and miscarriages as well as a largely unconscious resentment of her adored, engrossing child.[30]

The Brownings expressed in their poems both the connubial affection for which they became famous and also other impulses—his to be dependent, hers to repel claims on her love—that were harder to acknowledge. Browning's need for mothering was partly satisfied by their marriage and issued in only a few weak poems. Barrett Browning's rebellious impulse, which was repressed and thwarted to a much greater degree, shows itself in more poems and is generally a source of energy—sometimes mawkish, sometimes surprisingly violent, but often suggestive, powerful, and strange. Insofar as it is possible to assess the total effect of their marriage on their writing, we can say with confidence that it was highly salutary. Freed from isolation and paternal censorship, Barrett Browning was able to write on contemporary public themes such as the role of women, prostitution, and the Risorgimento, which increasingly absorbed her attention. *Sonnets from the Portuguese,* her first major work and her last on a wholly private, erotic theme, was written during their courtship, and *Aurora Leigh,* her other major work, when Pen was little. Browning wrote all of *Men and Women* and some of *Dramatis Personae,* and partly conceived, though he did not execute, *The Ring and the Book.* He wrote less, quantitatively, in the fifteen years they lived together than he did before or after, but what he did write was much better. Almost all his best work comes from those years, and his characteristic weaknesses—excessive length, apparent shapelessness, opacity of language—hardly appear at all. Perhaps Elizabeth's salutary critical influence was responsible, or perhaps while she was with him he did not have to fill the emptiness of his time with writing. The Brownings' love story became a sentimental legend in their own lifetime and continues to repel some readers from their poetry and incite others to find flaws in their absurdly celebrated happiness. The subjects on which they disagreed—politics, Pen's clothes, spiritualism—have been made to suggest serious rifts, especially by critics who seem to imagine that an argumentative wife would be intolerable. They had many serious troubles, the worst being Elizabeth's miscarriages and illnesses. But they both *thought* they were very happy together, and Browning said many times that his wife was the source and inspiration of his best poetry. What they gave each other as poets, it seems, was a psychic space in which they could work freely, and the confidence to explore previously repressed or inaccessible desires and fields of experience.

Notes

1.　Gerardine MacPherson, *Memoirs of the Life of Anna Jameson* (Boston: Robert Bros., 1878), pp. 228–29. Barrett Browning's illness is analyzed by George Pickering in *Creative Malady: Illness in the Lives and Minds of Charles Darwin, Florence Nightingale, Mary Baker Eddy, Sigmund Freud, Marcel Proust, Elizabeth Barrett Browning* (New York: Oxford University Press, 1974), pp. 245–65. The Brownings' life together is discussed in many biographies; see Dorothy Hewlett, *Elizabeth Barrett Browning* (London: Cassell, 1953); Gardner B. Taplin, *The Life of Elizabeth Barrett Browning* (New Haven: Yale University Press, 1957); Alethea Hayter, *Mrs. Browning: A Poet's Work and Its Setting* (London: Faber and Faber, 1962); Betty Miller, *Robert Browning: A Portrait* (New York: Scribners, 1952); Maisie Ward, *Robert Browning and His World*, 2 vols. (New York: Holt, Rinehart, and Winston, 1967–1969); William Irvine and Park Honan, *The Book, the Ring, and the Poet* (New York: McGraw-Hill, 1974); and Edward C. McAleer, *The Brownings of Casa Guidi* (New York: The Browning Institute, 1979).

2.　Leonard Huxley, ed., *Elizabeth Barrett Browning: Letters to Her Sister, 1846–1859* (London: John Murray, 1929), p. 11; Frederic G. Kenyon, ed., *The Letters of Elizabeth Barrett Browning*, 2 vols., 4th ed. (London: Smith, Elder, 1898), I, 306: *Twenty-Two Unpublished Letters of Elizabeth Barrett Browning and Robert Browning Addressed to Henrietta and Arabella Moulton-Barrett* (New York: United Feature Syndicate, 1935), p. 25; Kenyon, *The Letters of Elizabeth Barrett Browning* I, 427; *Twenty-Two Unpublished Letters,* p. 10; Huxley, *Letters to Her Sister,* p. 109; Kenyon, *The Letters of Elizabeth Barrett Browning* II, 85.

3.　Elvan Kintner, ed., *The Letters of Robert Browning and Elizabeth Barrett Barrett, 1845–1846,* 2 vols. (Cambridge: Harvard University Press, 1969), I, 319.

4.　Kintner, *The Letters of Robert Browning and Elizabeth Barrett Barrett* II, 1006, 960, 976; Peter N. Heydon and Philip Kelley, eds., *Elizabeth Barrett Browning's Letters to Mrs. David Ogilvy, 1849–1861, with Recollections by Mrs. Ogilvy,* (New York: Quadrangle/The New York Times Book Company, and The Browning Institute, 1973), p. 45.

5.　Kenyon, *The Letters of Elizabeth Barrett Browning* II, 134.

6.　Heydon and Kelley, *Elizabeth Barrett Browning's Letters to Mrs. David Ogilvy,* p. 136.

7.　Kintner, *The Letters of Robert Browning and Elizabeth Barrett Barrett* II, 894.

8. Kenyon, *The Letters of Elizabeth Barrett Browning* I, 410.

9. Ronald Hudson, "Elizabeth Barrett Browning and Her Brother Alfred: Some Unpublished Letters," *Browning Institute Studies* 2 (1974), 147. On the intense and often problematic relation of the Brownings to their son, see Maisie Ward, *The Tragi-Comedy of Pen Browning* (New York: Sheed and Ward, and The Browning Institute, 1972), especially the introduction by Robert Coles.

10. Kenyon, *The Letters of Elizabeth Barrett Browning* I, 421.

11. Paul Landis, ed., *Letters of the Brownings to George Barrett* (Urbana: University of Illinois Press, 1958), p. 359; *Twenty-Two Unpublished Letters*, p. 85; Huxley, *Letters to Her Sister*, p. 233; Thurman L. Hood, ed., *Letters of Robert Browning* (New Haven: Yale University Press, 1933), p. 48.

12. Huxley, *Letters to Her Sister*, p. 73.

13. Letter to Arabella Barrett (June 26, 1851), in the Henry W. and Albert A. Berg Collection, The New York Public Library, Astor, Lenox and Tilden Foundations. Quotations from letters in the Berg Collection are published by permission of The New York Public Library and John Murray.

14. Huxley, *Letters to Her Sister*, p. 125, 307, 305; Edward C. McAleer, ed., *Dearest Isa: Robert Browning's Letters to Isabella Blagden* (Austin: University of Texas Press, 1951), p. 36.

15. Letter to Arabella Barrett (May 25, 1852), in the Berg Collection.

16. Letter to Arabella Barrett (May 29–30, 1852), in the Berg Collection.

17. Betty Miller, ed., *Elizabeth Barrett to Miss Mitford: The Unpublished Letters of Elizabeth Barrett Barrett to Mary Russell Mitford* (New Haven: Yale University Press, 1954), pp. 241, 251, 179, 80, 172; Kintner, *The Letters of Robert Browning and Elizabeth Barrett Barrett* I, 3.

18. Kintner, *The Letters of Robert Browning and Elizabeth Barrett Barrett* I, 25, 87, 247; II, 757; I, 7.

19. "Two Autobiographical Essays by Elizabeth Barrett," *Browning Institute Studies* 2 (1974), 130.

20. Kenyon, *The Letters of Elizabeth Barrett Browning* II, 189.

21. See Bernice Fox, "Revision in Browning's *Paracelsus*," *Modern Language Notes*, 55 (1940), 195–97, and Edward Snyder and Frederic Palmer, Jr., "New Light on the Brownings," *Quarterly Review* 269 (1937), 48–63.

22. S. R. Townshend Mayer, ed., *Letters of Elizabeth Barrett Browning Addressed to Richard Hengist Horne*, 2 vols. (London: Richard Bentley and Son, 1877), II, 145–46.

23. Landis, *Letters . . . to George Barrett*, p. 187; Huxley, *Letters to Her Sister*, pp. 276–77.

24. Heydon and Kelley, *Elizabeth Barrett Browning's Letters to Mrs. . . . . Ogilvy*, p. 115; William Clyde DeVane and Kenneth Leslie Knickerbocker, eds., *New Letters of Robert Browning* (London: John Murray, 1951), p. 97; McAleer, *Dearest Isa*, p. 365.

25. *The Poetical Works of Elizabeth Barrett Browning* (Boston: Houghton Mifflin, 1974), XXI. All references to Barrett Browning's poems are to this edition.

26. See Jeannette Marks, *The Family of the Barrett: A Colonial Romance* (New York: Macmillan, 1938), for the history of the Barretts in Jamaica.

27. Browning, *The Poems*, ed. John Pettigrew, 2 vols. (New Haven: Yale University Press, 1981), "The Guardian-Angel," II. 18–21. All references to Browning's poems are to this edition.

28. Richard Curle, ed., *Robert Browning and Julia Wedgwood: A Broken Friendship as Revealed by Their Letters* (New York: Frederick A. Stokes, 1937), p. 137.

29. Kenyon, *The Letters of Elizabeth Barrett Browning*, I, 449.

30. For a survey of Barrett Browning's poetry about mothers and children that takes a somewhat different point of view, see Sandra Donaldson, " 'Motherhood's Advent in Power': Elizabeth Barrett Browning's Poems about Motherhood," *Victorian Poetry* 18 (1980), 51–60.

Casa Guidi Windows and Aurora Leigh:
The Genesis of Elizabeth Barrett Browning's
Visionary Aesthetic

Dolores Rosenblum

Recent feminist criticism has gone a long way toward rescuing Elizabeth Barrett Browning's masterpiece, *Aurora Leigh,* from more than a half-century of neglect.[1] Through this narrative of the growth of a female poet and the development of a female poetics, Barrett Browning, who urged the female poet to look for her poetic "grandmothers,"[2] has come to serve as a poetic grandmother herself, a model of the female poet whose imagination is epic in scope, and whose inner—and domestic—life fosters the poetic energy to tackle social and political mystifications. *Aurora Leigh* shows Barrett Browning working out an aesthetic which, first of all, identifies women as originators of meaning rather than as reflecting mirrors for the male poet's search for self-transcendence, and secondly, makes a claim for poetry as deeply revolutionary as that of the Romantic poets. But the politics of Barrett Browning's poetics has an earlier source in another long-neglected poem,[3] written some years before *Aurora Leigh,* but not before *Aurora Leigh* was in her mind:[4] *Casa Guidi Windows* (written 1848–49, published 1851). Less a narrative than a meditative essay on the vicissitudes of the Italian Risorgimento, *Casa Guidi Windows* deals with a specific moment in history, framed—literally—by Barrett Browning's window on the world. What links the two poems is the poet's conviction that ways of seeing can transform the world of action, and that the weight of patriarchal tradition, aesthetic or political, can paralyze the actors in human history. As a representation of the deadliness of patriarchal rhetoric as well as patriarchal politics, *Casa Guidi Windows* paves the way for Aurora Leigh's attempt to create a new mythos and a living language out of a deadening literary inheritance. In other words, what is mandated by the political vision of *Casa Guidi Windows* is a wholly new literary aesthetic.

In regard to *Aurora Leigh,* Barrett Browning once wrote that her aim was to come face to face with a living present, with the "Humanity" of the

Reprinted from *Tulsa Studies in Women's Literature* Vol. 4, No. 1, Spring 1985. © 1985, The University of Tulsa. Reprinted by permission of the publisher.

age.[5] In *Casa Guidi Windows* she in effect prepares herself for such a bold confrontation by first evaluating the view from the window: the processional of history in the making, "Humanity" betrayed by weak and faithless rulers and oppressed by a dead literary-political mythology. Barrett Browning does not reject, however, the poet's need for a tradition or culture's links with its heroic past. In both poems she is concerned with how the dead—fallen women, "shot corpses," useless myths, dead poets—can be made to serve the living.

It is useful to keep in mind that this connection has not been made in the history of Barrett Browning scholarship, which has tended to compartmentalize and seal off her "best" works—the *Sonnets from the Portuguese, Aurora Leigh*—from large tracts of presumed poetic wasteland. *Casa Guidi Windows* has been dismissed as politically naive, and misread as a record of Barrett Browning's disappointment in the Grand Duke Leopold's failure to become a charismatic hero.[6] Julia Markus's recent scholarly edition of the poem[7] goes a long way toward dispelling these misapprehensions, and her introductory essay is mandatory reading for the Barrett Browning scholar. In an attempt to offset the critical tendency to consider *Casa Guidi Windows* "a political poem written by an unknowledgeable and hysterical female" (xix), Markus carefully reconstructs the poem's historical context. Markus's main point is that the Brownings' new life of freedom in Italy coincided with the Florentines' hope for a new era of political freedom and the eventual unification of Italy, as signaled by certain freedoms granted by Grand Duke Leopold II of Tuscany and the newly elected Pope, Pius IX. Markus brings textual and contextual evidence to bear against the charge that Barrett Browning naively trusted the promises of the Duke and the Pope, and that her reaction against both leaders and people is a reaction against the Risorgimento itself. Markus points out, rather, that Barrett Browning's support of the Duke in 1847 and her disillusionment with him in 1849 "accurately reflect the attitude of all liberal Europe before and after the revolutions of 1848" (xvii). In fact, Markus makes a good case for the poem's being "one of the most detailed accounts of the political happenings in Florence in 1847 and 1849 that has come down to us" (xxx). As well as this "objective" accuracy, what is important to a rehabilitative reading of the poem is the double-nature of the speaker: the persona is both "I, a woman" and "I, the poet," a fusion that produces unique clarity and depth of vision. As this essay attempts to show, this vision is suited both to historical narrative and mythic epic. In *Casa Guidi Windows* a double-vision simultaneously "domesticates" the processional of history, focusing on lived experience in the present as opposed to a dead past, and places the lived moment within a cosmic perspective in which the present unfolds a dynamic future.

Casa Guidi Windows' cosmic-domestic perspective provides a foundation for *Aurora Leigh*'s discovery of a whole new way of seeing. Aurora Leigh sees herself developing an aesthetic that will be more adequate to the needs of a living people than are short-sighted social projects, precisely because the aesthetic irradiates the individual life *as* individual life. It would be simplistic to read *Aurora Leigh* as a response to the failures of active heroism as illustrated in *Casa Guidi Windows,* failures exemplary of patriarchal politics. Rather, we can see how in *Casa Guidi Windows* Barrett Browning is working out a conception of the struggle to recover the human from the abstract, the present from the past, radical vision from empty images. This conception is fully realized in *Aurora Leigh,* where the struggle is carried on by a woman poet who becomes a hero for humanity by virtue of her life-affirming visionary power. The rest of my essay elaborates a more detailed consideration of how the shifting perspective in *Casa Guidi Windows* leads to the crucial aesthetic reorientation of *Aurora Leigh.*

Part I of *Casa Guidi Windows* begins with a motion of the poet-speaker's mind, from her recollection of a child's song in praise of liberty, to her musings on the singers of the past who have commemorated Italy's sufferings. It is at this point, when she feels herself drawn to the beauty and melancholy of the past, that the poet announces her intention to break with their seductive rhetoric. The poem's images—here, in particular, female images—are fictions that mask the actuality of suffering: Juliet's empty tomb at Verona stands for "all images/Men set between themselves and actual wrong" (43–44). No matter how great the heritage—"Virgil, Cicero, Catullus, Caesar . . . Boccaccio, Dante, Petrarca . . . Angelo, Raffael, Pergolese" (176–81)—when these figures dry up into rhetoric they only enervate the living. As she is well aware, however, in Italy the past breaks into the present at every turn. Barrett Browning in fact shows great imaginative sympathy for the past, fully representing that seductive pull at the same time that she renounces it. When she visits a Florentine church, for instance, she can "see" exactly what Machiavelli saw: the beautiful terrified women at Plague time, "Rustling her silks in pauses of the mass,/To keep the thought off how her husband fell,/When she left home, stark dead across her feet" (325–27). It is just this ability to recreate that living moment that makes plain to her how easy it is to "reverence or lament" the past, and to turn away from the difficult present. To the extent that she is an apocalyptic thinker, Barrett Browning envisions a cleansing destruction of the old order to make way for the new. The living must go on with their present concerns, the making of a future, and remain strengthened by their links to the dead past, but not enthralled by it.

These meditations are followed by a description of the Grand Duke Leopold's triumphant procession through the streets of Florence. From her perspective at the window, as woman and poet, Barrett Browning sees the progress of a type of Carlylean hero, a hero for the people who demonstrate *their* heroism, in the Carlylean sense, by having chosen *him.* When she looks at the second actor in this pageant, Pius Ninth, she has more serious reservations. Here the past is put to a different use: her knowledge of the historic papacy, the "hierocratic empire," makes her doubt the new pope can transcend that history. He too is captive to death, the deadliness of his symbolic function. He hardens into the stone of his office, and the people who need a living man must be served by "half travertine" (1041). Still hopeful, however, the poet ends with a blessing from one on whom the images of Italy have had a deep and early influence and a valediction for Naples' "shot corpses," who are dead fruitfully, in a righteous cause. With all the rest of Italy, then, the poet awaits the fulfillment of the Risorgimento.

Part II registers the poet's reaction to Duke Leopold's betrayal of Italy to the Austrians, the feeble attempts of the Florentine people at nationalism, and the Duke's return to Florence with the Austrian military machine. Death, the stone-hardness Barrett Browning has represented in Part I as reaching out from the past, enters the present fully realized as the inexorable engines of war:

> cannons rolling on, /. . . each bestrode / By a single man, dust-white from head to heel, Indifferent as the dreadful thing he rode, / Like a sculptured Fate serene and terrible. (302–07)

As neither leaders nor people have acted courageously or wisely, she can exempt from complicity only the dead themselves, who now become the "seeds of life" (663) in a new birth that prefigures the revival of the corpse Earth in Book V of *Aurora Leigh*.[8] The end of the poem circles back to the beginning, with the poet still preoccupied with "graves" and "patriot['s] tombs" (724–25). But she also recalls that she had hope once because a child sang. This association focuses her attention on her own child as a prophetic symbol of rebirth. The Christlike child offers hope of escape from the cycle of history, and the domestic sphere becomes the place where cosmic destiny is at work, allowing the poet to believe that there is a design to human history, that "the blank interstices/Men take for ruins, He will build into/With pillared marbles rare" (756–58).

This transposition of a pattern of death and renewal from a historical sphere to a cosmic-domestic one prepares for a similar shift in *Aurora Leigh*. The central parallels are two. First, Barrett Browning's assertions in *Casa Guidi Windows* that Italy must throw off a crippling past, especially the mediations of a bankrupt rhetoric, prepare for her assertions about the poet's role in *Aurora Leigh* and her rejection of the empty rhetoric of a patriarchal poetic tradition. In Book V, for instance, she denounces the kind of poet who "trundles back his soul five hundred years" to commemorate an idealized past (in other words the Carlyles and the Tennysons) and announces her aim to write for the present, to "catch/Upon the burning lava of a song/ The full-veined, heaving, double-breasted Age" (V, 215–17). This impulse is the same one that stirs the poet to mistrust the uses of the past in *Casa Guidi Windows:* not a mistrust of Dante and Boccaccio in themselves, but in the way they come to signify, blurring our vision of the present. This oppressive past is obviously patriarchal and Barrett Browning comes to supplant it with a female aesthetic and a female history.

Second, in "planting" the dead as seeds for new life in *Casa Guidi Windows,* Barrett Browning prepares for a similarly fruitful "planting" in *Aurora Leigh.* In this case, however, rather than the death of the life-denying fathers, Barrett Browning takes as her base the death of the life-giving mothers. If the dead poets transmit useless myths, there are ways in which female death— female exclusion from the canon—can be made to signify. Like the corpse Earth, whom Christ revives by freeing her curled-back tongue, the poet in Aurora—and in her creator—is revived and set free in the course of the poem. The symbolic instrument of that resuscitation is Marian Erle, the woman who suffers social death as a consequence of her rape, pregnancy, and delivery. On a narrative level, the birth of Marian's child delivers her from her numbing exclusion from society; on the symbolic level, the woman who has been set beyond the boundaries of signification altogether—"fallen" to her death—becomes a powerful figure for the female as originator of meaning. Both through her ongoing relation with Marian and through Marian's narration of her personal history Aurora makes contact with a mythic past adequate to her present; encountering this mother, Aurora can at last experience herself as the mother of poems. On the one hand, Marian Erle has created her own domestic society that excludes as much as it is itself excluded from patriarchal culture; on the other, Aurora Leigh, while rejecting the deadening aspects of patriarchal poetics, has created her own aesthetic sphere which is uniquely inclusive.

While both *Casa Guidi Windows* and *Aurora Leigh* designate the proper sphere of poetic vision as the domestic-cosmic rather than the social-historic, Aurora Leigh holds out the possibility of keeping both spheres simultaneously in view. According to Aurora, the proper poet ought to "exert a double vision," to

see near things as comprehensively / As if afar they took their point of sight, / And distant things as intimately deep / As if they touched them. (V, 184–88)

On the surface, this looks like the standard Romantic tendency toward the visionary, a call to "see into the life of things." My argument, however, is that Barrett Browning's "double vision" requires constant shifts in focus that not only open up vistas, but also keep the gazer firmly rooted in the moment and the near-at-hand. In Book VI, just before her encounter with Marian Erle. Aurora articulates her resolve to "look into the swarthiest face of things" (VI, 148), and asserts that she will have nothing to do with an art that shrinks from the particularity of a beggar boy who hungers for oranges. The poet who looks and really sees this reality sees yet another: the beggar boy contains

both flowers and firmaments / And surging seas and aspectable stars / And all that we would push him out of sight / In order to see nearer. (VI, 194–97)

It is this realization of double focus that seems to facilitate Aurora's crucial recovery of Marian the beggar maid and her child. The "age" Aurora aims to reflect in her poetry seems problematically female, for Aurora's resolve to "look" will have to encounter Marian's sexual fall and death, a female *cultural* death. What such determination yields is a miraculous, or mythic, reality: the dead mother restored to life, accompanied by her sacred child—a little world that opens out into infinity. The kind of double focus I have described above is prefigured in *Casa Guidi Windows* as a shift in focus from the distant to the near, which may yet yield another distance: from the pageant outside the windows, to the child within the house, to the invisible heavenly city. It is fully realized in *Aurora Leigh* by the poet's ability to keep Marian in view simultaneously as a narrative character with a social destiny and as a mythic character with a cosmic destiny. Significantly, while the poet in *Casa Guidi Windows* remains framed in the window, looking out on the panorama of patriarchal history, or turns from that to her inner domain, the poet in *Aurora Leigh* moves freely in the crowded street and takes her vision where she finds it.

In his Nobel Lecture (1982), Czeslaw Milosz suggests that this double vision characterizes the poet whose quest is for "reality."[9] He tells how his model for the poet is a character in a children's fantasy by Selma Lagerlöf, who "flies above the earth and looks at it from above but at the same time sees it in every detail." Such double vision implies for Milosz two attributes of the poet: "avidity of the eye and the desire to describe that which he sees." I would suggest that such double vision as Barrett Browning and Milosz describe—the comprehensive and the close-up view—is specially, if not uniquely, female. The contrast between Robert Browning's and Barrett Browning's positions is instructive: as Nina Auerbach points out, for Robert Browning there is no single moment of epiphanic vision, only the multiple changing faces of his dramatis personae.[10] Robert Browning, then, with his ironic distance and shifting realities, would seem to be the more "modern" poet, less in the grip of Romantic projections. But as much as she, too, is committed to the deconstruction of Romantic projections, Barrett Browning is equally committed to the epiphanic vision which would empower all the oppressed—whether the Italian people or all women. It would seem that Barrett Browning turns Romantic vision to her own female purposes, emphasizing the necessary shift and re-shift from the near-at-hand to the distant overview. Because she, too, wants access to power, the female poet looks through appearances to the visionary distances; because she cannot forget female powerlessness, however, she keeps looking steadfastly at the close-up view, the swarthiest face of things.

Notes

1.   Notable are Cora Kaplan's introduction to her edition, *Aurora Leigh and Other Poems* (London: The Women's Press Ltd., 1978); Sandra Donaldson's " 'Motherhood's Advent in Power': Elizabeth Barrett Browning's Poems about Motherhood," *Victorian Poetry*, 18 (Spring 1980), 51–60; Barbara Gelpi's "*Aurora Leigh:* The Vocation of the Woman Poet," *Victorian*

Poetry, 19 (Spring 1981), 35–48; Virginia Steinmetz's "Beyond the Sun: Patriarchal Images in *Aurora Leigh,*" *Studies in Browning and His Circle,* 9 (Winter 1981), 18–41, and "Images of 'Mother-Want' in Elizabeth Barrett Browning's *Aurora Leigh,*" *Victorian Poetry,* 21 (Winter 1983), 351–67; Sandra Gilbert's analysis in *The Madwoman in the Attic: The Woman Writer and the Nineteenth-Century Literary Imagination* (New Haven and London: Yale University Press, 1979), as well as her "From Patria to Matria: Elizabeth Barrett Browning's Risorgimento," *PMLA,* 99 (March 1984), 194–209; and Dolores Rosenblum's "Elizabeth Barrett Browning's *Aurora Leigh:* Face to Face with the Nineteenth-Century Poets," *Victorian Studies,* 26 (Spring 1983), 321–38.

2. "England has had many learned women, not merely readers but writers of the learned languages, in Elizabeth's time and afterwards—women of deeper acquirement than are common now in the greater diffusion of letters; and yet where were the poetesses? The divine breath . . . why did it never pass, even in the lyrical form, over the lips of a woman? How strange! And can we deny that it was so? I look everywhere for grandmothers and see none. It is not in the filial spirit I am deficient, I do assure you—witness my reverent love of the grand-fathers!" *The Letters of Elizabeth Barrett Browning,* ed. Frederic G. Kenyon (New York: Macmillan, 1897), I, 231–32.

3. See Flavia Alaya's complex and insightful study of the Brownings and Italian politics in "The Ring, the Rescue, and the Risorgimento: Reunifying the Brownings' Italy," *Browning Institute Studies,* 6 (1978), 1–41.

4. Writing to Robert Browning in 1845, she mentions her projected "novel-poem." *The Letters of Robert Browning and Elizabeth Barrett Barrett. 1845–1846,* ed. Elvan Kinter (Cambridge, Massachusetts: Harvard University Press, 1969), I, 31.

5. *Letters of Robert Browning and Elizabeth Barrett Barrett,* I, 31.

6. See for instance Alethea Hayter's comments in *Mrs Browning: A Poet's Work and Its Setting* (London: Faber and Faber, 1962), 131–32, and William Irvine and Park Honan's evaluation in *The Book, the Ring, and the Poet* (New York: McGraw-Hill, 1974), 253–54.

7. Elizabeth Barrett Browning, *Casa Guidi Windows,* ed. Julia Markus (New York: The Browning Institute, 1977). Subsequent references to Markus's essay are cited parenthetically, and line numbers for *Casa Guidi Windows* refer to this edition.

8. Elizabeth Barrett Browning, *The Complete Works of Elizabeth Barrett Browning,* eds. Charlotte Porter and Helen Clarke (New York; Crowell, 1900; rpt. New York: AMS Press, 1983), V, 117–18. Subsequent references to *Aurora Leigh* refer to this edition, and book and line numbers are cited parenthetically in the text.

9. *The New York Review of Books,* 28: 3, 11–15.

10. Nina Auerbach, "Robert Browning's Last Word," *Victorian Poetry,* 22 (Summer, 1984). 161–73.

"Art's a Service":
Social Wound, Sexual Politics,
and *Aurora Leigh*

DEIRDRE DAVID

Elizabeth Barrett Browning's *Aurora Leigh* has become a key text for feminist critics concerned with nineteenth-century women writers. For some, *Aurora Leigh* is a revolutionary poem, a passionate indictment of patriarchy that speaks the resentment of the Victorian woman poet through a language of eroticized female imagery. For others, the poem is less explosive, and Barrett Browning's liberal feminism is seen as compromised by Aurora Leigh's eventual dedication to a life governed by traditionally male directives. In my view, however, *Aurora Leigh* is neither revolutionary nor compromised: rather, it is a coherent expression of Barrett Browning's conservative sexual politics, and I shall argue that female imagery is employed to show that the "art" of the woman poet performs a "service" for a patriarchal vision of the apocalypse. In *Aurora Leigh* woman's art is made the servitor of male ideal.

Locating Barrett Browning in the tradition of nineteenth-century women writers and analyzing "the centrality of female experience" in *Aurora Leigh,* Cora Kaplan reads the poem as a revolutionary text: "In spite of its conventional happy ending, it is possible to see it as contributing to a feminist theory of art which argues that women's language, precisely because it has been suppressed by patriarchal societies, re-enters discourse with a shattering revolutionary force, speaking all that is repressed and forbidden in human experience."[1] To be sure, the bold vitality of Barrett Browning's language and imagery in *Aurora Leigh* is undeniable; and the governing ideology of the poem is, indeed, revolutionary. However, revolutionary does not necessarily mean feminist in Barrett Browning's sexual politics: her novel-poem is an integrated expression of essentialist and ultimately non-feminist views of sex and gender, despite sharp attacks on sexual hypocrisy and devastating satire of women's education. Kaplan argues that because "the woman as speaker-poet," replaces "all male prophets" and "dominates the symbolic language of

Reprinted from *Browning Institute Studies,* now *Victorian Literature and Culture,* 13 (1985): 113–36. Used by permission of the publisher.

the poem," *Aurora Leigh* dynamically confronts patriarchal attitudes.[2] *Aurora Leigh* is certainly confrontational: its antagonist, however, is more the middle-class materialism which found a convenient ally in Victorian patriarchal formations than it is patriarchy itself. As I shall show, in assuming a mission to transcend materialist ideology, Aurora Leigh joyfully assumes a role inscribed in and by male-dominated culture and society.

As an essentialist in sexual politics, Barrett Browning unequivocally sanctioned the concepts of "masculine" and "feminine" intelligence: after the death of Margaret Fuller, she evaluated the bulk of her writings as "quite inferior to what might have been expected from so masculine an intellect."[3] To speak of a masculine intellect evidently presupposes a feminine one, and as far as one can judge from Barrett Browning's letters and poetry, the feminine is inferior. Harriet Martineau is consistently praised by Barrett Browning for the "male" qualities of her mind, and the following remarks about her fellow-invalid—addressed to Mrs. Martin in 1844—betray Barrett Browning's sanction of the Victorian allocation of men and women into categories of strong and weak thinkers: "No case of a weak-minded woman and a nervous affection; but of the most manlike woman in the three kingdoms—in the best sense of man—a woman gifted with admirable fortitude, as well as exercised in high logic, a woman of sensibility and of imagination certainly, but apt to carry her reason unbent wherever she sets her foot; given to utilitarian philosophy and the habit of logical analysis."[4] The model for intellectual superiority is the conventionally male one: Martineau is not nervous, possesses fortitude, and exercises the power of logical reasoning. When Barrett Browning wrote to H.S. Boyd that Martineau is "the most logical intellect of the age, for a woman" she believed—with her contemporaries—that it was unusual for a woman to be logical (*L.* EBB I, 225). In the Victorian discourse of sex and gender, logic is a male property, just as nurturance is a female one; and it is essential that Barrett Browning's employment of imagery associated with women's experience be located within the context of her entire sexual politics. To dislocate the imagery for celebratory purposes runs the risk of elaborating the same sexist, dualistic modes of thought which governed the dominant Victorian understanding of intellect, sex, and gender.

Barrett Browning believed woman the intellectual inferior of man. She emphatically announced herself not a "very strong partisan on the Rights-of-Woman-side of the argument . . . I believe that, considering men and women in the mass, there is *an inequality* of intellect, and that it is proved by the very state of things of which gifted women complain,—and more than proved by the manner in which their complaint is received by their own sisterhood."[5] In this tautological denigration of female mind, women are proved inferior by their record, which implies that if they *were* intellectually powerful, then feminists would have nothing to complain of. The manner in which feminists complain confirms woman's intellectual inferiority. The actual constraints placed upon the lives of Victorian women, the necessity of fitting female desire for intellectual autonomy to the shapes of male cultural authority, tend to be evaded or ignored in Barrett Browning's sexual politics. For example, that need for women to be educated in which women like Harriet Martineau so strongly believed is of little interest to her: she confided to Robert Browning that women have "minds of quicker movement, but less power and depth" than men: "there is a natural inferiority of mind in women—of the— intellect . . . the history of art and of genius testifies to this fact openly." She made no secret of her dislike of everything to do with "Women and their Mission" (her terms) and, as she confessed to Browning, early in her career she relinquished whatever interest she may have had in "the Martineau-doctrines of equality."[6]

Before her marriage to Robert Browning, Elizabeth Barrett made it clear that she shared his ambiguous assessment of women's intellectual and artistic capabilities: in a complex strategy of praise and criticism, Robert Browning deemed women too good to be in Parliament, implicitly too delicate for participation in the privileged rough and tumble of Westminster. In late June of 1846, he wrote to Elizabeth Barrett that it would be "exquisitely absurd . . . essentially retrograde a measure" for Harriet Martineau's call for female members of Parliament to become reality: "Parliament seems no place for originating, creative minds—but for the second-rate minds influenced by and bent on working out the results of these—and the most efficient qualities for such a purpose are confessedly found oftener with men than with women" (*L.* RB/EBB 2, 280). This is one form of the insidious praise of women that constitutes Victorian deification and degradation of the "softer sex." Parliamentary practice calls for "second-rate minds," practical rather than "originating, creative" ones: men are more likely to possess these practical second-rate minds than women. This opinion seems to score one for the female side, but such praise also implies that women are inadequate to sustained, administrative work. Elizabeth Barrett replied to Browning's views of women and Parliament by declaring that not only do women lack the physical strength for such work (which Browning had also suggested), but they "have not instruction, capacity, wholeness of intellect enough" to be in Parliament. Admittedly, this is a woman writing to the man she would marry in less than three months, and her letters in this period of their correspondence are more concerned with the joys and difficulties of their romance than with sexual politics: but the statement that women lack the "instruction, capacity, wholeness of intellect" to participate in the political life of their country is not the statement of a woman on her way to confronting patriarchy, nor is it pregnant with the promise of "speaking all that is repressed and forbidden in human experience," which is how Kaplan reads *Aurora Leigh.*

A poem that begins with the admonition from Ecclesiastes, "Of writing many books there is no end," *Aurora Leigh* is pervaded by metaphors of writing, the most notable being that employed by Aurora in likening man's soul to a multiply-inscribed text. Refuting Enlightenment beliefs in the soul as "clear white paper," she imagines it as:

> A palimpsest, a prophet's holograph,
> Defiled, erased and covered by a monk's—
> The apocalypse, by a Longus! poring on
> Which obscene text, we may discern perhaps
> Some fair, fine trace of what was written once,
> Some upstroke of an alpha and omega
> Expressing the old scripture.[7]

Richly invested with Barrett Browning's philosophical and political values, the lines signalize her recurrent preoccupation with the traditional Christian myth of lost unity. Man's soul is likened to a scripture which once possessed its own perfect form and its own internal coherence: as Christ declares in Revelation 1:8, "I am Alpha and Omega, the beginning and the ending," so man, in an ideal correspondence to this unity, once possessed a unified soul/text. But the soul/text which once resembled the holograph inscribed by a prophet, who was, in his turn, inspired by the original inscriber of all things, has been defiled by later writers: man's original soul/text has been debased from its primary, revelatory meaning and transformed from oracular revelation to pastoral romance (the apocalypse inscribed by a Longus). Implicitly proclaiming herself as God's new prophet and as God's new inscriber of the ideal world which will replace that sundered by a social "cleft," Barrett Browning, through Aurora Leigh, instructs man in discovering traces of the original text in the degenerate palimpsest. Aurora Leigh must perform the ideal mission which Barrett Browning described in her Preface to "A Vision of Poets," a lengthy homage to poets of the far and recent past and included in *Poems* (1844). She declares that the Victorian poet "wears better broad-cloth, but speaks no more oracles . . . the evil of this social incrustation over a great idea is eating deeper and more fatally into our literature than either readers or writers may apprehend fully" (2:147). Acting as cultural agent between a troubled society and transcendent values, the ideal poet performs an oracular function: if soul, text, and form have been debased through inscribed interpretation, erasure, and deformation, so, too, the alpha and omega of Victorian life have become obscured by the inscriptions of materialism and socialist politics. Empowered through vocation to reveal the organic connections between God, man, culture, and society which have been obscured in a secular world, the ideal poet is made a woman poet in *Aurora Leigh*. And the language of imagery derived from female experience is employed by that woman poet in an alignment of two powerful myths: the traditional myth of poet as witness to a transcendent order is aligned with the traditional myth of woman as moral servitor.

II

The *Westminster Review* in 1857 praised the mind that produced *Aurora Leigh* as one remarkable for "its abundant treasure of well-digested learning, its acute observation of life, its yearning sympathy with multiform human sorrow, its store of personal, domestic love and joy." This was a rare moment in an avalanche of negative criticism (including the rest of the *Westminster's* review) which roundly condemned Barrett Browning's prolixity, extravagant metaphors, eccentric rhymes, riotous metre, and, most significantly and pervasively, her use of "unfeminine" poetic language and her choice of poetic subject. She is labelled an "unchaste poet." Accused of depicting female types the critics seemed to prefer *not* depicted by a "poetess" beloved as much for her refined seclusion as she was for the delicacy of her verse, she had dared to parade before her astonished readers a lascivious aristocrat, a raped working-class girl, and an intellectually independent heroine. Charged with writing in a "high fever," of taking the literary field like Britomartis, an assertive, mythological maiden who escaped the sexual advances of Minos by leaping from a rock, Barrett Browning may be said to have leapt from her "respectable" rock, not, however, as frantic escape from male pursuit, but to immerse herself in the representation of subjects more usually treated by the novel: utopian politics, female sexuality, rape, urban misery, and woman's struggle for professional recognition.

She is accused of indelicately affecting "masculine" language, of becoming "coarse" in her desire not to be squeamish. *Blackwood's Magazine* adopted a thoroughly offended male stance, finding "the extreme independence" of Aurora detracting from the paucity of "feminine" charm she might possess and marring all interest that the reader might have in "so intellectual a heroine." If there is one critical thread that holds the negative reviews of the poem together, it is an accusation of coarseness of language and of theme. Propriety and good taste are particularly called into question in discussion of what *The Spectator* called "the 'Clarissa Harlowe' calamity": "The bar of the Old Bailey is the only place where we wish to hear of such things!"[8]

The plot of *Aurora Leigh* traces the development of its heroine from her Florentine childhood to eventual marriage to her cousin Romney. The child of an English father and Italian mother, she is sent to England to live with her aunt on the death of her parents at the age of thirteen. The aunt trains her in the conventional accomplishments of English young ladies and for marriage to her cousin. At the age of twenty Aurora refuses his proposal, inherits a small income on the death of her aunt, and moves to London determined to become a poet. Some ten years later (having achieved modest recognition of her work), she learns that the Christian socialism favored by Romney which she had scorned as insufficient to remedy social evil, has taken the form of intended marriage to a working-class girl, Marian Erle. In a stunningly visual depiction that calls to mind Hogarthian London, rich and poor meet at St.

James's Church where Romney vainly awaits his bride. Marian never arrives, having been persuaded to leave for Australia by Lady Waldemar, the woman who wants Romney for herself. Duped by the maid of this voluptuous aristocrat, and drugged in a French brothel, Marian is raped. Aurora learns her story two years after "the Clarissa Harlowe calamity" when she spots Marian, now the mother of a baby boy, in a Paris flower market. Aurora takes mother and child to Italy where they live happily together in the countryside of Aurora's childhood. Believing Romney to have married Lady Waldemar, Aurora is astonished to see him arrive on her porch one summer evening. The last two books of the poem are devoted to an extended dialogue between Romney and Aurora about the need to unify spiritual and material remedies for social ills. The poem ends with an apocalyptic vision of the New Jerusalem, Aurora having at last realized that Romney has been blinded by an injury received in the fire that destroys his utopian socialist community. The poem is punctuated by Aurora's lengthy meditations upon art; it contains an arresting amount of violent imagery; and by the time of Barrett Browning's death in 1861 it had gone through five editions.

Vigorously employing blank verse and multiple images of degradation and exploitation, Barrett Browning vividly places Marian's rape before the reader, if not in its details then in its absence. Social and literary decorum dictate that Marian's story remain unsaid, yet its marginal status intensifies its volatile content:

> We wretches cannot tell out all our wrong
> Without offence to decent happy folk.
> I know that we must scrupulously hint
> With half-words, delicate reserves, the thing
> Which no one scrupled we should feel in full.
> (6.1220–24)

Aurora becomes a mother to Marian, making those "half-words" whole, giving utterance to a character who has no social right of narrative, repairing as much as she is able the injury she has suffered, and in the way of all mothers described by Aurora in evoking her own Italian childhood, "kisses full sense" into what Marian cannot say.[9] In giving voice and protection to Marian, Aurora combats a social evil consistently attacked by Barrett Browning: the sexual hypocrisy of sexually respectable women. If there is one place where *Aurora Leigh* takes an unequivocal feminist stand, it is in its refusal to be silent about sexuality.

In 1861 Thackeray rejected one of Barrett Browning's poems, "Lord Walter's Wife" for the *Cornhill* on the grounds that "there are things my squeamish public will not hear," hastening to assure her that the wife of Browning and the mother of Pen was sacred to English readers. Barrett Browning's response was to the sexist point: "It is exactly because pure and prosperous women choose to *ignore* vice, that miserable women suffer wrong by it everywhere" (*L*.2, 244–45). Moreover, Barrett Browning had long held such pronounced views: twenty years earlier, in writing to Mary Russell Mitford, she berated respectable women who will "shrink from breathing the same air with a betrayed woman," yet will gracefully sit down to dinner with male adulterers (*L*. EBB/M I, 295). "Lord Walter's Wife" figures a quite different woman, one who makes a spirited attack on the prevailing sexual double standard. An engaged man declares to his friend's wife that he finds her "too fair." Deliberately encouraging his attentions, the woman, Lord Walter's wife, instructs him in the unhappy social truth that men treat all women as sexual commodities to be used and discarded. Had she succumbed to his advances he would no longer find her so desirable: "Too fair?—not unless you misuse us! and surely if, once in a while, / You attain to it, straight way you call us no longer too fair, but too vile" (6:31–32). The poem is vitalized by the woman's anger, felt not only by the aristocratic wife but on behalf of all women who are either deified or degraded by men.

During the Crimean War, Barrett Browning wrote to a friend from her girlhood years at Hope End, Mrs. Martin, that "there are worse plagues, deeper griefs, dreader wounds than the physical. What of the forty thousand wretched women in this city? The silent writing of them is to me more appalling than the roar of the cannons" (*L*. EBB 2, 213). In *Aurora Leigh* the wounds are both physical and symbolic: Marian is violently wounded by rape, and in a hellish scene of diseased bodies swelling the aisles of the church where Romney and Marian are to be married, all is an oozing "peccant social wound." The image of the wound is crucial not only to the poem, but also to Barrett Browning's work as a woman poet. In refusing to ignore the injuries suffered by prostitutes, in compelling society to look at the "offal" it makes of "fallen" women and of the poor, and in symbolizing social evil as social wound, she creates herself as a ministering healer to an infected world. If society has been cleft in two by a symbolic knife, if women are cleft by rapacious men, then Barrett Browning will, through her poetry, dress the wounds, address the means of cure. An imagery of wounding cuts into *Aurora Leigh* as powerfully as an imagery of maternal nurturance may be said to unify it.

When establishing the presence of "women's language" in *Aurora Leigh*, most feminist critics point to the poem's almost obsessive attention to suckling and its eroticized fascination with breasts: Aurora is symbolically suckled by the hills of her Italian childhood; she exhorts her fellow poets to "Never flinch, / But still unscrupulously epic, catch / Upon the burning lava of a song / The full-veined, heaving, double-breasted Age" (5.214–17); Romney feeds the great carnivorous mouth of the poor through his Christian socialism.[10] This mammocentric imagery, however, is ambiguous: the image of proper poetic practice invoked by Aurora implies conventionally male rather than female meanings, and maternal nurturance is invested with strangely unsettling qualities. Aurora, the woman poet, rather peculiarly figures the poet's task in conventionally male terms—as unflinching, aggressive work—and she makes the subject of the poem almost primordially female—full-veined, heaving, double-breasted. The poet must make a swiftly moving song out of an age which seems to be immutably stable in its connection with mother earth. As further complication of the breast imagery, Marian's nurturance of her baby is invested with an almost malevolent quality: as she suckles him, she seems to consume him greedily in an image of appropriation, "drinking him as wine."

Moreover, Lady Waldemar's breasts both attract and repel. They are an unspoiled source of life and an image of demonic eroticism: the paradox suggests that contradiction between the deification and degradation of women which Barrett Browning attacks in her poem, "Lord Walter's Wife." Lady Waldemar offers a dazzling display of ripe female sexuality:

> . . . How they told,
> Those alabaster shoulders and bare breasts,
> On which the pearls, drowned out of sight in milk,
> Were lost, excepting for the ruby clasp!
> They split the amaranth velvet-bodice down
> To the waist or nearly, with the audacious press
> Of full-breathed beauty. If the heart within
> Were half as white!—but, if it were, perhaps
> The breast were closer covered and the sight
> Less aspectable by half, too.
>
> (5.618–27)

Proceeding through a sequence of false appearances and concealed truth, the description shows that "aspectable" things are not what they seem. Nature herself (in the seductive shape of milky breasts) seems to drown out female ornamentation (the pearl necklace), yet the visible ruby clasp indicates Lady Waldemar's embellished sexuality. A single grey hair in her luxuriant bronze tresses contrasts ironically with the symbolism of her amaranth-velvet bodice (the purple color of a mythical flower which never fades). The display of vibrant sexuality implies its own degeneration and in terms of what Lady Waldemar does to Marian, the radiant whiteness of her breasts conceals the dark heart within. Lady Waldemar is what her name implies—the "weal" which "marrs" all she touches.

The depiction of women in *Aurora Leigh* is framed by Barrett Browning's employment of three interwoven color images: green, red, and white. The first symbolizes the serenity Aurora enjoys in the time she is freed from her aunt's instruction in English womanhood; the other two tend to express, even when employed by Aurora herself, the prevailing nineteenth-century fragmentation of woman into a creature fractured by seemingly irreconcilable, and therefore dangerous, attributes. Such fragmentation is figured most prominently in the portrait of Aurora's mother, painted with white face and

red dress, and appearing as "Ghost, fiend, and angel, fairy, witch and sprite"
to her daughter. Sometimes speaking this imagery of fragmentation, Aurora
moves from the green, calm (but stultifying) time of her young womanhood
to her mature, vibrant, fiery part in building the New Jerusalem:

> I had a little chamber in the house,
> As green as any privet-hedge a bird
> Might choose to build in, though the nest itself
> Could show but dead-brown sticks and straws; the walls
> Were green, the carpet was pure green, the straight
> Small bed was curtained greenly, and the folds
> Hung green about the window which let in
> The out-door world with all its greenery.
>
> (1.567–74)

In the serene, cool space of the English countryside, employing the bird
imagery that is everywhere in the poem, Aurora describes herself placidly
nesting in her green chamber/privet hedge.

The first significant employment of the red/white imagery occurs in
Aurora's description of her mother's portrait which was executed after her
death. The face, throat and hands possess a "swan-like supernatural white
life," yet the body wears a red brocade dress; and to the child Aurora the face
is "by turns" that paradoxical female face of so much Victorian art—the
angelic sprite who winds her hair around the neck of a knight in Water-
house's "La Belle Dame Sans Merci," the fiendish, contorted figure of Hunt's
"The Lady of Shalott," Rossetti's "Lady Lilith" whose massive neck and powerful jaw signalize an awful female mystery.[11] When Aurora hears of Marian's
flight from London, she relies upon the traditional symbolism of purity and
whiteness to reassure Romney: his lost bride will stay as pure as "snow that's
drifted from the garden-bank / To the open road." In Marian's own powerful
evocation of her despair, however, the color imagery becomes more complicated. She describes herself, pregnant and destitute, wandering the roads in
France:

> And there I sat, one evening, by the road,
> I, Marian Erle, myself, alone, undone,
> Facing a sunset low upon the flats
> As if it were the finish of all time,
> The great red stone upon my sepulchre,
> Which angels were too weak to roll away.
>
> (6.1269–74)

The raped woman, spoiled yet innocent, soon to give birth to a joyful
child from brutal rape, reddened by the blood of defloration which literally

and symbolically is "engraved" upon her white body, likens the setting sun to a red stone upon her sepulchre. In Marian's language, the red imagery links the dying day, the exhausted woman, and the weakened angels in a paradoxically fiery decline, suggesting a significant contrast to Aurora in her green chamber on her twentieth birthday. A radiant, vital and virginal Aurora, fresh from her vernal nest in the morning, foreshadows a depleted, violated Marian at sunset. On Aurora's morning, she is dressed in white, hopefully self-wreathed in ivy as symbol of the poetic power to come: "The June was in me, with its multitudes / Of nightingales all singing in the dark, / And rosebuds reddening where the calyx split" (2.10–12). The green calyx splits to reveal the ripening rose and suggests the departure of a maturing Aurora from the green enclosure of her room.

If Marian suffers a symbolical fiery ordeal as she feels the weight of "a great red stone" upon her grave, then Romney suffers a literal one when he is blinded in the fire set by local peasants, incensed by the "drabs and thieves" he has housed in his Phalanstery. He describes himself as "A mere bare blind stone in the blaze of day," a comparison which connects with Marian's evocation of a "great red stone" upon her sepulchre. Aligning the traditional myth of poet as witness to a transcendent order with the traditional myth of woman as moral servitor, Aurora repairs the injuries suffered by Marian and Romney.

The informing structure of wounding and healing in the poem is emphatically etched by imagery of knifing. "There, ended childhood" declares Aurora on the death of her father. Her life becomes "Smooth endless days, notched here and there with knives, / A weary, wormy darkness, spurred i' the flank / With flame, that it should eat and end itself / Like some tormented scorpion" (1.219–22). Barrett Browning sustains the imagery of knifing throughout the poem. Aurora describes her aunt's discipline as a "sharp sword set against my life," her aunt's gaze as "two grey-steel naked-bladed eyes" searching through her face, a young man at a dinner party as possessing "A sharp face, like a knife in a cleft stick" (1.691, 328; 5.629). Moreover, Aurora's sense of injured self is sometimes surprisingly gruesome: "So I lived" she says, "A Roman died so; smeared with honey, teased / By insects, stared to torture by the moon" (2.890–91); in London she likens the city sun to the "fiery brass" of cages used in Druidic sacrifice "from which the blood of wretches pent inside / Seems oozing forth to incarnadine the air" (3.172–75); and in justifying her refusal of Romney, she suspects that "He might cut / My body into coins to give away / Among his other paupers" (2.790–91).

Knifing and bleeding are prominent symbols in the severe condemnation of female sentimentality which Romney, somewhat imprudently for a suitor, issues to Aurora, and which quite plausibly consolidates her refusal to marry him:

> . . . Your quick-breathed hearts,
> So sympathetic to the personal pang,
> Close on each separate knife-stroke, yielding up
> A whole life at each wound, incapable
> Of deepening, widening a large lap of life
> To hold the world-full woe. The human race
> To you means, such a child, or such a man,
> You saw one morning waiting in the cold,
> Beside that gate, perhaps. You gather up
> A few such cases, and when strong sometimes
> Will write of factories and of slaves, as if
> Your father were a negro, and your son
> A spinner in the mills. All's yours and you,
> All, coloured with your blood, or otherwise
> Just nothing to you.
>
> (2.184–98)

From Romney's perspective of patriarchal socialism, women lack the male faculty of abstraction from personal experience to a general theory of society: wounded women give up their entire beings at one emotional "knife-stroke," leaving no room in their maternal laps for the woes of the world. Through Romney's sexist sermon, Barrett Browning seems slyly to respond to those critics who derided the poems *she* wrote about factories and slaves, and also to a powerful Victorian myth about women writers: if women can only write about what is "coloured" with their blood, can only think in terms of "yours and you," as Romney scornfully announces, then their intellectual lives must be symbolically stained by the somatic signs of their womanhood. In the success of *Aurora Leigh* and in her own career, Barrett Browning defies the ugly implication that the intellectual lives of women must be marred by biological destiny.

In proposing to Marian, the cutting edge, as it were, of Romney's imagery is deflected from disdain for women's sentimentality to a passionate plea for the class unity that will be realized through their marriage:

> . . . though the tyrannous sword,
> which pierced Christ's heart, has cleft the world in twain
> 'Twixt class and class, opposing rich to poor,
> Shall *we* keep parted? Not so. Let us lean
> And strain together rather, each to each,
> Compress the red lips of this gaping wound
> As far as two souls can . . .
>
> (4.122–28)

Assimilating Christian and socialist doctrine, Romney aligns the origin of class antagonism with the fall from unity which originated in the piercing of Christ's body. Despite the eventual insufficiency of Romney's materialistic remedy for social evil, Barrett Browning, through deploying this imagery, expresses that yearning for re-integration of the mythical bond between man and his world which she, in common with many of her Victorian contemporaries, believed had been stretched to its most "gaping" extent in the nineteenth century. Romney acknowledges that fallen, class-conscious man can do little more than "compress" the wound, and from the manner in which Barrett Browning imagines the Church scene where rich and poor come to witness this "compressing" marriage, it would seem there *can* be no successful healing. The social body is deeply infected. Employing a language of violence and pestilence which reminds us of the suffering scorpion burnt by flame, the Roman eaten by insects, and the Druidic human sacrifices, Barrett Browning paints a Brueghelesque picture.

The vision is infernal. How could a woman who had been secluded from society until the age of forty, and after that who had resided in Italy under the adoring protection of her husband, a woman who was a mother, who had written heart-rending poems about the untimely death of children and of female self-sacrifice such as "Isobel's Child" and "Bertha in the Lane"—how could this revered example of female virtue and delicacy describe that half of the wedding party which comes from "Saint Giles" in the following language?

> . . . Faces? . . . phew,
> We'll call them vices, festering to despairs,
> Or sorrows, petrifying to vices: not
> A finger-touch of God left whole on them,
> All ruined, lost—the countenance worn out
> As the garment, the will dissolute as the act,
> The passions loose and draggling in the dirt
> To trip a foot up at the first free step!
> Those, faces? 'twas as if you had stirred up hell
> To heave its lowest dreg-fiends uppermost
> In fiery swirls of slime, . . .
>
> (4.579–89)

As far as one can judge from reading her letters, the closest Barrett Browning ever got to such hellish faces was on a rare cab trip to Shoreditch in search of Flush, dog-napped from Wimpole Street. However, she was very close to such scenes of fiendish misery through her daily reading of newspapers, periodicals and novels of social realism, particularly of Sue, Hugo, and Balzac. Moreover, all readers of the London *Times* in the eighteen-forties would have read uncensored reports of testimony before the various Parliamentary committees investigating conditions in the factories, mines, and slum areas of the poor. The reports reveal a hellish world of stench, squalor, and disease, of open privies, of prostitutes and beggars living in dens which resembled animal lairs rather than human dwellings: it is a world consistently rendered in the language of the inferno where bodies tumble together in crowded hovels, dunghills dominate the landscape, and all is festering and pestilential.

In February 1843 Barrett Browning read the entire Report of the Royal Commission on the Employment of Children and Young Persons in Mines and Manufactories (one of its Assistant Commissioners was her close correspondent, R.H. Horne): as a consequence of that reading, she was compelled to write her first poem of social protest, "The Cry of the Children" (a poem of the "factory" species despised by Romney) which appeared in *Blackwood's Magazine* in August of that year. As an avid reader of virtually every kind of Victorian text, she was no stranger to representation of working-class suffering, and this, of course, is really the point—those faces "festering to despairs" come from her extensive reading. In itself, the informing relationship between reading and writing in a poet's life is hardly remarkable, but by virtue of the limitations of Barrett Browning's experience, her work was undoubtedly more structured by text than it was by direct observation and it seems as if these sections of *Aurora Leigh* are the hellish distillation of her readings in the Victorian discourse of the poor.

Romney's plans for his marriage have a carnivalesque aspect: rich and poor are to transgress convention by meeting in a Mayfair church and by enjoying a marriage feast together on Hampstead Heath:

> Of course, the people came in uncompelled,
> Lame, blind, and worse—sick, sorrowful, and worse—
> The humours of the peccant social wound
> All pressed out, poured down upon Pimlico,
> Exasperating the unaccustomed air
> With a hideous interfusion. You'd suppose
> A finished generation, dead of plague,
> Swept outward from their graves into the sun,
> The moil of death upon them.
>
> (4.542–50)

The metaphor of the "social cleft" is both repeated and literalized as the symbolic wound in the social body literally stinks, presses out its suppurating matter. The people clog the streets, ooze into the church "In a dark, slow stream, like blood," and Barrett Browning pushes her infernal imagery to a hideous conclusion as the movement of the crowd is likened to that of bruised snakes crawling and hissing out of a hole "with shuddering involution." As the stinking poor makes its serpentine procession, the upper classes sit with handkerchiefs to their noses, and Barrett Browning aligns her pestilential imagery with her poetics of healing by having one of the aristocrats observe that the present spectacle, "this dismembering of society," resembles the tearing apart of Damien's body by horses. The social wound, the ruptured body, the bloody procession, all seem to congeal in a dreadful vision of the dismembered body/social state. Aurora Leigh as woman poet is destined to work alongside Romney, curing the wounded social body, enacting Barrett Browning's ideal form of sexual politics.

III

As an intelligent girl confined to the provincial upper-middle class, Aurora Leigh has foisted upon her an education which is hardly apt apprenticeship for building the New Jerusalem. In a satiric feminist interrogation of the subjects thought suitable for women's minds, Barrett Browning shows Aurora acquiring a jumble of useless information and social skills designed to make her a desirable commodity in the marriage market. She learns the "collects and the catechism," a "complement of classic French," "a little Algebra," the "internal laws of the Burmese empire." And she is educated in the conventional male views of female intellectual ability: "I read a score of books on womanhood/To prove, if women do not think at all, / They may teach thinking" (1:428–30). In terms of my argument for the ultimately non-feminist nature of Barrett Browning's sexual politics, however, it is significant that in the angry arguments between Aurora and Romney about woman's contribution to remedying social evil and her potential for producing great art, the principal object of Aurora's contempt is less the male cultural authority which denigrates woman's mind, than it is male inability to feel. The angry woman utters a sentimental attack on male insensitivity. It is not Romney's politics that Aurora really objects to when she refuses his proposal, not his desire to fit women into the convenient social slots of wife, nurse, and helper, but rather that he is emotionally barren, as figuratively blind to Aurora's feelings as he is literally blind to her face at the end of the poem. To a sexually vibrant Aurora on her twentieth birthday morning, Romney is a cold fish.

In London ten years later, a successful Aurora muses on her solitary state. Praised by all the periodicals but bereft of physical love, she sits unhappily alone praying to God the Father / God the Artist, who understands her dilemma as woman poet. Despite a certain daring intimation of ungratified female sexual desire in these lines, they are, in my view, deeply conventional in the heartfelt praise of a patriarchal deity. This may be "women's language" that Aurora speaks but it can hardly be said to contribute to what Cora Kaplan sees as a "feminist theory of art which argues that women's language [speaks] all that is repressed and forbidden in human experience."

> O my God, my God,
> O supreme Artist, who as sole return
> For all the cosmic wonder of Thy Work
> Demandest of us just a word . . . a name,

> "My father!" thou hast knowledge, only thou,
> How dreary 'tis for women to sit still,
> On winter nights by solitary fires,
> And hear the nations praising them far off,
> Too far! ay, praising our quick sense of love,
> Our very heart of passionate womanhood,
> Which could not beat so in the verse without
> Being present also in the unkissed lips
> And eyes undried because there's none to ask
> The reason they grew moist.
>
> (5.434–47)

With a play upon the passionate beat of a woman's heart and the meter of her verse, Aurora implies that the creation of verse is unfulfilling to the woman poet unless she is sexually loved, kissed upon the lips. The making of poetry and the making of love are associated to show that woman's poetry is created from her sexuality, indeed that poetry and sexuality are part of the "cosmic wonder" that is God's "work." Having heard Marian's story, Aurora assumes that Romney has married Lady Waldemar. She regrets her own refusal of him, for in so doing she has refused God's gift of the power to make poetry through love, and love through poetry: "Now, if I had been a woman, such / As God made women, to save men by love,—/ By just my love I might have saved this man, / And made a nobler poem for the world / Than all I have failed in" (7.184–88). Questioning her womanhood, her failure to "save" Romney through sexual love, she denigrates her literary achievement by believing that to have "written" Romney in marriage she would have produced a "noble" text far superior to any she has composed. She then concludes that he is lost, "And, by my own fault, his empty house / Sucks in, at this same hour, a wind from hell / To keep his heart cold, make his casements creak / For ever to the tune of plague and sin" (7.190–93). Unmade into a "noble" poem by the "good" Aurora, that is to say not sexually loved by her, Romney's body is as an empty house, sucking in an evil wind. She has figured herself as passionately warm, her heart and verse beating with desire: Romney, also alone, is made cold by the dissonant "tune" hissed by the "evil" Lady Waldemar; hers is a cold sexuality manifested in those marble breasts designed for display, not warm nurturance.

Having evoked her own mature emotional life in rosy, vibrant, terms and that of Romney through cold, white imagery, Aurora suggests that women possess a quality which permits them to transcend the symbolized dualism: they can undo their own iconized fragmentation through a legendary female ability to relinquish identity to the more powerful sex. While explicitly praising woman's ability to transcend ugly, aggressive self, Aurora actually perpetuates the unfortunate myth that woman lacks a strong sense of individual identity: we women, Aurora says, "yearn to lose ourselves / And melt like white pearls in another's wine"; man "seeks to double himself by what he loves, / And makes his drink more costly by our pearls" (5.1078–81). At the end of the poem Aurora dismantles the dualism of red and white imagery by melting the purity of her art and sexuality (the white pearls) into Romney's vision (the wine), and Romney, in his turn, ceases to appropriate women's feelings to his male politics. The rosy Florentine dawn that concludes the poem anticipates the forthcoming expression of Aurora's sexuality in marriage with Romney and a dissolution of his emotional anaesthesia through that union.

The closing lines of *Aurora Leigh* constitute a densely allusive hymn to work, sexual love, and the vision of a new city built from the consummation of man and woman, intellect and feeling, blindness and vision. Romney praises "the love of wedded souls," which is the earthly counterpart of God's love:

> Sweet shadow rose, upon the water of life,
> Of such a mystic substance, Sharon gave
> A name to! human, vital, fructuous rose,
> Whose calyx holds the multitude of leaves,
> Loves filial, loves fraternal, neighbour-loves
> And civic—all fair petals, all good scents,
> All reddened, sweetened from one central Heart.
>
> (9.884–90)

Political and social action will originate in and be sweetened from their marriage, from the rose of sexual love which is consummated and celebrated in the Song of Solomon: Judaic wedding song, Christian doctrine, social action, all center in the rose image which evokes the vibrant twenty-year-old Aurora who feels the June within her, "rosebuds reddening where the calyx split," and the present, mature Aurora, a ripe and blooming flower. And Aurora is also the radiant light of the morning star, destined for tutelage by the darkened, weary, blind Romney in her contribution to their joint work. In terms which express Barrett Browning's vision of woman's art as servitor of patriarchy, Aurora is instructed by Romney to become the witnessing poet of Barrett Browning's aesthetic discourse:

> . . . Art's a service,—mark:
> A silver key is given to thy clasp,
> And thou shalt stand, unwearied, night and day,
> And fix it in the hard, slow-turning wards,
> To open, so, that intermediate door
> Betwixt the different planes of sensuous form
> And form insensuous, that inferior men
> May learn to feel on still through these to those,
> And bless thy ministration. The world waits
> For help.
>
> (9.915–24)

The artist labors to unlock doors of perception, to mediate between material and spiritual "planes," and the term "wards" implies not only the mechanisms of a lock, but also places of confinement of the individual to the stifling materialistic ideologies which Barrett Browning despised. The poet's function, and it is a hard function, is to recover the original text of man's soul debased by deforming interpretation, to trace the first writing of that "old scripture."

Aurora is exhorted by Romney "to press the clarion on thy woman's lips . . . And blow all class-walls level as Jericho's." Sandra Gilbert and Susan Gubar read these closing lines as a revolutionary fantasy too dangerous to be articulated by Aurora, and they suggest Romney's sanctification of revolution through marriage is a severe compromise of Barrett Browning's own politics: the "millenarian program Romney outlines is not, of course, his own; it is the revolutionary fantasy of his author—and of her heroine, his wife-to-be, discreetly transferred from female to male lips." That the program is revolutionary is undeniable, and Gilbert and Gubar are clearly correct in noting that all must be made new, even though "a divine patriarch, aided by a human patriarch and his helpmeet" are doing the renovation.[12] Yet what is to be made new, and the means of making it new, figured in highly traditional, even reactionary terms which, if placed in the context of Barrett Browning's sexual politics, make the ending of *Aurora Leigh* less a compromise than a fulfillment of her "revolutionary fantasy." It is important to examine the lines which follow Romney's call for Aurora to level class barriers: she must do so in order that all men and all women may be flattened to an equality of subjugation to God's will so they might ascend to an "unsexing" of their incarnate state. To be sure, this is revolutionary, but not, it seems to me, in any way that suggests an adjustment of Barrett Browning's beliefs: men's souls "here assembled on earth's flats" must "get them to some purer eminence":

> . . . The world's old,
> But the old world waits the time to be renewed,
> Toward which, new hearts in individual growth
> Must quicken and increase to multitude
> In new dynasties of the race of men;
> Developed whence, shall grow spontaneously
> New churches, new oeconomies, new laws,
> Admitting freedom, new societies
> Excluding falsehood: He shall make all new.
> (9.941–49)

New churches precede new economic systems and new laws in this taxonomy of Christian revolution: after all Romney has already decreed that there must be "fewer programmes . . . fewer systems": "Less mapping out of masses to be saved, / By nations or by sexes! Fourier's void, / And Comte absurd,—and Cabet puerile" (9.867–69). This is Romney's *and* Aurora's *and* Barrett Browning's vision—coherent with her sexual politics and inspired first and always by a patriarchal God who demands hard work from his woman poets. Work is a "key" word at the end of *Aurora Leigh*—the literal key which will enable the poet to unlock the symbolic wards which restrain man from seeing connections between "sensuous" and "insensuous" worlds. The woman poet labors in service to God, mankind, and man.

"I have *worked* at poetry—it has not been with me revery, but art. As the physician and lawyer work at their several professions, so have I, and so do I, apply to mine." Writing to Horne in 1844, Barrett Browning insists upon her professional status as working poet.[13] In one of the 1844 Poems, "A Fourfold Aspect," the speaker traces a child's fearful understanding of its mortality, gleaned from reading of the death of heroes. So awful are these stories that the child wakes shrieking in the night and spends its days mournfully preoccupied with the dead. The poem turns upon a lesson the child must learn: death leads to Heaven and in the mortal meantime man must pray, think, learn, and work: "Work: make clear the forest-tangles / Of the wildest stranger-land" (3:119–20). This imperative originates in the Victorian preoccupation with clearing the wilderness, that renovation of the wasteland imagined, for example, in "The Coming of Arthur," the first of Tennyson's *Idylls of the King* and figured in these lines, "And so there grew great tracts of wilderness, / Wherein the beast was ever more and more, / But man was less and less, till Arthur came."[14] And when Arthur does come, he drives out the "heathen," slays the beasts, fells the forest "letting in the sun." Tennyson's Camelot is one version of the Victorian New Jerusalem, the city built from barbarism, darkness, and despair. Indignantly refusing Romney's offer of marriage and partnership in practice of his despised social theory, Aurora declares "I too have my vocation,—work to do . . . Most serious work, most necessary work / As any of the economists" (2.455–60).

"Blessed is he who has found his work; let him ask no other blessedness," thunders Carlyle in *Past and Present:* he who works, makes "instead of pestilential swamp, a green fruitful meadow with its clear flowing stream."[15] Barrett Browning's enduring insistence on the cultural function of the poet *in* the political world originates in this imperative to work: the poet clears a symbolical path, unlocks a symbolical door, dissolves the encrustations of debasing materialism which cover man's soul. Carlyle's Gospel of Work is the good news elaborated by Aurora and Romney at the end of the poem: men, women, creatures all, must work: "Let us be content, in work," is repeated with slight variation in a hymn of praise sung throughout the night as Aurora and Romney await the new day. Aurora describes Romney crying out the litany which has united them:

> And then calm, equal, smooth with weights of joy,
> His voice rose, as some chief musician's song
> Amid the old Jewish temple's Selah-pause,
> And bade me mark how we two met at last

> Upon this moon-bathed promontory of earth,
> To give up much on each side, then take all.
> "Beloved!" it sang, "we must be here to work;
> And men who work can only work for men,
> And, not to work in vain, must comprehend
> Humanity and so work humanly,
> And raise men's bodies, still by raising souls,
> As God did first."
>
> (9.843–54)

The poem ends as the dawn signals a new beginning and chastened lovers dedicate themselves to clearing the wilderness and to liberating man (and woman) from materialistic values. As Aurora is married to Romney and female art wedded to male socialist politics, the novel-poem *Aurora Leigh* becomes a form-giving epithalamium for Barrett Browning's essentialist sexual politics. In this poem we hear a woman's voice speaking patriarchal discourse—boldly, passionately, and without rancor.

Notes

1. Cora Kaplan, Introduction to *Aurora Leigh With Other Poems* (London: The Women's Press, 1978), p. 11. The first important feminist analysis of *Aurora Leigh* is to be found in Ellen Moers, *Literary Women* (New York: Doubleday, 1976).

2. Kaplan, p. 35.

3. *Elizabeth Barrett Browning's Letters to Mrs. David Ogilvy 1849–1861,* with recollections by Mrs. Ogilvy, ed. Peter N. Heydon and Philip Kelley (New York: Quadrangle/The New York Times Book Co. and the Browning Institute, 1973), p. 32.

4. *The Letters of Elizabeth Barrett Browning,* 2 vols., ed. with biographical additions by Frederic G. Kenyon (London: The Macmillan Company, 1897), 1, 196–97. (Hereinafter abbreviated in the text as *L.* EBB).

5. *The Letters of Elizabeth Barrett Browning to Mary Russell Mitford 1836–1854,* 3 vols., ed. Meredith B. Raymond and Mary Rose Sullivan (Winfield, Kansas: Wedgestone Press, Armstrong Browning Library of Baylor University, The Browning Institute, and Wellesley College Library, 1983), 3, 81. (Hereinafter abbreviated in the text as *L.* EBB / M).

6. *The Letters of Robert Browning and Elizabeth Barrett Barrett 1845–1846,* 2 vols. (New York: Harper and Bros., 1899), 1, 116, 373, 357. (Hereinafter abbreviated in the text as *L.* RB/EBB).

7. *Aurora Leigh,* in *The Complete Works of Mrs. Elizabeth Barrett Browning,* ed. Charlotte Porter and Helen A. Clarke, 6 vols. (New York: George D. Sproul, 1901), 1.826–32. (All references in the text to the work of Elizabeth Barrett Browning are to this edition: citations are by volume and page number, except in the case of *Aurora Leigh* where citations are by book and line number[s]).

8. *Westminster Review,* 68 (1857), 399–415; *Blackwood's Magazine,* 81 (1857), 23–41; *The Spectator,* 29 (1856), 1239–40. The following reviews of *Aurora Leigh* are also of particular interest: *Saturday Review,* 2 (1856), 776–78; *Dublin University Magazine,* 49 (1857), 460–70; *National Quarterly Review,* 5 (1862), 134–48.

9. In her sensitive reading of Marian Erle's relationship to mothers and the meaning of Marian's own motherhood, Sandra Gilbert makes the point that Marian bears a likeness

"not only to the fallen woman Mary Magdalen but also the blessed Virgin Mary, whose immaculate conception was the sign of a divine annunciation." "From *Patria* to *Matria:* Elizabeth Barrett Browning's Risorgimento," *PMLA,* 99 (1984), 194–211.

10.   Sandra Donaldson, Barbara Charlesworth Gelpi, and Virginia V. Steinmetz offer closely related interpretations of the imagery of motherhood and suckling in *Aurora Leigh.* Donaldson links Barrett Browning's own motherhood and a more powerful poetry than that she had produced in her childless days: by the time of *Aurora Leigh* she uses the "metaphor of breasts boldly as a symbol of activity and vitality." "Motherhood's Advent in Power: Elizabeth Barrett Browning's Poems About Motherhood," *Victorian Poetry,* 18 (1980), 51–60. Focusing upon Aurora's ambivalent attitude towards her mother's portrait, Gelpi argues that Aurora finally trusts her own womanhood by the end of the poem. "*Aurora Leigh:* The Vocation of the Woman Poet," *Victorian Poetry,* 19 (1981), 35–48. Steinmetz's reading discusses the maternal images less positively and more psychoanalytically, and sees them as "negative symbols reenforcing the theme of deprivation and representing the poet's need to bring obsessive infantile desires into light where they could serve rather than dominate her." "Images of 'Mother-Want' in Elizabeth Barrett Browning's *Aurora Leigh,*" *Victorian Poetry,* 21 (1983), 351–67.

11.   Sandra Gilbert and Susan Gubar see these forms/faces in the portrait as "melodramatic, gothic, the moral extremes of angel and monster characteristic of male-defined masks and costumes." *The Madwoman in the Attic: The Woman Writer and the Nineteenth-Century Literary Imagination* (New Haven: Yale University Press), p. 19. Dolores Rosenblum argues that when Aurora sees Marian's face in Paris, she *re*-sees the iconized female face of nineteenth-century poetry, and is thereby liberated to a full expression of her art. "Face to Face: Elizabeth Barrett Browning's *Aurora Leigh* and Nineteenth-Century Poetry," *Victorian Studies,* 26 (1983), 321–38. Nina Auerbach splendidly dissects the contradictory "faces" of Victorian woman in *Woman and the Demon: The Life of a Victorian Myth* (Cambridge, Mass.: Harvard University Press, 1983).

12.   *The Madwoman in the Attic,* pp. 579–80.

13.   *Letters of Elizabeth Barrett Browning to Richard Hengist Horne,* with Preface and Memoir by Richard Henry Stoddard (New York: Worthington Co., 1889), p. 263.

14.   See John D. Rosenberg's *The Fall of Camelot: A Study of Tennyson's "The Idylls of the King"* (Cambridge, Mass.: The Belknap Press of Harvard University Press, 1973) for a reading of the poem as apocalyptic vision and for examination of the *Idylls'* contribution to the Victorian literary concern with clearing the wasteland.

15.   Thomas Carlyle, *Past and Present,* ed. Richard D. Altick (Boston: Houghton Mifflin Company, 1965), p. 197.

Cursing As One of the Fine Arts:
Elizabeth Barrett Browning's Political Poems

MARJORIE STONE

In her letters to Robert Browning written before their marriage, Elizabeth Barrett is wont to satirize the judgments and pronouncements of the "critical Board of Trade" (Kintner 1: 58). Her metaphor still applies very well to the school of literary critics that habitually attempts to fix literary values, manipulate supply and demand, promote the monopoly of the canon, or police the plenitude of texts. Such self-appointed policers are responsible for works like *Fifty Works of Literature We Could Do Without,* an Index Librorum Prohibitorum that includes Dickens' *Pickwick Papers* and Barrett Browning's *Aurora Leigh.* No doubt we all have our own secret dismal catalogues of such works, but a more creative pastime might be to speculate on literary works we don't have but could do *with.* One such would be an essay by Barrett Browning entitled "On Cursing Considered as One of the Fine Arts," along the lines of Thomas DeQuincey's subtly perverse essay "On Murder Considered as One of the Fine Arts." Cursing has a better claim than murder to be viewed as a fine art, both because its practitioners do not stoop to crude implements like axes and daggers, and because it is an art often practised by poets who, like witches and prophets, weave dire spells with words. And Barrett Browning is the most likely author of such an essay, among the Victorian poets at least. She not only curses more often than her male contemporaries, when they are speaking in their own voices; she also curses more daringly and resoundingly, yet at the same time with finesse and feeling.

The range and ingenuity of Barrett Browning's cursing are indeed remarkable. She is capable of turning the cry of children or the silent gesture of a statue into a curse. She shows how blessings can function as curses, and how the very act of revoking a curse can have all the force of pronouncing it. Moreover, she is capable of writing a curse that can be recycled in different polemical contexts, yet lose none of its force. Her poetry also reveals her

Reprinted from *Dalhousie Review* 66, nos. 1–2 (Spring/Summer 1986): 155–73. Used by permission of the publisher.

exploiting the full range of meaning in the term "curse," which can refer to the act of pronouncing a malediction, the malediction itself, or the evil effects engendered by it, as well as to profane or blasphemous language or the act of uttering it. Most often, however, and particularly in the poems written after her elopement and escape from a repressively patriarchal home, Barrett Browning tends to focus on the act of cursing in the strong sense of pronouncing a malediction, and to depict women engaged in this act. At first, the women articulating curses in her poems are fictive figures, initially carefully dissociated from the poet herself, and subsequently more closely allied to her own voice and vision. But in the poems of her maturity—most notably in "A Curse For a Nation"—she speaks out boldly in her own voice, cursing the corruptions of her times with the passion and thunder of the Old Testament prophets whom she emulates in all but her gender. In this late poem there is no attempt at the male impersonation characteristic of some of her earlier works, such as "The Battle of Marathon." Barrett Browning makes it very clear that "A Curse For a Nation" is delivered by a woman.

As the poem opens, the voice of an angel commands a poet to " 'Write a Nation's curse for me, / And send it over the Western Sea' " (*Works* 3: 354). The reference to the Western sea, combined with other details in the poem and its initial publication in the Boston abolitionist magazine *The Liberty Bell* in 1856, indicates that the nation addressed is America and that the curse is both the curse of and a curse against the evil of slavery. Commanded by the angel to "write," the poet at first falters at his harsh imperative, pleading that " 'I am bound by gratitude, / By love and blood, / To brothers of mine across the sea' " (lines 9–11). When the angel overturns this objection, she—though at this point in the poem there is no clear indication that the poet is female—then objects that there are sins enough to write of in her own country. The angel over-rules this objection too, as well as the third and most telling one: " 'To curse, choose men. / For I, a woman, have only known / How the heart melts and the tears run down' " (38–40). But the overbearing angel is unrelenting, arguing that the poet's gender, like her love for her brothers across the sea and her consciousness of her own country's sins, is not an obstacle but a justification for her writing the curse.

> "Therefore," the voice said, "shalt thou write
> My curse to-night.
> Some women weep and curse, I say
> (And no one marvels), night and day.
>
> "And thou shalt take their part to-night,
> Weep and write.
> A curse from the depths of womanhood
> Is very salt, and bitter, and good.
> (41–48)

As these powerful lines reveal, Barrett Browning was well aware that nobody in her time marvelled at women weeping and cursing "night and day" in futile privacy or, like Bertha Rochester in *Jane Eyre,* screaming and cursing locked up in an attic. What was unprecedented was for a woman to curse publicly and politically like the Old Testament prophets—not only to "weep," but also to "write" and publish a curse that is "for a nation," yet one that nevertheless springs from the depths of a woman's personal experience. Through her fusion of weeping and cursing, Barrett Browning emphasizes that she is producing not the salt tears conventionally associated with woman's melting "heart," but salt and bitter curses springing from "the depths of womanhood," the depths of woman's oppression, as well as of her anger and passion.

Like the "salt, and bitter, and good" curse in this poem, most of the curses portrayed or pronounced in Barrett Browning's works have political dimensions, whether the politics at stake be those of nations or the politics of gender—or both, as in "A Curse For a Nation." A consideration of the nature and frequency of cursing in a number of poems written throughout her career can help to show how Barrett Browning came to express her increasingly interconnected political and feminist views with more radical directness and rhetorical sophistication in her later poems. Paradoxically, as her curses move out of the private realm conventionally associated with women and become more explicitly political, they also become more personal, and are more often uttered in her own voice. This paradox is in part explained by her realization that, as contemporary feminists like Adrienne Rich and Marge Piercy stress, the personal *is* the political. For Barrett Browning such a realization was a part of the "deepest truth" in her own heart and head that she felt compelled to utter as an artist, in the spirit of her credo that art is "essential truth that makes its way through beauty into use" (Kenyon 2: 383). But such intense truth-telling in the public sphere of politics was not without its risks, particularly when Barrett Browning, an English wife and mother, assumed the prerogative of polemical cursing traditionally monopolized by male prophets and a male God. The risks are reflected in the exclusion of Barrett Browning's many historically significant political poems from the Victorian literary canon for more than a century following her death in 1861—with the telling exception of "The Cry of the Children," the work in which the poet's political act of cursing is most indirect.

I

Next to "A Curse For a Nation," where the word "curse" appears twenty-four times in one hundred and nineteen lines, *A Drama of Exile* is the work by Barrett Browning in which cursing is most frequent. This lyrical drama modelled on classical Greek tragedy is the most ambitious work in her two-volume *Poems* published in 1844, a publication that led Edgar Allan Poe to dedicate *The Raven and Other Poems* (1845) "To the Noblest of Her Sex—Elizabeth Barrett Barrett" (Quinn 485). Unconcerned with the politics of nations, *A Drama of Exile* is very much concerned with gender politics. But the assumptions it reflects about the relation of women to language and power are very different from those manifested in a later work like "A Curse For a Nation." The differences reveal how much Barrett Browning's vision evolved in the space of little more than a decade.

Elizabeth Barrett begins in *A Drama of Exile* where Milton leaves off in *Paradise Lost,* as the gates of Eden close upon Eve and Adam. That this is perilously lofty subject matter for a woman she acknowledges in her Preface, an elaborate apology for daring to tread on Milton's sacred ground. She justifies her venture in part by emphasizing that her work gives special attention to "Eve's allotted grief" and her guilty consciousness of originating the Fall, emotions "imperfectly apprehended hitherto, and more expressible by a woman than a man" (*Works* 2: 143–44). These emotions indeed constitute a thematic concern in *A Drama of Exile:* Eve bewails her grief and guilt again and again in the longest and most moving speeches given to any of the characters. Eve has brought God's curse down upon Adam and herself, and upon Earth and all things on it. Worse, as the Earth Spirits remind her in a haunting refrain, Eve is "bringer of the curse" on all future generations (lines 1658, 1692, 1698).

Eve is always the accursed, never a curser in this drama that might well have been entitled "A Drama of Curses," since curses and cursing are mentioned thirty-six times, far more often than exile. God curses, although we never see His divine dignity compromised by the act. The weight of God's curse on Eve and Adam for their transgression broods over the play. Lucifer, accursed though he is, nevertheless curses copiously and felicitously himself. Adam at least threatens to curse Lucifer, although he chivalrously refuses to curse Eve when, mortifying herself in abasement, she begs him to strike her down with a curse as God has struck both of them down with His. But Eve, who is "crazed with curse" like the Earth (911) and who calls herself Adam's "cursemete" instead of his helpmate, never curses (1305). She does not yield to the temptation to curse even when Lucifer taunts her by sneering that "she could curse too—as a woman may—/ Smooth in the vowels" (664–65). Neither does Eve bless, as Christ and Adam do in the drama, Adam blessing Eve and Christ blessing a humanity that shall be redeemed.

In her emphasis on the guilt-crazed Eve's self-abasement, Elizabeth Barrett was apparently trying to arouse in her male readers as much sympathy as possible for fallen womanhood. If only all men were as chivalrous as her Adam is shown to be in refraining from cursing Eve! But Barrett was well aware they were not. Adam acknowledges how in the fallen world to come women will suffer "pressures of an alien tyranny / With its dynastic reasons of

larger bones / And stronger sinews" (1865–67). This euphemistically cir-
cuitous description of wife-battering is replaced in the later *Aurora Leigh*
(1857) by a blunter reference to wives whom men "kick like Britons" (8.
921); but like her Eve, Elizabeth Barrett eschewed such bluntness in *A
Drama of Exile*. A cursing Eve, even an Eve cursing Lucifer, could hardly
arouse the protective chivalry Barrett seeks to inspire, even as she implicitly
and subversively criticizes the "alien tyranny" of bone and muscle power that
makes it necessary. Indeed, another poem published in the 1844 volumes
reveals that she knew very well a cursing woman was apt to be seen as a
witch.

In the strangely intense romantic ballad "The Lay of the Brown Rosary,"
we find not just a cursing woman but a cursing nun—or rather, the ghost of
one. Alive, the nun had " 'mocked at the priest when he called her to shrive' "
(line 47); consequently, she was buried, still alive, in a wall for her sin, where-
upon she " 'shrieked such a curse' " that her own abbess swooned to death at
the sound (48–50). Dead, the nun carries a mysterious brown rosary and acts
as a corrupt mother confessor to the young heroine of the ballad, Onora, leading her to repudiate simultaneously God, her dead father, and her priest in
conventional witch fashion: " 'Aroint thee, father mine!' " (214). The cursing
nun is undoubtedly portrayed as an evil figure by Elizabeth Barrett, yet the
poem remains ambiguous in its moral implications. Is this nun one of the
"Hags" whom Mary Daly celebrates in *Gyn/Ecology,* we wonder? For the nun
only curses the priest because she is going to be buried alive, and Onora only
falls under the nun's influence because God the Father has mysteriously condemned her to die just as she is about to wed her young lover. And quite naturally, both women wish to live.

Despite these troubling ambiguities, however, it is clear that, as a
woman poet, Elizabeth Barrett took care to dissociate herself from the cursing nun in "The Lay of the Brown Rosary," and indeed from cursing in general in her poems of and before 1844. This tactic is particularly apparent in
one of the strongest poems included in the 1844 volumes, "The Cry of the
Children," which concludes with a rhetorically complex and resounding curse
articulating the poet's own thoughts and feelings, but doing so indirectly.
"The Cry of the Children" is a poem that deserves to be ranked with Blake's
subtly bitter "Songs of Experience," and like some of those lyrics, it focusses
on the image of children weeping. It is also very much a polemical poem,
written and published first in 1843 immediately after Elizabeth Barrett read
her friend Richard Horne's "Report on the Employment of Children and
Young Persons in Mines and Manufactories" (3: 362). The poem builds to a
palpably intense impression of the children's physically and spiritually suffo-
cating environment amidst the endless turning of factory wheels, the wheels
that produce their weeping. As the poet articulates their silent suffering, the
children cry:

For all day the wheels are droning, turning;
    Their wind comes in our faces,
Till our hearts turn, our heads with pulses burning,
    And the walls turn in their places:
Turns the sky in the high window, blank and reeling,
    Turns the long light that drops adown the wall,
Turn the black flies that crawl along the ceiling:
    All are turning, all the day, and we with all.
And all day the iron wheels are droning,
    And sometimes we could pray,
"O ye wheels" (breaking out in a mad moaning),
    "Stop! be silent for today!"

                (77–88)

Driven in these dark whirling mills, the children know no words of prayer except "Our Father," but they despair of addressing God even with these words because they are told that their masters are made in God's image:

"Go to?" say the children,—"up in Heaven,
    Dark, wheel-like, turning clouds are all we find.
Do not mock us; grief has made us unbelieving:
    We look up for God, but tears have made us blind."

                (129–32)

As the children weep, the poet asks, "Do you hear the children weeping and disproving / O my brothers, what ye preach?" (133–34). But she does not rest simply with an appeal to the pity of these "brothers" who own and run the factories and mines, and who preach in the churches that justify economic exploitation. Knowing that many will hear and not be moved, she transforms the weeping image at the close of the poem into a forceful curse: " 'But the child's sob in the silence curses deeper / Than the strong man in his wrath.' " Moreover, she does not show the children speaking this curse, nor does she articulate it herself. The words are spoken by "angels in high places" who utter God's wrath (151). This displacement of children by angels, accompanied by the metaphoric transformation of weeping into cursing (the same transformation later used in "A Curse For a Nation"), is very effective rhetorically because it permits Elizabeth Barrett to pronounce a curse upon the employers and their justifiers without either speaking a curse herself or making the suffering children curse. Thus she ends her poem with a bang, not a whimper, stealing a little of God's thunder to arouse dread in her "brothers," while at the same time maintaining the appeal to pity.

The same combined rhetorical appeal is evident in a later polemical poem written in 1854, "A Song For the Ragged Schools of London"—this one Shelleyan rather than Blakean in its imagery, with notable echoes of "The Mask of Anarchy." Barrett Browning wrote this now completely neglected poem for a benefit bazaar organized by her sister Arabella Barrett to raise money for the Ragged Schools; it was sold at the bazaar, bound together with a poem by Robert Browning entitled "The Twins" (6: 364). Since women were actively involved in charitable work in and for the Ragged Schools, Barrett Browning knew that much of her immediate audience was female, and thus it is not surprising to see her addressing not her "brothers," but her "sisters" in this poem. Again, she takes it upon herself to speak for the inarticulate suffering children, this time pauper children "Spilt like blots about the city," as she ironically describes them (line 46). And again, she appeals to pity, imploring her "sisters" to imagine the children's plight and to "take them into pity" (93, 128). Her appeal gathers added resonance from its echo of a line in a section of *The Iliad* that she translated in which Andromache pleads with Hector not to go to war but to " 'take me into pity' " (6: 158).

Both the appeal and the Homeric passage it echoes reflect Barrett Browning's increasingly woman-centered consciousness, yet the "Song For the Ragged Schools" is not a poem addressed only to women or relying upon only an appeal to pity. The poem begins with a bold satire of the "ruins worse than Rome's" at the heart of the ascendant British Empire, human ruins in the form of England's paupers whom the poet envisions from her vantage point among the ruins of Rome much as Shelley envisioned England's anarchy in the Peterloo Massacre while he "lay asleep in Italy" (line 1). Barrett Browning decries the corruption and violent order of English society as Shelley does in "The Mask of Anarchy," but with fewer poetic abstractions and less visionary hope. Thus in Shelley's poem, the masses for whom he speaks are envisioned with "Science, Poetry, and Thought" as their "lamps," and accordingly they do not "curse" their lot (254–57). In Barrett Browning's grim satire of England's human ruins, she does not take it upon herself to speak for the adult impoverished because, as she forcefully says to her middle and upper class readers, "women leering through the gas" and "men, turned wolves by famine"—"Those can speak themselves, and curse you" (41–44). In *Aurora Leigh,* these paupers, taught cursing from the time when they hang like rags "[f]orgotten on their mother's neck" (4. 576–77), curse Aurora from their tenement windows when she ventures into their slums (3. 767); moreover, even the idealistic Christian socialist Romney Leigh finds himself "cursed" for his attempts to reform the poor in his phalanstery (8.893).

Like some sections of *Aurora Leigh,* both "A Song For the Ragged Schools" and "The Cry of the Children" attack evils in Barrett Browning's own country. But in "The Runaway Slave At Pilgrim's Point," her most powerful polemical poem before "A Curse For a Nation," she treats the evils of another country, and perhaps for that reason is more outspoken, sympathetically presenting a cursing woman for the first time. "The Runaway Slave" was written in late 1846 at the request of an American anti-slavery friend. Barrett Browning said it was "too ferocious, perhaps, for the Americans to publish"

(Kenyon 1: 315). But *The Liberty Bell,* the Boston abolitionist publication in which "A Curse For a Nation" later appeared, did print it in the 1848 issue, which was for sale that same year at a mammoth anti-slavery bazaar in Boston (3: 385).

If ferocity can be measured by curses, "The Runaway Slave" is certainly more ferocious than Barrett Browning's previous poems. As the title implies, it is a dramatic monologue, or more accurately a dramatic romance, in which a runaway female slave ends her flight at Pilgrim's Point, where she addresses first the spirits of the pilgrim fathers and then their "hunter sons" in the flesh as they close in around her in pursuit (line 204). The slave's past is revealed and relived as she speaks: a love affair with another slave; forced separation from him, followed by his death; her subsequent pregnancy after being raped by her white master; her strangling of the baby that is born because when she looked down to her breast she saw "The *master's* look, that used to fall / On my face like his lash" (144–45); the flogging she received as punishment; and finally her flight and arrival at Pilgrim's Point. As the woman speaks, she also recalls the curses she uttered in the past, and she adds to these curses in the present. To the spirits of the dead pilgrim fathers she declares that she has come to Pilgrim's Point to "curse" in their names the land they blessed in the name of freedom (20–21). She strangles her white-faced child in order to "save it" from her curse (147). She curses the descendants of the pilgrim fathers as they hunt her down and one lifts the first stone, wishing each of them "for his own wife's joy and gift / A little corpse" like the corpse of her strangled baby (213–14). She recalls how she made no sound as they flogged her—"only cursed them all around / As softly" as she might have cursed her own child had she not buried it in the kind blackness of the earth (227–28). (This "soft" cursing is evidently the type Lucifer refers to in *A Drama of Exile* when he taunts Eve about the way women curse "smooth in the vowels.") But the slave woman does not always curse softly. "Whips, curses; these must answer those!" she declares to her hunters, thereby locating the cause of her curses in the white sons of the holy pilgrim fathers (232).

In the course of her monologue, the slave questions and finally discards her faith in the benevolence of the white man's God with his "fine white angels." She is as little able to believe in such a divinity as are Blake's little black boy and Elizabeth Barrett's crying children (157). More rebellious and outspoken than they are, however, she asserts near the end that white men are not gods nor "able to make Christs again / Do good with bleeding" (239–43). Blacks who bleed and who hang "too heavy" for their cross are suffering martyrs, but their martyrdom brings destruction not redemption (244).

Unexpectedly, yet in keeping with her final focus on Christ, suddenly at the end of the poem and her life the slave revokes her curse on the white masters:

> In the name of the white child waiting for me
> In the death-dark where we may kiss and agree,
> White men, I leave you all curse-free
> In my broken heart's disdain!
>
> (250–53)

However much one might wish to see the slave as adopting a doctrine of Christian forgiveness here, her last words are surely a case of reiterating her curse and absolving herself of it too. Indeed, the final wrenching reference to her "broken heart's disdain" assumes additional force because it appears in an extra last line, breaking the pattern of seven lines maintained throughout the poem's thirty-seven stanzas. Barrett Browning recognized in an earlier poem entitled "A Valediction" that human blessings, even when well-intentioned, can "curse and kill" (2: 279, line 31); and in the slave's case we cannot be sure of benign intent. There is none of Eve's meek self-abnegation in this fierce woman who compares herself to the "black eagle" (208), and who rises in the moral loftiness of her heart's disdain as she falls into the welcoming blackness of death. She does not accept the curse on Eve as a cause of her oppression as a raped and impregnated woman any more than she accepts the curse on Ham as a cause of her oppression as a slave. Like the white man's God and His prophets, she is the one who curses and who, serene in the authority of her righteousness, revokes her curse at her will.

Barrett Browning was herself a member of a family that, like Mr. Rochester's in *Jane Eyre,* derived part of its fortune from West Indian slave plantations, and there is little doubt that she felt closer to the guilty white masters than she liked to contemplate. In a letter to John Ruskin written nine years after "The Runaway Slave," she said, "I belong to a family of West Indian slaveholders, and if I believed in curses, I should be afraid" (Kenyon 2: 220). However, as a woman who in December of 1846 had recently rebelled against the patriarchal master in her own house, the father who forbade any of his children to marry, her sympathies were obviously with the black woman she treats so heroically. "Oh, and is it possible that you think a woman has no business with questions like the question of slavery?" she asked her friend Mrs. Jameson with respect to Harriet Beecher Stowe's *Uncle Tom's Cabin.* "Then she had better use a pen no more. She had better subside into slavery and concubinage herself, I think, as in the times of old, shut herself up with the Penelopes and the 'women's apartment,' and take no rank among thinkers and speakers" (Kenyon 2: 110–11).

Casa Guidi Windows (1851), focusing on the 1848 revolutions in Italy and their aftermath, is Barrett Browning's first major attempt to take a rank as a speaker on political subjects. Strikingly original in form and conception, this work can be assigned to no established genre. It is perhaps best described by Barrett Browning's turn-of-the-century editors, Charlotte Porter and Helen A. Clarke, as a "condensed lyrical epic of a modern nation's birth" (3: xv). In her critical edition of *Casa Guidi Windows* (1977), Julia Markus notes as particularly unprecedented the "daring subjectivity" with which Barrett Browning fuses her personal experience as poet and mother with the political upheavals of a nation struggling to be born (xix). Not surprisingly, then, in *Casa Guidi Windows* Barrett Browning first curses in her own voice. She utters "the poet's curse" on art critics who scorn the achievement of early Italian painters like Cimabue simply because they have not reached the "heights of Raffaelhood" (Markus ed. Pt. 1, lines 351–57). This curse is presented warily, however: behind a mask of sorts still ("the poet's"), and in the sphere of the arts where Barrett Browning was confident of her authority, not in the political sphere that forms the more immediate focus of the poem. She clearly recognized the complex interaction between these two spheres, as well as the connections between the politics of nations and gender politics. Thus she satirizes the hackneyed tropes of Italian patriots: "Bewailers of an Italy enchained," who perpetuate their country's oppression by casting her either as a barren woman or a shamed one—"Cursing her beauty to her face, as brothers / Might a shamed sister's" (1. 21–26). But while she implies that there are subtle connections between art and politics, she does not directly address them. Nor does she pronounce political curses. The curses that she does depict in the political sphere are paradoxically silent curses, articulated by the poet but not pronounced by her. Emphasizing the silent response of the Florentines to their renewed suppression by the Austrian overlords, she writes:

> Meantime, from Casa Guidi windows, we
> Beheld the armament of Austria flow
> Into the drowning heart of Tuscany.
> And yet none wept; none cursed, or, if 'twas so,
> They wept and cursed in silence. Silently
> Our noisy Tuscans watched the invading foe;
> They had learnt silence.
>
> (2. 352–58)

No doubt Barrett Browning's experience as a woman who had also "learnt silence"—at least insofar as expressing her anger was concerned—contributed to her imaginative identification with the oppressed Italians. The motif of silence speaking recurs in her poetry, most notably in "Lady Geraldine's Courtship," where a statue of silence is the central symbol. In *Casa Guidi Windows* too, a statue is associated with the most complex instance of silence speaking when Barrett Browning uses a statue in snow to articulate an artist's curse on a political tyrant. Narrating the story of how Michelangelo was ordered to erect a snow statue to serve the mocking pleasure of the ruler of Florence, she depicts the great artist creating a statue erect as Jove with "The right hand raised . . . as if it cursed," then watching his creation melt and the hand drop, "a mere snowball" (1. 117–18). This raised hand initially seems to articulate Michelangelo's silent curse on the tyrant who mocks him, but as Barrett Browning develops the image, the raised cursing arm reduced to a mere snowball finally becomes a symbol of the heavyhanded oppression of the tyrant. Like Shelley's Ozymandias, the sneering tyrant is the one whose fame is obliterated, while the story of the ephemeral statue built by the artist endures as a sign to succeeding generations of "what is true princedom" (1. 143). Michelangelo's snow statue thus resembles the statue of a Greek slave sculpted by one of Barrett Browning's contemporaries, which she celebrates in one of her best sonnets, "Hiram Powers' 'Greek Slave.' " The Greek slave is mute and passive in stone, yet the statue's "Ideal beauty" and the evil of slavery it symbolizes "shame the strong / By thunders of white silence, overthrown" (3: 178). Powers' "Greek Slave" epitomizes Barrett Browning's vision of art as "essential truth that makes its way through beauty into use."

II

Barrett Browning's vision of art did not change in her later works, but her acceptance of silence did. In her poems after *Casa Guidi Windows* and most notably in "A Curse For a Nation," she no longer limits herself to thundering in "white silence," to cursing indirectly through gestures and silent cries or, if aloud, in fictive voices not her own. She asks in one of her late poems, "Where's Agnes?", whether a "low and soft" voice can "Take open and actual part / With Right,—maintain aloft / Pure truth in life or art. . . ?" (6: 31, lines 55–60). Her changing treatment of cursing as a speech act reflects her answer to this rhetorical question. I have already shown how in the dialogue between the angel and the poet forming the "Prologue" to "A Curse For a Nation" she dramatically foregrounds the fact that the poet is a woman. There is no reason to interpret this woman as anyone other than Barrett Browning herself, speaking out here for the first time as boldly as her runaway slave. Barrett Browning's pet name among her family and intimate friends such as her mentor John Kenyon was "Ba." But as Elizabeth Barrett confessed to Robert Browning in 1845, "Mr. Kenyon & I agreed the other day that there was something of the tigress-nature very distinctly cognizable under what he is pleased to call my 'Ba-lambishness' " (Kintner 1: 225). This "tigress" no longer wears lamb's clothing in later works such as *Aurora Leigh* and "A Curse For a Nation," where Barrett Browning assumes the role of a Miriam or a Cassandra, the two figures in the Jewish and Classical traditions respectively upon whom she modelled herself as her poetry became more woman-centered and outspoken. "I am Cassandra you know, & smell the slaughter in the bathroom," she said to Robert Browning (Kintner 1: 240). In "A Curse For a Nation" she becomes a Cassandra in earnest, and writes at the angel's behest "The Curse" that makes up the main part of the poem, emphasizing her act of writing with the refrain that thunders at the close of each of the ten stanzas: "This is the curse. Write."

" 'Oh, Ba, such dreadful curses!' " was the response of Barrett Browning's own sister Henrietta to this fiery poem, a response that the poet said she "couldn't help laughing at" (Kenyon 2: 376). Her laughter implies a measure of detachment from even this work, a poem that more than any other reflects the "poetical devil" she described as burning in her (Kenyon 2: 369). And indeed, precisely because she writes such "dreadful curses" in "A Curse For a Nation," she takes care to frame the poem with fearful symmetry. It is tightly structured, controlled in tone, subtle in its rhetorical strategies, and measured in its ironies. Structurally, it falls into three parts, with successively longer stanzas in each part: the "Prologue" presenting the dialogue between the poet and the angel, the first section of "The Curse" setting forth the reasons for the curse, and the second section prophesying its consequences.

The rhetorical strategies determining this tripartite structure become apparent if one considers how it contributes to the forcefulness and complexity of the curse Barrett Browning "writes." The introductory dialogue with the angel not only dramatizes and justifies the fact that a woman has been chosen to "write" the curse, but also invests her words with all the authority of patriarchal Christianity. The angel is emphatically male and masterful, and he is the one who sanctions the woman's right to curse. In fact, the right becomes an obligation, and she becomes no more than the mouthpiece of the host. This apparent reduction of the woman to a subservient vessel by no means represents a capitulation of Barrett Browning's feminist vision. The use of the angel as a commanding muse may instead be seen as a calculated manoeuvre, the pragmatism of which is apparent in the context of a political and ethical distinction noted by Wayne Booth: the distinction between "*freedom from* external restraints and the power of others to inhibit our actions, and *freedom to* act effectively when restraints disappear" (Booth 52). Barrett Browning appears to surrender her freedom from the authority of the patriarchal tradition, but only in order to gain the freedom to pronounce the sort of curse women were conventionally not permitted to utter. And despite her apparent capitulation, she subverts the tradition that empowers her, in part through her use of the male angel and in part through the manner in which she progressively complicates the origin and nature of the curse as she writes. Who is responsible for the curse? we find ourselves asking. The woman? The angel? Or the nation itself?

The question of origin and responsibility becomes particularly complex as we encounter the refrain—"This is the curse. Write." Who speaks the command and who acts in response? The final stanza of the "Prologue" indicates that the poet herself has written the curse ("So thus I wrote"); it is therefore she who most obviously issues the command "Write" to the wrongdoers in

the nation she addresses. But the refrain also reminds us that she is responding to the angel's command to write, just as presumably the angel is responding to God's command. Insofar as the command is addressed to the nation,
either by the poet or by the angel acting through the poet, Barrett Browning
implies that the nation that perpetuates wrongs such as slavery in effect
"writes" or causes its own curse. Moreover, she reinforces this implication by
emphasizing the notion of causation in the first section of "The Curse" (all
three stanzas here begin with "Because"), and by playing upon the pun of
"Write" and "Right." This pun is activated by the juxtaposition of the final
word "wrong" in the second-last line of the first stanza in "The Curse" with
the final word "Write" in the last line:

> BECAUSE ye have broken your own chain
>   With the strain
> Of brave men climbing a Nation's height,
> Yet thence bear down with brand and thong
> On souls of others,—for this wrong
>   This is the curse. Write.
>
>   (53–58)

Thus the imperative in the refrain becomes a command to the nation that
causes or "writes" its own curse through its wrongs to right those wrongs.

If the nation fails to right the curse that it in effect writes through its
acts, then it will suffer the evil consequences Barrett Browning presents in
the second section of "The Curse." Here she further exploits the polysemy of
the refrain by playing upon the various senses of the term "curse" and the
ambiguity of the demonstrative pronoun "This." The reference of "This"
shifts as she moves into Part II of "The Curse," just as the reference of "curse"
shifts from a malediction or cause to its evil effects. The most agonizing effect
is the nation's consciousness of its own evil, of the curse that stains it, as Barrett Browning emphasizes in six stanzas that describe first what the nation
will "watch," and then what it will hear (three for each mode of perception).
She thus implies, with acute psychological insight, that consciousness of the
curse *is* finally the curse. This guilty consciousness "writes" the curse that is
engraved on the conscience of the nation. But the same guilty consciousness
is also the only way of ending the curse by righting it. Hence the write / right
pun continues through this section up to the envoy in the seventh stanza,
where Barrett Browning further complicates the polysemy of the refrain and
extends the consciousness of the curse:

> Go, wherever ill deeds shall be done,
> Go, plant your flag in the sun
>   Beside the ill-doers!
> And recoil from clenching the curse
> Of God's witnessing Universe

> With a curse of yours.
>   THIS is the curse. Write.
>   (113–19)

Here an important distinction is introduced between the "curse / Of God's witnessing Universe"—in effect, the righteous curse the angel asks the poet to write—and the self-confirming evil curse of anger, which is for the first time directly attributed to the nation that has created it. Only if the nation "clenches" God's curse with its own will the curse continue in a vicious echoing circle. As the ambiguous "THIS" in the final lines suggests, the nation can choose which curse to "write."

When one considers how the meanings of the keyword "curse" and of the entire refrain are altered and complicated in "A Curse For a Nation," it becomes apparent that Barrett Browning was strictly accurate when she maintained in one of her letters that *she* did not curse any nation in the poem. She left such cursing to Rome's "Holy Father," she wryly remarked; "the poem only pointed out how the curse was involved in the action of slaveholding" (Kenyon 2: 367). The title of the poem supports her assertion, since it implies that she writes not a curse *on* a nation but "A Curse *For* a Nation," not a curse expressing hate or anger but one written out of love. As the angel expressively puts it, " 'From the summits of love a curse is driven, / As lightning is from the tops of heaven' " (15–16).

Barrett Browning's contemporary readers heard the thunder of her curses, but not many seemed to see the "lightning" of love generating them. Nor did they perceive the poet as being as uninvolved in the cursing as she maintained she was. Ironically, however, it was not her American audience that was shocked and incensed at the curse "for" their nation. It was her own countrymen. As Leonid M. Arinshtein and Robert W. Gladish have shown, English readers took little notice of "A Curse For a Nation" when it was initially published in the 1856 issue of *The Liberty Bell*. But when Barrett Browning reprinted it as the final poem in her 1860 volume *Poems Before Congress,* there was a violent uproar among English reviewers. Many of the poems in this highly polemical volume were harshly critical of England's timeserving non-intervention in the Italian liberation movement. Even more outrageous for patriotic English readers was the high praise Barrett Browning accorded Napoleon III of France in *Poems Before Congress* for his initial support of the Italian nationalists—this at a time when many Englishmen had paranoid fears of a French invasion, and when Tennyson, Poet Laureate, had recently published a ranting, jingoistic poem in *The Times* (May 9, 1859) urging, "Form! form! Riflemen, form! / Ready, be ready to meet the storm! / Riflemen, Riflemen, Riflemen, form!"

Because of her praise for Napoleon III and her criticisms of England in *Poems Before Congress,* most reviewers of the volume assumed that Barrett Browning was cursing her own country in the final poem, and they fulminated at the idea of an English wife and mother engaging in such an act. The *Saturday Review* reviled her as an "illogical renegade," a "denationalized fanatic," and denounced "A Curse For a Nation" for its "hysterical antipathy to England," its "delirium of imbecile one-sidedness" (quoted in Arinshtein 38–39). *Blackwood's* deplored the intervention of a woman in politics: "we love the fair sex too well, to desire that they should be withdrawn from their own sphere, which is that of adorning the domestic circle, . . . to figure in the public arena." It held up the example of Florence Nightingale for Mrs. Browning's edification, and reminded her that "to bless and not to curse is woman's function" (quoted in Taplin 377). Barrett Browning summarized the hysterical response to *Poems Before Congress* and especially to "A Curse For a Nation" by noting that she had been "held up at the end of a fork as the unnatural she-monster who had 'cursed' her own country" (Kenyon 2: 380). Even her longtime friend Henry Chorley, writing in the *Athenaeum,* had censured "A Curse For a Nation" as "improper and unpatriotic" (Kenyon 2: 364), leading Barrett Browning to observe that she had been "dishonored before the 'Athenaeum' world as an unnatural vixen, who, instead of staying at home and spinning wool, stays at home and curses her own land." She sardonically added, "If, indeed, I had gone abroad and cursed other people's lands, there would have been no objection. That poem, as addressed to America, has always been considered rather an amiable and domestic trait on my part. But England! Heavens and earth! What a crime! The very suspicion of it is guilt." On the same occasion (in a letter to Isa Blagden), she also privately acknowledged that certain stanzas in "A Curse For a Nation" "do 'fit' England 'as though they were made for her,' which they were *not* though" (Kenyon 2: 374–75). Barrett Browning had insisted to Henry Chorley that the poem was addressed to America and that her reviewers were mistaken in interpreting it as a curse aimed at England. However, her private remark reveals that, like the Old Testament prophets, she was not averse to employing the same formula in different rhetorical contexts.

Barrett Browning was well aware that much of the furor excited by "A Curse For a Nation" derived from her violation of the taboo against women prophesying and cursing. Of her treatment in *Blackwood's* she said to a woman friend, "you and all women, though you hated me, should be vexed on your own accounts" (Kenyon 2: 387). *Blackwood's* might praise women such as Florence Nightingale, but Barrett Browning was caustically sceptical of such fulsome sentiments. After meeting Florence Nightingale in London, she praised her as "an earnest, noble woman," but also criticized the idealization of nursing her work brought about as a "retrograde" step, "a revival of old virtues! . . . Every man is on his knees before ladies carrying lint, calling them 'angelic she's,' whereas, if they stir an inch as thinkers or artists from the beaten line (involving more good to general humanity than is involved in lint), the very same men would curse the impudence of the same women and stop there. . . . I do not consider the best use to which we can put a gifted and accomplished woman is to *make her a hospital nurse*. If it is, why then woe to us all who are artists! The woman's question is at an end" (Kenyon 2: 189).

Barrett Browning expressed these opinions in 1855, but her remark about men cursing women who "stir an inch as thinkers or artists from the beaten line" proved prophetic in her own case. All of her political poems, and particularly her later more outspoken ones, represent a swerving from the "beaten line" laid down for women in her century and persisting into our own. That may be one reason why her political poetry has been suppressed, with the occasional exception of "The Cry of the Children," the early political poem in which the rhetorical strategies and subject matter most accord with conventional views of women's sphere. Although critics such as Gladish, Arinshtein, and Gardner B. Taplin have examined the controversy surrounding the publication of "A Curse For a Nation" in *Poems Before Congress,* they do not consider how the gender bias and patriotic hysteria of the reviewers obscured the artistry and complexity of the poem. In fact, they give no attention to the poem as a work of art, or to *Poems Before Congress* as a carefully orchestrated series of poems recording Barrett Browning's changing views of Napoleon III, the Italian liberation struggle, and the European political situation. Other political poems by Barrett Browning—even a major work such as *Casa Guidi Windows*—have received even less attention from mainstream critics.

The neglect of such a large and historically significant body of political poems is a notable example of how, as Edward Said observes, canons of standard literary texts often have "very little historical accuracy to them" (23). Indeed, the failure to consider Barrett Browning's achievement as a political poet has led to some startling omissions and distortions in the treatment of the Victoria period. Most notably, in a study of "Politics and the Poet's Role" in Victorian poetry John Lucas fails to mention any of her major political poems or collections of poems; he briefly discusses "The Cry of the Children" only to dismiss it as a "specific polemic" (29–30, 37). E.D.H. Johnson, in a now classic study, can speak of *The Alien Vision of Victorian Poetry* in part because he omits to consider the social and political engagement of Barrett Browning and of many other women poets in the period, poets responsible for much of the Victorian poetry of social protest, as Kathleen Hickok points out (156). Even more disturbing is the assertion by Donald A. Davie in 1982 that feminist criticism has never considered the concept of patriotism: "An Italian woman may well, we must suppose, be an Italian patriot; but where, in the current vocabulary of feminists, is that dimension of her 'woman-ness' allowed for?" (40). The question overlooks, among much else, the recovery and analysis of *Casa Guidi Windows* in 1977–78 by Julia Markus and Flavia Alaya, and the reprinting of Barrett Browning's fine late poem "Mother and Poet" by Cora Kaplan in *Aurora Leigh and Other Poems* (1978). "Mother and Poet" is a moving tribute to the Italian poet and patriot Laura Savio by the feminist poet who was herself accorded the highest praise as an Italian patriot by the citizens of Florence on her death (Alaya 21).

The critical distortions obscuring Barrett Browning's achievement as a political poet do not spring only from omission, however. Flavia Alaya has incisively shown that a canonical critical myth has been created and perpetuated, depicting Barrett Browning as an unstable and emotional political observer whose blind hero worship of Napoleon III of France and other ardent polemical excesses were the cause of numerous disputes with her more judicious and politically astute husband. A full consideration of how and why this extraordinary myth has developed is beyond the scope of this essay. But clearly it has functioned to promote Robert Browning's reputation at the expense of his wife's, it reflects and reinforces stereotypical assumptions about women held by a predominantly male hegemony, and it accords with the New Critical axiom that poetry should be apolitical. The myth may also be a reaction formation against Barrett Browning's forceful and radical expression of her feminist political vision in her later poems, manifested in her increasing mastery of the fine art of political cursing.

Like so many women writers, Barrett Browning was faced by the dilemma summarized by Sandra M. Gilbert and Susan Gubar in "Sexual Linguistics." Citing Xaviere Gauthier, they observe "that 'as long as women remain silent'—that is, as long as women remain linguistically 'female'—'they will be outside the historical process. But if they begin to speak and write as men do, they will enter history subdued and alienated'" (521). In Barrett Browning's case, however, the choices were slightly more complex. She could choose to remain conventionally female in her poetic speech acts, as she was careful to do in "The Cry of the Children" by cursing indirectly through the children and the mediation of God's wrathful angels. Or she could attempt to speak like a man, either disguising her own sex in the process as she did in her early poems, or asserting it as she did in late poems like "A Curse For a Nation." Every choice involved suppression and alienation. If she was conventionally female, she faced marginalization outside the male mainstream of major poets. If she wrote like a man, but disguised her sex, she did so at risk of being alienated from her own womanhood. If she wrote like a man, simultaneously declaring her womanhood, she did so at risk of being suppressed for her assumption of male power.

She chose the last risk in her later poems and, predictably, she has been suppressed. The canon politely acknowledges the lady who asks, "How do I love thee? Let me count the ways." But with the exception of feminist scholars who, since 1970, have made their way on to the "critical Board of Trade," the canon-makers have steadfastly ignored the woman-poet who maintained that "the liberation of a people and the struggle of a nation for existence" will always be "right arguments for poetry" (Kenyon 2: 380), the woman-poet who seems to have asked herself how she might address nations and powers so as to change the course of history. The canon-makers have ignored the woman who evidently asked, "How can I curse, creatively? Let me explore the ways."

Works Cited

Alaya, Flavia. "The Ring, the Rescue, and the Risorgimento: Reunifying the Brownings' Italy." *Browning Institute Studies* 6 (1978): 1–41.

Arinshtein, Leonid M. "A Curse for a Nation: A Controversial Episode in Elizabeth Barrett Browning's Political Poetry." *Review of English Studies* ns 20 (1969): 33–42.

Booth, Wayne C. "Freedom of Interpretation: Bakhtin and the Challenge of Feminist Criticism." *The Politics of Interpretation*. Ed. W.J.T. Mitchell. Chicago: University of Chicago Press, 1983, 51–82.

Browning, Elizabeth Barrett. *Aurora Leigh and Other Poems*. Ed. Cora Kaplan. London: The Women's Press, 1978.

———*Casa Guidi Windows*. Ed. Julia Markus. New York: Browning Institute, 1977.

———*The Complete Works of Elizabeth Barrett Browning*. Ed. Charlotte Porter & Helen A. Clarke. 6 vols. New York: Thomas Y. Crowell, 1900.

Davie, Donald A. "Poet: Patriot: Interpreter." *The Politics of Interpretation*. Ed. W.J.T. Mitchell. 38–49.

Gilbert, Sandra M. & Susan Gubar. "Sexual Linguistics: Gender, Language, Sexuality." *New Literary History* 16 (1985): 515–543.

Gladish, Robert W. "Mrs. Browning's 'A Curse for a Nation': Some Further Comments." *Victorian Poetry* 7 (1969): 275–80.

Hickok, Kathleen. *Representations of Women: Nineteenth-Century British Women's Poetry*. London: Greenwood Press, 1984.

Kenyon, Frederic G., ed. *The Letters of Elizabeth Barrett Browning*. 2 vols. New York: Macmillan, 1897.

Kintner, Elvan, ed. *The Letters of Robert Browning and Elizabeth Barrett Barrett 1845–1846*. 2 vols. Cambridge, Mass.: Harvard University Press, 1969, Vol. 1.

Lucas, John. "Politics and the Poet's Role." *Literature and Politics in the Nineteenth Century*. Ed. John Lucas. London: Methuen, 1971. 7–43.

Quinn, Arthur H. *Edgar Allan Poe: A Critical Biography*. New York: Appleton-Century Crofts, 1941.

Said, Edward W. "Opponents, Audiences, Constituencies, and Community." *The Politics of Interpretation*. Ed. W.J.T. Mitchell. 7–32.

Shelley, Percy B. "The Mask of Anarchy." *Shelley: Poetical Works*. Ed. Thomas Hutchinson. Rev. new ed. G. M. Matthews. London: Oxford University Press, 1970. 338–44.

Taplin, Gardner B. *The Life of Elizabeth Barrett Browning*. New Haven: Yale University Press, 1957.

Combating an Alien Tyranny:
Elizabeth Barrett Browning's Evolution
As a Feminist Poet

Deborah Byrd

The drama of woman lies in this conflict between the fundamental aspirations
of every subject (ego)—who always regards the self as the essential—and the
compulsions of a situation in which she is the inessential.

(Simone de Beauvoir xxxiv)

The name [of poet]
Is royal, and to sign it like a queen
Is what I dare not,—though some royal blood
Would seem to tingle in me now and then,
With sense of power and ache.

(Aurora Leigh 1. 934–38)

'Tis Antidote to turn—
To Tomes of solid Witchcraft—

(Emily Dickinson, #593)

"Speed and energy, forthrightness and complete self-confidence—these are
the qualities that hold us enthralled" as we read Elizabeth Barrett Browning's
Aurora Leigh, wrote Virginia Woolf in 1932 (I.212). As Woolf points out,
these qualities emanate not so much from Aurora as from her creator, whose
strong and lively presence so pervades the poem that "Again and again . . .
Aurora the fictitious seems to be throwing light upon Elizabeth the
actual. . . . [making it] impossible for the most austere of critics not sometimes to touch the flesh when his [*sic*] eyes should be fixed upon the page"

Reprinted from *Browning Institute Studies,* now *Victorian Literature and Culture,* 15 (1987): 23–41.
Used by permission of the publisher.

(212). And as Woolf observes, the "flesh" the critic touches is that of a woman who knows that the royal blood of poets flows through her veins. "Elizabeth the actual" is a subject, speaking boldly of the world as she perceives and experiences it.

Wit and verve, directness and energy, an authorial voice radiating a firm sense of self and a firm sense of purpose—these are the salient characteristics not only of *Aurora Leigh* but of most of the poems that Barrett Browning wrote after 1845. In such works the poet "use[s] the woman's figures naturally" and often is "plain at speech, direct in purpose" when critiquing patriarchy (*AL* 8. 1127–31); in some instances, she even transforms poetic forms that her contemporaries considered the exclusive province of men into vehicles for the expression of female and feminist concerns. Since Barrett Browning's reputation as a major Victorian poet rests primarily on these late woman-centered poems, it is important to identify the experiences that furthered her development of a feminist consciousness and aesthetic. Foremost among these experiences were the poet's encounters with literary texts.[1] Aware of Barrett Browning's erudition, numerous scholars have drawn attention to specific ways in which the poet draws upon or swerves from male writers, especially the acknowledged "masters" of European verse.[2] But with the exception of a few studies of Barrett Browning's debts to Sand, DeStaël, Gaskell, and Charlotte Brontë, surprisingly little has been written about the poet's artistic interaction with women authors, particularly women poets.[3]

It is quite true that Barrett Browning's favorite poets were men. She believed that England had produced no "poetess before Joanna Baillie [1762–1851]—poetess in the true sense," and she regarded no nineteenth-century woman poet as highly as she did Wordsworth, Byron, Browning, and Tennyson (Kenyon I:30). Barrett Browning's dissatisfaction with English women poets does not mean, however, that she did not participate in a female poetic tradition.[4] As numerous scholars have shown, the nineteenth-century woman writer generally searched for and was empowered by her discovery of literary foremothers and sisters. Even when she chose to modify or depart from the practices of her female predecessors and contemporaries, she often defined herself in relation to other literary women—attempting to avoid making their mistakes, trying to accomplish where they had failed.[5]

Barrett Browning was no exception. She was an avid reader of poems, essays, and fiction by women and took a keen interest in the lives of other professional women writers.[6] Moreover, as a poet she frequently imitated or responded critically to literary texts by other women, regarding such "Tomes of solid Witchcraft" as sources of sustenance as well as instruction. The women poets of her own century and country played a particularly crucial role in Barrett Browning's development, for when she began emulating these poets in the late 1830s she took the first step towards transforming herself into a woman-identified poet.[7]

Throughout her career Barrett Browning engaged in conversations with writers of both sexes, particularly other poets. Identifying the texts she read and chose to respond to is important, for it can help account for the marked changes in style and vision that characterize each distinctive stage of her career. I cannot in short compass describe all the ways in which this self-proclaimed "book-ferret" was influenced by other writers (Raymond and Sullivan 1:117). But I will provide an overview of Barrett Browning's poetic evolution, drawing attention to the ways in which her aesthetic principles and practices change as her reading habits and literary tastes alter.

Initially imitating women novelists, then treading closely in the footsteps of her poetic forefathers, in the late 1830s Barrett Browning turned her attention once again to women writers, this time to women poets. In this transitional stage of her career, she sometimes modeled her poetic efforts on those of other women; at other times she attempted, not always successfully, to synthesize aspects of the two distinct (though of course related) poetic traditions to which she was heir. At the height of her powers, Barrett Browning came to view her task as that of writing as "a woman & man in one," a feat she believed her friend Mary Russell Mitford and her idol George Sand had accomplished. She brings into harmony the potentially discordant elements of her dual literary heritage, writing authentically of her own and other women's experiences with the "forthrightness and self-confidence" she considered to be more characteristic of male than of female writers.[8]

Surprising as it may seem, the first stage of this precocious poet's literary career spans the brief period from 1814 to 1817, ending when the eleven-year-old became the pupil of Daniel McSwiney. In 1814, at the age of eight, Barrett Browning was designated by her father "Poet-Laureat [sic] of Hope End" (Kelley and Hudson 1:10), a position she took seriously for years, considering it her duty to compose poems on birthdays and other important family occasions. Yet it was not until the age of eleven that the Poet Laureate exhibited a decided preference for composing in verse. The longest and most ambitious works of her childhood are written in prose, not surprisingly, for once she had outgrown her taste for fairy tales, reading and "studying" novels became Elizabeth's "most delightful" pastime (Kelley and Hudson 1:349–50). Significantly, the novels that she knew and liked best (novels generally selected by her mother) were by women authors such as Maria Edgeworth, Charlotte Smith, and Amelia Opie. Barrett Browning particularly admired the fiction of Edgeworth, in which the woman who gives free rein to her passions and "forgets womanly duties in the personality of a man" is criticized, and the young woman who exhibits "too much sense" to be considered a "heroine" is presented as a character worthy of emulation (Kelley and Hudson 1:33–34).[9]

As long as she sought to emulate women novelists, and as long as she wrote for as well as about women (most of these early works were directed to

Elizabeth's mother or other female relatives), Barrett Browning could write with both authenticity and confidence. Without anxiety she could imagine the kind of woman she would like to become, could attempt to write her own story, to chart the course her future would take. But in 1817 she suddenly began to regard novels as a form of light entertainment and decided to seek her fame as a writer of poems and essays (Kelley and Hudson 1:33, 350).

Had she begun to read and imitate poems and non-fiction prose by women, Barrett Browning might have continued to assert her subjectivity and might not have suffered—or suffered as intensely—from that female malady that Sandra Gilbert and Susan Gubar term "the anxiety of authorship" (*Madwoman* 48–49). But internalizing the patriarchal standards of literary excellence espoused by McSwiney, she began to study and imitate her poetic forefathers—only to feel "the whole extent of my own immense & mortifying inferiority" (Kelley and Hudson 1:351). Essentially, Barrett Browning began to undergo the process that Judith Fetterley calls "immasculation," began to experience

> not simply the powerlessness which derives from not seeing one's experience articulated, clarified, and legitimized in art, but more significantly, the powerlessness which results from the endless division of self against self, the consequence of the invocation to identify as male while being reminded that to be male—to be universal— . . . is to be *not female* (xiii).[10]

Thus during the second stage of her literary career, which roughly spans the years 1818 to 1838, Barrett Browning writes as a divided self. The fragmentary "Essay on Woman" (ca. 1822) shows that she was quite capable of identifying and criticizing writers who espoused patriarchal values. Writing as a disciple of Mary Wollstonecraft, she openly reproaches poets who depict women as timid and subservient creatures, poets who "Paint . . . The trembling, melting voice of tenderness, / And all that Mother, Sister, Wife impart / To nurture, solace and subdue the heart" of man.[11] Proclaiming that her goal is "To bend to nobler thoughts the British fair" by "Found[ing] the proud path, where . . . [Woman] stands the equal of her Master Man," Barrett Browning leads us to expect that henceforth she will present women as resourceful and self-reliant beings.

Yet it was not until the late 1830s that Barrett Browning began to compose poems in which female characters act assertively and independently. Indeed, most of the poems she wrote before 1838 center on the experiences of men. When the poet does write about real or imaginary women, she generally depicts them as relative creatures, as associates of men of courage and nobility of character. For example, she praises Riego's widow for behaving in a way that enhances our appreciation of her patriot husband's integrity and valor, urges a young girl to heed the advice her father gives her as she sits meekly at his feet, and tells Bettine, "The Child-Friend of Goethe," that having her existence acknowledged by a man of genius should adequately compensate her for any suffering she has experienced or any sacrifices she has made as the poet's worshiper.[12] Moreover, in the few poems in which men are criticized for treating women like chattel or for being fickle or self-serving, women tend to die of grief or passively bemoan their fate; the poet regards such characters sympathetically, but she presents them as helpless victims rather than as active combatants of patriarchy.[13]

Most of these poems about women are sentimental, lacking the emotional power that comes from writing authentically out of one's own experience of the world. Barrett Browning had written elsewhere that she spurned "that subserviency of opinion which is generally considered necessary to feminine softness" and regarded as the most "odious" of creatures "a damsel famed in story for a superabundance of sensibility" (Kelley and Hudson 1:354–55). Moreover, she did not sit humbly at the feet of her own father, nor was she content to achieve fame as the adoring child-friend of the classical scholars Boyd and Price.[14]

To understand why it took Barrett Browning over three decades to write poems that reflect the reality of her own and other women's lives, one must turn once more to "Essay on Woman." Despite its overtly feminist themes, the poem suggests that henceforth Barrett Browning often will write as a male-identified poet. Indeed, she does so to a certain extent in this poem, for although she refutes Pope's belief in woman's inferiority, she feels compelled to demonstrate that she has mastered "Pope's" verse form, the heroic couplet. In other words, Barrett Browning seems to assume that to be a great poet she must compete with male predecessors on their terms, must excel in the poetic modes that men have considered most valuable. Accepting the patriarchal notion that some verse forms are inherently more noble than others, she apparently does not realize that the idea of a hierarchy of literary forms historically has been used to disparage and to exclude from the literary canon much of the verse written by women.

Or perhaps Barrett Browning did realize that women poets do not fare well when judged by patriarchal standards of literary excellence. Perhaps she failed to finish "Essay on Woman" because as a teenager, she was incapable of positing critical standards that would allow her to argue persuasively that the accomplishments of her poetic foremothers were as significant as those of her forefathers. After all, of the four women authors cited in the poem only Anne Dacier and Hannah More wrote in verse, and evidence suggests that Barrett Browning considered both to be second-rate authors.[15] Moreover, if the poet truly believed More and Dacier to be women of genius (as the final stanza of the poem implies), why does she describe her own task as that of *founding*— rather than treading in or enlarging—the poetic path in which woman stands the equal of man? And why did she not complete the poem, giving her predecessors the opportunity to reply to the charge that women, including women poets, are doomed to sigh in obscurity?

I believe that Barrett Browning failed to finish "Essay on Woman" because in the process of writing the poem, she came to the dismal and frightening conclusion that none of her literary foremothers had been a poet of major stature and that therefore the burden of proving that women could excel in poetic composition rested squarely on her own shoulders. Convinced that poets could learn much from imitating their precursors but not wanting to follow in the footsteps of poets whose works she regarded as second-rate, until the late 1830s Barrett Browning equated poetic excellence with and measured her own progress as a poet in terms of her ability to equal or best the literary efforts of the male poets whose artistic achievements she most admired. Not surprisingly, she found it almost impossible to depict women as fully autonomous beings and to express authoritatively her own vision of the world while drawing upon and responding almost exclusively to poetic texts by men, texts that generally convey the authors' assumption that the perspective, concerns, and experiences of men are central and quintessentially human.

At the height of her powers Barrett Browning was to rewrite in original and daring ways and from a woman's point of view some of the "masterpieces" of the Western European poetic tradition. But as works such as *The Battle of Marathon, An Essay on Mind,* and *The Seraphim* reveal, the poet's earliest attempts to write long poems led her to ignore, marginalize, or trivialize the experiences of women.[16] The fact that Barrett Browning wrote such poems at all, however, testifies to her audacity and rebelliousness. For in composing epics, verse dramas, and long philosophical-didactic poems, the poet was deliberately violating the existing norms governing the relationship between gender and genre. Refusing to restrict herself to the portrayal of domestic life and the expression of the affections, she insisted on being read and judged as a poet rather than as a "poetess"—insisted on writing about subjects that interested her, even if these subjects were ones about which a middle-class Victorian woman was supposed to be uninformed.[17]

In the third stage of her literary career, represented primarily by the two-volume collection of 1844, Barrett Browning continues to allude and respond to her poetic forefathers. But having discovered and begun to participate in a female poetic tradition, she no longer is so overwhelmed by the influence of male precursors that she adopts a male perspective on reality. On the contrary, she generally writes as a woman-identified woman, proclaiming that her central subject—the consciousness of woman—is a subject "more expressible by a woman than a man."[18]

"An Island," one of the best poems of the *Seraphim* volume, helps to account for Barrett Browning's transition from an immasculated to a woman-identified poet. In this poem a woman dreams of escaping from the violent and hierarchically-ordered world of patriarchy; she longs to settle with a few select others on an island which has neither weapons nor rulers. This peaceful and egalitarian island is clearly a motherland: it is a realm reserved for "Those who would [ex]change man's voice and use / For [a female] Nature's way and tone," a land of undulating, breast-like hills where maternal cows gaze approvingly upon "The warm mouths milking them for love" (111–112, 72). If she lived in this nurturing environment, the speaker proclaims, she could compose poems freely and easily, almost "Unconsciously" (143). She predicts that in the sweetness of their music her songs would rival those of Pindar, Æschylus, and Homer; indeed, she avers that her poetry would be superior to that of her forefathers because she would depict a world of harmony rather than one of strife and discord. In the concluding stanzas, however, the woman not only sadly acknowledges that her "island-place" does not exist, but she also expresses her fear that her fantasy of a world in which women's creativity is valued and nurtured is the product of a sinful mind, the dream of a woman who should be content to accept the world and the role that God has chosen for her.

Despite its ambiguous conclusion, "An Island" reveals that by 1836 Barrett Browning longed to ally herself with "two or three" who shared both her utopian dreams and the dissatisfaction with patriarchy that had prompted them. Fortunately, at about the time she composed "An Island" the poet found such an ally in Mary Russell Mitford, a writer who played an essential role in Barrett Browning's evolution as a feminist poet. For although she was to remark in 1850 that she could "never *count* upon her [Mitford] in poetry, of which, in my mind, she does not apprehend the essential qualities," it certainly was Mitford who urged Barrett Browning to study and consider emulating such popular and prolific poets as Letitia Landon, Felicia Hemans, Anna Barbauld, Mary Howitt, Joanna Baillie, Eliza Cook, Fanny Kemble Butler, Sara Clarke Lippincott, Anna Seward, Caroline Norton, Georgiana Bennet, and Maria Jane Jewsbury—poets from whose failures as well as successes Barrett Browning was to learn a great deal (Heydon and Kelley 20).[19] Moreover, it was in the pages of *Findens' Tableaux,* which Mitford edited in the late 1830s and early 1840s, that Barrett Browning first seems to have experimented self-consciously with the literary modes and devices that characterize some of the best and most representative poems by late eighteenth- and early nineteenth-century women writers.[20]

It is important to note, however, that Barrett Browning's debts to these poets are quite different in kind from her debts to her poetic forefathers. For rather than borrowing details from a particular poem or entering into a dialogical relationship with a specific female precursor, Barrett Browning writes about the subjects which interested her literary sisters and does so by using the tropes, imagery, and rhetorical strategies that distinguish much of the poetry written by women of the period 1780–1850 from that composed by men of the age. When drawing upon English women poets Barrett Browning generally responds not to particular texts but to an entire body of poetry, working within the confines of and expanding the possibilities of recognizable and distinctively female *types* of poems.

The female poetic tradition in which Barrett Browning began to participate is one in which authors take as their central subject matter and draw their metaphors from the lives of women. It is a tradition in which authors attempt to define the rights and duties of the Christian woman, portray the struggles and accomplishments of women artists, evaluate heterosexual relationships, depict the benefits of sisterhood, examine the process of female socialization, and ponder the degree to which women do and should participate in the economic and political life of the country. In addition, it is a tradition in which authors sometimes demonstrate their awareness that the fabric of Western society is woven of the intertwined threads of sexism, racism, and imperialism. Most English women poets of the period 1780–1850 write not only of the subjection of women, but also—and sometimes simultaneously—of the plight of Blacks, Native Americans, Irish Catholics, the poor, and politically-oppressed nations of the past and present.

To be sure, none of the poets mentioned above was a consistently vocal critic; in fact, each wrote a number of poems in which woman is presented as fragile and pure, as the obedient helpmate or helpless victim of man. Yet each also wrote a number of "protest poems" in which patriarchal values and institutions are criticized, though usually in indirect and covert rather than explicit ways. For example, these poets generally attribute heroic stature not to their English contemporaries, but to individuals of distant times or places who attempt to subvert existing power structures. In other poems, particularly those with contemporary settings, they encode rebellious sentiments in seemingly conventional texts; in such works, statements that seem to endorse patriarchal ideology are voiced ironically or ambiguously or are called into question by the poem's imagery or structure.

As is revealed by such explicitly topical protest poems as "The Cry of the Children" and "Lady Geraldine's Courtship," both of which appeared in the 1844 *Poems,* Barrett Browning soon was to become dissatisfied with such a palimpsestic method of recording her own and other women's concerns. Concluding that "puckerings in the silk," even when stitched by clever literary seamstresses, were more imprisoning than liberating, by late 1844 she was declaring to friends that in the future she was going to meet "face to face & without mask the Humanity [or Inhumanity?] of the age" (Kintner 1:31).[21] But in many of the poems published in the 1844 collection she uses the strategies of indirection as well as the tropes that characterize much of the verse of her poetic sisters and foremothers.

For example, these poets write frequently of a young girl's joyous appreciation of or an older woman's nostalgia for time spent alone—and usually creatively—in a bower, garden, or other spot in nature.[22] In such poems, the youthful female is not, like Tennyson's Lady of Shalott, "half sick of shadows" (71); on the contrary, she finds her privacy and her escape from social and domestic duties delightful. And the older woman does not, like the persona of Wordsworth's "Intimations Ode," celebrate and yearn for a time of "obstinate questionings / Of sense and outward things" (142–143). She *is* nostalgic, but what she laments is the loss of her belief that as an adult she could engage in meaningful, personally-chosen activities. Moreover, unlike the male personae of many of Wordsworth's poems, this middle-aged woman does not believe that she has received "Abundant recompense" for her loss ("Tintern Abbey" 88), nor does she characterize her experience as an inevitable and universal (that is, genderless) one. In "The Lost Bower" and "The Romance of the Swan's Nest" (1844) and "Hector in the Garden" (1846) Barrett Browning carries on this female tradition of articulating in a metaphorical and some-what veiled way the sadness a woman experiences when she realizes that for women, the transition from childhood to adulthood generally entails a loss of hope, self-esteem, and imaginative freedom.

Similarly, in poems like "The Romaunt of the Page" and "The Rhyme of the Duchess May," Barrett Browning follows her poetic sisters into the Mid-dle Ages, often envisioned by female poets as a time in which at least some women had control over their property and destiny and the courage to ven-ture into the "male" arenas of politics and war.[23] In such poems, Barrett Browning, like other women poets, uses an historical setting, the romance form, and in the case of "The Romaunt of the Page," ambiguous wording to hide from the unsympathetic reader the fact that she is protesting against middle-class Victorian definitions of the good wife and good daughter. In these poems the poet urges her female readers, as Carlyle had urged male readers of *Sartor Resartus* and *Past and Present,* to cast off their ill-fitting clothes and to benefit from both the wisdom and the mistakes of their forebears, in this case foremothers.

Countless other poems in the 1844 collection—"A Soul's Expression," "The Seraph and the Poet," "Work and Contemplation," "The Lay of the Early Rose," "Wine of Cyprus," and the two sonnets to George Sand, for example—reveal that as Barrett Browning began to view herself as carrying on a female as well as male poetic tradition her conception of God and of the poet began to change, to become more woman-centered. Perhaps the poem that best reveals the poet's growing determination to assert her independence from her poetic forefathers is *A Drama of Exile.*

A poetic drama that depicts the frame of mind of Adam and Eve imme-diately after they have been expelled from the Garden of Eden, *A Drama of Exile* is far from being a consummate artistic whole. Yet it is an unsuccessful poem precisely because the poet is determined to wrestle with the massive figure of Milton, with whom she closely identifies as a Christian but whose view of woman's subordinate status she wishes to refute. The product of this struggle is a poem that contains conflicting views of woman's rights and duties, a drama in which characters lack internal consistency, and a work in which passages vary greatly in poetic power, fluidity and grace. But though *A Drama of Exile* is riddled with the kind of ambiguity that detracts from rather than contributes to a poem's artistic success, it is a key text in Barrett Browning's poetic evolution and a poem that gives us great insight into the anxieties suffered by the woman poet working in a patriarchal society and within a male-dominated literary tradition. The same can be said of "The Lay of the Brown Rosary," a poem in which Barrett Browning unsuccessfully tries to fuse aspects of the female Gothic tradition with technical and thematic elements of poems by Keats, Wordsworth, and Coleridge.

If *Poems* of 1844 is the volume of a woman who is still suffering from anxieties of influence and who finds it somewhat "easier to gaze . . . On mournful masks and sad effigies / Than on real, live, weak creatures crushed by strong" (*Casa Guidi Windows* 1:46–48), *Poems* of 1850 is the volume of a poet who is drawing in a sophisticated way upon her dual poetic heritage, the work of a feminist who can be witty and playful as well as express righteous indignation. In "The Runaway Slave at Pilgrim's Point" Barrett Browning not only vehemently protests against slavery but also clearly spells out the connections between racism and sexism; in the companion poems "A Woman's Shortcomings" and "A Man's Requirements," she humorously but with equal directness and artistic skill exposes inequities in relationships between Victorian women and men. Moreover, having married a man who shared her desire to identify and combat the evils of patriarchy, she has the courage to make public *Sonnets from the Portuguese,* a poem in which she honestly recounts the vacillation between feelings of fear and joy, self-abasement and self-worth, that she experienced when she began to fall in love with Browning.

Reaffirming in another 1850 poem that the reed rather than the trumpet is her emblem, Barrett Browning announces that henceforth she will be the voice of women, children, and the common man rather than blast forth the "hollow" sounds of "priest or king" ("A Reed" 3–4). Pan, whom the poet associates with freedom, eroticism, and egalitarianism, is not so dead as the last poem of the 1844 collection seems (but only seems) to declare him to be. Moreover, by re-adopting as her symbol the reed of Pan, the playmate of nymphs who was bested by the more aloof and refined Apollo, Barrett Browning prepares us for her attempt to "blow all class-walls level as Jericho's" (*Aurora Leigh* 9.932) and for the literal and metaphorical union of female and male, pagan and Christian, that is at the heart of her subsequent and greatest poems.

One of these poems is *Casa Guidi Windows.* Writing with confidence about contemporary European politics, Barrett Browning unabashedly stakes her claim to a land into which most of her poetic foremothers had feared even to tread. In so doing, the poet weaves an ornate tapestry out of the three thematic strands that so frequently appear in her earlier poetry: the duties of the artist, the responsibilities of the Christian, and the rights of the oppressed. Having learned to value the wisdom and strength of mothers and to discriminate between good and bad fathers, in this poem Barrett Browning frankly and gratefully acknowledges her literary debts to "dead masters" yet proclaims: "We do not serve the dead" (1.217). Similarly, Barrett Browning the Christian invokes the aid of Christ and the Virgin Mary but castigates a Pope who has betrayed his charges, and Barrett Browning the citizen defends the dedicated freedom fighters of her adopted motherland while exposing the cowardice of a "paternal Duke" and the hypocrisy and crass materialism of her powerful fatherland. Finally, Barrett Browning the feminist praises the Italian women and men who are working together to combat their oppressors, but bitterly notes that in "liberal nations" there is "No help for women sobbing out of sight / Because men made the laws" (2.638–39). Almost succumbing to despair at the poem's conclusion, she recovers faith in the possibility of constructive change only when she remembers that some children, among them her own son, are being reared by parents committed to the establishment of a more egalitarian and just society.

In *Aurora Leigh,* an even more ambitious work, the formal and thematic characteristics of both male and female predecessors are welded into a unique, magnificent structure. A "verse novel" that owes much to the author's extensive reading of poems, fiction, and non-fiction prose by women; a first-person account of the growth and development of a woman poet's mind; "a Don Juan, without the mockery & impurity" of Byron, "admitting of much philosophical dreaming & digression" but "having unity, as a work of art" (Raymond and Sullivan 3:49); and a distinctively female envisioning of the kind of personal and societal paradise that has been lost and the means by which it may be regained, *Aurora Leigh* is certainly one of the most important long poems of the Victorian period. It also is one of the major works of the female literary tradition in English, for in *Aurora Leigh* the poet demonstrates that the epic mode can accommodate the experiences, language, and viewpoint of women.

Having proclaimed in *Aurora Leigh* that it is the task of great poets to represent both the glory and the corruption of "this live, throbbing age" (5.203), Barrett Browning continues in *Poems Before Congress* to write openly about the controversial social and political events of her time. But rather than sharing with her readers the observations and meditations of a woman safely ensconced in a Florentine apartment, the poet ventures into the more public arenas of "Italy and the World" and explicitly directs her comments to those who have the power to shape world affairs. Praising rulers who are helping to "deliver" Italy from the womb of a nation that has failed to nurture her, paying tribute to one Italian woman who nurses with equal tenderness dying freedom fighters of varying nationalities, and praising another who not only makes French soldiers regard Italian women with respect but who also creates an atmosphere in which French and Italian soldiers are moved to kiss one another "mouth to mouth," in *Poems Before Congress* Barrett Browning boldly advances a notion that had been covertly suggested in the political poems of many of her poetic foremothers and sisters: that the "mother-want about the world" (*Aurora Leigh* 1.40) can be eliminated only if individuals and nations become more womanly.[24] No longer asking—as she had in *Casa Guidi Windows*—to be absolved of an ardent idealism and emotionalism that she explicitly had labeled female, she firmly declares her belief that "A curse from the depths of womanhood / Is . . . good," essential to the apocalyptic transformation of society ("Prologue" to "A Curse for a Nation" 47–48).

Cursing of the power-hungry, apathetic, and cowardly is less evident, however, in the verses on Italy that appear in the posthumously published *Last Poems* (1862). The change in tone is due in part to the poet's belief that the Italian struggle for independence was succeeding, but even more to her growing awareness of the tragedy of war, even one fought for noble ends. Not surprisingly, the horrors of war are most powerfully depicted in poems that focus on the experiences of Italian women, the poet suggesting in both "Parting Lovers" and "Mother and Poet" that "daughters give up more than sons" when nations experience their "birth-pangs" ("PL" line 52, "MP" line 93).

But it is not just sympathy for the women of Italy that produces the best poems of Barrett Browning's last years; it is compassion for all women living in patriarchy. For example, in "Where's Agnes?" and "Lord Walter's Wife," the poet criticizes men who cannot or will not regard women as autonomous human beings and who therefore view women either as angelic creatures who "scarcely tread the earth" or as harlots, "mere dirt" ("Agnes" 86–87). And in poems such as "Void in Law," "Bianca Among the Nightingales," and "Amy's Cruelty," she openly characterizes men as selfish, untrustworthy, and exploitative, warning women that unless they use great caution when selecting a mate they may "forfeit all things" by loving ("Amy's Cruelty" 34). Thus Barrett Browning concludes her poetic career by firmly rejecting the notion that she had challenged only tentatively in *A Drama of Exile:* the notion that women, including women poets, must passively endure the "pressures of an alien tyranny / With its dynastic reasons of larger bones / And stronger sinews" (lines 1865–67).

Notes

1. Throughout her life Barrett Browning believed that emulating authors one admired benefited rather than harmed a writer. "There is no vanity, but rather wisdom, in following humbly [in] the footsteps of perfection," the poet announces in the preface to *The Battle of Marathon* (Porter and Clarke 1:9). She expresses the same sentiment thirty years later in *Casa Guidi Windows,* claiming that she could not "sing this song, / If my dead masters had not taken heed / To help the heavens and earth to make me strong" (1:432–34).

2. See, for example, Kaplan; Gilbert and Gubar, esp. 70, 189, 391, 547; Cooper, "Theory"; Zimmerman; Rosenblum; Mermin; and Hayter.

3. EBB's debts to women prose writers are explored in Kaplan; Donaldson; Hickok, " 'New Yet Orthodox' "; Holloway; Thomson; and Moser. Cooper comments on EBB's artistic interaction with other nineteenth-century women poets in Chapter 2 of her dissertation and discusses ways EBB's poetry differs from that of her literary sisters in "Working into Light."

4. As Showalter remarks, a woman writer "confronts both paternal and maternal precursors and must deal with the problems and advantages of both lines of inheritance. . . . The female tradition can be a positive source of strength and solidarity as well as a negative source of powerlessness; it can generate its own experiences and symbols which are not simply the obverse of the male tradition" (265).

5. See, for example, Miller's discussion of Emily Dickinson's revisions of the poems of her female contemporaries, especially Chapter 9.

6. For the most part, Barrett Browning shared her interest in the lives and writings of women authors with other women—initially with her mother, later with friends such as Anna Jameson, Mary Russell Mitford, Harriet Martineau, and Eliza Ogilvy. The influence that female relatives and friends exerted on Barrett Browning's development is a subject that needs to be explored further, particularly since Kelley and Hudson have demonstrated that it was Mary Moulton-Barrett rather than the poet's father who was "the prime motivator in EBB's early poetic development" (1:xxxiv).

7. To date, the only book-length study of early nineteenth-century English women's poetry (much of which is out of print) is Hickok's *Representations of Women.* My own study of the poetry women published in England during the period 1780–1850 was made possible by a grant from the Committee on Advanced Study and Research of Lafayette College, to whom I express my appreciation.

8. The phrase "a woman & man in one" appears in an 1844 letter to Mitford in which EBB notes that it is "a hard & difficult process for a woman to get forgiven for her strength by her grace. . . . [E]very woman of letters knows it is hard" (Raymond and Sullivan 3:38). In this paragraph I am not arguing that to be a great poet a woman *must* draw upon the works of predecessors of both sexes, but I believe that EBB held this view and that in many of her finest poems she works out of both a female and a male poetic tradition.

9. Although the phrase "forgets womanly duties in the personality of a man" is applied by EBB to Scott's Diana Vernon, it also describes the behavior of many of the female characters Edgeworth criticizes in her novels. For a thoughtful analysis of the way Edgeworth responds as a writer to her father's literary productions and views of women, see Hawthorne.

10. For other discussions of "immasculation" see Gilbert and Gubar; Cooper's "Theory"; Homans; Diehl; and Flynn and Schweickart, especially the essays by Schweickart, Schibanoff, and Fetterley (31–62, 83–106, 147–64).

11. A transcription of EBB's manuscript poem "Fragment of an 'Essay on Woman' " appears in *SBHC* 12 (1984), along with Moser's discussion of the ways EBB drew on *A Vindication of the Rights of Woman* when writing this poem.

12. The poems referred to are "On a Picture of Riego's Widow," "The Little Friend," and "To Bettine." The first was published with *An Essay on Mind* in 1826; the others appeared in the *Seraphim* volume. See also "To a Poet's Child" and "Isobel's Child," published in the collections of 1833 and 1838 respectively.

13. Among the poems in this category are "The Poet's Vow," "The Romaunt of Margaret," and "A Romance of the Ganges."

14. EBB's ambivalent feelings about her father are conveyed particularly well in a poem addressed to him on his thirty-third birthday (in which she subtly compares him to Pitt, "who made blest freedoms weep / His name") and in an untitled essay of 1827, written after her father had called her latest production "most wretched" (Kelley and Hudson 1.59–60, 361). The poet had no need to abase herself before Uvedale Price, who treated her with respect, but she had to actively combat the temptation to become the docile handmaiden of Hugh Stuart Boyd, who often behaved selfishly and maliciously. EBB's hostility towards Boyd is recorded frequently in her diary of 1831–32; see, for example, pp. 39 and 148 (Kelley and Hudson *Diary*).

15. In "The Book of the Poets" (1842), More is one of the writers EBB cites when arguing that during the second half of the eighteenth century England produced no great poets

(Porter and Clarke 6:298). Similarly, in a letter of December 1842 EBB asserts that Dacier was "a learned writer" but not "a woman of genius" (Raymond and Sullivan 2:136).

16.   In *The Battle of Marathon* (1820), Barrett Browning praises the Athenian warriors who defended their city-state against the Persians; the fact that the rights and privileges of Athenian democracy did not extend to women does not seem to disturb her. Moreover, the Greek commander, whom the poet repeatedly and without irony terms "sage," responds scornfully to the rousing speech of a patriotic Greek matron and steels his warriors for battle by proclaiming that the Persians "not as heroes, but as women fight; / Grovelling as proud, and cowardly as vain" (756–60, 977–78). Women are totally excluded from *An Essay on Mind* (1826), a work in which Barrett Browning pays tribute to countless males who have furthered the intellectual development of Western "man," and issues of gender are avoided in *The Seraphim* (1838), the poet viewing the crucifixion through "seraphic" rather than human eyes.

17.   In Book 2 of *Aurora Leigh,* Barrett Browning vehemently protests against those who urge women poets to limit themselves to expressing emotions with grace and delicacy and who then argue that poetry by women is inherently inferior to that by men.

18.   In the preface to the 1844 *Poems* EBB claims that Eve's state of mind after the fall is "more expressible by a woman than a man"; however, the phrase applies equally well to the other poems about women that appear in this collection.

19.   As the poem "Felicia Hemans" reveals, before meeting Mitford EBB was familiar with the verse of Hemans and Letitia Landon, the two most highly regarded English women poets of the 1820s and 1830s. But she does not seem to have read extensively or attentively poetry by other nineteenth-century women writers, most likely because she had internalized her male contemporaries' disparaging view of the productions of poetesses. Women poets are a frequent topic of discussion in EBB's letters to Mitford, however.

20.   EBB published the following poems in *Findens' Tableaux:* "A Romance of the Ganges," "The Romaunt of the Page," "The Dream" (later entitled "A Child Asleep"), and "Legend (later "The Lay") of the Brown Rosary."

21.   Although the second quotation comes from a February 1845 letter to Browning, EBB expresses the same desire to approach "the conventions of vulgar life . . . & touch this real everyday life of our age" in a December 1844 letter to Mitford (Raymond and Sullivan 3:49). The phrase "puckerings in the silk" is one spoken by Aurora Leigh, who frequently uses sewing as a metaphor for composing poetry. Aurora tells Romney: "I'm plain at speech, direct in purpose; when / I speak, you'll take the meaning as it is, / And not allow for puckerings in the silk / By clever stitches" (8.1127–30).

22.   Following is a partial list of this kind of "nature poem": Eliza Cook's "The Waters," "The Old Water-Mill," "The Old Mill Stream," "The Forest Brake," "When I Wore Red Shoes," and "Stanzas by the Sea-Side"; Maria Jane Jewsbury's "I am Come Back from my Bower," "A Remembered Scene," and "A Summer Eve's Vision"; Felicia Hemans' "To the Mountain Winds"; Letitia Landon's "Erinna," "A History of the Lyre," and "The Enchanted Island"; and Anna Barbauld's "Verses Written in an Alcove." The bower motif appears frequently in women's fiction as well as in women's poetry, as is demonstrated by Annis Pratt and her co-authors.

23.   The idea that women poets often wrote of the Middle Ages and were particularly fond of presenting female characters who disguised themselves as male pages was so common a notion that Frances Trollope could mock the phenomenon in her satirical *The Mother's Manual; or, Illustrations of Matrimonial Economy. An Essay in Verse* (64). Examples of this kind of poem include Landon's "The Vow of the Peacock," "Inez," and "The Castilian Nuptials," and Sara Clarke Lippincott's [alias Grace Greenwood] "Dreams." For other depictions of women of the Middle Ages see Hemans' "The Abencerrage," "The Widow of Crescentius," "Woman on the Field of Battle," "The Effigies," and "The Lady of Provence."

24.   References are to these poems: "Napoleon III. in Italy," "A Court Lady," and "The Dance."

Works Cited

Cooper, Helen. "Working Into Light: Elizabeth Barrett Browning." *Shakespeare's Sisters: Feminist Essays on Women Poets.* Ed. Sandra Gilbert and Susan Gubar Bloomington: Indiana UP, 1979, 65–81.

Cooper, Helen Margaret. "Elizabeth Barrett Browning: A Theory of Women's Poetry." Diss. Rutgers U, 1982.

de Beauvoir, Simone. *The Second Sex.* Ed. and trans. H.M. Parshley. New York: Random House, 1952.

Dickinson, Emily. *The Complete Poems of Emily Dickinson.* Ed. Thomas H. Johnson. Boston: Little, Brown, 1960.

Diehl, Joanne Feit. " 'Come Slowly—Eden': An Exploration of Women Poets and Their Muse." *Signs* 3 (1978): 572–87.

Donaldson, Sandra M. "Elizabeth Barrett's Two Sonnets to George Sand." *SBHC* 5 (1977): 19–22.

Fetterley, Judith. *The Resisting Reader: A Feminist Approach to American Fiction.* Bloomington: Indiana UP, 1978.

Flynn, Elizabeth A., and Patrocinio P. Schweickart, eds. *Gender and Reading: Essays on Readers, Texts, and Contexts.* Baltimore: Johns Hopkins UP, 1986.

Gilbert, Sandra, and Susan Gubar. *The Madwoman in the Attic: The Woman Writer and the Nineteenth-Century Literary Imagination.* New Haven: Yale UP, 1979.

Hawthorne, Mark D. *Doubt and Dogma in Maria Edgeworth.* U of Florida Monographs, The Humanities, 25. Gainesville: U of Florida P, 1967.

Hayter, Alethea. " 'These Men Over-Nice': Elizabeth Barrett Browning's 'Lord Walter's Wife'." *BSN* 8 (1978): 5–7.

Heydon, Peter N., and Philip Kelley, eds. *Elizabeth Barrett Browning's Letters to Mrs. David Ogilvy 1849–1861.* New York: Quadrangle and The Browning Institute, 1973.

Hickok, Kathleen. *Representations of Women: Nineteenth-Century British Women's Poetry.* Westport, CT: Greenwood, 1984.

Hickok, Kathleen K. " 'New Yet Orthodox': The Female Characters in *Aurora Leigh*." *International Journal of Women's Studies* 3 (1980): 479–89.

Holloway, Julia Bolton. "*Aurora Leigh* and *Jane Eyre*." *Brontë Society Transactions* 17 (1977): 126–32.

Homans, Margaret. *Women Writers and Poetic Identity: Dorothy Wordsworth, Emily Brontë, and Emily Dickinson.* Princeton: Princeton UP, 1980.

Kaplan, Cora. Introduction. *Elizabeth Barrett Browning: Aurora Leigh and Other Poems.* London: The Women's P, 1978.

Kelley, Philip, and Ronald Hudson, eds. *The Brownings' Correspondence.* 4 vols. Winfield, KS: Wedgestone Press, 1984–.

———. *The Unpublished Diary of Elizabeth Barrett Barrett, 1831–1832.* Athens: Ohio UP, 1969.

Kenyon, Frederic G., ed. *The Letters of Elizabeth Barrett Browning.* 2 vols. New York: Macmillan, 1899.

Kintner, Elvan, ed. *The Letters of Robert Browning and Elizabeth Barrett Barrett 1845–1846.* 2 vols. Cambridge, MA: Harvard UP, 1969.

Mermin, Dorothy. "The Female Poet and the Embarrassed Reader: Elizabeth Barrett Browning's *Sonnets from the Portuguese*." *ELH* 48 (1981): 351–67.

Miller, Ruth. *The Poetry of Emily Dickinson.* Middletown, CT: Wesleyan UP, 1968.

Moser, Kay. "Elizabeth Barrett's Youthful Feminism: Fragment of 'An Essay on Woman'." *SIB* 12 (1984): 13–26.

Porter, Charlotte, and Helen A. Clarke, eds. *The Complete Works of Elizabeth Barrett Browning.* 6 vols. New York: Thomas Y. Crowell, 1900.

Pratt, Annis, and others. *Archetypal Patterns in Women's Fiction.* Bloomington: Indiana UP, 1981.

Raymond, Meredith B., and Mary Rose Sullivan, eds. *The Letters of Elizabeth Barrett Browning to Mary Russell Mitford 1836–1854.* 3 vols. Winfield, KS: Armstrong Browning Library of Baylor University, The Browning Institute, Wedgestone Press, and Wellesley College, 1983.

Rosenblum, Dolores. "Face to Face: Elizabeth Barrett Browning's *Aurora Leigh* and Nineteenth-Century Poetry." *VS* 26 (1983): 321–38.

Showalter, Elaine. "Feminist Criticism in the Wilderness." *The New Feminist Criticism: Essays on Women, Literature, and Theory.* New York: Pantheon, 1985.

Thomson, Patricia. *George Sand and the Victorians: Her Influence and Reputation in Nineteenth-century England.* New York: Columbia UP, 1977.

Trollope, Frances. *The Mother's Manual: or, Illustrations of Matrimonial Economy. An Essay in Verse.* London: Treuttel and Würtz, 1833.

Woolf, Virginia. *"Aurora Leigh." Collected Essays of Virginia Woolf.* Ed. Leonard Woolf. New York: Harcourt, Brace and World, 1953.

Wordsworth, William. *The Poetical Works of Wordsworth.* Ed. Paul D. Sheats. Boston: Houghton Mifflin, 1982.

Zimmerman, Susan. *"Sonnets from the Portuguese:* A Negative and a Positive Context." *Mary Wollstonecraft Newsletter* 2 (1973): 1–11.

Stirring "a Dust of Figures":
Elizabeth Barrett Browning and Love

Angela Leighton

> This word is not enough but it will have to do.
>
> (Margaret Atwood, "Variations on the Word *Love*," 83)

Not only is the word "love" not enough; it is also too much. Its meaning is prolific. Love serves, as Atwood specifies, for the lacy, heart-shaped card, the expensive body lotion, the patriotic war song; even, perhaps, for the cool copulation of slugs. "Then," she adds, "there's the two / of us" (83).

Variations on the word "love" range from a creed to a cliché, a psychosis to a social contract, a pious mysticism to a crude commercialism. Personal or political, holy or obscene, literal or metaphorical, to talk about love as opposed, for instance, to sex, marriage or desire, is to have a constant problem of reference. It would be easier not to talk about it at all. Yet this problem of reference is part of the point. Love, in a way, includes sex, marriage and desire, but it also suggests something more: a residue—sentimental and nostalgic, maybe—of all the quantifiable terms of our social and sexual politics. Love is something left over:—just a superfluous word, perhaps.

The twentieth century's reaction against the Victorians, as well as its obsession with them, tends to focus on the problem of love. The continuing popularity of works such as *The Barretts of Wimpole Street,* for instance, bears witness to our own fascination with hypocrisy and repression. We flatter ourselves at the spectacle of the Victorians' sexual mystifications. We *enjoy* the "repressive hypothesis" (Michel Foucault, 10) which seems to confirm our superior sexual enlightenment. Yet, it may be, that far from being the detectives of the Victorians' hidden *crimes passionnels,* we are, ourselves, the criminals; ourselves, the "Victorians." The theory of repression is one which depends on reducing the open possibilities of love to the closed meaning of sex.

Reprinted from *Browning Society Notes* 17, nos. 1–3 (1987/88): 11–23. Used by permission of the publisher.

Meanwhile, however, our own repression goes unnoticed. Having made no secret of sex, we have, perhaps, to invoke Foucault again (35), made a verbose and degraded secret of love. Sentimentalised, commercialised or simply ridiculed, love is, it may be, our own peculiarly obsessive taboo. We speak of it scornfully, guiltily or coyly. Yet, somehow, we do go on speaking about it. In all its debased and specific variations, love offers us still a possibility of meaning—a precarious idealism. It is, as Atwood concludes:

> a finger-
> grip on a cliffside. You can
> hold on or let go.
>
> (83)

Psychoanalytical and feminist discussions of love, while assimilating it into the Oedipal drama, on the one hand, or into the discourse of sexual politics, on the other, have also, often, felt something unaccounted for. Freud has influentially linked love with narcissism, but both Lacan and Kristeva have since wanted to loosen that connection. "The lover is a narcissist with an *object*" (250), Kristeva declares. Feminist critics, particularly in the early seventies, have been emphatic in denouncing the oppressive ideology of romantic love. Shulamith Firestone, for instance, asserts that "love, perhaps, even more than childbearing, is the pivot of women's oppression today" (142), and Kate Millett, similarly, dismisses love as no more than a pious Victorian excuse for "sexual activity" (37), particularly the sexual activity of women. Other feminist critics, however, have sought to distinguish love from the social and psychological inequalities which vitiate it. Love, for de Beauvoir, when "founded on the mutual recognition of two liberties" (677), might still be an ideal for the future. Thus, however much decried or explained, love continues to suggest something over and above the calculable power-structures of society or of the mind—something, perhaps, to be desired.

It is this superfluity of meaning which Roland Barthes celebrates in *A Lover's Discourse*. Rejecting the antagonistic or reductive descriptions of love in Christian, psychoanalytical and Marxist discourse (211), he turns, in his linguistic bereavement, to the language of imaginative literature. In particular, he turns to the wordy, profligate, posturing conventions of the literature of Sensibility. It is Goethe's *Werther* which, above all, offers innumerable examples of the discourse of love. Such a discourse, which indulgently "puts the sentimental in place of the sexual" (178) is, in fact, Barthes claims, the scandalous subject of today.

This reversal of priorities reiterates the principles of a long tradition. As Denis de Rougemont argues in *Love in the Western World*, romantic love, which is rooted in the courtly literature of the twelfth and thirteenth centuries, constantly resists its material expenditure in either sexual satisfaction or social bonding (15). It is a sentiment, satisfied in the indefinite postponement of its final gratification. In that postponement, the lover finds time to speak. "Passion and expression are not really separable" (173), de Rougemont claims. Rather, it is a passion *for* expression which characterises romantic love. In this tradition, "the sentimental" does not aim to become "the sexual," but rather to postpone it.

Juliet Mitchell, in an essay on "Romantic Love," complains that de Rougemont generalises entirely from the experience of the male. The love of women is different, she claims. For, while man's love is "the poetic utterance of a free, aspiring subject," woman's love remains the "opiate of a trapped sexual object" (108). The trouble with this distinction, however, is that it confirms as an absolute the very difference it would condemn. Mitchell's assertion that the "romantic love of women looks forward, forward to marriage" (114) is one which seems to assign to women only the bourgeois domestication of love, and denies them its rebellious, imaginative energies. The evidence of women's literature, from the letters of Heloise to the poems of Adrienne Rich, tells a different story.

"Marriage in the abstract," Elizabeth Barrett Browning wrote to Miss Mitford in February 1846, at a time when her thoughts might well have been running on marriage, "has always seemed to me the most profoundly indecent of all ideas. . . ." She adds: "I have always been called romantic for this way of seeing" (III, 160). It is one of the sad ironies of EBB's reputation as a poet that later generations have called her "romantic" for quite different reasons. She has gone down in literary history as the invalid poetess, who was swept off her couch, and rescued from a tyrannical father, by a charming poet with whom she eloped to Italy. As testimony to this eminently satisfying romance, she wrote, everyone knows, *one* poem: "How do I love thee? Let me count the ways" (Sonnet XLIII). Many of EBB's most appreciative critics have found the *Sonnets from the Portuguese* something of a stumbling block. For instance, Alethea Hayter complains of having a "Peeping Tom sensation" (105) when reading the Sonnets, though, surprisingly, she never feels it when reading the "love letters" (106). Recent feminist critics, such as Gilbert and Gubar and Cora Kaplan, tend to pass over these ideologically unfashionable poems. Somehow, their subject and their inspiration, which lack the larger sexual politics of *Aurora Leigh,* strike contemporary critics as naked and naive. They are, it is said with wearying regularity, simply too "sincere."[1]

However, it may be that sincerity is an inhibition of our own expectations, rather than a fault of the poems. The story of the popular romance continues to overshadow our reading. But the emotional drama of the Sonnets has, in fact, little to do with a despotic father, an invalid daughter and a miraculous elopement. Instead, that drama is to be found in the close and self-conscious connection with the love letters—themselves a highly *written* text. It is as a literary performance, rather than an autobiographical statement, that I want to look again at the writing of these poems.

To read the Sonnets afresh, in conjunction with the letters, is to become aware of an intricately answering and over-wrought writing of love. In both poems and letters, sincerity of feeling is not so much the motivation as the point in question. The correspondence, which has been hailed as one of the great documents of romantic love, is in fact as prolix and literary as any other substitution of "the sentimental" for "the sexual." The passion of these letters is a passion of too many words, at odds with life and the heart's true feelings. For all their intimate wrangling, the general effect of the letters is of a highly constructed and self-referential piece of collaborative writing.

It is true that Robert's are the more contorted, defensive and equivocal letters. But the idea that Elizabeth was the inspirationally simpler and sincerer poet of the two reflects, as Daniel Karlin (52) points out, much more on Robert's need to idealise her than on any quality of her verse. She no more "communicates with godlike directness" (205) than he does. The *Sonnets from the Portuguese,* in particular, elaborate many of the anxieties of the letters about the possibility of communicating the heart's true feelings. The theatrical landscapes and stylised imagery of these poems distances them, strangely, from the real scene of love. Furthermore, there is a certain, quietly playful instability of reference in the Sonnets, which gives them an air of being very often only half serious.

> BELOVED, thou hast brought me many flowers
> Plucked in the garden, all the summer through
> And winter, and it seemed as if they grew
> In this close room, nor missed the sun and showers.
> So, in the like name of that love of ours,
> Take back these thoughts which here unfolded too,
> And which on warm and cold days I withdrew
> From my heart's ground. Indeed, those beds and bowers
> Be overgrown with bitter weeds and rue,
> And wait thy weeding; yet here's eglantine,
> Here's ivy!—take them, as I used to do
> Thy flowers, and keep them where they shall not pine.
> Instruct thine eyes to keep their colours true,
> And tell thy soul their roots are left in mine.
>
> (Sonnet XLIV)

As Elizabeth waited during those many months of courtship for Robert to visit her, or for his letters to arrive, she wrote the poems which she offered in return for all his flowers, but which she did not show him until three years after their marriage. However, it is not only his actual gifts of flowers which she remembers and requites in this last of her Sonnets, but also the many shared double meanings of flowers throughout the correspondence. Flowers are the connecting image of love and poetry, of passion and expression. The first gift was Robert's, in that opening letter with its extraordinarily direct declaration of literary esteem: "so into me has it gone, and part of me has it become, this great living poetry of yours, not a flower of which but took root and grew—oh how different that is from lying to be dried and pressed flat, and prized highly and put in a book . . ." (I, 3). Yet, of course, the having been "put in a book" is precisely the original tenor of these flowers, just as it will be their last in EBB's sonnet. Flowers begin as poems, "pressed flat and put in a book," and only later spring roots in the heart.

This opening gambit supplies both correspondents with a wealth of playful variations on the theme of flowers. In them, the usual priorities of what is lived and what is written are upset. Poetry, Elizabeth declares, "is the flower of me." She adds that "the rest of me is nothing but a root, fit for the ground and the dark" (I, 65). Between the flower and the root, between poems and life's "ground," there is a discrepancy; just as later, in the sonnet, there is a break between the flower's expression and the "heart's ground" from which it comes. These flowers, though once grounded, have been plucked. Obedient to her imagery, Robert repeats the idea: "this is all the flower of my life which you call forth and which lies at your feet" (I, 352). But the flower which is uprooted is not really life's; it is poetry's and love's. Robert tells her: "this is my first song, my true song—this love I bear you" (I, 352). Love is already the song, and the flower is already what it might become: a poem. For Elizabeth it did; and, as if in proof of what flowers might be, she returned, so many years later, her own small "anthology" of poems, which she had not yet dared "put in a book."

The play on flowers throughout the courtship offers a continual, delight-ful, metaphorical substitution of one thing for another: poems, flowers, life, love, memories, flowers and poems, again. The "ground" of these figurative transformations ought to be the heart, but it is just as often already a book of poems. Heart and book are subtly interchangeable, as if in quiet acknowl-edgement of the fact that they were interchangeable at the start: "I love your verses with all my heart, dear Miss Barrett" (I, 3). This witty and self-conscious play on flowers, however, throws into dark relief that comment of Robert's, when he remembered how a "strange, heavy crown, that wreath of Sonnets (was) put on me one morning unawares" (*Robert Browning and Julia Wedgwood*, 114). Whether the "wreath" was one of laurels for her, or of death to himself, remains to be guessed.

The *Sonnets from the Portuguese* were published in 1850 and, as William Going has noted, they resuscitated an outworn genre (19). The amatory son-net sequence, before the Victorian flowering of the form, was largely confined to the sixteenth century. It is, therefore, as Cynthia Grant Tucker points out, a "literary mode" clearly associated with "a bygone age," and riddled with "old generic postures and conventions" (353). One of these "generic postures" which the Victorians revived, for reasons that may have been socially contem-porary as well as imaginatively nostalgic, was that of the woman who waits.

One particular poem, which stands at the threshold of the age, seems to have been profoundly influential in the recovery of this pose:

> All day within the dreamy house,
> The doors upon their hinges creak'd
> The blue fly sung in the pane; the mouse
> Behind the mouldering wainscot shriek'd,
> Or from the crevice peer'd about.
> Old faces glimmer'd thro' the doors,
> Old footsteps trod the upper floors,
> Old voices called her from without.
> She only said, "My life is dreary,
> He cometh not," she said;
> She said, "I am aweary, aweary,
> I would that I were dead!"
>
> (Tennyson, "Mariana," 90)

Tennyson's "Mariana" captures, not only the ennui of the woman's waiting, but also the pressure of a literary tradition behind that waiting. Only a woman could be so trapped in hopelessness. But at the same time, Mariana's is no more than an old literary pose—a waiting, in the courtly tradition, which is almost for its own sake. Tennyson's poem is ghostly with literariness. Not only is it a text, written on the inspiration of another text; but it also seems to want to go back in time to its literary original. The house suffers from the dilapidation of ages, and the past haunts its precincts in those "Old faces," "Old footsteps," "Old voices." The "dreamy house" is actually a house *of* dreams: from the antique. Although the atmosphere of courtly love is curiously decadent for the Victorian poet, and the passion of expectation somehow stale, the "old generic postures and conventions" are the same: Mariana waits.

Dorothy Mermin writes that a "woman poet who identified herself with such a stock figure of intense and isolated art would hardly be able to write at all" (68).[2] But this is not quite true. "I am like Mariana in the moated grange and sit listening too often to the mouse in the wainscot" (I, 87), Elizabeth informs Robert. The figure of Mariana offers her both a literally apt, and a subtly desirable, description of herself. "For have I not felt twenty times the desolate advantage of being insulated here and of not minding anybody when I made my poems? . . . and caring less for supposititious criticism than for the black fly buzzing in the pane?" (I, 263), she asks. Tennyson's imagery of fixation and distraction offers EBB, as it will Christina Rossetti, an eerily appropriate picture of her self. To be the maiden in the tower, the woman at the window, the dreamer in the prison, is to inhabit a literary tableau which is very close to the facts of life. Certainly, Elizabeth waited, and kept Robert waiting. Christina Rossetti made a life's work of waiting—and turned away any lovers who did come. Her poem "Day-Dreams" is "Mariana" from another, equally disconcerting, angle:

> Cold she sits through all my kindling,
> Deaf to all I pray:
> I have wasted might and wisdom,
> Wasted night and day:
> Deaf she dreams to all I say.
>
> ("Day-Dreams," 333)

It is as if these women poets sometimes choose to inhabit the "dreamy house" of Mariana, but with attention turned inwards to its poetic possibilities: to the "Old voices" which still echo in the ruined house of love. The "lover's discourse," Barthes claims, "is no more than a dust of figures stirring according to the unpredictable order, like a fly buzzing in a room" (197).

If the love poetry of the Victorians very often stirs "a dust of figures" from the antique, EBB's *Sonnets from the Portuguese,* which have by turns delighted or embarrassed readers for their sincerity, are certainly no exception.

> THOU hast thy calling to some palace-floor,
> Most gracious singer of high poems! where
> The dancers will break footing, from the care
> Of watching up thy pregnant lips for more.
> And dost thou lift this house's latch too poor
> For hand of thine? and canst thou think and bear
> To let thy music drop here unaware
> In folds of golden fulness at my door?
> Look up and see the casement broken in,
> The bats and owlets builders in the roof!
> My cricket chirps against thy mandolin.
> Hush, call no echo up in further proof
> Of desolation! there's a voice within
> That weeps . . . as thou must sing . . . alone, aloof.
>
> (Sonnet IV)

This is much more Mariana in the moated grange than it is EBB in Wimpole Street. The imagery of courtly luxury and mouldering decay belongs to a long tradition of romantic love, which the poet inhabits like the ruined house itself. She sits, picturesquely, amid a scene of desolation, listening, like her prototype Mariana, for the "lifted latch," and aware of too many echoes. The whole poem is a stage-setting of love in some "far countree" of the imagination. Singing, playing, dancing, weeping, are all decorous items of a drama self-distanced in time and feeling. It is this tapestried effect of the language which gives to the *Sonnets from the Portuguese* their atmosphere of a "bygone" passion. This is not a spontaneous, but a remembered and remote poetry of love, haunted by figures stirring from another time, another literature: "bats and owlets builders in the roof!"

However, at their best, these Sonnets also have a quietly discordant sense of humour. They are not just period pieces. "My cricket chirps against thy mandolin" is a welcome interruption of that too consistently "golden" music, attributed to Robert, the serenader. Thus the courtly or mythological imagery is frequently subjected to small witticisms and pranks of action. The moments when the instrument proves out of tune, angels collide, a god turns out to be a porpoise, the poet's hair is liable to catch fire, or a mystic shape draws the speaker familiarly "by the hair"—these are moments when the static iconography of courtly love is playfully disrupted, and the once immovable lady is caught up in a quite lively drama. It remains, however, a bookish drama, dependent on the written tangles of the letters, much more than on the actual events in Wimpole Street. The minstrels, princes, angels, palm trees and porpoises of these Sonnets belong to that rarefied, but fertile, drama of the correspondence, where the two poets find occasion to be both in love, and also practising for poems.

To fix the *Sonnets from the Portuguese* as an autobiographical record of a true romance is to miss their literary playfulness, their in-jokes, even, at times, their competitive ingenuity. But above all, it is to miss their sense of the other, remote, difficult language of love, which is inherited from a long-ago of literature, and which threatens to substitute its "Old voices" for the new; its flowers of poetry for real flowers. This is the danger, but also the "desolate advantage," of writing about love. Through the gruellingly *written* story of the letters and the Sonnets there is felt, in counterpoint to love's earnest, love's other language, which is separate, strange and insincere.

"As for me," Elizabeth writes at one point, "I have done most of my talking by post of late years—as people shut up in dungeons, take up with scrawling mottos on the walls" (I, 13). The scene of writing, for this woman poet, is the prison; so that, she suggests, all her letters will have the desperate and dissociated quality of a writing on the wall. This, already at the beginning, rejects Robert's idealisation of her as the poet of unmediated expression. Her woman's confinement means that all her writing will seem like vivid, but hardly decipherable, "mottos." Certainly, the experience of reading Elizabeth's letters must soon have disabused Robert of his idealising simplification. As he admits, he was frequently bewildered by her twists of logic. Often, she puts him " 'in a maze' " (I, 474); he is jealous of her "infinite adroitness" (I, 533); he is beaten by her seeming to turn his "illustrations into obscurations" (I, 558); till, at one point, he turns on her almost violently, with the declaration: "Sometimes I have a disposition to dispute with dearest Ba, to wrench her simile-weapons out of the dexterous hand ... and have the truth of things my way and its own way, not hers" (I, 562). This peevish insistence on the truth being his own betrays the extent to which Robert felt threatened by Elizabeth's own rhetoric. The "truth of things" is at risk in the very similes she wields so dexterously and combatively.

The quarrels of these lovers are not so much quarrels of feeling, as of ety-mologies and meanings. They censor each other's scripts, and cavil at each other's turns of phrase. They both, also, contend passionately to have the last word. "I *must* have last word," Robert insists, "as all people in the wrong desire to have—and then, no more of the subject" (I, 80). But immediately, Elizabeth makes her own claim to be last: "but suffer me to say as one other last word, (and *quite, quite the last this time!*) . . . " (I, 82). As each new dispute develops between them, the imposition of a last word continues to be laid down. "Therefore we must leave this subject—and I must trust you to leave it without one word more." She adds, with pointed vagueness, "too many have been said already" (I, 179). Too many words is the danger and the temp-tation of romantic love. Towards the end of the correspondence, Robert admits how often his letters have "run in the vile fashion of a disputatious 'last word', 'one word yet' " (II, 1058). Yet, the continuing drama of the last word was to prove a fecund source of poetry to him. The poem he wrote, years later, to thank Elizabeth for her Sonnets, affectionately recalls the con-tentious wordiness of the letters: it is "One Word More."

The literature of romantic love is always, in a sense, a word too many. Self-expression becomes its own goal. As de Rougemont puts it, romantic love "tends to self-description, either in order to justify or intensify its being, or else simply in order to keep *going*" (173). One word more is one more poem. Yet, this very creative resourcefulness of words risks being at odds with a sense of the truth. It is perhaps to Elizabeth that Robert ascribes the weary plea of that other poem of a last word, which recalls the furious verbalising of the letters. The speaker of "A Woman's Last Word" begs:

> Let's contend no more, Love,
> Strive nor weep:
> All be as before, love,
> —Only sleep!
> ("A Woman's Last Word", I, 539)

Love may be, on the one hand, a rhetoric of too many words, but, on the other hand, love also seeks to put an end to words altogether. "I love you because I *love* you" (I, 245), Robert insists, offering the redundancy of the logic as an emotional security. But such security is achieved at the cost of words. As Barthes puts it, "I love you because I love you" is a line that marks "the end of language, where it can merely repeat *its last word* like a scratched record" (21). Yet, a poem must be more than "a scratched record." There are times when Robert sounds trapped between the minimalist statement of love, which Elizabeth demands of him, and the one word more that must be writ-ten, if poems are to continue. "I turn from what is in my mind," he declares, "and determine to write about anybody's book to avoid writing that I love and love and love again my own, dearest love—because of the cuckoo-song of it" (I, 329).

When EBB attempts to write the "cuckoo-song," the reductive obviousness of it risks spoiling the poem:

> SAY over again, and yet once over again,
> That thou dost love me. Though the word repeated
> Should seem "a cuckoo-song," as thou dost treat it,
> Remember, never to the hill or plain,
> Valley and wood, without her cuckoo-strain
> Comes the fresh Spring in all her green completed.
> Belovèd, I, amid the darkness greeted
> By a doubtful spirit-voice, in that doubt's pain
> Cry, "Speak once more—thou lovest!" Who can fear
> Too many stars, though each in heaven shall roll,
> Too many flowers, though each shall crown the year?
> Say thou dost love me, love me, love me—toll
> The silver iterance! only minding, Dear,
> To love me also in silence with thy soul.
>
> (Sonnet XXI)

Between the silence of the soul and the poem's proliferating figures— between words which are not enough and those which are too much—the poet lover must negotiate a kind of truth. In this sonnet EBB fails to find it, perhaps for insisting too much on the "cuckoo-song" at the expense of a more playful rhetoric.

There is one delightful passage in a letter of Elizabeth's where she directly confronts the problem of living and loving so much in words. She is correcting Robert's "The Book of the Duchess" and is puzzled at having seemed to have lost a "bad line" which she cannot locate in the poem. She realises, with undisguised pleasure, that she must have written the line herself. "And so it became a proved thing to me," she relates, "that I had been enacting, in a mystery, both poet and critic together—and one so neutralizing the other, that I took all that pains you remark upon to cross myself out in my double capacity . . . and am now telling the story of it notwithstanding. And there's an obvious moral to the myth, isn't there? for critics who bark the loudest, commonly bark at their own shadow in the glass, as my Flush used to do long and loud . . . and as I did, under the erasure." She continues, irresistibly: "And another moral springs up of itself in this productive ground; for, you see . . . quand je m'efface il n'y a pas grand mal' " (I, 145).

In this fine piece of structuralism before its time, the "productive ground" of meaning is the act of writing itself. From that "productive ground" many flowers may grow, and many kinds of morals may spring. It is indeed a fertile origin. Thus, as Elizabeth cancels her own line, she also cancels herself, her face in the mirror, her role as critic and her role as bad poet. But, in the end, as she gaily tells, someone is left over from all the cancellations, to tell "the story of it notwithstanding." Out of a "bad line" she spins a good tale, and out of her self-effacement she irresistibly pursues the proliferating figures of a game of words. In any case, one might ask, what was she doing *writing* in Robert's poem?

" 'Quand je m'efface il n'y a pas grand mal.' " The lover's discourse, according to Barthes, "proceeds from others, from the language, from books." He concludes, "no love is original" (136). The "dreamy house" is haunted by other voices. The text of feeling has been written already. This *déjà vu,* or rather, *déjà écrit,* inevitably turns the lover's passion into a pose; the lover's poem into another, older one. Feeling suffers the anxiety of having been preempted by literature.

The innumerable references to other texts in the letters, as well as the innumerable self-references to the act of writing, bear witness to this pressure. For instance, it is not only Tennyson's "Mariana" which supplies a figure of love, but also EBB's own poem "Catarina to Camoens." Catarina was the courtly lady loved by the poet Camoens, but she died while waiting for him to return from his long travels. The poem is the last and only word of one who experienced love so entirely in the "sentimental" that all she experienced was a set of lovely phrases. As she repeats the line from one of Camoens' own songs: " 'Sweetest eyes were ever seen!' " (3, 124), she wonders what use to her either the sweetness of her eyes, or the sweetness of his poem, will be, once she is dead.

Sonnets from the Portuguese, as is well known, is the title that was suggested by Robert, as a disguise. It hints at a translation—specifically, it hints at Camoens, some of whose works had been translated by Felicia Hemans, and who was well known to the Victorian public in Strangford's translation as well. The title thus serves as a distraction from the autobiographical origins of the Sonnets. But the title hints at Camoens by way of EBB's own, very popular, "Catarina to Camoens." In a sense, therefore, "from the Portuguese" means, not only from Camoens, but also from Catarina—the woman who waited, to no avail. Like Christina Rossetti, in her *Monna Innominata* sonnets, EBB seems to speak from the generic pose of the unknown lady of the courtly tradition—anonymous and foreign—whose indefinitely postponed love becomes the occasion for poems instead. The title thus stresses the effect of distance, in time and place, which the language of the poems themselves underlines.

That the *Sonnets from the Portuguese* take their place in a long, self-conscious tradition of literary writing about love is also suggested by one other possible connotation of the title. In 1678, there appeared in English translation a series of five letters, written allegedly by a Portuguese nun to her unfaithful lover. The *Portuguese Letters,*[3] as they were known, started a vogue for writing "à la portuguaise,"—in a style of declamatory despair which later became the stock-in-trade of the literature of Sensibility. Through the posturing rhetoric of the nun's grief there runs a vein of almost self-satisfied achievement. "And it is not your Person neither that is so dear to me," she asserts, "but the Dignity of my unalterable Affection" (17). It is in the cause of love alone, that she is driven to tell "at every turn how my Pulse beats" (21). That the *Portuguese Letters* were probably fictitious, and not written by a nun at all, only makes them the more characteristic of a literature in which feeling is a matter of fine words, and truth a matter of convention. The very name of the nun is resonantly premonitory of that most stereotypical name in the literature of Sensibility: "Ah wretched *Mariane!*" (5) she exclaims.

Thus the title, *Sonnets from the Portuguese,* is one that teases with a wealth of literary connotations. It proposes a translation; it remembers another poem; it echoes, perhaps, the highly literary disposition of the Portuguese nun herself. However, the sense of derivativeness—the sense of a text remembering some other original—is a connotation which finds support, not only in these specific references, but also in a recurring anxiety about the language of feeling, expressed in the letters of both poets. The "dust of figures stirring" in the title of *Sonnets from the Portuguese* is not just a dust flung in the eyes of "Peeping Tom" readers. It is not just a decoy. It is also a quiet revelation. The idea of translation—of mediating what is remote and foreign—of writing at a distance from the original—is an idea that finds considerable support in certain preoccupations of both Robert's and Elizabeth's letters.

Elizabeth's early descriptions of herself as a prisoner "scrawling mottos on the walls," with its admission of a displaced intensity and of an alienated sensibility, is one which then gathers a cluster of related images in the course of the correspondence. Taking her cue, at first, from Robert's unnerving declarations of having a double nature, Elizabeth gradually recognises the same doubleness in herself. Far from being the prototype of the inspirationally direct poet, she too knew the discrepant passage from consciousness to writing, from love to love poetry. That Robert also eventually recognised this equivalent obliquity in *her* work is perhaps revealed by one of those characteristically answering images between the letters and the poems. Near the start of the correspondence, Elizabeth acknowledges that all Robert's verse is a dramatic displacement of himself: "your rays fall obliquely rather than directly straight," she admits, and adds, humbly, "I see you only in your moon" (I, 22). This sense of the moon, as the indirect reflector of light, is remembered, and returned, perhaps, in that resonant line from "One Word More," where Robert calls Elizabeth: "my moon of poets!" (I, 742). She too, he seems to admit, has her unknown, dark side, and her own mediations of the light.

The idea that feeling is often refracted, and expression mediated, is one which finds a recurring description in the letters. After Elizabeth returned that first, over-enthusiastic letter of Robert's, in which, it seems, he declared his feelings for her too impetuously or fulsomely, he retaliated by assuring her, in his reply, that she had mistaken both him and his intentions. Cruelly driving the message home, he stressed that there were "huge layers of ice and pits of black cold water" in his character, and that those were his "true part" (I, 74). Elizabeth was haunted by the implications of this simile for years. At the time, however, she answered with unaggrieved dignity: "Well—if I do not know you, I shall learn, I suppose, in time. I am ready to try humbly to learn—and I may perhaps—if you are not done in Sanscrit, which is too hard for me" (I, 79). A little later, in her frustration at being idealised out of her own true nature, she retorted with a similar image, and begged Robert to "determine to read me no more backwards with your Hebrew, putting in your own vowel points without my leave" (I, 87). He, in his turn, jumped at the opportunity offered by her mis-reading and mis-correcting one of his poems: "So you can decypher my *utterest* hieroglyphic?" (I, 153) he mocked, hinting again that the language of his true self might be indecipherable.

The idea of the illegible script, the strange text, the foreign language, frequently has a double reference, to the heart and to the book, to the self and the poem. Reading and writing thus become the primary gestures of love's drama, subject to all the tricky and deceptive calligraphies of the heart. The difficulty of knowing the true from the false, the sincere from the convention, the familiar from the foreign, is a dilemma exacerbated by the very verbal nature of romantic love. The more the difference is insisted on, the more elusive does it become. Thus, even as Robert expresses his ambition to write the perfectly self-expressive, unmediated text—" 'R.B. a poem' " (I, 17)—he is frustrated by the difference between the two. The self does not translate easily into poetry. For when he reads "the language" of himself to himself, he reads a "spiritual Attic" (I, 38), communicable to none.

But it is not only Robert who defensively distances himself in doubleness and foreignness. The same split is felt by Elizabeth. When, towards the end of *Aurora Leigh*, Romney enthusiastically claims to have understood her at last, after reading her poems, Aurora answers curtly:

> You have read
> My book, but not my heart; for recollect,
> 'Tis writ in Sanscrit, which you bungle at.
> (*Aurora Leigh*, VIII, 475–7)

That "recollect" goes all the way back to the letters, and is Elizabeth's pointed response to the fear that Robert himself was "done in Sanscrit."

Thus, the idea that the language of the heart is hard to learn, easily misunderstood, dauntingly foreign, is one that runs through the letters. Such a language is likely to be archaic and difficult—perhaps permanently beyond reach. Elizabeth might assure Robert that "you could turn over every page of my heart like the pages of a book" (I, 274–5), but she cannot promise that the language in which the book is written will be understood. The evidence of many of the letters is that it will not. For if "writ in Sanscrit," it is "too hard." It will remain untranslatable.

The language of romantic love, even when written in the heart, is a language likely to be foreign, strange, dead. It is written already, out of old codes, old conventions, old poems, perhaps. The difficulty of making it legible again is the constant anxiety of the lover poet. To write about love, originally and uniquely, might be, in fact, to engage in an act of translation. "I have done some work," Elizabeth responds evasively, "only it is nothing worth speaking of . . . lyrics for the most part, which lie written illegibly in pure AEgyptian" (I, 145). Her own suggested title for the Sonnets is only another obstructively remote and puzzling derivation to add to all these others: "from the Bosnian" she proposed.

This, then, is the troubling legacy of romantic love. It is the legacy, not of an original passion, but of an old language; not of a sincere feeling, but of a poem. The literature of romantic love, even as it seeks to be the heart's expression, is likely to be something else: mottos, hieroglyphs, Sanscrit, Hebrew, Attic, AEgyptian, Bosnian:—a "dust of figures." To these one must add the distant, literary, untranslated derivation of EBB's own love Sonnets: "from the Portuguese."

Notes

1. For two exceptions, see Dorothy Mermin, "The Female Poet and the Embarrassed Reader: Elizabeth Barrett Browning's *Sonnets from the Portuguese*," *English Literary History*, 48 (1981), 351–67, and Angela Leighton, *Elizabeth Barrett Browning* (Brighton, Harvester, 1986), chapter five.

2. Dorothy Mermin, "The Damsel, the Knight, and the Victorian Woman Poet," *Critical Inquiry*, 13 (1986), 64–80.

3. I am grateful to a member of the audience at the "Victorians and Love" conference, April 1987, for directing me towards these.

Bibliography

Atwood, Margaret, *True Stories* (London, Jonathan Cape, 1982).

Barrett Browning, Elizabeth, *Aurora Leigh,* intro. Cora Kaplan (London, The Women's Press, 1983).

———— *The Complete Works of Elizabeth Barrett Browning,* 6 vols, ed. Charlotte Porter and Helen A. Clarke (New York, Thomas Y. Crowell, 1900).

———— *The Letters of Elizabeth Barrett Browning to Mary Russell Mitford: 1836–1854,* 3 vols, ed. Meredith B. Raymond and Mary Rose Sullivan (New York, The Browning Institute and Wellesley College, 1983).

———— *The Letters of Robert Browning and Elizabeth Barrett Barrett: 1845–1846,* 2 vols, ed. Elvan Kintner (Cambridge, Mass., Harvard University Press, 1969).

Barthes, Roland, *A Lover's Discourse: Fragments,* trans. Richard Howard (New York, Hill and Wang, 1978).

Browning, Robert, *The Poems,* 2 vols, ed. John Pettigrew, supplemented and completed by Thomas J. Collins (Harmondsworth, Penguin, 1981).

——— *Robert Browning and Julia Wedgwood,* ed. R. Curle (London, John Murray, 1937).

de Beauvoir, Simone, *The Second Sex,* trans. H.M. Parshley (Harmondsworth, Penguin, 1972).

de Rougemont, Denis, *Love in the Western World,* trans. Montgomery Belgion, revised and augmented edition (Princeton, N.J., Princeton University Press, 1983).

Firestone, Shulamith, *The Dialectic of Sex: The Case for Feminist Revolution* (1970; revised edition New York, Bantam, 1972).

Foucault, Michel, *The History of Sexuality,* vol. I, trans. Robert Hurley (Harmondsworth, Penguin, 1981).

Gilbert, Sandra M. and Gubar, Susan, *The Madwoman in the Attic: The Woman Writer and the Nineteenth-Century Literary Imagination* (New Haven and London, Yale University Press, 1979).

Going, William, *Scanty Plot of Ground: Studies in the Victorian Sonnet* (Paris, Mouton, 1976).

Hayter, Alethea, *Mrs Browning: A Poet's Work and its Setting* (London, Faber, 1962)

Karlin, Daniel, *The Courtship of Robert Browning and Elizabeth Barrett* (Oxford, Oxford University Press, 1987).

Kristeva, Julia, "Freud and Love: Treatment and Its Discontents," in *The Kristeva Reader,* ed. Toril Moi (Oxford, Blackwell, 1986).

Leighton, Angela, *Elizabeth Barrett Browning* (Brighton, Harvester Press, 1986).

Mermin, Dorothy, "The Damsel, the Knight, and the Victorian Woman Poet," *Critical Inquiry,* 13 (1986), 64–80.

——— "The Female Poet and the Embarrassed Reader: Elizabeth Barrett Browning's *Sonnets from the Portuguese,*" *English Literary History,* 48 (1981), 351–67.

Millett, Kate, *Sexual Politics* (London, Virago, 1977).

Mitchell, Juliet, "Romantic Love," in *Women: The Longest Revolution* (London, Virago, 1984).

The Portuguese Letters, in *The Novel in Letters: Epistolary Fiction in the Early English Novel 1678–1740,* ed. Natascha Wurzbach (London, Routledge & Kegan Paul, 1969), 3–21.

Rossetti, Christina, *The Poetical Works of Christina Georgina Rossetti,* ed. William Michael Rossetti (London, Macmillan, 1928).

Tennyson, Alfred, *The Poems of Tennyson,* ed. Christopher Ricks (London, Longmans, 1969).

Tucker, Cynthia Grant, "Meredith's Broken Laurel: *Modern Love* and the Renaissance Sonnet Tradition," *Victorian Poetry,* 10 (1972), 351–65.

"Some Interchange of Grace":
"Saul" and *Sonnets from the Portuguese*

MARY ROSE SULLIVAN

That Robert Browning and Elizabeth Barrett Browning had an influence on each other's poetry is difficult to doubt but more difficult to prove; their similar backgrounds and shared experiences, and a reticence in both to discuss their working habits, generally make attempts to fix possible influences between them problematic at best.[1] Two periods of their shared lives, however, do provide an unusually clear record of the way each affected and was affected by the other's writings: the first, from their introduction in January 1845 until their marriage in September 1846, during which time Browning completed the last two numbers of his *Bells and Pomegranates* series and Elizabeth Barrett wrote her *Sonnets from the Portuguese,* and the second in 1855, when Browning published *Men and Women.* Their courtship letters show that they considered themselves engaged in a unique poetic as well as personal partnership, and their poetry of this time, together with Browning's 1855 volume, reveals that their creative interaction was more extensive than even they realized. Of particular note is the way that Browning's first version of "Saul" helped to shape the theme and imagery of *Sonnets from the Portuguese,* which in turn influenced his later conclusion to "Saul."

The idea that, as working poets, their correspondence should be an even-handed exchange of poetic views is set up immediately in Elizabeth Barrett's response to Browning's initial letter. EBB (as she signed herself) gracefully acknowledges Browning's admiration for her *Poems* (1844) by noting that of all "commerce" done in the world, "the exchange of sympathy for gratitude is the most princely thing" (*Letters,* Kintner 4). Thus is the keynote of "exchange" struck: each poet has something to offer the other, both will benefit and neither will be a debtor. He will make suggestions for her retranslation of Aeschylus, and she will respond, after his "own example & pattern" (136), with criticisms of poems in preparation for *Dramatic Romances and*

Reprinted from *Browning Institute Studies,* now *Victorian Literature and Culture,* 15 (1987): 55–68. Used by permission of the publisher.

Lyrics. For her help with the latter, Browning thought of repaying EBB by dedicating the volume to her on its publication in November 1845, but by then the complexities of their personal situation, including the need to keep their relationship secret, prevented his doing so. The dedication remained, as he said, understood between them (until "One day!" [242]) as did, for the same reasons, the dedication of his next volume in April 1846, for which EBB performed similar service.

As their involvement deepened and exchanges between them extended far beyond poetic critiques, they consistently invoked the original *quid pro quo* principle, by which all favors received—whether flowers, pictures, or books—were understood to be strictly "exchange." EBB, for example, slyly applies Horace's *Ars Poetica* dictum of poetic "giving and taking by turns" to Browning's request for a lock of hair; she will not "*give*" it but only "exchange it for another thing. . . . It shall be pure merchandise or nothing at all" (291). Primarily, however, the medium of exchange between them is words, the written words of their letters and poems. Not only do they keep close account of who is owed what, in number and length of letters, but they take turns repeating lines from each other's poetry, returning quotation for quotation (EBB had his manuscripts in her possession much of the time, and he wrote with a volume of her poems open on his desk), and they echo each other with reverberations, expanding on and playing with the other's thoughts and expressions. Both seized on, and constantly recurred to, the phrase in Landor's sonnet, "To Robert Browning," about the Siren's "singing song for song" with Browning—EBB playing in their minds the Siren's role—because it captured so neatly the idea of a constant poetic give-and-take between them.[2]

The persistent echoing of each other—often from letters written months earlier—proves how acutely conscious each was of the other's particular form of discourse, poet's ear and lover's ear combining in each to produce a hypersensitivity to the sound of the other's "voice" on paper. EBB responded, for instance, to Browning's written expression of love by describing her emotion at "hearing such words said . . . by such a speaker" (216), as if reading a dramatic monologue.[3] Their written exchange is in fact a dramatic dialogue, but often their voices blend so completely that neither is certain which one originated an idea or phrase, since the rules of the exchange, clearly, called not merely for repeating words but for adapting, reforming, and returning them ever more freighted with meaning. Before long, what started in their correspondence as a playful figure of speech, of "bartering" word for word, had become a firmly-entrenched custom—even a mental habit—of considering verbal formulations passed between them as a kind of community property, to be used freely by either without reference to individual proprietary rights.

Such a notion inevitably spilled over into their composition of poetry. EBB suggests as much when she admits ruefully to discovering that in correcting Browning's manuscripts for *Dramatic Romances and Lyrics* she had worked and re-worked one line before realizing that it was not his but one she had invented herself (145). With his the only work in progress between them in the courtship period, his poetry naturally became the focus of their attention, and her attitude toward revising it shows how closely she had come to identify with his expressions and mannerisms. Early on he had proposed that they collaborate on a poem ("I should like to write something in concert with you" [56]), to her pleasure ("*I* should like it still better" [58]) and, although no formal collaborative work ever materialized, both believed that in readying his poems for publication they were in fact working in concert. For these manuscripts EBB wrote some fifty-six pages of suggested revisions.[4] Her shrewdly practical comments—ranging over such points as whether an "or" should appear in a given line (136–37) and whether the word should be "stomp" or "stamp" (154)—were editorial rather than substantive but of invaluable help to Browning, still suffering from an early reputation for obscurity, in providing a way to hear his own voice and learn how habits of elision and "clogged" meter could obscure his meaning, even for someone as sympathetically attuned to his thoughts as EBB. Duly grateful, he adopted the suggestions wholesale and looked eagerly to return the favor ("your turn comes now" [262]). EBB was, as it turned out, deeply involved just at that point in writing poems of her own, a series of sonnets recording the dramatic changes wrought by Browning's entrance into her life; but with the outcome of their relationship still in doubt she chose to keep the poems' existence temporarily a secret from him. The very nature of their exchange, with all its verbal borrowings and transformations, made it inevitable, however, that those sonnets—later to form the sequence titled (at Browning's suggestion) *Sonnets from the Portuguese*—most of them completed at the very time she was working with him on *Dramatic Romances and Lyrics,* would bear discernible traces of Browning's style.[5]

For only one of his poems from this period was she called on for substantive rather than editorial help, which makes it ironic that for that one poem—"Saul," for which he could not find a suitable conclusion—she could offer no tangible assistance. Deeply impressed with the opening nine stanzas he had completed ("I cannot tell you how the poem holds me & will not let me go until it blesses me" [173]), she repeatedly urged him to go on with it ("& so, where are the 'sixty lines' thrown away? I do beseech you . . you who forget nothing, . . to remember them directly, & to go on with the rest" [173]). When it became clear, however, that he was effectively stymied at finding a way to end the poem, she suggested publishing it as a fragment: " 'Saul' is noble & must have his full royalty some day. Would it not be well, by the way, to print it in the meanwhile as a fragment confessed . . . ?" (252). After he took her advice and included it as it stood in *Dramatic Romances and Lyrics,* she waged a campaign to have it completed: "And do *you* remember of the said poem, that it is there only as a first part, & that the next parts must certainly follow & complete what will be a great lyrical work—now remember" (315). In the ensuing months she repeatedly invoked the name of their friend John Kenyon, reporting that he "hoped, very earnestly I am sure, that you would finish 'Saul' . . . which you ought to do, . . must do—" (508), and again, that he "asked of 'Saul' & whether it would be finished in the new number," adding that he "hangs on the music of your David" (536). Since Browning was regularly talking to Kenyon himself at this time, EBB's enlisting their friend's aid seems disingenuous, perhaps a strategy for diverting attention from her own intense interest in having the poem concluded.

"Saul" seems to have held a personal significance for her that she was as yet hesitant to reveal to Browning.[6] The poem's genesis and development coincided, in what must have seemed to her a strangely portentous fashion, with the progress of her relationship with Browning. He began writing "Saul" in January 1845 just at the time he began writing to her; he told her of the poem in May at the time he first called on her (immediately after which he wrote a declaration of love that so shook EBB that she returned his letter); he showed her the manuscript in late August at the time she first acknowledged her feelings for him. In September and October, while he struggled to find a conclusion for the poem, she struggled with the decision—presented by her doctors as a life-or-death choice—about whether to go to Italy for the winter. Both Browning and EBB lost their respective struggles, he sending "Saul" to press unfinished and she yielding to her father's opposition to the Italian trip. But, just as "Saul" appeared in early November, she gained courage to ask Browning for return of the offending love-letter (which as it happened he had long since destroyed) and by this gesture—of reaching to recover writing of his which, she said, "belongs to me" (257)—signified that Browning had won out over her doubts and he and she would ultimately go to Italy together.

Even if the production of "Saul" had not been so intimately linked with her own fate, certain parallels between her relationship with Browning and Saul's with David in the poem could hardly have escaped her notice. The absence in her letters, after first mention of "Saul," of quotations or any specific allusions to the poem is noteworthy, in light of her well-established habit of referring to favorite lines in his poems. This reticence perhaps reflects a self-consciousness about its theme—of a gifted singer working a miracle of restoration on a despairing soul. Occasionally she seems to raise the possibility of a personal application as when she tells Browning: "you come out into the desert here to me, you whose place is by the waters of Damascus" (290), or when she notes how his flowers live on in her room where flowers usually "die of despair" (348), a phenomenon she might well have associated with David's lilies, "still living and blue" ("Saul" line 12) despite the desert heat. Browning seems not to have picked up such hints, if hints they were, that he was playing David to her Saul, and EBB turned to the poems she was writing in that crucial autumn and winter of 1845 to express the wonder of what was happening to her—poems which bear evidence that "Saul" was echoing in her mind.

Her language in these *Sonnets* is markedly similar to the language of "Saul." She uses the same terms for poetic creation—"life," "breath," "spirit," "touch," "soul," "song," "gift," "star"—and for love—"heart," "hand," "eye," "lips," "kiss," "name," "tears," "prayer"—a convergence that might be attributable to poetic conventions. Other repetitions are less easily accounted for on such grounds, particularly the whole cluster of royal orientalisms—terms like "king," "silver," "gold," "rubies," "lilies," "wine," "grapes," "sparkles," "sword," "pine," "altar," "bier," "desert"—which are natural to the biblical setting of "Saul" but unexpected in the context of the Wimpole Street sickroom. Where EBB's terms are not identical to Browning's they are often closely related, as with her "pearls" for his "jewels," "lute" for "harp," "palace-floors" for "pavilion," "chanted joy" for "glad chaunt," "ashen greyness" for "sand burnt to powder." The most obvious parallel is that between Browning's David and EBB's poet-lover. Her hero is, like David, princely: "noble and like a king" (*Sonnets* XVI), fit to wear "gold / And purple" (VIII), and with "chrism" (III) on his brow. He is a "Most gracious singer of high poems" (IV), a "chief musician" (III) who heals body and soul with his "Antidotes / Of medicated music" (XVII). He finds her in a state remarkably like that in which David found Saul, who was "drear and stark, blind and dumb" in the "blackness" of his "enclosure," helpless to help himself, "caught in his pangs . . . till deliverance come / With the spring-time" ("Saul" 19–33). She too is "faint and blind" (*Sonnets* XXVI) with grief as she waits "amid the darkness" (XXI) in her "close room" (XLIV), at the "dreadful outer brink / Of obvious death" (VII). But then her lover comes and, working God's will, his loving patience and "divinest Art's / Own instrument" (XLI) draw her forth into light and new life in a transformed world.

Browning's Saul did not, however, achieve this release and transformation in the poem EBB read in 1845; that triumphant conclusion came only in 1855. Hence, the parallels between the ending of the *Sonnets* and the ending of "Saul"—which include a number of strikingly similar descriptions of quickening and renewal—represent a reversal of influence, with Browning's poetry now indebted to EBB's for theme and imagery as hers had earlier been to his. EBB, it appears, finally showed her *Sonnets* to him late in the summer of 1849 at Bagni di Lucca, hoping to lift him out of the depression brought on by the shock of his mother's death.[7] The love poems had the desired effect, judging by his beginning to work within weeks on *Christmas-Eve and Easter-Day;* more to the point, in putting into Browning's hands the little book of manuscript poems, EBB also put into his hands the key to how to end "Saul."

While EBB's religious views have generally been credited with inspiring Browning to end "Saul" finally on such a positive note, it is more likely to have been the images of love and art in the *Sonnets* that allowed that breakthrough. For one thing, evidence from her poetry shows that religion generally, and the Incarnation specifically, played far less a role in her thinking after

1845 than before. For another, Browning must have intended from its incep-
tion to conclude "Saul" with a prophecy of the Incarnation: he was aware of
the scriptural tradition of David's vision[8] and began the poem after reading
Christopher Smart's "Song of David," which invokes the Christ-vision at its
end. Clearly, the difficulty about the ending in 1845 was not *whether* to show
David foreseeing the Incarnation but how to account for, and render dramatically, his foreseeing it and sharing it with Saul. Neither scripture nor Smart is
of help here; both merely link Christ with the house of David without explanation. EBB addressed just this difficulty—how to convincingly portray
David's moving from the natural plane to the supernatural—when she wrote
that since the nature of Saul's torment is vague, then "the consolation is not
obliged to be definite" (*Letters,* Kintner 173) either; in other words, perhaps
the curing of Saul by art and love is essentially poetically inexpressible and
Browning should admit as much and do as scripture and Smart do. But
Browning was illustrating in "Saul" the creative process and could hardly be
content to pass over its climax as indescribable. His David was the type of the
highest creative artist, subjective and objective at once, whose act of seeing
and making others see was what Browning held to be at the heart of his own
artistic vocation.

In the various figurative representations of the poetic process that
Browning had been trying out over the years, an image that regularly
recurred was that of the poet as a "mimic-creator" who, like God in the garden of Eden, breathes life into, or "resuscitates,"[9] human forms. In *Pauline,*
which begins with an allusion to the occult philosopher Cornelius Agrippa
who resuscitated corpses, the poet-speaker describes himself as figuratively
wandering through an underworld, holding a lamp "Over the dead, to call
and to awake" them to life (*Pauline* 968); in *Paracelsus* the poet Aprile longs to
"select some shape" from among the ghostly spirits awaiting his "summons"
to life (*Paracelsus* pt. 2. 578, 601); in *Sordello* the poet-narrator boasts the trick
of "Catching the dead" and making them re-enact the historical past: "now
view / The host I muster!" (*Sordello* bk. I. 36, 44–45). Common to these aspiring artists is the sense of themselves exercising, with god-like detachment,
magical life-restoring powers on inert or disembodied forms. What is new in
the David-poet is his intense sympathy with and affection for the object of his
ministrations, who has already realized a greatness, now temporarily abeyant,
and whom his servant David longs to see restored to his former glory. Far
from feeling god-like, David—at the conclusion of "Saul"—acknowledges
the limitations of his human art and prays for a way to help Saul, to transfer
his own overflowing creative energy and joy to the despondent king, and the
answer to his prayer comes, unexpectedly, by way of Saul.

Here is a new dynamic in the creative process for Browning: the artist,
no longer concerned merely to demonstrate his power but rather to use it in
the service of another, reaches his fullest creative potential only with the help
of the one he serves. In the poem the interaction comes about when the

hitherto-immobilized Saul, moved by David's music to resume his old royal "motions and habitudes," lays his hand "with care / Soft and grave, but in mild settled will" ("Saul" 208, 227–28) on David's head as he looks searchingly into his eyes. The kingly look and touch, an unlooked-for return of love and gratitude, ignite in David a burning desire to give his lord more abundant life, even at the cost of his own: "And oh, all my heart how it loved him!" ("Saul" 232). As his love blazes forth, the vision bursts upon him, as much a leap of logic as of faith: If he, David, a mere mortal, would sacrifice life for one he loves, then so would God, so *will God,* sacrifice himself to take on human flesh and "throw open the gates of new life" ("Saul" 312) to his creatures.

All his life, as Browning told EBB, he had been asking "what connection there is between the satisfaction at the display of power, and the sympathy with—ever-increasing sympathy with—all imaginable weakness" (*Letters,* Kintner 270). He had just re-read her 1844 sonnet of resigned acceptance, "Past and Future," which affected him, he said, "more than any poem I ever read," and which caused him to see his serving her (making "that beloved hand shake the less") as supplying that "connection" he sought and resolving the conflict he had felt between exercising power and sympathizing with weakness. Whatever he could do for her would be, "as with all power," the working of "God thro' the weakest instrumentality" (272). The linkage here of his service with her need, like the linkage of her poetry with his poetic aspirations, is a thread running through all his letters, but the particular formulation of himself as poet-lover discovering that his true vocation is to serve as God's instrument for restoring her to life adumbrates in almost every respect David's "curing" of Saul; it lacks only the concept of reciprocal love as the vehicle for accomplishing the transference of life-restoring energy. Browning's formulation also constitutes one more example of the strangely reflexive fashion in which his and EBB's "exchanges" operated. Her immediate response to his power-and-weakness linkage, for a further example, was to write another sonnet, alluding to the bleak conclusion of "Past and Future" and recanting it, because now she knows that her poet-lover will, in her words, "write me new my future's epigraph" (*Sonnets* XLII). The interchange here is intricate indeed: his prose statement (inspired by her poem) moving her to re-write her poem (as he "re-writes" her life) and make it the keystone of a larger poetic design (the whole sonnet sequence)—a design that will then be adapted by Browning to complete (in a sense "re-write") *his* poem.[10]

In the *Sonnets* as a whole we can trace the stages, in that larger design, by which love and art are integrated and see how they must have crystallized Browning's thoughts on the process. First there is the concept of poet as god-like resuscitator who, says the sonnet-speaker,

> hast lifted me
> From this drear flat of earth where I was thrown,

And, in betwixt the languid ringlets, blown
A life-breath.

(XXVII)

Other images emphasizing the inequality between lover and beloved—"We
are not peers, / So to be lovers" (IX)—appear but are gradually submerged in
the concept of the beloved's transformation by love, which gives a "vindicat-
ing grace" and convinces her that "therefore if to love can be desert, / I am
not all unworthy" (XI). The next stage sees the beloved enabled to envision
equality of interchange between them: "If I leave all for thee, wilt thou
exchange / And be all to me?" (XXXV). She has learned to respond, because
his "earnest eyes" (XII) and "touch upon the palm" (VI) have brought their
"souls to touch" (XL) (as Saul's benediction of "look" and "touch" unite him
with David): "I should not love withal, unless that thou / Hadst set me an
example, shown me how" (XII). She feels this union as a form of radiant
energy so powerful that it arcs back from her to him with redoubled intensity: "Fire is bright," "And love is fire," "I stand transfigured, glorified aright /
With conscience of the new rays that proceed / Out of my face toward thine"
(X). It is an energy that galvanizes the whole universe: "The face of all the
world is changed" and she is "caught up into love, and taught the whole / Of
life in a new rhythm" (VII). The language here of all nature quickened, as if
by electric currents, is echoed in Browning's description of David's world
after his vision, in which the stars "beat," "tingled," "shot out in fire," in a
reflection of the "tumult" and "rapture" in his own heart ("Saul" 319–23).
Finally, in the *Sonnets,* comes the realization that love transcends time—"I
shall but love thee better after death" (XLIII)—and that human love leads
ineluctably to divine love—"Because God's gifts put man's best dreams to
shame" (XXVI)—ideas which find expression in David's understanding of
the God that Saul will "love and be loved by, for ever" ("Saul" 311).

That Browning was conscious of the role such images from the *Sonnets*
played in his completing "Saul" is clear from the dedicatory poem to *Men and
Women* (1855) in which the completed "Saul" finally appeared. "One Word
More" is the public dedication—"To E.B.B."—which had to remain unwritten in 1845–46 and *Men and Women* is the major work he had promised her
then. The first line of "One Word More"—"There they are, my fifty men and
women"—is intended to recall her line about life "before him"—"I lived with
visions for my company, / Instead of men and women" (*Sonnets* XXVI)—and
the following lines recall, obliquely but unmistakably, her *Sonnets from the Portuguese,* with their praise of a "certain volume" ("One Word" 6) which proved
that the "lady of the sonnets" (12) had turned her lover into a poet. The
repeated phrases "Here in London" and "You and I" hark back to their first
collaboration a decade earlier: EBB would not fail to realize that these dedicatory lines were written exactly ten years after that September of 1845 when
they pledged their love and he promised that "ten years hence as now" (*Let-*

ters, Kintner 200) he would be there to serve her. She would also catch in his "yourself my moon of poets" ("One Word" 188) invocation the echo of another letter from that time (*Letters,* Kintner 142), just as she would recognize in his poet-prophet Moses an allusion to her David-like hero of the *Sonnets.*[11] And she would read his line, "Heaven's gift takes earth's abatement" ("One Word" 73), as a typically Browningesque recasting of her own line, "God's gifts put man's best dreams to shame." Most significantly, she would understand that he was presenting his poems to her as an "exchange," acknowledging what she had given him in her love *and* in her poetry. The last of her *Sonnets* described them as poems offered in return for "flowers": "Take back these thoughts which [. . .] I withdrew / From my heart's ground" (XLIV). *His* last poem, in *Men and Women,* is offered as the continuing exchange of gift for gift, as signified by the echoing of "take": "Take and keep my fifty poems finished" ("One Word" 141). (And would she not have detected, one wonders, a particular note of satisfaction in that word "finished," as he gave her at last the whole of that "Saul" she had so wished to see finished?)

Later re-readings of their courtship letters must have made it clear to EBB, if she were not aware of it from the start, that, in their infinitely complex *Ars Poetica* "giving and taking by turns," much of what he gratefully "took" from her was essentially a re-working of ideas that had originated with him. Even the key notion of love as a kind of transferable and infinitely renewable thermodynamic force was something he was gradually formulating almost from the first moment he knew EBB. On her side, she avowed the ruling *quid pro quo* principle of their relationship but often doubted its possibility: "There is no possible return" from her to him (*Letters,* Kintner 376); the good comes to her from him but "will not go back again" (577); "Shall I ever, ever, ever, be of any use or good to you?" (643). Her ultimate conclusion, in the *Sonnets,* that he could in some way benefit from their relationship—that "new rays" could proceed out of her face and illumine his—was a victory for his faith over her doubts. He, on the other hand, never doubted the reciprocity in their relationship—"poetry is not the thing given or taken between us," he insisted, but what "you glorify and change and, in returning then, give *me!*" (278). And yet many of EBB's most memorable phrases from the *Sonnets* can be seen emerging first in Browning's letters: he tries, for example, to "count how many other ways" (364) he may serve her or express the "depth and breadth" of his love (396), and he even tries a *sortes* (in an Italian grammar!) and finds this prediction: "*If we love in the other world as we do in this, I shall love thee to eternity*" (450). EBB, always convinced that his was the more powerful poetic imagination, would readily acknowledge the source of her ideas in him, the whole thrust of her *Sonnets* being to demonstrate his effect on her life and art.[12] Browning, however, would undoubtedly feel it impossible to distinguish in their interchange whose idea was root and whose branch, all their giving and taking being in his eyes one and the same.

We, nevertheless, can discern rather clearly what was given and what taken in their works, at least in the period when she dwelt on the first stanzas of "Saul" as she shaped *Sonnets from the Portuguese* and he in turn thought on the *Sonnets* as he shaped the last stanzas of "Saul." The whole process of their composition is oddly like the "transference of energy" process both believed was operating between them in their lives and art. The evidence of mutual influence in this one limited period of their careers may have implications for the larger works that each produced later; at the very least, such evidence gives added meaning to one aspect of *The Ring and the Book*—the invocation to EBB at the end of Book I (lines 1383–1408). Browning's prayer to his "lyric Love"—the epithet encompassing the poetic and private sides of their relationship—acknowledges that she was God's instrument for making him a poet, but in suggesting that "What was, again may be" Browning also seems to acknowledge that he has done and, with his new work, will continue to do some good for her in return. The convoluted syntax of this passage, which makes it difficult to determine who is offering and who receiving the "blessing back," is perhaps one more demonstration of Browning's conviction that at the heart of his relationship with Elizabeth Barrett was not the "thing given or taken" but, always, just this: "some interchange of grace."

Notes

1. An early study of their influence on each other's poetry by Snyder and Palmer examines manuscripts of EBB that suggest revisions to Browning's last two *Bells and Pomegranates*. They find her influence "demonstrably far greater than has been supposed" (62), although confined to corrections of rhyme and meter. Most recent studies of parallels in the Brownings' poetry deal, like Flavia Alaya's, with similarities in viewpoint. Daniel Karlin makes a close study of the psychological rather than literary interaction in the letters.

2. Landor's line is first mentioned 20 November 1845, and allusions to it appear over the next several months; see *Letters*, Kintner 273, 277, 284, 349, and 481. Landor sent the sonnet to Browning after reading *Dramatic Romances and Lyrics*. The concluding lines read:

> the breeze
> Of Alpine heights thou playest
> with, borne on
> Beyond Sorrento and Amalfi,
> where
> The Siren waits thee, singing song
> for song.

For the complete poem, see Wheeler II 387–88.

3. At this point EBB was restricting all such declarations by Browning to letters; it was not until several weeks later that she allowed him to voice his feelings in their face-to-face meetings.

4. The manuscripts of her revisions were later separated from the letters to Browning but have been reproduced in part in F.G. Kenyon's edition of their poetry.

5. Internal evidence from the courtship letters makes it almost certain that the sonnets were composed between August and December 1845 except for those appearing as the final two in the published version, both of which were probably written in early 1846. The published version seems to reflect, on the basis of the letters, generally if not strictly the chronology of their composition, except for Sonnet XLII which was written earlier. See note 10 below.

6. Snyder and Palmer argue for "The Flight of the Duchess" as the poem having the most personal significance in the courtship, but the fact that much of the poem was already in print (in *Hood's Magazine* of April 1845) before EBB worked on it and the rest was completed before her father's opposition surfaced argues against her and Browning's reading into it parallels with her situation in Wimpole Street.

7. Browning describes the occasion in a letter of 1857 to Leigh Hunt (*Letters*, Hood 48).

8. See, for example, Acts 2:30.

9. These terms are not actually used until later, in Book I (lines 712 and 733) of *The Ring and the Book*, but they describe an idea Browning long held.

10. Although EBB's "retraction" appears late in the published version, as XLII, it was originally placed much earlier in the sequence, as XVII, and clearly represents a turning-point in her conception of their relationship. It was removed before publication, apparently because of Browning's fear that its cross-reference to EBB's "Past and Future" would point too clearly to EBB as the poet-speaker in the *Sonnets*, but it was restored, in its new place, in the 1856 edition of the *Sonnets*.

11. See Eleanor Cook for a discussion of the tradition of Moses as poet-prophet (234–38).

12. Once their relationship was resolved, it should be noted, EBB seems to have intended to show the sonnet sequence to Browning. See, for example, her remark of 22 July 1846: "You shall see some day at Pisa what I will not show you now" (*Letters*, Kintner 892).

Works Cited

Alaya, Flavia. "The Ring, the Rescue, and the Risorgimento: Reunifying the Brownings' Italy." *Browning Institute Studies* 6 (1978): 1–41.

Browning, Elizabeth Barrett. *A Variorum Edition of Elizabeth Barrett Browning's "Sonnets from the Portuguese."* Ed. Miroslava Wein Dow. Troy, New York: Whitston Publishing, 1980.

Browning, Robert. *The Complete Works of Robert Browning.* Ed. Roma A. King, Jr. et al. Athens: Ohio UP, 1969.

———. *Letters of Robert Browning Collected by Thomas J. Wise.* Ed. Thurman L. Hood. London: John Murray, 1933.

———. *The Letters of Robert Browning and Elizabeth Barrett Barrett.* Ed. Elvan Kintner. 2 vols. Cambridge: Harvard UP, 1969.

———. *New Poems by Robert Browning and Elizabeth Barrett Browning.* Ed. F.G. Kenyon. London: Smith, Elder, 1914.

Cook, Eleanor. *Browning's Lyrics: An Exploration.* Toronto: U of Toronto P, 1974.

Karlin, Daniel. *The Courtship of Robert Browning and Elizabeth Barrett.* Oxford: Clarendon, 1985.

Landor, Walter Savage. *The Poetical Works of Walter Savage Landor.* Ed. Stephen Wheeler. 3 vols. Oxford: Clarendon, 1937.

Snyder, Edward, and Frederic Palmer, Jr. "New Light on the Brownings." *Quarterly Review* 269 (1937): 48–63.

The Vision Speaks:
Love in Elizabeth Barrett Browning's
"Lady Geraldine's Courtship"

Glennis Stephenson

Among Elizabeth Barrett Browning's contemporaries, one of the popular poems in her 1844 collection was "Lady Geraldine's Courtship." The ballad was warmly admired by Carlyle, Martineau, and the Rossettis, among others, and frequently singled out for particular praise by the critics. Barrett Browning, who had written the poem hastily to meet a publisher's deadline, was amused and surprised by its success and believed that it had attracted "more attention than its due."[1] Modern critics have wholeheartedly agreed, and done more than enough to compensate for any overindulgence on the part of nineteenth-century readers. The poem now rarely attracts critical attention, and, when it does, it is usually dismissed as no more than a particularly uninspired example of Barrett Browning's early ballad romances.[2]

But "Lady Geraldine's Courtship," the last of the romances to be written, actually bears only the most superficial resemblance to the other ballads; both thematically and stylistically, the poem reveals a significant advance in Barrett Browning's treatment of the main subject of this group of poems: the subject of love. The other early ballads almost consistently focus on the failure of love; the heroines are repeatedly frustrated in their attempts to establish lasting and satisfying relationships by the intervention of death, the inconstancy of their lovers, or—most importantly—the passive roles imposed upon them by conventional notions concerning the proper behavior for women in love. Even when Barrett Browning does write of a happy, although short-lived, union in "Rhyme of the Duchess May," she makes little attempt to suggest the nature of the love which drives May to elope with Sir Guy. She sweeps right past the initial joys of love and fixes firmly on its eventual sorrows. The other early ballads may be primarily concerned with romance, but the romances they present are rarely emotionally complex.[3]

In "Lady Geraldine's Courtship," Barrett Browning is interested in bringing love to life for the reader, not in tracing the reasons for its demise.

Reprinted from *Victorian Poetry* 27 (1989): 17–31. Used by permission of the author.

For the first time, the nature of a successful romantic relationship becomes the focus of her attention, and the relationship is shown to succeed primarily because the heroine is not confined to that restrictive position of passive and silent beloved against which Barrett Browning's earlier female characters so vainly rebelled. There is a new emphasis on the woman's potential to be the active subject in a narrative, the "lover" rather than merely the "beloved"—an emphasis which leads to a deliberate confounding of traditional lovers' roles. The title itself, "Lady Geraldine's Courtship," piquantly raises this issue in providing us with no context by which to ascertain whether this is grammatically an objective or subjective genitive: it could equally mean "The Courtship of Lady Geraldine (by Bertram)" or "Lady Geraldine's Courtship (of Bertram)." The poem at large demonstrates that the genitive leans more to the subjective than the objective and that Geraldine is the active lover. Along with this new emphasis on woman as lover rather than beloved, there is a movement away from a preoccupation with plot to a concern with relationship and a resulting interest in experimenting with sensuous language to convey the physical and the spiritual nature of the relationship; "Lady Geraldine's Courtship" consequently marks an important turning point in Barrett Browning's conception and treatment of the question of love.

The main narrator of this romantic tale is Bertram, a poor poet who is invited by the wealthy and powerful Lady Geraldine to Wycombe Hall. Lady Geraldine and Bertram spend many hours discussing such topics as the primary importance of the soul and the basic nobility of all men, and Bertram comes to believe she is sympathetic to his radical social theories; he falls in love with her, but assumes his passion to be hopeless. One morning, he overhears Geraldine tell an overly persistent suitor, an earl, that she will marry only a wealthy and noble man. "I shall never blush," she claims, "to think how he was born" (l. 264).[4] Bertram, misunderstanding her words, angrily rushes into the room, denounces her for scorning the common man, and declares that he has dared to love her. His passionate tirade over, he hears Lady Geraldine say his name, and swoons away at her feet; when he awakens in another room, he begins to write the letter to a friend which comprises the main body of the poem. In a brief conclusion, Barrett Browning adopts an omniscient narrator to describe Geraldine as she comes to Bertram's room and declares her love for him, and the poem ends with Bertram kneeling before Geraldine while she whispers triumphantly: "It shall be as I have sworn. / Very rich he is in virtues, very noble—noble, certes; / And I shall not blush in knowing that men call him lowly born" (ll. 410–412).

This "Romance of the Age," which replaces exotic landscapes and ancient days with the Victorian drawing room, may not be as colorful as "A Romance of the Ganges," or as thrilling as "The Romaunt of the Page," but it is psychologically far more interesting. In the other early ballads, Barrett Browning generally employs an omniscient narrator, but rarely takes advantage of the opportunity this provides to suggest the thoughts and feelings of her characters or to explore their emotional responses to each other; as is usual in traditional literary ballads, the events of the story take precedence over the developing inner lives of the characters. In "Lady Geraldine's Courtship," the inner life predominates; the poem "has more mysticism (or what is called mysticism) in it," Barrett Browning wrote to Mary Russell Mitford, "hid in the story . . . than all the other ballad-poems of the two volumes."[5] It is actually more like a dramatic monologue than a ballad: Bertram's perceptions, and in particular his responses to Geraldine, become of far greater significance than the actual events he describes.

The main narrative, the letter written by Bertram, is complicated by the presence of three different perspectives. First, there are the two perspectives provided directly by Bertram. The young man who records the events of the preceeding days is painfully aware of his love for Lady Geraldine and believes she scorns him as lowly born; his resulting bitterness and cynicism frequently emerge to color his narrative. He is trying, however, to convey not only his present unhappiness, but also his thoughts and feelings as he lived through these experiences. Consequently, as he becomes caught up in his memories, Bertram also appears as the idealistic romantic, smitten by the woman he sees as representative of "all of good and all of fair" (l. 30). These two perspectives rarely emerge as distinctly as I have presented them, and as a result, the young poet's narrative is sometimes marked by contradiction or ambivalence; descriptions of lingering tenderness can be quickly succeeded by, or mixed with, the bitter recriminations of a lover scorned.

Bertram's dual perspective, however, does not dominate the poem completely. Barrett Browning actually creates two distinct strands of narrative: Bertram's story, which is given directly, and Geraldine's, which must be deduced. As Bertram describes Lady Geraldine and recalls what she said and did, the reader pieces together a second, and more accurate, underlying narrative which tells of Geraldine's responses to, and growing love for, the young poet. Since Bertram tells the story, his narrative obviously appears to dominate the text, but Barrett Browning continually distances the reader from his perspective and encourages the construction of the alternative narrative. Geraldine never becomes lost as the silent passive object in Bertram's story; she is too clearly established as the active speaking subject in her own.

In attempting to distance the reader from Bertram, Barrett Browning ensures that he does not always appear as a sympathetic character. His most objectionable feature stems, somewhat paradoxically, from his most admirable. Bertram's democratic views allow for no distinction to be made on the grounds of birth, wealth, or social position. The primary importance of the soul and the irrelevance of worldly trappings is a subject of which he never tires. It forms the basis for both a scornful summary of British social law (ll. 125–132) and an ironic lecture on the "wondrous age" of progress which is more concerned with the development of iron than the development of man's spirit (ll. 197–212). As he indicates when, enraged, he suggests Lady

Geraldine needs to show "more reverence . . . not for rank or wealth . . . / But for Adam's seed, MAN!" (ll. 297–299), he is convinced of the basic nobility of all men. Everyone, he grandly announces, is stamped with "God's image," and has "God's kindling breath within" (l. 300).

But Bertram is an inverted snob. Although his scorn for Lady Geraldine's fashionable friends seems to be justified, he nevertheless frequently appears to have a weighty chip on his shoulder. He is much too quick to dismiss the wealthy and nobly born with disdainful generalizations. Barrett Browning's attempt to distance the reader from Bertram is perhaps overly successful when she depicts him storming into the room to denounce Geraldine. In Bertram's presence, Geraldine displays the conventional signs of love: she trembles and is alternately flushed and pale. Bertram's response is unforgivable, even if his pride has been hurt; he is just too smug: "'tis so always with a worldly man or woman / In the presence of true spirits," he sneers, "what else *can* they do but quail?" (ll. 279–280).

Not surprisingly, the peasant poet has not proved to be one of Barrett Browning's more popular creations. Edmund Stedman, for one, found him unbearable. In "Lady Geraldine's Courtship," Stedman wrote, Barrett Browning succeeded only in "showing us how meanly a womanish fellow might act"; Bertram, he assures us, is a "dreadful prig, who cries, mouths, and faints like a school-girl, allowing himself to eat the bread of the Philistines and betray his sense of inequality, and upon whom Lady Geraldine certainly throws herself away."[6] Stedman's response is extreme, however, and his understanding of the poem questionable. Barrett Browning does not aim to create a strong and spotless white knight for Geraldine, and Bertram comes alive for the reader so vibrantly precisely because his eager idealism is so endearingly flawed.

Barrett Browning also encourages the continual construction of Geraldine's alternative narrative by revealing Bertram to be an unreliable narrator and a poor interpreter of Lady Geraldine. Initially he seems to attribute her flattering attentions to a taste for poetry and sympathy with his democratic views. After overhearing her conversation with the earl, he assumes that she is no better than her companions and has only been idly amusing herself. He was no more, he tells his friend with bitter regret, than a momentary diversion, a household pet like her greyhound, a dog whose antics are encouraged when it is convenient but who is scorned and sent home as soon as he becomes tiresome.

Geraldine's response to the earl never misleads the reader. Her attraction to the poet and her scorn for society's values are immediately recognizable as soon as she singles Bertram out with an invitation to Wycombe Hall. The invitation, extended in the presence of her friends, results in a sudden telling silence. Geraldine colors, and although Bertram interprets this as a momentary blush of shame, her subsequent words indicate it is more likely to be a flush of anger. "I am seeking," she says with cold deliberation, "More distinction than these gentlemen think worthy of my claim" (ll. 55–56); "these gentlemen" are obviously thinking quite the opposite, and her cool polite formality only thinly veils an aggressive challenge to their arrogant pretensions.

Geraldine's attraction to Bertram becomes even clearer after his arrival at Wycombe Hall. On the very first morning of his visit, she leads him and her other guests directly to the statue of Silence in her garden. Her following commentary on the statue suggests that this scene has been carefully staged—and staged entirely for Bertram's benefit. She is eager to demonstrate that she too is unimpressed by outer show and concerned only with spiritual excellence. While the typical statue of Silence has her left hand's index finger on her lips to say "Hush," Geraldine's Silence is asleep; her finger has fallen on her cheek and her symbol rose is held only slackly. This particular interpretation of the conventional form, Geraldine says, suggests how "the essential meaning growing may exceed the special symbol" (l. 121). The statue may no longer display all the expected attributes of a typical figure of Silence, but it has become a truer representation of the concept of silence. This, she continues, "applies more high and low. / Our true noblemen will often through right nobleness grow humble, / And assert an inward honour by denying outward show" (ll. 122–124). Bertram gives Geraldine no opportunity to continue and to explain how the concept applies to the low—although he might have found this instructive. His favorite topic has just been raised, and in he jumps, determined to prove Geraldine wrong. The result is a verbal tug of war. While Geraldine is vainly struggling to convey a personal conviction to Bertram, he views the discussion purely on a general level. " 'Let the poets dream such dreaming! madam, in these British islands / 'Tis the substance that wanes ever, 'tis the symbol that exceeds' " (ll. 129–130). Geraldine is not about to give up, and insistently returns the subject to the personal:

> Not so quickly . . . I confess, where'er you go, you
> Find for things, names—shows for actions, and pure gold for honour clear:
> But when all is run to symbol in the Social, I will throw you
> The world's book which now reads dryly, and sit down with Silence here.
>
> (ll. 133–136)

While the reader may see a subtle message of encouragement for the young poet in Geraldine's argument, Bertram misses the point entirely. He may hold democratic views in theory, but—quite understandably—the possibility that the wealthy and powerful Lady Geraldine might be romantically interested in him, a lowly born poet, never enters his mind. Before Bertram can recognize that she not only seriously accepts his democratic theories but is quite prepared to put them into practice, Geraldine must literally become the active subject in the narrative. She must take the initiative and explicitly declare her love.

As this resolution to the poem indicates, the active role of lover in "Lady Geraldine's Courtship" is not restricted to Bertram; the roles of lover and beloved are as interchangeable as the positions of narrative subject and object. This is one of the most significant ways in which "Lady Geraldine's Courtship" differs from Barrett Browning's previous medieval ballads—and possibly one of the reasons it is "A Romance of the Age." Although the earlier ballads focus primarily on the female perspective, they show the roles of men and women to be firmly, and often fatally, fixed according to traditional standards. As Dorothy Mermin has shown, the women in these poems are generally passive and powerless; the men do all the choosing and the acting. The women who do attempt to step out of their assigned roles—to become the active subjects or lovers in their own narratives—inevitably meet with disaster (pp. 99–112). Barrett Browning now moves away from these early ballads and in the direction of the later poems by suggesting an interchangeability of roles in the lovers' relationship and showing a hero and heroine who are equally suited to the roles of both lover and beloved.

Initially, the reader no doubt approaches the poem with the standard expectation that Bertram will appear as the lover and Geraldine the beloved, and the opening stanzas seem to confirm such an assumption by placing Bertram in the most conventional of lover's roles: the troubadour, the poet-lover "singing" to the beautiful noble lady whom he apparently has no hope of winning. The most notable features of this traditional lover are his romantic deification of the beloved and his accompanying conviction of unworthiness. Bertram quickly demonstrates he conforms to the type. There is an important distinction, however, between the inequality present in social roles and lovers' roles, and the difference is made quite clear when Bertram first describes Lady Geraldine to his friend:

> There are none of England's daughters who can show a prouder presence;
> Upon princely suitors' praying she has looked in her disdain.
> She was sprung of English nobles, I was born of English peasants;
> What was *I* that I should love her, save for competence to pain?
>
> I was only a poor poet, made for singing at her casement,
> As the finches or the thrushes, while she thought of other things.
> Oh, she walked so high above me, she appeared to my abasement,
> In her lovely silken murmur, like an angel clad in wings!
>
> (ll. 13–20)

When Bertram considers the social inequality which divides him from Lady Geraldine, his tone is bitter; with those numerous alliterative *p*'s, he almost seems to be spitting out his scorn for the system. He is echoing the views of the majority, not his own, but is convinced that these are the views that will prevail; he has little hope of seeing his dream of a more democratic world realized. Gradually, however, the bitterness disappears and is replaced by a sense of wonder and reverence. The language softens as he dwells on a vision of Geraldine, who first appears to him in that highly traditional role of an angel from heaven, silent save for the murmur of her silks. Bertram as social creature may have little use for class distinctions, but as Barrett Browning shows, the experience of romantic love inevitably creates its own set of distinctions, its own levels of inequality. Bertram as poet and lover sees Geraldine as a superior being not because he is dazzled by her wealth and position, but, quite simply, because he loves her.

The romantic deification of the beloved emerges throughout Bertram's letter. At first, he believes that he loves Geraldine because she is a Platonic form of ideal beauty and he, as a poet, "could not choose but love her" (l. 29). "I was born to poet-uses," he tells his friend,

> To love all things set above me, all of good and all of fair.
> Nymphs of mountain, not of valley, we are wont to call the Muses;
> And in nympholeptic climbing, poets pass from mount to star.
>
> (ll. 29–32)

When he overhears Lady Geraldine's conversation with the earl, however, and the hopes he has unconsciously been harboring are dashed, Bertram recognizes that he has loved Geraldine not just as a "heavenly object"—in the same way he "loved pure inspirations, loved the graces, loved the virtues" (l. 215)— but also as a woman. Her declaration, therefore, is particularly painful for him; not only does Geraldine confirm his belief that she would never marry such as he, but her apparent arrogance also detracts from his image of her perfect goodness; the beauty seems to be detached from the virtue. His vision of Geraldine no longer appears to match the reality.

Geraldine feels as unworthy of Bertram as he does of her, and is not above indulging in a little nympholepsy herself. She has woods in Sussex, she announces when inviting the young man to Wycombe, with "some purple shades at gloaming / Which are worthy of a king in state, or poet in his youth" (ll. 59–60). The royal purple she believes to be equally suited to king and poet, and by directly equating the two, she explicitly reveals her attitude towards Bertram. While he is the lowly poet worshipping the divine lady, she is the young girl adoring the superior soul with his great poet-heart. As they sit among the daisies on the hillside and Geraldine encourages Bertram to speak on the spirit or pleads with him for a poem, she becomes like a schoolgirl eager to learn from, and please, her teacher. And when she finally goes to Bertram's chamber, her sense of unworthiness is unmistakable. "Dost thou, Bertram, truly love me?" she asks in wonder, "Is no woman far above me / Found more worthy of thy poet-heart than such a one as I?" (ll. 399–400).

The experience of romantic love, Barrett Browning suggests, precludes any possibility of a conviction of equality in a relationship. It is the lover's belief in the infinite superiority of the beloved that, when love is discovered to be returned, results in that elevating sense of wonder which later pervades the *Sonnets from the Portuguese* and which is experienced by both Bertram and Geraldine in "Lady Geraldine's Courtship."

Bertram's angry tirade is the means by which Geraldine learns he returns her love, and it is apparently his declaration of love, not his bitter recriminations, that she primarily hears and to which she eventually responds. When the passionate flow of words abruptly ends, she looks up "as if in wonder, / With tears beaded on her lashes, and said—'Bertram!'—It was all" (ll. 327–328). The joyful surprise and wonder experienced by Bertram upon discovering Geraldine loves him are described less directly but in more detail. When Geraldine comes to his chamber—surely a daring step—she is silently smiling, crying, and blushing. She approaches Bertram with "her two white hands extended as if praying one offended, / And a look of supplication gazing earnest in his face" (ll. 391–392). There can be little doubt what her presence means. Consequently, Bertram is simply unable to believe that she is really with him. He assumes he is dreaming, conjuring up a "vision . . . of mercies" (l. 375); the implications of her actual presence would be overwhelming. As Geraldine glides closer to him, he desperately clings to his conviction that she is a vision; "No approaching—hush, no breathing!" he pleads, "or my heart must swoon to death in / The too utter life thou bringest, O thou dream of Geraldine!" (ll. 395–396). Only when Geraldine touches him and with "both her hands enfolding both of his" says, "Bertram, if I say I love thee, . . . 'tis the vision only speaks" (ll. 407–408), is he forced to acknowledge her actual presence. For both the reader and Bertram, Geraldine rises far above the traditional role of the angelic beloved, passive, silent and unobtainable in her perfection; the vision and the woman merge.

Although "Lady Geraldine's Courtship" ends with Bertram kneeling before Geraldine in the conventional pose of the lover adoring his lady,[7] for the greater part of the poem he is actually the lover only in the most figurative sense. His letter is full of the images commonly associated with love-melancholy. Love is seen as a wound inflicted by Geraldine in the alternately blessed and cursed woods of Sussex. The arrows which inflict the wound come from Geraldine's hypnotic eyes which "undo" (l. 377) Bertram and draw him on, and from her "lips of silent passion, / Curved like an archer's bow to send the bitter arrows out" (ll. 387–388). Like the most conventional of lovers, Bertram is left "mad and blind" (l. 72) with an almost painfully acute sensitivity to the presence or voice of his beloved. He reads the poems of Petrarch, among others, to Geraldine and avoids the company of her guests whenever possible, preferring to languish alone and listen to Geraldine's "pure voice o'erfloat the rest" (l. 88) or to muse over the poems of Camoëns, another lover cruelly separated from his lady by society. Shakespeare's Rosalind could teach this particular lover little.

Although Bertram is certainly a perfect literary lover, his only active courting of Geraldine is contained, ironically, in the angry lecture to which he subjects her. As he listens to Lady Geraldine and the earl, he literally sees red (l. 271); he feels within him the "conventions coiled to ashes" (l. 270) and suddenly becomes quite capable of openly speaking his mind. He reveals not only his anger, but also his love, and his lecture on the equality of all men gradually becomes a series of bitter compliments to Geraldine on her "lovely spirit face" (l. 306) and "voice of holy sweetness" (l. 308). As Bertram's passions build and Geraldine does not respond, he quickly works up to a full declaration of his feelings:

> Have you any answer, madam? If my spirit were less earthly,
> If its instrument were gifted with a better silver string,
> I would kneel down where I stand, and say—Behold me! I am worthy
> Of thy loving, for I love thee. I am worthy as a king.
>
> (ll. 313–316)

This climactic moment is tinged with irony for the reader; Geraldine has already vainly tried to indicate to Bertram that he is indeed, in her eyes, the equal of a king.

Geraldine is far more active in the role of lover than Bertram. She may even be seen as the female version of that noble Duke on a red roan steed that Barrett Browning's other early heroines, such as Little Ellie in "The Romance of the Swan's Nest" and May in "Rhyme of the Duchess May," either dream about or love. Bertram, conversely, with his tears, his tenderness, and his sensitivity, displays numerous "feminine" qualities which are appropriate to both lover and beloved. Geraldine's more active role is, admittedly, partly the result of the differences in their social positions. In spite of all Bertram's theories, he could never initiate the relationship. It is essential that Geraldine should make the first move and invite him to Wycombe. Nevertheless, throughout the poem Barrett Browning continually undercuts the importance of social position.

This was, indeed, Coventry Patmore's major objection to the poem. Quite certain that such an ill-matched pair as Geraldine and Bertram could never be happy, Patmore as self-appointed marital expert reminds us just how strongly early nineteenth-century society would object to such a "mesalliance." Geraldine would be forced to relinquish her *station in society,* he observes with distaste, and this point is not made clearly enough in the poem. If Barrett Browning meant to show the nobility of Geraldine, he writes,

> in leaving the condition in which she had passed her life, for the sake of passing it henceforward in the unsophisticated company of an uneducated poet, and his friends and relations, she ought, in order to have brought out her meaning artistically, to have shown that the Lady was not only fully aware of the sacrifice she was making, but that she was also capable of enduring it to the end, with all its trying circumstances of social contempt and dissonance of habits.[8]

Patmore is obviously more concerned with the effects of social position than the effects of love. The middle-class reading public, though it could accept the romantic notion of the marriage of a man to his social inferior—a Cinderella or a Pamela—still reacted strongly against the idea of a highborn woman stooping to conquer. This was precisely because such a situation implies an active sexuality on the woman's part. Barrett Browning does not hesitate to create an actively sexual heroine and, despite the grim mutterings of such critics as Patmore and Stedman, she successfully romanticizes the feminine plot of desire. Patmore's objections to the story surely stem from his uneasy recognition that Barrett Browning is quite clearly showing how unimportant social standing can become once a woman is permitted to feel normal sexual desire.

As Barrett Browning undercuts the importance of social position in the poem as a whole, so she minimizes its significance as a cause of Geraldine's active love-making. Geraldine is a strong woman with an independent mind and a healthy disregard for convention; in courting Bertram she is as defiant as he would be in courting her. And her active wooing is not confined to the obvious examples of inviting Bertram to Wycombe and going to his chamber to declare her love; she attempts to win him in various subtle ways. Once she has the poet at Wycombe, she continues to pay him particular attention. Repeatedly, she coaxes him to join her and her friends, and, when he lingers behind, apparently draws on all her charms to encourage him. Her conversation is always obviously directed to Bertram and her other guests seem forgotten. In the midst of a large gathering, Geraldine manages to transform the time she spends with Bertram into intimate moments.

This sense of intimacy pervades "Lady Geraldine's Courtship" and clearly reflects Barrett Browning's primary concern with the nature of Bertram and Geraldine's love. The poem may be, as she explained in a letter, "a 'romance of the age,' treating of railroads, routes, and all manner of 'temporalities' " (Kenyon, 1:177), but the romance is far more important than the railroads. For the first time in her career, Barrett Browning has shifted her interest away from the excitement of plot and has concentrated specifically on the nature of a romantic relationship.

As Barrett Browning becomes more interested in the intricacies of love than of plot, she also searches for new ways to convey the nature of the love she describes, and, to a great extent, she relies on the effects of highly sensuous language and imagery. The rendering of sensuous experience in "Lady Geraldine's Courtship" becomes a true register of both erotic and emotional attraction, and a means of providing the reader with access to the inner lives of her characters. There is little sensuous description in the previous ballads, a telling reflection of the frustration of desire pervading the poems, and when it does occur, it usually suggests desire displaced. There is more of the sensual, for example, in Duchess May's caressing the red roan steed on which she escapes from that abhorrent—yet sexually magnetic—villain, Lord Leigh than there ever is in her relationship with the stiff picture-book knight she marries.

In "Lady Geraldine's Courtship," an abundance of sensuous description brings the love of the poet and the lady alive for the reader, and it clearly establishes that, despite Bertram's nympholeptic leanings, he does not love an ideal or a vision, but an actual woman. There are two sides to Geraldine's character—the regal, awe-inspiring lady, and the playful, often child-like woman. Bertram apparently finds her highly desirable in both roles. As the high-born lady, Geraldine is kingly, princely, and owns vast properties; it is not her wealth or position that attract Bertram, however, but the power and strength they bestow upon her, her consequent ability to "threaten and command." This Geraldine is associated with luxurious surroundings, the "crimson carpet" and the "perfumed air" (l. 6) and the finest jewels in the land. When she rejects her numerous suitors, she deals with them as "imperially as Venus did the waves" (l. 222). Her demonstration of power and control enables Bertram to feel more acutely her superiority—and the attitude of worship is, for both him and Geraldine, erotically satisfying.

As she demonstrates when inviting Bertram to Wycombe, Geraldine can play the role of the grand lady with great style. She deals with the obvious disapproval of her friends with a "calm and regnant spirit" (l. 49), and when she leaves the room, resembles "one who quells the lions" (l. 67). Her magnificence leaves Bertram quivering with silent pleasure. Even in this scene, however, she reveals the other side to her character when she softens visibly as she turns to Bertram. Lady Geraldine, lion-tamer, is replaced by Geraldine, lover. Sharp coldness is succeeded by an overflowing warmth, a welcoming smile, and an almost flirtatious tone when she says:

> I invite you, Mister Bertram, to no scene for worldly speeches—
> Sir, I scarce should dare—but only where God asked the thrushes first:
> And if *you* will sing beside them, in the covert of my beeches,
> I will thank you for the woodlands,—for the human world, at worst.
>
> (ll. 61–64)

While Geraldine as lady is most closely associated with courts, castles, and ancient halls, Geraldine as woman and lover is associated with these woodlands, with hills, forests, swans, and fawns. She appears as an integral part of the natural sensuous world, and as Bertram writes his letter, the sound of the woods that he connects with Geraldine haunts him as much as her "fair face" and "tender voice" (l. 72).

Since this face and voice drive Bertram "mad and blind" (l. 72), it is fitting that his sensuous perceptions of Geraldine are revealed primarily through visual and aural images. The sound of Geraldine as she moves is seductively rendered by such alliterative and onomatopoeic phrases as "lovely silken murmur" (l. 20) and "sudden silken stirring" (l. 48). While primarily aural, these images also embrace the tactual, and this mingling of the senses is particularly appropriate since the sound of Geraldine is something Bertram feels intensely. His vision of Geraldine as angel may initially suggest he resembles the poet of the traditional romantic lyric with its masculinist plot of distance and desire, but the sensuous imagery he employs eliminates the traditional sense of separation and emphasizes instead a sense of intimacy and the unmistakable proximity of a flesh and blood woman. Bertram registers an acute, almost physical sensitivity to Geraldine's presence; the sound of her arrival, he records, "touched my inner nature through" (l. 48).

Geraldine's voice has a similar effect. Unlike the other women, whose voices Bertram scorns as "low with fashion, not with feeling" (l. 75), Geraldine has a "pure" and "tender" voice of "holy sweetness" which turns "common words to grace" (l. 308). Her "sudden silver speaking" (l. 47) can leave Bertram weak and helpless, and he is easily bound by her "silver-corded speeches" (l. 85). The effect of Geraldine's voice is never shown more clearly than at the climax of his passionate tirade:

> But at last there came a pause. I stood all vibrating with thunder
> Which my soul had used. The silence drew her face up like a call.
> Could you guess what word she uttered? She looked up, as if in wonder
> With tears beaded on her lashes, and said—"Bertram!"—It was all.
>
> (ll. 325–328)

The passage is reminiscent of Herbert's "The Collar," in which the raving of the rebellious soul ends with a simple call from God. Bertram's violent rush of passion is subdued by a single word. He is struck by the "sense accursed and instant, that if even I spake wisely / I spake basely—using truth, if what I spake indeed was true" (ll. 341–342). The sound of Geraldine's voice crushes him; in spite of his previous conviction that his anger is justified, he suddenly instinctively feels he is wrong. Geraldine's feelings for Bertram are obviously conveyed through her voice, and Bertram is therefore left thoroughly confused; the message that he seems to detect in the voice is completely at odds with his rational estimation of the situation. At this climactic moment, it is perhaps not so surprising that he should faint away at Geraldine's feet.

Geraldine's appearance is clearly as captivating as her voice, and Bertram frequently interrupts the flow of his letter to dwell on the vision of her beauty. Every smile and every movement is lingered over and described in detail; even the movement of her garments is noted when Bertram remembers her wandering in the gardens:

> Thus, her foot upon the new-mown grass, bareheaded, with the flowing
> Of the virginal white vesture gathered closely to her throat,

> And the golden ringlets in her neck just quickened by her going,
> And appearing to breathe sun for air, and doubting if to float,—
>
> With a bunch of dewy maple, which her right hand held above her,
> And which trembled a green shadow in betwixt her and the skies.
>
> (ll. 93–98)

Once again the tactual emerges. The passage may have a primarily visual appeal, but Bertram still conveys the impression that he is actually feeling the wetness of the maple, the pressure of Geraldine's foot on the grass, and the soft flicker of her hair on her neck—Barrett Browning is already well aware of the potential sexual suggestiveness of woman's hair and will later use such images to even greater effect in *Aurora Leigh* and *Sonnets from the Portuguese*.

It is the effect of the eyes, however, that is most fully explored in "Lady Geraldine's Courtship." Geraldine's "shining eyes, like antique jewels set in Parian statue-stone," Bertram claims, "undo" him (ll. 377–378). That steady serene glance which can quell in a moment can also appear soft and inviting. When she turns and looks at Bertram, he remembers, "she drew me on to love her / And to worship the divineness of the smile hid in her eyes" (ll. 99–100). Those deep blue eyes "smile constantly, as if they in discreetness / Kept the secret of a happy dream she did not care to speak" (ll. 103–104). Geraldine's eyes, like her voice, reveal her love, and Bertram consequently finds her glances a mystery.

The visual and the aural finally become merged in the description of Geraldine singing. As Bertram and Geraldine sit alone on the hillside, they often tire of books and grow silent. The silence gives Bertram a pleasant, yet disconcerting, awareness of Geraldine's presence which is "felt with beatings at the breast" (l. 170). Geraldine, apparently similarly disturbed, breaks the silence by bursting into song. "Oh to see or hear her singing!" Bertram writes,

> scarce I know which is divinest,
> For her looks sing too—she modulates her gestures on the tune,
> And her mouth stirs with the song, like song; and when the notes are finest,
> 'Tis the eyes that shoot out vocal light and seem to swell them on.
>
> Then we talked—oh, how we talked! her voice, so cadenced in the talking,
> Made another singing—of the soul! a music without bars.
>
> (ll. 173–178)

Geraldine herself becomes the song, and what is sung is indistinguishable from the singer; Bertram responds with the senses and the spirit.

Both the presentation of Geraldine as song and singer and the mingling of the sensuous and the spiritual in this central passage become a reflection of Barrett Browning's larger concern within the poem to create and celebrate a successful romantic relationship. The lines which traditionally divide poet from lady, subject from object, lover from beloved, and sensuous from spiritual gradually dissolve and, as they do, the barriers which left Barrett Browning's earlier heroines frustrated, able to find satisfaction in love only by accepting God as substitute-beloved, are overcome. As Barrett Browning's first detailed evocation and dramatization of a growing love, "Lady Geraldine's Courtship" marks a crucial turning point between the early ballads, with their pessimistic and rather superficial handling of romance, and such later works as *Sonnets from the Portuguese* and *Aurora Leigh*, with their more mature and complex investigation of the experience of love.

Notes

1. Frederic G. Kenyon, ed., *The Letters of Elizabeth Barrett Browning*, 2 vols. (London, 1897), 1:211. For contemporary views of the poem see Kenyon, 1:199–204; Gardner B. Taplin, *The Life of Elizabeth Barrett Browning* (New Haven, 1957), pp. 127–131, 237–238; Alethea Hayter, *Mrs Browning: A Poet's Work and Its Setting* (London, 1962), pp. 84–86. This paper derives from my thesis on the concept of love in the works of Elizabeth Barrett Browning, and I would like to acknowledge the support of a SSHRCC doctoral fellowship in writing this thesis.

2. See, for example, Hayter, pp. 85–86; Virginia Radley, *Elizabeth Barrett Browning* (New York, 1972), pp. 60–62.

3. For the best discussion of these early poems, see Dorothy Mermin, "Barrett Browning's Stories," *Browning Institute Studies* 13 (1985): 99–112, to which I am indebted. While the poems are not emotionally complex, they are, as Mermin shows, frequently concerned with complex social and cultural issues.

4. Barrett Browning's poetry is quoted from *The Complete Works of Elizabeth Barrett Browning*, ed. Charlotte Porter and Helen A. Clarke, 6 vols. (New York, 1900).

5. *The Letters of Elizabeth Barrett Browning to Mary Russell Mitford. 1836–1854*, ed. Meredith B. Raymond and Mary Rose Sullivan, 3 vols. (Winfield, Kansas, 1983), 3:49.

6. Edmund Clarence Stedman, *Victorian Poets* (Boston, 1891), pp. 130–131.

7. The woman's new freedom to act, combined with the traditional male worship of the woman, recalls Ellen Moers's discussion of Barrett Browning being similarly worshiped by her admiring father. See *Literary Women* (New York, 1985), p. 7.

8. Coventry Patmore, "Mrs. Browning's *Poems*," review of *Poems* (1856), *North British Review* 26 (February 1857): 445.

The Death of Pan:
Elizabeth Barrett Browning
and the Romantic Ego

Margaret M. Morlier

During the past two decades Elizabeth Barrett Browning has become most appreciated for her 1856 feminist epic *Aurora Leigh,* a poem in which she asserted her "highest convictions upon Life and Art." Before publishing *Aurora Leigh,* however, she said that one of her most important poems was "The Dead Pan." When she published her two-volume collection of *Poems* in 1844, she insisted that "The Dead Pan" be placed last for emphasis. This poem of thirty-nine stanzas, each ending with some variation of the phrase "Pan is dead," is often overlooked today in discussions of Barrett Browning's development probably because its theme appears outdated to modern readers. Beginning with a catalogue of classical deities—such as Juno, Apollo, and Cybele—shocked by the crucifixion of Christ, the poem depicts the death of these classical gods along with their representative, Pan. In the final third of the poem they are replaced by the Christian god and his martyred son. Then the refrain "Pan is dead" changes in meaning: no longer the lament of the classical gods, the refrain becomes a joyful proclamation of the Christian poet. On a first reading, "The Dead Pan" seems simply to celebrate orthodox Christianity; it is still generally remembered as a Victorian expression of pietism or, in Douglas Bush's facetious words of 1937, a poem in which the "Greek gods are brought face to face with Christian truth and put to rout" (268). . . .

[Yet] revisionary use of Christian materials appears throughout Barrett Browning's poetry. Her poetry draws from non-institutional forms of Christianity, like an 1844 sonnet that recalls the mystical tradition of likening the voice of the Christian Savior to a "mother's mouth" and "breast" that allow the believer to be "love-reconciled" ("Comfort" 12–13). And the poet's later

Reprinted from *Browning Institute Studies,* now *Victorian Literature and Culture,* 18 (1990): 131–55. Used by permission of the publisher.

attraction to Spiritualism—a movement involving mediums and séances, and which Vieda Skultans calls a female religious enterprise because of its domestic settings and its predominantly female leaders—further puts a radical coloring on the poet's interpretation of Christianity. In short, her poetry reveals a feminist revision of Christianity.

The Christian conception of divine passion, a passion that shares feeling with others empathetically, has the appeal of the kind of epistemology that, according to psychologist Carol Gilligan, women tend to employ. Gilligan concludes that

> For boys and men, separation and individuation are critically tied to gender identity since separation from the mother is essential for the development of masculinity. For girls and women, issues of femininity or feminine identity do not depend on the achievement of separation from the mother or on the progress of individuation. (8)

As a result, women tend to view morality not in terms of objective ideals as much as in "a context of human relationship" (17); in addition, "the underlying epistemology correspondingly shifts from the Greek ideal of knowledge as a correspondence between mind and form to the Biblical conception of knowing as a process of human relationship" (173). Consequently, because he typified empathetic knowledge, Christ remained central in Barrett Browning's moral vision as a theological and psychological ideal.

Equally central in her moral vision was the figure of Pan. The evolution of this character in her poetry provides a record of her evolving understanding of evil. Barrett Browning's attitude toward the classical goat-god, like her artistic vision of Christianity, is not typical in Victorian literature. Typical nineteenth-century treatments use Pan to represent a pre-civilized, natural world and an innocent psychological state: invoking the spirit of Pan, poets like Blake, Wordsworth, Keats, and Shelley assumed a critical position outside of the structures of civilization and offered revolutionary critiques of those structures. The typical post-Romantic treatment lamented the loss of an intuitive spirit in the Victorian technological world, a loss represented by the unfortunate death of Pan. In contrast Barrett Browning's "The Dead Pan" distinctively celebrates Pan's death.[1] Robert Buchanan published a poetic response to Barrett Browning's poem, reasserting, "O Pan, great Pan, thou art not dead" but alive in the "gleam of some forgotten life" ("Pan: Epilogue" 10, 40). Buchanan's poem is a representative Victorian lament for the modern suppression of intuitive feelings; in fact, his sentiment strikingly parallels the one expressed in a different context by Matthew Arnold in "The Buried Life." For most nineteenth-century artists, both before and after Barrett Browning, Pan might have represented an outworn creed, but they would rather be suckled in his innocence than in industrialization.

What then is the difference between the Romantic celebration of intuitive knowledge and Barrett Browning's celebration of empathetic knowledge? The Romantic regard for feeling might conceivably empower a woman speaker, especially in a culture that educated women rather than men to develop strong emotional skills. Why, then, does Barrett Browning so distinctively celebrate Pan's death? The tradition that proposed the male goat-god as a figure of the artist might instead be resisted by a woman poet. But the issue is more complex. In the figure of Pan, Barrett Browning explored the problem of the female poet and Romantic egoism. In particular she identified something sinister, especially for women, in the Romantic privileging of imagination over nature. Writing about the problem of identity for the female poet, Margaret Homans points out that the Romantic "Mother Nature" was the "object of the [male] poet's love" and the "necessary complement to his imaginative project, the grounding of an imagination so powerful that it risks abstraction without her"; in reality, however, Homans adds, "Mother Nature" is "no more than what [the male poet] allows her to be" (13). Nature is under the control of the male poet's imagination. The female poet had to contend with being seen as a human embodiment of the same feminine principle as "Mother Nature" and to contend with the male poet's accompanying ambivalence. From the vantage of a female poet, Barrett Browning likewise saw the Romantic desire for consummation with some feminine principle—Nature or an internal *anima*—expressed artistically in terms of a desire to control it. Politically, this desire would be played out in terms of control over nature and real women. Furthermore, as Gilligan explains, male socialization to individuation, if excessive, can lead to a strong ego but can also lead to aggression, violence, and control if individuation threatens to become "dangerous isolation" (43). In Barrett Browning's poetry, Pan represents the potential for aggression, violence, and control in Romantic egoism. . . .

Granted, the division between Christian and "pagan" gods in "The Dead Pan" sounds suggestively like the basis for imperialistic thinking; from her room on Wimpole Street in 1844, Elizabeth Barrett might have shared some imperialistic attitudes about foreign cultures with her Victorian contemporaries.[2] However, "The Dead Pan" also complains about the imposition of imagination over reality, which, as Edward W. Said has argued, is a kind of imperialism in itself. "Texts," writes Said, "are a system of forces institutionalized by the reigning culture at some human cost to its various components" (53). Barrett Browning's poem shows that the texts of her culture—classical to Romantic—are seductive but dangerous. The lethargy of classical gods appears blissful, as if it were caused by the influence of "lotus" (13), "slumber" (15), "poppies" (17), or "wine" (19), but this lethargy seduces one into impotence and death, for the gods are also "stagnant" (22), "blind" (68), and "deaf" (101) against the reality of the crucifixion. Meanwhile opposed to this pageant of inanimate past gods, nature is alive in the present:

> Not a word the Naiads say,
> Though the rivers run for aye;
> For Pan is dead. . . . Now a word the Dryads say,
> Though the forests wave for aye;
> For Pan is dead.
>
> (40–42, 47–49)

Consequently the poem's opposition of Christian and classical gods should alert readers to the evangelical values that would also lead Tennyson to imperialistic assertions.

One might argue that the course of her life, later moving to foreign lands, saved Barrett Browning from this strand of thought, yet her evangelicalism was early qualified by a feminist questioning of cultural power. "The Dead Pan" in particular compares most easily with Tennyson's "The Lotos–Eaters" in portraying the seductiveness of art, and her poem clearly privileges reality over imagination:

> Truth is fair: should we forgo it?
> Can we sigh right for a wrong?
> God Himself is the best Poet,
> And the Real is His song.
> Sing His truth out fair and full,
> And secure His beautiful!
> Let Pan be dead!
>
> (246–252)

This second theme, about the political power of a culture's imaginative texts, continued to interest Barrett Browning, especially in her poems involving the myths of Pan. As a woman, she approaches the issue from the point of view of a victim of cultural distortions, as one of Said's "various [excluded] components" rather than as one of the "reigning culture." Pan becomes in her poetry a figure that enacts various forms of ideological control.

Pan did not die so easily in 1844; in addition to an early allusion to Pan, Barrett Browning composed whole poems centered on the Pan myths, like "A Reed" (1846), "Mountaineer and Poet" (1847), and her most well-known poem about the goat-god, "A Musical Instrument" (1860). Each of these subsequent poems seems a response to specific Romantic versions of the classical figure. When the Pan poems are read together, a consistent portrait emerges: Pan typifies a whole cluster of moral problems that can stem from egocentrism manifest in a variety of ways in British culture—in general, in its Romantic egoism that would later become Victorian colonialism and paternalism. In Said's recent work he refers to the "twin origin of the Higher Crit-icism and of Orientalism" in which "the passing of divine authority enables the appearance of European ethnocentrism" so that "the methods and the dis-course of Western scholarship confine inferior non-European cultures to a position of subordination" (47). One might also note the twin origin of Higher Criticism and the excesses of Victorian domestic patriarchy. No longer secure in his identity as an image of god, the Victorian patriarch sought it through comparison with other males, for example by looking for "touch-stones" of great literature by past male writers, in part to establish a canonical context for his individual existence. Similarly, no longer assured of his central-ity in the order of creation, he could take comfort in control over others—domestic as well as foreign—who were less politically powerful. As one of the less powerful and as an artist, Barrett Browning would resent the conception of artistic greatness as a solely masculine privilege; however, as her poetry matured, so did her understanding of the philosophical issues underlying the imbalance of literary tradition.

In rejecting Pan, Barrett Browning rejected a well-established literary tradition associating Pan with Christ and with the artist. These two traditions are worth briefly retracing here. Originally, as Patricia Merivale has shown, Pan was simply the goat-god of Arcadian shepherds, but because of a linguis-tic error, writes Merivale, "Pan" came to mean "all" (9). Then in early Chris-tian texts, a legend developed involving Pan and Christ. According to this legend, at the moment of Christ's crucifixion, a wail was heard on the Aegean Sea calling "Pan is dead." As a result, two traditions developed. In one, Pan is associated with Christ, and the cry "Pan is dead" laments Christ's death on the cross. In the other tradition, Pan is associated with Satan, and the wail heard on the Aegean Sea proclaims that Christ has killed the pagan gods by his martyrdom (Merivale 12–13). Barrett Browning's poetry draws from the latter tradition, as is obvious by her refrain in "The Dead Pan." . . .

Barrett Browning also inherits the figure of Pan as the (male) artist or poet, a tradition based upon the myth of Pan and Syrinx. The significance of this myth for a woman artist will be immediately apparent. In the most well-known version of this story, by Ovid (*Metamorphosis* 1.689–712), Pan desires sexual possession of a female nymph named Syrinx. She runs to avoid the lust of the male goat-god, and when she arrives at a river and can run no farther, she begs for help from the river nymphs, who respond by changing her into a bed of reeds. When Pan arrives, he attempts to capture and embrace Syrinx, but finds himself with arms full of reeds. So he fashions the reeds to make his pipes, and from then on he is accompanied by his instrument, his Syrinx, which he uses to create enchanting songs about his "tragic" loss. Pan thus became a traditional metaphor for the poet. A second and equally important source for the association of Pan and the poet is "Pan's role as a master of cer-emonies in pastoral drama" (Merivale 18). In some medieval and renaissance popular dramas, Pan appeared as the controlling spirit (or consciousness) of the play. By extension, Pan was the guiding consciousness of a work of art, and Pan came to be synonymous with the poet.

British Romantic poets drew from this whole set of traditions to have Pan represent intuitive inspiration from nature that works through the unconscious, pre-civilized part of humanity. Moreover, the "spirit of Pan" or poetic inspiration guides the consciousness of the poet. For Wordsworth, Pan is an all-pervading nature-spirit; for Shelley, in his "Hymn of Pan," Pan's pursuit of Syrinx is like the poet's quest for a kind of *anima;* and for Keats, in "I stood on tip-toe . . ." and Book 1 of *Endymion,* Pan is a poetic muse. In Keats's most famous but subtle allusion, Pan is the invisible spirit with his "soft pipes" who mediates between the past piper and the living poet to create those "unheard melodies" in "Ode on a Grecian Urn." Such is the cultural environment and its implicit assumption that the artist is male. In reaction, Barrett Browning's poetry explores the role of Syrinx in the mythological drama. More importantly, in sharp contrast to the traditional stories about Pan, Barrett Browning brings to the foreground the themes of violence (from the attempted rape) and arbitrary power (from the relative, controlling consciousness) that are the tradition's undercurrents.

"The Dead Pan" was written in specific response to an English paraphrase of Schiller's *Die Götter Griechenlands* made by John Kenyon, friend of the Barrett family. Schiller's poem did not mention Pan, but lamented the loss of poetic perception with the loss of pagan myths (Merivale 103). Kenyon added Pan to represent both the collection of lost gods and the loss of inspiration in the materialist, utilitarian world of Victorian England:

> Pan! the Wood-nymphs! all are gone!
> Bright as yet were, bright Fictions!—now—
> Ye live in Poet's dream—alone.
> (qtd. in Merivale 104)

In a letter to her literary confidante, Mary Russell Mitford, Barrett Browning wrote that she found Kenyon's poem to be "an eloquent Lament for the Gods of Greece & the ancient mythology" but that her poetic response takes "the contrary side of the question" to show "the false Gods well gone"; she added somewhat flippantly, "*Pan* signifies 'all,' besides his individual goat-godship" (*Letters,* Raymond and Sullivan 2: 205). . . .

Barrett Browning mainly used Pan to criticize the aesthetics of both Keats and Wordsworth, whom, ironically, she admired more than any of her predecessors. "The Dead Pan" itself resembles Keats's "Ode on a Grecian Urn," with its meditation on Hellenic culture, its images of deities frozen inanimate like figures on the urn, and especially its final couplet, "Hold, in high poetic duty, / Truest Truth the fairest Beauty" (271–72). Like Keats, Barrett Browning recognized a seduction of art that in Keats's words could "tease us out of thought"; yet this seduction from reality by a "Cold Pastoral" is what she rejected, partly because the masculine artistic tradition did not completely speak the truth to her that the urn apparently does to the controlling consciousness of Keats's "Ode." Instead of an antique urn or the values of an antique culture, "The Dead Pan" advises looking to present experience for "Truest Truth."

Barrett Browning's poetic and critical responses to Wordsworth, too, suggest that even the benevolent egoism of the Grasmere poet has something sinister in its epistemology, because it imposes a view on reality, including the reality of other people. Wordsworth, in fact, becomes a strong case for this position because his benevolence is so attractive. In "Mountaineer and Poet," published in 1847, the Wordsworthian Pan is more realistically rendered as a "simple goatherd" (1) who sees his enlarged shadow in a light refraction phenomenon that occurs when someone in the mountains casts a shadow into mountain mists. In this phenomenon (called "mountain glory" or "glory"), with certain angles of light the vapor in the mists causes the shadow to appear larger than human and sometimes causes the head of the shadow to appear to be surrounded by circles of color. *The Prelude,* which contains Wordsworth's use of the "glory" image, was not published in its entirety until after the laureate's death in 1850, and there is no firm evidence that Barrett Browning was familiar with any of its parts before 1847. However, she knew Wordsworth's probable source, James Thomson's 1746 *The Seasons,* in which the autumn landscape includes a shadow that the "shepherd stalks gigantic" (3.727). She may also have been familiar with Coleridge's "Constancy to an Ideal Object," which revises this image as well as the treatment that he found in the 1805 *Prelude.* In Wordsworth's 1805 version, the sight of a shepherd when "glorified / By the deep radiance of the setting sun" (8.404–405) leads to a celebration of human imaginative power; man is then "Ennobled outwardly before mine eyes" (8.411), and the shadow becomes "an index of delight, / Of grace and honour, power and worthiness" (8.415–16).

For Coleridge the image of the shepherd's shadow in mountain glory also represents the power of the human imagination, but he slightly modifies Wordsworth's treatment. Use of the motif in "Constancy to an Ideal Object" might have been inspired by the verb "to stalk," employed by both Thomson and Wordsworth, which means both "walking after" and "attempting to overtake." Coleridge's poem, about an insatiable obsession with the ideal, likens the ideal to a shadow that a shepherd sees before him, "an image with a glory round its head" (30). The speaker of the poem concludes that "The enamoured rustic worships its fair hues, / Nor knows he makes the shadow he pursues!" (31–32). This poem recognizes that the ideal of human imagination is also created by human imagination. In her study *Victorian and Modern Poet-*

ics, Carol Christ sees a general Victorian reaction to the Romantic self-created ideal and concludes that for the Romantic poet, the "mind's realization of its own autonomy as it attempts to approach the objects of its consciousness brings . . . both a tragic awareness of the solitary self and a compensatory exaltation of the imagination's power" (5), a conclusion well illustrated by the irony of Coleridge's poem. The poet as an "enamoured rustic" worships the glorified shadow before him, but the poet as speaker of the poem is aware that he "makes the shadow he pursues." As the Romantic imagination subsumes reality in itself, however benevolent a Pan it might be, it also entraps itself within itself. Coleridge's forethinking poem laments the implied isolation of Romantic individualism. Barrett Browning's responding use of the glory motif exposes the political implication of this entrapment only hinted at by Coleridge: an individual projects an imaginative glorification of *him*self, and with Pan there is emphasis on the gender of the pronoun, and then claims that this exclusive image is an objective human ideal. Unlike her male predecessors, her perspective on this aesthetic issue, outlined below, is not that of one trapped within his vision but of one trapped outside of the social power that the vision evokes.

Wordsworth, Coleridge, and, as I shall soon show, Shelley all use "mountain glory" to glorify the human ego. Yet in Barrett Browning's "Mountaineer and Poet," the real goatherd, or poet, who when "between Alp and sky" sees his shadow "in that awful tryst, / Dilated to a giant's on the mist" (1–3) is not a Pan who exults in his control of the world around him: he "Esteems not his own stature larger by / The apparent image" (4–5). This real goatherd, rather, "more patiently / Strikes his staff down beneath his clenching fist" (5–6)—the "staff" suggesting the poet's pen or writing staff—to continue to work to glorify the universe of which the poet is a part. The final lines of the poem state this theme explicitly, addressing all would-be poets:

> Ye are not great because creation drew
> Large revelations round your earliest sense,
> Nor bright because God's glory shines for you.
> (12–14)

In terms of the present discussion, these lines address Wordsworthian aesthetics, maintaining distinction between the mind as a means and an end of art. Her poem, along with Coleridge's, recognizes that the mind can become a means of projecting and celebrating itself; however, Barrett Browning's poem asserts that it can celebrate a moral reality outside of itself. Obviously this reality must be known by alternative epistemological means. . . .

Despite her reservations, Elizabeth Barrett Browning's admiration for Wordsworth was matched only by Robert Browning's corresponding regard for Shelley, who also influenced her development. The benevolence that expressed itself on the individual level with Wordsworth also expressed itself in Shelley's social activism, which Barrett Browning admired without being able to embrace its materialist implications. . . . [H]er 1846 poem entitled "A Reed" addresses the ethics she found in Shelley's work.

Shelley draws from the Pan and Syrinx myth for "Hymn of Pan," which Barrett Browning also uses in "A Reed" and later in "A Musical Instrument." In Shelley's poem, Pan's pursuit of Syrinx is likened to the poet's pursuit of an *anima* that can only be captured in art; his Pan complains, "I pursued a maiden and clasped a reed" (31). Barrett Browning not only gives voice to the reed, but also, instead of complaining about the fate of Syrinx, proposes that the role of any poet should be like the reed, mediating moral reality rather than, like Pan, presuming to create it. In one sense, then, "A Reed" and "A Musical Instrument" reveal a critique of the empiricist/materialist strand that links Shelley with Victorian ethics.

In 1840 Elizabeth Barrett had been given a copy of Shelley's *Essays, Letters from Abroad, Translations and Fragments,* which, as James Thorpe has shown, she annotated heavily, especially *A Defense of Poetry.* Although she was unable to follow Shelley into what she perceived as theological skepticism and doubt, Elizabeth Barrett's annotations indicate that she agreed with or qualified some of his ideas, especially his discussion of the moral function of poetry. Drawing from empiricist ethics, Shelley argued that poetry has the moral function of exercising human sympathy:

> A man, to be greatly good, must imagine intensely and comprehensively; he must put himself in the place of another and of many others; the pains and pleasures of his species must become his own. The great instrument of moral good is the imagination; and poetry administers to the effect by acting upon the cause. (7: 118)

Shelley's poet creates imaginative visions with which the reader can exercise sympathetic faculties, while for Barrett Browning the process of creation itself involves the artist in empathizing with others. She was particularly interested in Shelley's analysis of the dramatic poet, for empathy has a dramatic, role-taking aspect. To Shelley's comment that "tragedy delights by affording a shadow of the pleasure which exists in pain" (7: 133), she responded with the following marginalia:

> . . . all passionate emotion breaks down or has a tendency to break down, that defence of habits & conventionalisms which the finite has erected between itself & the infinite . . . to shield its overdazzled vision—It is the tendency of all passionate emotion to shake selfism to its foundation—to shape selfism by selfism—& [thru] the rents made in the convulsion to display the infinity ever beyond—(qtd. in Thorpe 457)

Her notes reveal two points worth remarking. First, while Shelley was mainly concerned with the effect of art on the auditor, Barrett Browning was also concerned with its effect on the artist and even more with the ways that art connects artist and auditor. What results is a very different view of the relationship between artist and society. The artist is not some variation of high-priest imposing order on the world; the artist is connected metaphysically and equally with other members of society. In addition, she was interested not only in the psychological effect of art but also in its metaphysical implications—in an aesthetics that includes a passionate sympathy so intense that it leads the self to glimpse "the infinity ever beyond." Only by getting beyond the psychological, or "the finite," can one begin to escape its prejudices. . . .

Although she admired Shelley's revolutionary impulse, Barrett Browning could not accept what she perceived as his ethical atheism; even further, her work implies that the failure to recognize spirituality leads to exclusionary ideologies. In "A Reed" and "A Musical Instrument" she too draws on the Pan and Syrinx myth, empathizing with the female who was changed into the artist's instrument and using the position outside of the dominant cultural ideology to show its moral weaknesses. In fact, "A Reed" seems almost to address Shelley's *Defense* directly. In his final paragraph, Shelley referred to poets as "trumpets which sing to battle, and feel not what they inspire; the influence which is moved not, but moves" and as "the unacknowledged legislators of the world" (7: 140). These images underscore an Aristotelean (the poet as "unmoved mover") strand of his thought as well as a separation of the poet (as legislator) from his audience. As if to emphasize her cultural position, the speaker of "A Reed" repeats the same line—"I am no trumpet, but a reed"—at the opening of each stanza:

> I am no trumpet, but a reed;
> No flattering breath shall from me lead
> A silver sound, a hollow sound:
> I will not ring, for priest or king,
> One blast that in re-echoing
> Would leave a bondsman faster bound.
>
> (1–6)

On the surface, this stanza might seem consonant with Shelley's revolutionary philosophy because the speaker announces her independence from hierarchical ideologies that enslave, whether the religious hierarchy of the priest or the political hierarchy of the king. But her opening line directly contrasts her role with that of the trumpet, like Shelley's trumpets which sing to battle.[3]

Moreover, in her annotations of Shelley's *Defense,* Barrett Browning commented on Shelley's analysis of the proper role of art in society. Writing of Homer's art, Shelley implied that morality results from social imitation:

> [T]he sentiments of the auditors [of Homer's poetry] must have been refined and enlarged by a sympathy with such great and lovely impersonations, until from admiring they imitated, and from imitation they identified themselves with the objects of their admiration. (7: 116)

In the margin next to this part, Barrett Browning asked, "Does not the feeling of *identification* follow the *admiration* and precede the *imitation?* (qtd. in Thorpe 456). Her question sounds like a quibble, but it reveals a crucial distinction about the relationship between art and political ethics. According to Shelley's analysis, morality results from imitation of beauty, and ethical behavior leads to moral goodness; conversely, Barrett Browning responded by writing that morality is innate, and that the "feeling of *identification*" with moral goodness causes good behavior (imitation). In other words, in her aesthetic theory, the function of the artist is to evoke the innate goodness of the reader by showing beauty (Shelley's "lovely impersonations"). The belief that human ideologies are the primary reality is a materialist position, represented by Pan in Barrett Browning's poetry.

A recent analysis of *mimesis* and ontology by René Girard sheds additional light on this characterization of the goat-god. In his critique of Freud, Girard argues that imitation stems from the "intense desires" of one person to possess the being perceived to be in another; this perception is an illusion fostered by the physical fact that one sees the other from the outside and the solid form appears to have a permanence that one's perceived internal fluidity lacks. In Girard's words, the "subject thus looks to that other person to inform him of what he should desire in order to acquire that being" (146). Girard concludes that this desire can lead to social violence if the subject and the person imitated both believe that they require possession of the same thing. In this context, the ethics outlined by Shelley stems from a desire to possess or control the perceived being of those "lovely impersonations" in Homer's art—"from admiring they imitated." Barrett Browning's critique clarifies the potential for violence and tyranny in this aesthetic; she responded that the beauty of Homer's art, to the contrary, appeals to some innate moral sense within the auditor. The distinction that she makes here parallels her distinction between a passion to possess or control another—epitomized by the lust of Pan for Syrinx—and a passion that liberates by sharing a common humanity or a common moral sense with another—epitomized in her poetry by the empathetic passion of Christ.

Consequently, as much as Barrett Browning admired Shelley's revolutionary disdain for convention, she also rejected what she perceived as the materialist/empiricist, even imperialist, implications of his philosophy. In the first stanza of "A Reed," the reed/speaker is opposed to "priest" and "king," religious and political hierarchies respectively. In the second stanza, the "broken reed" becomes the voice for those who are most vulnerable in a patriarchal culture, a "little maid" and a "child." More significantly, however, the reed asks in the third and final stanza to be left alone by all so-called "fishers"—which I interpret to mean representatives of any institutional religion:

> I am no trumpet, but a reed;
> Go, tell the fishers, as they spread
> Their nets along the river's edge,
> I will not tear their nets at all,
> Nor pierce their hands, if they should fall:
> Then let them leave me in the sedge.
>
> (13–18)

The "fishers" certainly suggest Christian disciples who were told in the Bible and repeatedly in sermons to be "fishers of men" for converts to Christian ideology, but by the mid-nineteenth century there were numerous sects or ideologies, each believing itself to have the "true" fishers of men. . . .

[T]he poem exposes the political dimension of religious and artistic traditions. In this poem, the reed is opposed to the king, the priest, and the fishers, all of whom share the same epistemological assumptions—that they have divine authority to hold political power over others. Pan indirectly typifies this illusion of authorized political power because in the original myth to which the poem alludes, the reed resists possession by Pan. Furthermore, if this poem is a response to Shelley, as I suspect it is, as odd a combination as it seems to modern readers, Shelley is linked with the cluster of political power because of his perceived materialism. "A Reed" implies that Pan represents all those, even poet-priests and poet-legislators, who construct and impose artificial ideologies on others.

Pan the artificer is the central character in another poem, "A Musical Instrument," from her *Last Poems*. This one begins with a question: "What was he doing, the great god Pan, / Down in the reeds by the river?" (1–2). The answer: "Spreading ruin and scattering ban, / Splashing and paddling with hoofs of a goat" (3–4). Pan is shown to be breaking down natural harmony in order to construct an artificial one. After tearing a reed from the river bank, Pan "hacked and hewed" it with "his hard bleak steel" (another image of the writer's pen) ". . . Till there was not a sign of the leaf indeed / To prove it fresh from the river" (15–18). The reed is then cut short and its pith, like "the heart of a man" (21), drawn out; next Pan "notched the poor dry empty thing / In holes" (23–24). In the fifth stanza Pan laughs, saying that all of this violent distorting of nature is " 'The only way, since gods began / To make sweet music' " (27–28), and then the whole creative process ends when

Pan "blew in power" (30) to the reed. Yet the goat-god does not have the last word in this poem. After Pan's song, the poet ends the poem by referring to "the true gods" who "sigh for" and remember the natural reed as it was but is no more:

> Yet half a beast is the great god Pan,
> To laugh as he sits by the river,
> Making a poet out of a man:
> The true gods sigh for the cost and pain,—
> For the reed which grows nevermore again
> As a reed with the reeds in the river.
>
> (37–42)

This final stanza and final treatment of the Pan myth looks forward—even in similar language of "cost and pain"—to Said's analysis quoted earlier: "Texts are a system of forces institutionalized by the reigning culture at some human cost to its various components" (53).

Of all of Barrett Browning's poems about Pan, "A Musical Instrument" is the most anthologized, and it is the only one with a critical history, however modest. In 1895 Hiram Corson published a reading in *Poet-Lore,* concluding that the poet reiterates Shelley's theme that the suffering of the poet must be "refined and exalted" to produce an expression of "sympathy and relationship" with the world (259). Corson identifies the natural reed as the merely "potential poet" (261) who must be shaped by Pan, a personification of universal poetic sensibility. After admitting difficulty with the final stanza, he concludes,

> The meaning . . . seems to be that Nature, though the great medium of the divine to Man, is unconscious, and sympathizes not with her poetic offspring; the "true gods," that is, the conscious spirits of the world . . . , sympathize with the poet in the severe ordeal he must pass through, and strengthen and uphold him. (262)

As interesting as his reading is, Corson does not acknowledge that the reed, Syrinx, is the victim of Pan's aggressive lust in the classical myth and that it is for her that the "true gods sigh." Merivale's 1969 reading begins to approach my own. After pointing out a technical similarity to Shelley's "Hymn of Pan" (83), she also suggests that Barrett Browning had "grave moral doubts as to the value of what Pan stands for" (84). She concludes that the theme is that "suffering is necessary to art" even though "art does not justify suffering" (84). More recently, Joanne Feit Diehl is the first to point out that Pan's words in the poem appear in quotation marks, distinguishing them from the poet's words, but she also sees Pan as an inspiring, male muse, one that both attracts and threatens to overcome the poet (584–85).

All of these readings assume that Pan represents an idealization of poetic inspiration, whatever the character of that inspiration for a woman poet, but in the context of Barrett Browning's other treatments of the mythical figure, I suggest that Pan presents an image of the poet with which Barrett Browning was never comfortable and which she resisted for reasons of morality if not gender. Among other things, Pan represents the privileging of imagination over reality. As a victim of reductive images of woman, and aware of female reality, this poet, even as an artist, is uneasy about this privilege. Dorothy Mermin concludes similarly that Barrett Browning "had not wanted to speak from the place of the victim unless that place could be redefined . . . as the locus of power"; then Mermin reads "A Musical Instrument" in particular as a "reluctant acknowledgment that great poetry" need not come from "participation in male superiority and cultural dominance, but from exclusion and pain" (245). I add, however, that Barrett Browning's poems question not only male superiority but also the epistemology that necessitates anyone having power over another. The process of Pan is not the process of "true gods," the "simple goatherd," or true poets; in fact the destruction of nature for the building of artifices is the process of science. Barrett Browning distinguished her poetics from those of Wordsworth and Shelley because their projections of ego over nature are analogous to the encroachment of an unbalanced civilization over reality, of science over poetic sensibility, of materialism over spirituality, and even of the male-created poetic tradition over a serious woman poet.

Her critique of her Romantic predecessors is in a broader sense a critique of the culture that they represent and the injustice that they maintain, however unintentionally, against serious women poets. This injustice can be seen explicitly in the exclusive masculinity of the Pan persona. Diehl identifies a "brute, masculine, destructive force" embodied by the Pan of "A Musical Instrument" that "suggests a hidden resentment of the male poet" (585). Yet the problem is more subtle. Barrett Browning recognized the difference between an ideology and individuals who practice it: for example, she commented to Robert Browning that her father was deluded "below all those patriarchal ideas" but that as an individual, "there never was (under the strata) a truer affection in a father's heart." She added, "The evil is in the system" (*Letters*, Kintner 169). Her resentment likewise is not for the male poet in particular but for his traditional epistemological assumptions that are powerful because they have gone unquestioned. Part of Barrett Browning's artistic success comes from continually questioning the meaning of Pan—and, by extension, the meaning of art—from outside of the authorized tradition. That she revises the Pan/Syrinx story to give voice to the nymph who escapes ravishment only by becoming a tool and an object of art suggests some bitterness about the roles that women are forced into by the assumptions of the male tradition. In fact, the tearing and piercing by Pan's "hard bleak steel" in

"A Musical Instrument" suggest not only a figurative crucifixion but also a figurative rape or defilement of the female reality. This violence together with her pleas in both "A Reed" and "A Musical Instrument" that the reed be left some integrity as a living, natural reed further suggests resentment, not so much of male poets, but of the kind of epistemology that Pan personifies and that the Romantic ego glorified.

This resentment can be seen further in the shifting tone of the phrase "the great god Pan," repeated in each stanza of "A Musical Instrument." The technique of repeating a phrase from stanza to stanza so that it shifts in tone with each renewed context was a favorite of this poet. She had used it to change the value of "Pan is dead" in "The Dead Pan."[4] In "A Musical Instrument," the phrase "the great god Pan" seems initially to accord with the usual Victorian praise for the figure. Then by the sixth repetition at the end of the poem the speaker announces, "Yet half a beast is the great god Pan" (37), a line that undercuts the absolute authority earlier allowed the figure. The poem implies that the poet typified by Pan is likewise "half a beast" and that his poetic authority is not absolute. Moreover, there are echoes here from earlier interpretations of Pan: in the final "great god Pan" one ironically hears both the flippant tone of "his individual goat-godship," from her comment to Mary Russell Mitford about "The Dead Pan," and the serious assertion that "Ye are not great" from "Mountaineer and Poet." And finally, one hears Robert Browning's artist Fra Lippo Lippi admitting, "You understand me: I'm a beast, I know" (270).[5] As her last poetic statement about the classical figure, "A Musical Instrument" portrays the death of Pan's absolute power. Still the poem does not simply reassign power to the female reed; it ends by directing attention beyond the "finite" with the words, sympathy, and power of the "true gods," who are neither male nor female.

Even further, a reader of the epic *Aurora Leigh* will find Romney, Aurora's cousin, described as bearing the "Genius of the Vatican . . . Upon the torso of the Dancing Faun" (3.514, 517). This comic/grotesque description is offered by Lady Waldemar, in one sense the cynical voice of the epic, who reveals her own obsessive lust for Romney in her description of him as half-beast. Yet the image indirectly suggests the goat-god Pan, and in the narrative as a whole, it is Romney who wants Aurora to give up her writing because it can never be the "best" art, since it is written by a woman. The allusion to Pan, however indirect, has resonances from throughout Barrett Browning's poetry because the nostalgia for Pan consistently means replacing divine authority with male authority and its philosophical assumptions. In the figure of Pan, the longed-for intuitive knowledge was confused with feelings of pleasure—at the expense of controlling others—rather than empathy.

This sort of epistemology, in which self-justification is based on a desire for power over others or, worse, on self-gratification, is the "sin" that Pan personifies. And in Barrett Browning's mature poetry it is a sin that can be practiced by men and women, as the exploits of Lady Waldemar illustrate. Likewise, Romney is not himself a villain, but his attempt to fashion the world after his own image is morally unsound. Accordingly, Barrett Browning's critique goes beyond complaining about exclusive masculine dominance to analyzing the potential for both kindness and control in the strong, individual ego. Her analysis of the individual benevolence of Wordsworth and of the social benevolence of Shelley are, in fact, condensed in her portrait of Romney and his good intentions. Still, her sustained critique of Pan throughout her poetic career exposes the assumptions of the Romantic ego that would contribute to the paternalistic, materialistic, and ultimately imperialistic Victorian society. Disguising a feminist qualification of Romantic aesthetics, "The Dead Pan" of 1844 is not outdated for modern readers. The poem perhaps masked this qualification from the poet herself at that point in her career, but an awareness of the political power of the products of the imagination would become a more overt theme as her poetry progressed. . . .

Notes

1.   The only notable exception is Charles Mackay's "The Death of Pan," published, coincidentally, within a few months of "The Dead Pan," in *Hood's Magazine and Comic Miscellany*. See Merivale 107–108, and see *Letters*, Kintner 382, 383n, and 387 for the Brownings' remarks on this coincidence.

2.   In fact, Dorothy Mermin has located an imperialist strand in one of the poet's 1833 poems. In the context of discussing heroism, Mermin describes "The Appeal" as "a grotesque and dreadful poem urging the 'Children of our England' to stand together and 'Shout aloud' (the phrase is repeated four times) Christian truth to heathens in distant lands" (55).

3.   The opposition between trumpet and reed might also suggest the difference between epic and lyric poet, but Barrett Browning had aspired since a child to be a female Homer and of course became one. Consequently, I do not think that this poem refers to a rejection of the epic voice.

4.   Barrett Browning used this technique most strikingly when repeating "The nightingales, the nightingales" at the end of each stanza of "Bianca Among the Nightingales," another late poem that also obviously responds to Romantic aesthetics.

5.   This point was made explicitly, although in a playfully bawdy statement, to T. A. Trollope. Isa Blagden showed the poet an interpretation and criticism of "A Musical Instrument" by Trollope's brother, which the poet assumed to be by T. A. Trollope, himself. At the end of her rejoinder, Barrett Browning reassured the critic that Pan "is a beast up to the waist; yes, Mr. Trollope, a beast. He is not a true god" (Trollope 396).

Works Cited

Barrett Browning, Elizabeth. *The Complete Works of Elizabeth Barrett Browning*. Ed. and introd. by Charlotte Porter and Helen A. Clarke. 6 vols. New York: Thomas Y. Crowell, 1900. Rpt. New York: AMS Press, 1973.

————. *The Letters of Elizabeth Barrett Browning to Mary Russell Mitford 1836–1854*. Eds. Meredith B. Raymond and Mary Rose Sullivan. 3 vols. Winfield, Kansas: Wedgestone Press, 1983.

————. *The Letters of Robert Browning and Elizabeth Barrett Barrett 1845–1846*. Ed. Elvan Kintner. 2 vols. Cambridge, Mass.: Harvard UP, 1969.

Buchanan, Robert. "Pan: Epilogue." *The Complete Poetical Works of Robert Buchanan*. London: Chatto & Windus, 1901. 1: 185.

Bush, Douglas. *Mythology and the Romantic Tradition in English Poetry*. Cambridge, Mass.: Harvard UP, 1937.

Christ, Carol T. *Victorian and Modern Poetics*. Chicago: U of Chicago P, 1984.

Coleridge, Samuel Taylor. *Samuel Taylor Coleridge*. Ed. H. J. Jackson. Oxford: Oxford UP, 1985.

Corson, Hiram. "The Cost of a Poet: Elizabeth Barrett Browning's 'A Musical Instrument.' " *Poet-Lore* 7 (1895): 259–63.

Diehl, Joanne Feit. " 'Come Slowly—Eden': An Exploration of Women Poets and Their Muse." *Signs* 3 (1978): 572–87.

Gilligan, Carol. *In a Different Voice: Psychological Theory and Women's Development*. Cambridge, Mass.: Harvard UP, 1982.

Girard, René. *Violence and the Sacred*. Trans. Patrick Gregory. Baltimore: Johns Hopkins UP, 1977.

Homans, Margaret. *Women Writers and Poetic Identity: Dorothy Wordsworth, Emily Brontë, and Emily Dickinson*. Princeton: Princeton UP, 1980.

Merivale, Patricia. *Pan the Goat-God: His Myth in Modern Times*. Cambridge, Mass.: Harvard UP, 1969.

Mermin, Dorothy. *Elizabeth Barrett Browning: The Origins of a New Poetry*. Chicago: U of Chicago P, 1989.

Said, Edward W. *The World, the Text, and the Critic*. Cambridge, Mass.: Harvard UP, 1983.

Shelley, Percy Bysshe. *The Complete Works of Percy Bysshe Shelley*. Eds. Roger Ingpen and Walter E. Peck. 10 vols. New York: Gordian Press, 1965.

Skultans, Vieda. "Mediums, Controls and Eminent Men." In *Women's Religious Experience: Cross-Cultural Perspectives*. Ed. Pat Holden. London: Croom Helm, 1983.

Thomson, James. *The Seasons and the Castle of Indolence*. Ed. James Sambrook. Oxford: Clarendon Press, 1981.

Thorpe, James. "Elizabeth Barrett's Commentary on Shelley: Some Marginalia." *MLN* 66 (1951): 455–58.

Trollope, Thomas Adolpus. *What I Remember*. New York: Harper & Brothers, 1888.

Wordsworth, William. *William Wordsworth: The Prelude 1799, 1805, 1850*. Eds. Jonathan Wordsworth, M. H. Abrams, and Stephen Gill. New York: W. W. Norton, 1979.

Aurora Leigh: An Epical *Ars Poetica*

HOLLY A. LAIRD

Ellen Moers called the Victorian period the "epic age" of women's writing (a phrase she picked up from Virginia Woolf)—that historic period when a new nation of literature by women received its foundations. Yet Moers wrote also that Elizabeth Barrett Browning's Aurora Leigh "may always be a heroine of limited appeal: the literary woman's heroine," in spite of her prior claim that the pen and printing press were the first means widely available to women to make themselves heard, to change their world, or to live a life of heroic "action."[1] It is always worrisome to find this kind of contradiction in claims made for women, and this is an especially thorny one: why is it not "appealingly" heroic to achieve stature as a writer? Moers probably felt that a contemplative heroine—more specifically, a woman of letters—could not be popular among women readers of the twentieth century. If not, this is our loss, and if there is anything the feminist critic can do to recover it, she should try. But as Janice Radway has shown, women readers even of Harlequin Romances read to satisfy a thirst for heroines—heroines who are often writers—and these readers admire Harlequin authors, frequently aspiring to follow them to authorship.[2] Moers's casual dismissal of the literary heroine, still more worrisomely, calls to mind the masculinist assumption that heroism belongs to traditionally virile efforts, which writing ceased to be when invaded by women. As it happens, one of the most influential writers of the Victorian age, Carlyle, believed that one could achieve modern heroism only through the pen, a belief whose most obvious descendant in the twentieth century is Marshall McLuhan's claim for the cultural primacy of modern media. To discard Barrett Browning's heroism is thus to discard the distinctive vision nineteenth-century thinkers had of themselves, a vision to which we remain indebted in our own information-happy age.

It is certainly no mistake that a woman writer appears at the center of Browning's epic, and Aurora Leigh is as convincingly courageous a heroine as has ever been created. As remarkable as its heroine, moreover, is the poetics

Reprinted from Suzanne W. Jones, ed., *Writing the Woman Artist: Essays on Poetics, Politics, and Portraiture*, (Philadelphia: University of Pennsylvania Press, 1991), 353–70. Used by permission of the publisher.

she articulates: a poetics in which the central concern is with her "epic" age and the "heroic" artist. Ellen Moers could well have grounded her own theories about women's writing in Browning's earlier effort. It is odd that—popular as this work was in its own time, crucial as it remains in reconstructing the history of women's writing—its contribution to literary criticism has been so thoroughly overlooked by contemporary feminist theorists.[3] Again, I suspect this has something to do with twentieth-century attitudes to Victorian thought, about which the twentieth-century reader has frequently been ambivalent.[4] The poetics of *Aurora Leigh* belongs on any syllabus that already includes Wollstonecraft and Woolf. It belongs in any anthology of "The History of Criticism: Plato to the Present" (as long as we go on having such anthologies), even though it might never quite fit an anthology and excerpts would not do it justice.[5] Although I do not want to claim—as Lawrence Lipking has appeared to do for Madame de Staël—that Browning is the first or best claimant to the title of Aristotle's sister,[6] I do want to indicate the trenchancy, range, and relevance of the poetics contained in *Aurora Leigh,* to sketch in the place Browning should all along have held as a theorist among her famous male compatriots, both Romantic and Victorian. I will argue that, in the context of Carlylian thought, Browning devised what she called a "twofold" vision of heroism in art and in life, an unironic vision of differences well suited to a feminist aesthetic. She created not merely a powerful philosophy for epic poetry, a poetics, but an epical enactment of that philosophy, an embodied *ars.*

Browning developed something quite different from the Romanticist poetics for which Lipking argued by way of de Staël, herself an important and acknowledged precursor to Browning. Lipking's aim was to decipher a model for a "woman's poetics" not by turning to a field outside English studies—philosophy, psychoanalysis, or history—but rather by adopting terms from an Aristotelian tradition, a poetics logically induced from literature. The classic defenses of poetry are not in fact autonomous, not without philosophical, psychological, and historical assumptions; nonetheless, the Aristotelian tradition offers a convenient place to begin evaluation of *Aurora Leigh* because Browning herself spoke this language. In addition, since Lipking's Romanticist views are familiar to today's critics and still attractive, and since Lipking's model represents an important strand in feminist thought—arguing for an alternative poetics grounded in women's experience and in recognition of their "abandonment" by men—a brief review of his conclusions provides a useful foil for Browning's.[7]

Through reading de Staël (and a number of men writing on women), Lipking reached three important conclusions, all of which often crop up in feminist defenses of women's literature: first, that a poetics of women's literature would take as the chief purpose of literature "expression" not "imitation," hence, its central feature would be "speech" and "discourse" rather than plot; second, following from the first, that poetry is personal and passionate rather than impersonal or disinterested, and to speak confers privilege and power, interests and rights, which have not historically been neutrally allocated; and finally, that literature is written within and for communities rather than by and for a sequence of heroic individuals, that traditions of writing are and should be linked by "affiliation" not only by "authority" (something made possible, according to Lipking, by the advent of the printing press and the democratization of writing). A poetics that includes these three criteria provides both a description of what men's literature reveals about women and a reformative vision of what literature can do for disenfranchised women. But summarized in this way, Lipking's claims look more universal than they are— and than they have appeared to feminist readers of his essay.[8] The effect of his argument is to recolonize women, to allow them personal expression rather than heroic authority, to hear them speaking as agonized sufferers but not as proud suffragists, and to discover no other Aristotelian voice among them than that of de Staël.

But the literary woman was a triumphant figure in the nineteenth century; such women had risen above the norm, could speak their minds, and win the respect of all. Neither the heroine nor the author of *Aurora Leigh* was an abandoned woman speaking of her private woes to a small community. She seemed to speak for her age. She also spoke for a poetics distinct from and in some ways more comprehensive than that of Wordsworth, of Lipking's de Staël, or even of Carlyle, though it is Carlyle alone of these three whom Aurora explicitly mentions in her discourse on poetry in Book V of *Aurora Leigh*. The debt to Carlyle is obviously profound: what one finds in Browning's heroine is a revised version of Carlyle's theory, widely held by others of this period, of the modern hero as a man of letters.[9] His or her compelling desire is to challenge formulaic positions, whether the conservative ideas of an old aristocracy or the new socialism of Charles Kingsley, to struggle against systemized thought of any kind for the sake of a lived philosophy (for Carlyle, a transcendentalist vitalism, for Browning, a Christian humanism). To be heroic is to struggle through the written word: to write one's life and to write it as heroic struggle.

Browning confronted the same challenges faced later by Arnold, as he tried to cope with the differences he perceived between Classics and Romantics: how to balance social duty with aesthetic interest, how to restore ancient epic actions to a contemporary literature absorbed in self-expression, how to move from a failure of belief to renewed belief or from the failure of previous systems of thought to a workable philosophy, how to reconcile the heritage of the past with the changes of the present, how to ground subjective perceptions in a persuasively disinterested stance. To these conflicts Browning responded quite differently from either Carlyle or Arnold, though she resembles Carlyle more than Arnold in her response since, like Carlyle, she avoided both Arnold's reactive neoclassicism and Pater's radical aestheticism, choosing instead to view these conflicting demands as compatible—choosing a

dualistic vision. Browning follows Carlyle's precedent in an especially important respect, in moving from a worry about either/or choices (the Carlylian
opposites of chaos and order, belief and unbelief, usefulness and pleasure, past
and present) to the risky acceptance of both/and (the Carlylian vision of the
coexistence of antagonistic possibilities). And, of course, she added to this list
of conflicts the struggle between man and woman.

She wrote—as she believed her husband Robert also wrote—straddling
Arnold's two worlds: in early correspondence with Robert, she praised him in
terms that she would clearly have liked to hear applied to herself, "you have
in your vision two worlds—or to use the language of the schools of the day,
you are both subjective and objective in the habits of your mind. You can deal
both with abstract thought and with human passion in the most passionate
sense."[10] But she differs even from her husband in this vision, first, as Meredith Raymond explains, by insisting on the "poet's unique role" and "individuality" in "gathering" inspiration rather than on the primal, Platonic source
alone,[11] and second, as Dolores Rosenblum argues, by adhering to *un*ironic
vision:

> Robert Browning, then, with his ironic distance and shifting realities, would
> seem to be the more "modern" poet, less in the grip of Romantic projections.
> But as much as she, too, is committed to the deconstruction of Romantic pro-
> jections, Barrett Browning is equally committed to the epiphanic vision which
> would empower the oppressed—whether the Italian people or all women. . . .
> Because she, too, wants access to power, the female poet looks through appear-
> ances to the visionary distances; because she cannot forget female powerless-
> ness, however, she keeps looking steadfastly at the close-up view, the swarthiest
> face of things.[12]

Paradoxically, it would seem that Elizabeth Barrett Browning differs from
Robert both in her greater concern with the knotty problems of the present
and in her greater investment in visionary transcendence. She differs from
Robert Browning, Arnold, and Carlyle in her greater capacity for reconciling
discordant viewpoints.

Yet the philosophy gradually articulated by Aurora Leigh and the poetics she unfolds at the center of the poem in Book V are not only revisions of
Carlylian thought.[13] Her point of departure is a series of conflicts that include
Carlyle's ideas as one side of an intellectual debate. In *Aurora Leigh,* Browning's central *aesthetic* choice and worry appears to be between the Wordsworthian advocacy of a solitary songster inspired by the deep urgings of
nature[14] and the Carlylian demand for a didactic writer with urban concerns
that he records through rhetorical narratives. Of course, Wordsworth and
Carlyle actually developed somewhat more complex scenarios than this, such
that, paradoxically, we see Wordsworth finding solace both in the visions that
come when he is alone and in the prospect of extending this vision to a larger

community; while Carlyle's outspoken hero is often depicted as a wandering and visionary outcast who acquires stature and influence in the present age only through the written word. But neither Wordsworth nor Carlyle was able to urge this particular set of opposed possibilities with equal fervor. Browning confronts the choice quite directly, and she comes up with a poem and a poetics to embrace both.

Her poetic hero is a Carlylian character with the power to teach, persuade, and prophesy,

> poets should
> Exert a double vision; should have eyes
> To see near things as comprehensively
> As if afar they took their point of sight,
> And distant things as intimately deep
> As if they touched them.
> (V:183–88)

yet is also soulful, vulnerable, sensitive, and capable of a long, gradual growth of the mind: "And take for a worthier stage the soul itself" (V:340). Her hero-poet lives both in country and city, indulges in both ethical discussion and ecstatic inspiration, is keen both to aesthetic beauty and to social truth, and is both personally interested in events around her and cautious to see them from more than one side. Her story takes form both as a mimetic narrative and an expressive poem (Browning called it a "novel-poem"[15] as well as "unscrupulously epic" [V:214]). Later in the poem, Aurora summarizes its character as both an "imitation" of nature and "archetypal" in its symbolism (VII:835–43). In short, this is a poetics that gives equal weight to action and character, to mimesis and expressive form, to the double aim to teach and to delight. Why and how the poem achieved aesthetic success in having it both ways is not something I have space to explore in this essay except to note that it was addressed to an audience happily alive to the appeal of large, baggy, multi-purposed poems; many readers in *Aurora Leigh*'s Victorian audience responded to the formal aspects of the poem, to its richly imagistic lyricism and large-spirited narrative, with great enthusiasm.[16]

While this concern with a double vision deeply informs Aurora's professed poetics and is, as I will further argue below, its most distinctive feature, the discourse on poetry in Book V officially begins, like previous classic defenses of poetry, with a more specific issue likely to concern all writers of her time: the question whether she was living in an age in which heroical epic poetry could be written. She addresses the problem convincingly and wittily, first by cutting the classics down to the size of the present:

> The critics say that epics have died out
> With Agamemnon and the goat-nursed gods;

> I'll not believe it. I could never deem,
> As Payne Knight did . . .
> . . . .
> That Homer's heroes measured twelve feet high.
> They were but men:—his Helen's hair turned grey
> Like any plain Miss Smith's who wears a front;
> And Hector's infant whimpered at a plume
> As yours last Friday at a turkey-cock.
> (V:139–50)

Second, she appeals to the possibility for heroism in any age and time:

> All actual heroes are essential men,
> And all men possible heroes: every age,
> Heroic in proportions, double-faced,
> Looks backward and before, expects a morn
> And claims an epos.
> Ay, but every age
> Appears to souls who live in't (ask Carlyle)
> Most unheroic. Ours, for instance, ours:
> (V:151–57)

Finally, she places the responsibility for recognizing heroism squarely with the poet: "the poets abound / Who scorn to touch [the age] with a finger-tip" (V:158–59). Browning joins another common debate of her age in arguing that the poet's subject should be the present rather than Carlyle's fabled past, and she argues that this is a noble subject against his tendency to see the present primarily as an object for satire. The task of seeing the age in this way remains with the poet: whether the age is great or not depends on whether or not its poets can see from two perspectives at once, see the world small and see it large.

In the course of this general argument, Aurora also indicates, indirectly, where to find epic battlegrounds in the present. The great battles of the age are waged, as Aurora's must be waged, in verbal debate:

> Nay, if there's room for poets in this world
> A little overgrown (I think there is),
> Their sole work is to represent the age,
> Their age, not Charlemagne's,—this live, throbbing age,
> That brawls, cheats, maddens, calculates, aspires,
> And spends more passion, more heroic heat,
> Betwixt the mirrors of its drawing-rooms,
> Than Roland with his knights at Roncesvalles.
> . . . .
> . . . King Arthur's self
> Was commonplace to Lady Guenever;

> And Camelot to minstrels seemed as flat
> As Fleet Street to our poets.
>
> (V:200–13)

Browning is humorously, yet correctly, specific about where epic debates predominantly occurred: in the social arena of women's drawing rooms and in the bookshops of Fleet Street. Although she does not reiterate them here, the rest of her poem is devoted to the social issues most debated: between the classes, between the sexes, between poetry and social science, between belief and agnosticism. These, in addition to her aesthetic choices, are the proper subject of her poem.

Nonetheless, her avowed aim is not finally to dramatize or announce the victory of any one side of these various issues over the other. Her key terms—as resonant for her as Arnold's "disinterestedness," Wordsworth's "feeling," or Aristotle's "mythos"—are the "twofold," "double vision," and "double-faced."[17] Her use of these terms anticipates the obsession of twentieth-century criticism with the terminology of irony, double perspective, binary opposition, différance. In contrast to New Critical irony and structuralist binarism, whose self-cancellations enable the critic to achieve a transcendent detachment, and in contrast to Derridean différance with its endlessly radicalizing erosions, Browning's terminology enacts embrasure, enfolding possibilities, multiplying choices, permitting alternatives. Browning's usage in particular of "twofold" and "double vision" anticipates a number of contemporary feminist theorists, who have adopted the vocabulary of "doubleness" to call for a similarly syncretic criticism. A notable difference here is that contemporary feminists tend to use such terms to indicate the difficult dilemmas in which they find themselves, to indicate, for example, the necessity for women to see as men but also as women, to see as women but also as different women—as African-Americans, lesbians, Third-World women—to see as women but also beyond gender, or to see from within an experience but also from without. Browning adopts yet another term, expressive of difficulty, but she again translates it into a word for conciliated opposites. More provocative than "twofold" is the conventionally duplicitous "double-faced," which Browning transforms by continually placing the term in contexts in which it is redefined and revalued as an expression for empathetic vision. For Browning, to see with a "double vision" does not, however, occur without struggle: it is to be able, in another of her formulations, to stand "face to face" with the world, confronting and accepting, opening oneself to and recognizing all that is other to oneself.[18]

Browning's terms receive very various applications in Aurora Leigh's hands. The age is "double-faced" in the citation above, in that, while inhering in the present moment, it looks into both the past and the future. More important, Browning believed that to lead others to a larger vision, she must meet "face to face & without mask the Humanity of the age"[19] and "exert a double vision" (V:184) by seeing both near and far. The artist must strive for a "twofold" life ("O sorrowful great gift / Conferred on poets, of a twofold life, / When one life has been found enough for pain!" V:380–82); that is, she must both be and see, to "stand up straight as demigods" (V: 384). Rearticulating these premises in Book VII, Aurora Leigh sums up in an impressive monologue:

> a twofold world
> Must go to a perfect cosmos. Natural things
> And spiritual,—who separates those two
> In art, in morals, or the social drift,
> Tears up the bond of nature and brings death
> . . . .
> We divide
> This apple of life, and cut it through the pips:
> The perfect round which fitted Venus' hand
> Has perished as utterly as if we ate
> Both halves. Without the spiritual, observe,
> The natural's impossible—no form,
> No motion: without sensuous, spiritual
> Is inappreciable,—no beauty or power:
> And in this twofold sphere the twofold man
> (For still the artist is intensely a man)
> Holds firmly by the natural, to reach
> The spiritual beyond it,—fixes still
> . . . man, the twofold creature, apprehends
> The twofold manner, in and outwardly,
> And nothing in the world comes single to him,
> A mere itself,—cup, column, or candlestick
>   (VII:762–805)

Even in her twofold nature, then, the poet does not in fact transcend her fellow creatures, but remains "man, the twofold creature." To be fully "twofold" may be extraordinary, but it can be achieved by anyone with enough will and aspiration; thus, at the end of the poem, even Aurora's hitherto antivisionary cousin Romney, who has devoted his life to everyday problems and practical reforms, can—though as blind as Milton—see with a poet's vision the New Jerusalem.

But the thorniest dialectic of all in this poem is the twofold *gender* of "man." Without the intense, personal experience of writing always in relation to men—in conflict with Romney's desire for a wife, in the shadow of his prejudices about women poets, and in competition with the great male poets of past and present—Aurora's (and Browning's) "twofold" philosophy might never have emerged. Aurora's struggle and ambition as a female animates all the other issues in the poem, most obviously in what she sees as possible "near" and "far" for herself and other women. The poem's feminism clearly has fueled the controversy surrounding it—Browning's gender carried much of the blame for flaws perceived by critics of her day[20]—and most feminist scholars consider the gender issue to be the most distinctive feature of Aurora/Browning's aesthetics. A woman artist is the subject of this poem, and her gender is her major obstacle in setting out on a career. Aurora's speculations about gender literally surround the poetics of Book V, constituting its narrative frame: her thoughts are most directly focused on gender when she is struggling with the fact of being female in her world, but being female is also her most recurrent worry when trying to write.

Even so, whether as a personal, sociological, or aesthetic problem, femaleness is seen by Aurora as a provisional, man-made obstacle that can be overcome. Aurora dedicates herself unhesitatingly to writing as well as any male ever wrote:

> Measure not the work
> Until the day's out and the labor done,
> . . . .
> And, in that we have nobly striven at least,
> Deal with us nobly, women though we be,
> And honor us with truth if not with praise.
> (V:77–83)

Every artist has a gender (since the artist is "intensely a man"), but writes both in and beyond gender. Aurora does not see herself (and neither, of course, did Browning) as writing exclusively for or about women. She writes as a literate and thoughtful woman for and about both men and women. Speaking in anger to Romney, she makes her position clear,

> You misconceive the question like a man,
> Who sees a woman as the complement
> Of his sex merely. You forget too much
> That every creature, female as the male,
> Stands single in responsible act and thought
> As also in birth and death. Whoever says
> To a loyal woman, "Love and work with me,"
> Will get fair answers if the work and love,
> Being good themselves, are good for her—
> . . . .
> But *me* your work
> Is not the best for,—nor your love the best,
> Nor able to commend the kind of work
> For love's sake merely. . . .
> For me,
> Perhaps I am not worthy, as you say,
> Of work like this: perhaps a woman's soul
> Aspires, and not creates: yet we aspire,

> And yet I'll try out your perhapses, sir,
> And if I fail . . . why, burn me up my straw
> Like other false works—I'll not ask for grace;
> Your scorn is better, cousin Romney. I
> Who love my art, would never wish it lower
> To suit my stature.
>
> (II:434–94)

Her poetics could not, then, be seen as an "alternative" poetics exclusively for women: it is a poetics for everyone, feminist in that it sees everyone as gendered, and everyone as in need of re-education about women's capacities.

The poem thus to some extent provides its own theoretical context for its celebrated imagery of childbearing women—imagery that forces us literally to see Aurora's ambitions for the female artist, and to see physical femaleness as twofold, sometimes grotesque, sometimes ennobled, and capable of the most diverse symbolism.[21] At the climax of her speech about the possibility for a contemporary epic, she depicts the age itself as female:

> Never flinch,
> But still, unscrupulously epic, catch
> Upon the burning lava of a song
> The full-veined, heaving, double-breasted Age:
> That, when the next shall come, the men of that
> May touch the impress with reverent hand, and say
> "Behold,—behold the paps we all have sucked!
> This bosom seems to beat still, or at least
> It sets ours beating. This is living art,
> Which thus presents and thus records true life."
>
> (V:213–22)

Aurora does not argue for a gender-free art but for an art that is great with life, and women may represent (flesh out) that life quite literally.

Aurora's epic poetics would not slip easily, however, into a standard anthology of "The History of Criticism" because, of course, it is embedded in a narrative context. *Aurora Leigh* is an extensive *ars poetica,* and although its poetics appears to emerge primarily from a (male) Aristotelian tradition, its *ars* emerges from the modern (woman's) novel.[22] Aurora's theory of art and the artist in Book V takes place while she is writing her books, philosophizing about them, trying to make a living, and suffering from solitude. A nonwriter reading the entire poem could glean from it an accurate description of a successful writer's life, of a lengthy career struggle, of writer's blocks, of postwriting depression, and of a writing woman's solitude, courage, self-doubt, and lucky chances. It is precisely through this contextualization that Browning's poetics works for and, in my view, reaches her most far-flung goals. Browning places her theory in action; she refuses to divorce philosophical rationalization from practical contexts; hers is meant to be a "living" word.

The poetics of Book V is placed at the center of the poem (complete with an invocation to the Muse). Structurally, this gives Aurora's poetics prominence and tends to lift it out of context. Book V is the "visionary" book of the epic. But it is as carefully located in a narrative context as any other section of the poem—more precisely, it is placed at the high point in Aurora's career. When Book V opens, Aurora has been in London for several years,[23] struggling for a living, and she has reached the point where she is nearly ready to write an epic. After calling for new inspiration and reiterating her desire to write as well as any man has ever written, she reviews her career up to this point, her ballads, her sonnets, her descriptive poems, and her pastorals; and she concludes that she will have failed in her ambitions if she does not go on to attempt the highest form, the form in which she must recreate her world in its entirety, an epic. From this humbling recognition she moves immediately to a justification of the epic form itself. When 200 lines later, she returns to herself, to her personal struggles and long working days, and announces to us and to herself "Behold, at last, a book" (V:352), we see in retrospect that her poetics has served a double purpose. While we have been listening to her apology for epic poetry, she has been conceiving her poem—writing her *Aurora Leigh.* Her poetics is a way of thinking out loud as she talks herself into writing this poem, justifying it not only to us but to herself. She then returns to meditating on the poem and the artist for another seventy lines or so, until again she returns to her personal life; and it appears in retrospect that she has meanwhile been revising, putting the final touches not only on her theory, but on her epic poem. In *Aurora Leigh,* philosophy and poetry go literally hand in hand.

This deft interlacing of Aurora's thoughts with her actions means that when she turns almost immediately in the fifth book from writing her poem to mourning the failures of her personal life as a woman, the transition is less abrupt, less contradictory than it might seem in a simple plot summary. Nothing now is left to Aurora to achieve in her career, and she remains a lonely woman, lonelier still with her great work complete; she is ripe for a postpartum depression. Aurora herself explains the shift in terms familiar to us from her previous theorizing about art: "To have our books / Appraised by love, associated with love, / While *we* sit loveless!" (V:474–76). Since she had meant, like most nineteenth-century poets, to produce an art embedded in life and life-giving, her own dismal life must undercut the success of her book. In perfecting one at the expense of the other, she has risked injuring both. True to her insistence on a Johnsonian appeal from art to nature, her ideas are subjected to skeptical questioning and proof by her subsequent experiences of solitude and eventual reunion with Romney.

Unlike Rasselas's, both her theories and her poetic creations survive their long test and receive fresh application when she comes face to face with Romney. The ending has provoked as much controversy as any other element in the book, for Aurora's new eagerness to serve Romney who all along has stood as her opposite (earthy while she is ethereal, a leader of men while she is a mere woman, a social activist while she insists on poetry), for the symbolic castration of the blinded Romney, and for the fact that both of these contribute to the striking but unacknowledged resemblance to the ending of *Jane Eyre* (which Browning appears to have forgotten when she echoed it here). The issues are perhaps too complex to explore thoroughly in this essay, but the ending may at least be reevaluated in light of Aurora's own poetics. While as acute a critic as Rachel Blau DuPlessis believes that because Aurora seeks to serve a "castrated" Romney in the end, this work "did not change the nineteenth-century convention of representation that saw the price of artistic ambition as the loss of femininity,"[24] what is most striking about this ending—when read in the context of Aurora's ideas—is her triumph in having it all: she has fame *and* Romney, Romney's love *and* respect, a new reason for working *and* a companion for her work (she will now work to embody the visions of them both). In the clear symbolism of this ending, Romney has learned to respect the visionary poet, while Aurora (without ceasing to write) can have a nitty-gritty life of her own. The difficulty of achieving all this is almost as great in our own time as it was in Browning's, though many more women are now trying. I suspect that, whatever other reasons readers have had for doubting this ending, its overflowing optimism has amazed them and, in some minds, marked it "female." But this was Aurora's vision, a vision that Browning herself realized, and the possibility for its triumph is one which the feminist reader should surely wish to grasp as her own.

Whatever our judgments of the way *Aurora Leigh* ends, the "twofold," "double-faced" character of Aurora's reasoning—of speculation wrestling with her own experimental life—remains one of the most compelling, though elusive, aesthetic features of this poem; it may also be the most useful feature to any feminist interested in binding *theoria* to *praxis*. A poetics emerges from its context in the poem in such a way as to resist being abstracted from its practical consequences. Moreover, while the poetics I have detailed belongs to the fictional Aurora, we are urged to believe with the first readers of the poem that Aurora was a portrait of the artist, and not to flinch from looking with a double vision at the artist in her art. We owe it as much to ourselves as to Browning to reconstruct this epical encounter of a woman's mind with *herstory*. Aurora is witness to the fact that Browning, at least, knew her achievement for what it was even as she wrote it: an unscrupulous epic by a woman poet.

Notes

1. Ellen Moers, *Literary Women* (Garden City, N.Y.: Doubleday, 1977; rpt. New York: Oxford University Press, 1985), pp. 14–15, 41.

2. Janice Radway, *Reading the Romance: Women, Patriarchy, and Popular Literature* (Chapel Hill: University of North Carolina Press, 1984). While professors of English are carefully training their students to appreciate Wordsworth, it is appalling to see a modern critic discard *Aurora Leigh* even for the educated reader, as did Virginia Radley: "the poet is to be commended for her effort, and for the sporadic but brilliant results that effort yielded. There is no question, however, that the total work is unwieldy, shapeless, amorphous, and philosophically untenable. While it will continue to be of interest to literary historians, it will never have much appeal for the general reading public (although an educated one) or, for that matter, for the mass of graduate students in English who seek a thesis topic with the urgent specter of 'Time's winged chariot' behind them," *Elizabeth Barrett Browning* (New York: Twayne, 1972), p. 125.

3. Although among feminist scholars and Victorianists there is resurgent interest in Browning's poetics, there are no accounts of *Aurora Leigh* as a comprehensive *ars poetica*, and I know of no contemporary outline for, or overview of, a feminist aesthetic that taps Browning's ideas or mentions her precedent.

4. Virginia Woolf may have initiated such a response in the case of *Aurora Leigh* when she gave a mixed review of the poem's success, overlooking and thus undermining Browning's own defense. But *Aurora Leigh* anticipates many of the issues that worry Woolf in *A Room of One's Own,* including most prominently the basic needs for a room of one's own and (in Aurora Leigh's day) £300: "You're richer than you fancy. The will says, / *Three hundred pounds, and any other sum / Of which the said testatrix dies possessed*" (emphasis in text). (ll. 300–302). See Virginia Woolf, "*Aurora Leigh,*" in *The Second Common Reader* (New York: Harcourt, Brace, & World, 1960), pp. 182–92; Elizabeth Barrett Browning, *Aurora Leigh,* II:987–89, in *The Complete Works of Elizabeth Barrett Browning,* ed. Charlotte Porter and Helen A. Clarke, vols. 4 and 5 (1900; rpt. New York: AMS Press, 1973). Subsequent citations of *Aurora Leigh* refer to this edition and appear parenthetically in the text.

5. Standard classroom anthologies by male editors cannot be counted on to contain representative selections of women's theories: Walter Jackson Bate includes a single text, Woolf's "Modern Fiction" in his *Criticism: The Major Texts* (New York: Harcourt Brace Jovanovich, 1970); no women theorists are included in Hazard Adams, *Critical Theory since Plato* (New York: Harcourt Brace Jovanovich, 1971). For a more representative selection of women critics (not, however, including Browning), see *Literary Criticism and Theory: The Greeks to the Present,* ed. Robert Con Davis and Laurie Finke (New York: Longman, 1989).

6. Lawrence Lipking, "Aristotle's Sister: A Poetics of Abandonment," *Critical Inquiry* 10 (September 1983), 61–81. Lipking has incorporated this essay in an expanded form into his *Abandoned Women and Poetic Tradition* (Chicago: University of Chicago Press, 1988).

7. As Josephine Donovan points out, Lipking's discussion replicates the efforts of women theorists—including Susan S. Lanser, Evelyn Torton Beck, Michele Barrett, and Elaine Showalter—to establish, in Showalter's terminology, a "gynocriticism." Donovan criticizes Lipking for extracting this poetics, somewhat contradictorily, from men's writing about women and from the European sentimentalist tradition, in which young heroines are typically seduced and abandoned. (Donovan follows Nancy K. Miller in this last description of the "heroine's text.") Donovan argues that a poetics should be grounded wholly in works by women and that it should be a "women's" not a "woman's" poetics, reflecting women's diverse experiences. Even so, Lipking's emphasis on women's suffering and solitude, the constriction of their lives to the private sphere, their understanding of and insistence on the importance of their personal lives when they finally do speak, and their yearning for community are often cited prominently in feminist discussions of women's experiences. See Josephine Donovan's "Toward a Women's Poetics," in *Feminist Issues in Literary Scholarship,* ed. Shari Benstock (Bloomington: Indiana University Press, 1987), pp. 98–109.

8. See, for example, Joan DeJean, "Fictions of Sappho," *Critical Inquiry* 13.4 (1987), 787–805; Donovan, "Toward a Women's Poetics," pp. 99–100, 105–7; and Jane Marcus, "Still

Practice, A/Wrested Alphabet: Toward a Feminist Aesthetic," in Benstock, *Feminist Issues in Literary Scholarship*, pp. 81–84.

9. Carlyle's ideas about heroism appear throughout his works, but most comprehensively in *On Heroes, Hero-Worship, and the Heroic in History* (1841; rpt. New York: AMS Press, 1969). While several critics have noted the influence both of a Carlylian work ethic and of his attack on materialism in Aurora Leigh's philosophy, none have recognized the relevance of the Carlylian (Wo)Man of Letters to this poetics. See Helen Cooper, *Elizabeth Barrett Browning, Woman and Artist* (Chapel Hill: University of North Carolina Press, 1988), p. 162; Deirdre David, " 'Art's a Service': Social Wound, Sexual Politics, and *Aurora Leigh*," *Browning Institute Studies* 13 (1985), 133–34; Alethea Hayter, *Mrs. Browning: A Poet's Work and Its Setting* (London: Faber & Faber, 1962), p. 159; and Dorothy Mermin, *Elizabeth Barrett Browning: The Origins of a New Poetry* (Chicago: University of Chicago Press, 1989), p. 202.

In constructing her "epic," Browning was by no means indebted to male writers alone. A number of critics argue that the unique shape of her "novel-poem" arises from her combination of aspects of women's novels and of men's poems; I will argue something similar below. For discussions of sources for the narrative of *Aurora Leigh* in works by both men and women writers, see especially Kathleen Blake, "Elizabeth Barrett Browning and Wordsworth: The Romantic Poet as a Woman," *Victorian Poetry* 24 (winter 1986), 387–98; Hayter, *Mrs. Browning*, pp. 159–62; Julia Bolton Holloway, "*Aurora Leigh* and *Jane Eyre*," *The Brontë Society* 17.2 (1977), 126–32; Cora Kaplan, *Aurora Leigh and Other Poems* (London: The Women's Press Ltd., 1978), pp. 5–36; Mermin, *Elizabeth Barrett Browning*, pp. 183–224; Dolores Rosenblum, "Face to Face: Elizabeth Barrett Browning's *Aurora Leigh* and Nineteenth-Century Poetry," *Victorian Studies* 26 (spring 1983), 321–38, and "*Casa Guidi Windows* and *Aurora Leigh:* The Genesis of Elizabeth Barrett Browning's Visionary Aesthetic," *Tulsa Studies in Women's Literature* 4.1 (1985), 61–68; and Marjorie Stone, "Genre Subversion and Gender Inversion: *The Princess* and *Aurora Leigh*," *Victorian Poetry* 25 (summer 1987), 101–27.

10. *The Letters of Robert Browning and Elizabeth Barrett Barrett 1845–1846*, ed. Elvan Kintner (Cambridge: Harvard University Press, 1969), vol. 1, p. 9.

11. Meredith Raymond, "Elizabeth Barrett Browning's Poetics 1845–1846: 'The Ascending Gyre,' " *Browning Society Notes* 11 (1981), 2.

12. Dolores Rosenblum, "*Casa Guidi*," pp. 66–67. Nina Auerbach conducts a provocative analysis of the literary "marriage" of the Brownings, in which Robert's irony operates at the expense of Elizabeth, in "Robert Browning's Last Word," *Victorian Poetry* 22.2 (1984), 161–73.

13. Lipking extols the prospect for a woman's poetics to "repair the balance of theory," but he believes this means that a feminist aesthetic must be necessarily reactive and that this is not entirely satisfactory: "Insofar as [a poetics of 'abandonment'] accurately represents the strategies of female authors within and against the dominant culture, it stands for a history of subordination and reaction that many women oppose more strenuously than they do the patriarchs themselves" (p. 78). Like Lipking's poetics, Browning's is reformative rather than anarchic or revolutionary, but it is not the plight of women alone to find themselves "reacting" at the moment of attempted "origination"; male critics are as burdened in this way as women.

14. Kathleen Blake demonstrates important parallels between Browning and Wordsworth, but I must disagree with her that Browning refutes Victorian objectivity in favor of Romanticist subjectivism: Victorian authors (notably, Arnold, Carlyle, Tennyson, and Robert Browning) viewed the claims of objectivity and subjectivity as in conflict and believed that a reconciliation should be achieved; Browning was as deeply invested in this problem as any of her peers. Blake's essay reflects the persistent critical tendency to privilege Wordsworth's aesthetics over any other in the nineteenth century. See Blake, "Elizabeth Barrett Browning and Wordsworth," pp. 387–98. The allusion to Wordsworth's "Immortality Ode" in the opening lines of the poem has been widely recognized by critics, but following on its heels is Byronic

satire (as Alethea Hayter points out, *Mrs. Browning,* p. 162), a kind of satire in which Carlyle also specialized. Aurora refers reverently to Keats in Book I, ll. 1003–15, but later she chooses epic poetry over the Keatsian lyricism with which her career began.

15. *Letters,* vol. 1, p. 31.

16. Amply documented by critics is the immediate and enormous popularity of the work; the enthusiasm of progressive writers, such as D. G. Rossetti, Swinburne, Landor, and others; and the anxiety expressed by the major quarterlies over its strong views and strong language. As Cora Kaplan reminds us, "everybody in polite society read it, even the Queen, and Barrett Browning was delighted by reports that it had corrupted women of sixty and been banned by horrified parents" (p. 12). But, as mentioned above, praise for the poem has often been mixed. As Radley notes, the reviews "affixed to the Porter-Clarke edition of the works, contain such diametrically opposed critical opinions as to make the reader wonder if the reviewers could possibly be discussing the same work" (*Elizabeth Barrett Browning,* p. 124). Both Virginia Woolf and Moers, for example, enjoyed reading *Aurora Leigh,* for its "speed and energy, forthrightness and complete self-confidence," "*Aurora Leigh,*" p. 184; quoted in Moers, *Literary Women,* p. 59. Woolf, however, also thought *Aurora Leigh* would have made a first-rate novel without the poetry; while Moers decided it would be first-rate poetry if it were less of a novel: "we need to slow down, to stop running against conventions" and "retreat into solitude, silence, decorum, and rhymed obscurity with Emily Dickinson" (p. 60). Although complex circumstances must have affected such discrepant evaluations, the most compelling discussions I know of Browning's challenge to genre boundaries in this poem are those of Susan Stanford Friedman, "Gender and Genre Anxiety: Elizabeth Barrett Browning and H.D. as Epic Poets," *Tulsa Studies in Women's Literature* 5.2 (1986), 203–28; Dorothy Mermin, "Gender and Genre in *Aurora Leigh,*" *The Victorian Newsletter* 69 (spring 1986), 7–11; and Stone, "Genre Subversion and Gender Inversion," pp. 101–27.

17. Rosenblum argues that Barrett Browning's "double vision" affects even her technique and "requires constant shifts in focus" from near to far and back again ("*Casa Guidi,*" p. 65). In addition to recognizing the importance of the "twofold" in Browning's poetics, Raymond points to a lesser "three-fold division" of "the poetic power" among "the senses, the intellect, and the soul," which in the fully successful poet may be united (p. 1), but this latter set of distinctions sinks from view in *Aurora Leigh.*

18. In a discussion of Eliza Haywood's literary criticism, Kristina Straub employs the vocabulary of doubleness (of "double vision," seeing "double," "double position" as woman and critic, doubled "perspective," "double writing," and "double reading"), not directly from Haywood, but by inference, and she cites parallel instances in the theories of Joan Kelly, Naomi Schor, and Bonnie Zimmerman. The notion of "doubleness" is pervasive in current feminist criticism. Browning's idea of the "double-faced" should similarly be contrasted with a necessary "duplicity" discussed by Straub, Schor, and Jonathan Culler, among others. See Kristina Straub, "Women, Gender, and Criticism," in *Literary Criticism and Theory: The Greeks to the Present,* pp. 859–66, 871–76. Also see Jonathan Culler, "Reading as a Woman," *On Deconstruction: Theory and Criticism after Structuralism* (Ithaca, N.Y.: Cornell University Press, 1982), pp. 43–64; Joan Kelly, "The Doubled Vision of Feminist Theory," in *Sex and Class in Women's History,* ed. Judith L. Newton, Mary P. Ryan, and Judith Walkowitz (London: Routledge & Kegan Paul, 1983), pp. 259–70; Naomi Schor, "Reading Double: Sand's Difference," in *The Poetics of Gender,* ed. Nancy K. Miller (New York: Columbia University Press, 1986), pp. 248–69; and Bonnie Zimmerman, "What Has Never Been: An Overview of Lesbian Feminist Criticism," in *The New Feminist Criticism: Essays on Women, Literature, and Theory,* ed. Elaine Showalter (New York: Pantheon Books, 1985), pp. 200–24.

19. *Letters,* vol. 1, p. 31.

20. Browning's contemporary Sydney Dobell wrote, for example, that *Aurora Leigh* "contains some of the finest poetry written in the century; poetry such as Shakespeare's sister might have written if he had had a twin. . . . But it is no poem. No woman can write a poem";

quoted in Jerome Buckley, *The Victorian Temper* (Cambridge: Cambridge University Press, 1981), p. 63.

21. On the imagery of motherhood and manhood in this poem, see, for example, Sandra Donaldson, " 'Motherhood's Advent in Power': Elizabeth Barrett Browning's Poems about Motherhood," *Victorian Poetry* 18 (spring 1980), 51–60; and Virginia Steinmetz, "Beyond the Sun: Patriarchal Images in *Aurora Leigh*," *Studies in Browning and His Circle* 9 (winter 1981), 18–41, and "Images of 'Mother-Want' in Elizabeth Barrett Browning's *Aurora Leigh*," *Victorian Poetry* 21 (winter 1983), 351–67.

22. For accounts of other aspects of the structure of this poem—which has otherwise received little attention—see C. Castan, "Structural Problems and the Poetry of *Aurora Leigh*," *Browning Society Notes* 7.3 (1977), 73–81; and Cooper, *Elizabeth Barrett Browning,* pp. 153–55. Two particularly interesting discussions of character changes in Aurora may be found in Barbara Gelpi, "*Aurora Leigh:* The Vocation of the Woman Poet," *Victorian Poetry* 19 (spring 1981), 35–48; and Sandra Gilbert, "From Patria to Matria: Elizabeth Barrett Browning's Risorgimento," *PMLA* 99.2 (1984), 194–211.

23. The precise number of years is uncertain. Castan and Cooper both believe that the narrating Aurora is 27 years old from the opening of the poem through Book V, until in ll. 1171–76 the narrated Aurora catches up with the narrator and they remain together to the end of the poem. But the poem moves back and forth between past and present when narrating the writing of Aurora's epic in Book V, from, for example, "Alas, I still see something to be done, / . . . / Behold, at last, a book" to "I laboured on alone" (V:344–52, 421), suggesting the "journalistic" style that Cooper describes in Books VIII and IX, pp. 153, 201, n. 17.

24. Rachel Blau DuPlessis, *Writing Beyond the Ending: Narrative Strategies of Twentieth-Century Women Writers* (Bloomington: Indiana University Press, 1985), p. 87.

Mapping Sublimity:
Elizabeth Barrett Browning's
Sonnets from the Portuguese

JEROME MAZZARO

For a Renaissance scholar and modernist like Robert B. Heilman, Elizabeth Barrett Browning's sonnet "How do I love thee?" (43) with its "piling up of abstractions and generalizations . . . gives a positive effect of insincerity." It "is as embarrassing as all platform rhetoric." He compares the poem's matter to Goneril's similar protestation of love for her father in Shakespeare's *King Lear* (I.i.58–62), distorting the inappropriateness of Goneril's emotions for a parent into an attack on Barrett Browning's verse technique.[1] Certainly, as T. S. Eliot remarks in "The Metaphysical Poets" (1921), between Shakespeare and Barrett Browning a change or "dissociation of sensibility set in." No longer, as in the poetry of Edmund Spenser, were emotions to be set off by the poet's constructing an external and conventional emblem or image to which a reader's emotions would sympathetically respond. Rather, as William Wordsworth noted in his Preface to *Lyrical Ballads* (1800), poems and their subjects would rise internally from a "spontaneous overflow of powerful feelings." In the case of the Romantic poets, whom Barrett Browning succeeded, the emotion most often sought was that of the sublime, situated, as religious writers like Robert Lowth held, in terror and shrinkage associated with contemplating divinity, eternity, etc. or, as Wordsworth maintained, in mentally expansive moments amid primitive nature or, as in his "Upon the Sight of a Beautiful Picture" (1815), amid the modest and commonplace.[2] Wordsworth's own evocations of the sublime in his poetry in terms of terror, transgressed boundaries, and spatial metaphors have been ably argued,[3] and in *Sonnets from the Portuguese* (1850) Barrett Browning seems intent on adapting the terror and physicality of these metaphors to her own encounter late in life with love. In so doing, she is not always involved, as Heilman infers that she might be, in expressing literary sincerity.

Reprinted from *Essays in Literature* 18, no. 2 (Fall 1991): 166–79. © 1991 Western Illinois University. Used by permission of the publisher.

Barrett Browning's interests in sublimity are everywhere evident in her Prefaces. She not only uses them to reject the opinion "that poetry is not a proper vehicle for abstract ideas" but speaks of poetry and its aims in moral superlatives. In the Preface to *The Battle of Marathon* (1819), for instance, she calls poetry the "noblest" human production: it "elevates the mind to heaven, kindles within it unwonted fires, and bids it throb with feelings exalting to its nature." She chooses to model her own work on Homer, "the sublime poet of antiquity," hoping, like him, to awaken audiences "to the praise of valour, honour, patriotism, and, best of all, to a sense of the high attributes of the Deity, though darkly and mysteriously revealed." Seven years later, she invokes the "sublime" Dante, wishing that, in *An Essay on Mind,* "the sublime circuit of intellect . . . had fallen to the lot of a spirit more powerful than [hers]," so that the work's "vastness" of design and "infinite" subject might have been better embraced. Longinus, "the Homer of critics," is invoked in the Preface to *The Seraphim* (1828) to counter a generation of critics who "believed in the inadmissibility of religion into poetry." Stating that "the very incoherences of poetic dreaming are but the struggle and the strife to reach the True in the Unknown," she claims for herself these "sublime uses of poetry, and the solemn responsibilities of the poet." In the 1844 Preface to her *Poems,* she again laments "the tendency of the present day . . . to sunder the daily life from the spiritual creed," having earlier, in her Preface to *Prometheus Bound* (1833), faulted Longinus for not having recognized Aeschylus's creating in Prometheus "the sublime of virtue" which her own verse translation seeks to preserve.[4]

Nor is there any question that, as biographers have pointed out, expansive as well as terrifying moments accompanied the successful suit and daily life on which *Sonnets from the Portuguese* is built. Elizabeth Barrett was thirty-nine at the time of her first meeting with Robert Browning and already a highly regarded poet. She had suffered the deaths of her mother and brother and had reconciled herself to ill health, opium addiction, and the foregoing of many of the rewards that an active life offers. She was reclusive, bookish, contemplative, and intellectual, and, although not the "confined" and "almost hermetically sealed" figure that R. H. Horne describes in *A New Spirit of the Age* (1844), she had turned her thoughts toward death.[5] Now, she was forced by Browning's insistence to consider turning these thoughts back toward life, surrendering her chastity, marrying, and devoting herself once again to the risks and disappointments of an active existence. In doing so, she would be defying a dictatorial father who characteristically would oppose the action and who, since her brother's death, had not reproached her for her part in it. Moreover, by the union, she would be giving up a direct relationship that she had forged with God in order to stand, as Saint Paul observed, in relation to a husband as that husband did to God and as the church does to Christ (Ephesians 5:21–24). Rather than the vividness and gentle agitations of beauty, the conflict, implications, and resolutions of these possibilities affected her deepest being.[6]

There is no question, either, that formally some of the techniques that Renaissance poets used to assert sincerity in their sonnets are used by Barrett Browning in realizing parts of the sequence. With their rigorous *abbaabbacdcdcd* Petrarchan rhyme scheme and Miltonic disregard of line end and division into octave and sestet, the poems suggest that, much as in the sonnets of John Donne and John Milton, violations to form occur because the emotions or thoughts are in excess of or different from what convention allows. The failure of the content of Donne's "At the round earth's imagined corners," for instance, to fit neatly the *abbaabbacdcdee* rhyme scheme that he provides is, in part, a tribute to the forcefulness of the poem's vision of world end and a reinforcement of the destruction and transformation that take place. Both he and Milton accepted the sonnet form as *lingua franca* for ideas and strong emotions and saw their formal violations of it as acceptable, more truly personally reflective weddings of form to content.[7] Barrett Browning, like Wordsworth before her, seems, in contrast, to have to justify not adjustments to form but the very idea of the sonnet as an adequate embodiment of or vehicle for true emotion. Wordsworth's comparisons of the form to a prison which "no prison is" and to what in Milton's hands "became a trumpet" that let him blow "soul-animated strains" are here relevant. At times, in the *Sonnets from the Portuguese,* form and content are so deliberately left at odds to mark not excess but empty and artificial boundaries that periodically, on grounds independent of sincerity, critics other than Heilman have called the competence of Barrett Browning's verse technique into question.

These critics see in Barrett Browning's submissions to a system of measure (line) and closure (rhyme) that does not measure or close and in her appeals for authority and convention to biblical and literary antecedents that do not quite correspond an impetuosity, faulty judgment, or misplaced ingenuity. They cite the "Latinate horrors, strained conceits, and specious supernatural intervention" that generally mar her verse and note, in the failure of these poems to observe line endings and divide neatly into octet and sestet, "the straining muscles and suffused countenance of the prisoner in the straitjacket." In the much praised Sonnet 5 ("I lift my heavy heart up solemnly"), for example, they are united in pointing out the imprecision of Sophocles's Electra as a correlative for the poet's feelings about her dead brother. Electra is mistaken about Orestes's being dead, and a reader's knowledge of this fact confuses the poem's impression. Critics are similarly embarrassed by the false self-depreciation that occurs in Sonnets 3 and 4 and by images that seem to make sense only as they are explained by the poet's life and letters. They have also objected on occasion to the poet's choice of language and the exaggerated nature of many of her contrasts. These failures in presenting precise correlatives for emotion have led even supporters of her work like Alethea

Hayter to call the result a "cornucopia" of "rich confused fruits" and pronounce the "much-praised" sequence "not her best work" because in it "she is dealing with an emotion too new and powerful for her to transmute . . . into universally valid terms."8

Moreover, as a result of gender, temperament, or a decision to follow history, the poems do not adhere either to the stereotypes of Victorian romance or to most Renaissance love sequences. Victorian social conventions provided no ready serious models for centering on an active older woman in love. They dictated, rather, that "good" women in love be young, submissive, devout, attractive, patient, helpless, and passive. Their function was to lift "carnal" man into a "higher life." Nor were Renaissance conventions with their cupids, arrows, and love sickness more accommodating. Love did not enter by the eye and take root in the heart. Nor was the speaker—like the speakers of so many older sequences—the initial pursuer languishing in pain at a beloved's cruelty. Rather, as Dorothy Mermin points out, the sequence confounds what "earlier love poetry had kept separate and opposite: speaker and listener, subject and object of desire, male and female." It begins with the sudden intrusion of love and the reasons why it must or should not occur. The sequence then moves to love's acceptance in calls for closeness and union that are repeatedly imaged as occurring between the "darkness" of the speaker's life before love entered and her views of God and eternity. By Sonnet 22, love is accepted, and with the exception of Sonnet 35, the last half of the sequence bears no indications of regret. In Sonnet 35, the speaker wonders briefly whether, having invited disowning, she will miss home and family. It is the sequence's celebration of joy as a reversal of fortune and a joint reflection on real life happiness that prompted its early appeal. In addition to a sign of divine favor, the successful overcoming of impediments, differences, and distances is, as Glennis Stephenson remarks, the substance of "all great love stories" and makes "the consummation, when it occurs, . . . appear all the more moving and perfect."9

Nonetheless, while true and significant, the poet's supposed impetuosity and the sequence's failures to adhere to Victorian and Renaissance love conventions explain less some of its oppositions of content and form and occasional absences of sincerity than do Lowth's characterizations of the sublime. In *Lectures on the Sacred Poetry of the Hebrews* (1787), Lowth cites not only the presence of "elevated sentiments" and bright, animated, energetic, and uncommon language but also the reluctance of the text "to fix on any single point." The mind moves "continually from one object to another," suddenly and frequently changing persons, especially in addresses and expostulations and, at times, in the very act of uttering, catches suddenly at a new and sometimes redundant expression that appears more animated and energetic. Likewise occurring at these times are frequent changes or variations in tense. In dealing with deity, Lowth remarks that "nothing . . . is nobler or more majestic" than a description "carried on by a kind of continued negation."

Boundaries "are gradually extended on every side, and at length totally removed; [and] the mind is insensibly led on towards infinity." Citing as "the most perfect example . . . of the sublime ode" a text "which possesses a sublimity dependent wholly upon the greatness of the conceptions, and the dignity of the language, without any peculiar excellence in the form and arrangement," he prepares the way for statements like S. T. Coleridge's that "nothing that has a shape can be sublime except by metaphor *ab occasione ad rem*" and the belief that forms like the sonnet might become a series of boundaries whose inability to contain a writer's "utmost faculties and grandest imagery" contributes to a feeling of majesty and the sometimes inexpressible majesty of God.[10]

This emphasis on the sublime would directly affect sincerity by affecting the sequence's ability to create and sustain character. First, character resides in a grammar of coherence, and the sudden shifts in person, tone, tense, emotion, and diction which Lowth details detract from a central identifiable focal point. But even if this point were to be manifest, a common trait of sublimity is a feeling of transport out of one's characteristical focus. In the case of Shakespeare's characters whose transports derive not from sublimity but from passion, Dr. Johnson notes that they so come to act and speak under "the influence of these general passions and principles by which all minds are agitated" that they manifest "nothing characteristical." The choice for an editor's "correctly" assigning speeches to a specific actor hinges on extrinsic evidence. Indeed, sublime transport differs markedly from both the internally consistent unifying voice, lifestyle, outlook, and behavior of the secular Renaissance love sequence and the violations of form and emotionally based meditational transports of its religious poetry. In the sonnets of Donne, for example, the elevated passions of the sestet are prepared for by the octet's equally intense context- and self-defining interactive language and central binding image. Thus, while "escapist," they are, nonetheless, "in character" with the octave psychologically and theologically. In the sonnets of George Herbert, where, as in those of Barrett Browning, the opacity of verbal interaction is weaker and no distanced persona emerges, the degree that a unified or sincere self occurs is gauged outside the poem in weighing the poem's language against the poet's other works or life.[11]

In the opening two sonnets of *Sonnets from the Portuguese*, one can see how these elements of the sublime are incorporated into the sequence. The first sonnet takes the reader from the comfortable and bounded imaginative realm of literary reminiscence into the frightening and unbounded realm of mystical appearance:

> I thought once how Theocritus had sung
> Of the sweet years, the dear and wished for years,
> Who each one in a gracious hand appears
> To bear a gift for mortals, old or young:

> And, as I mused it in his antique tongue,
> I saw, in gradual vision through my tears,
> The sweet, sad years, the melancholy years,
> Those of my life, who by turns had flung
> A shadow across me. Straightway I was 'ware
> So weeping, how a mystic Shape did move
> Behind me, and drew me backward by the hair,
> And a voice said in mastery while I strove . . .
> "Guess now who holds thee?"—"Death," I said. But there,
> The silver answer rang . . . "Not Death, but Love."

The poem opens on a figure who thinks of life in terms of art, in this instance, of life as imaged by Theocritus in Idyll 15 (ll. 102–05). The allusion is precise and, indeed, an adequate translation of the Greek. In the Idyll, the lines appear as part of a song that is sung by an accomplished female poet and contrast with the everyday chatter of the two women who pause to hear the singer. Their "dear and wished for years" not only revive briefly the annual return of Adonis from the dead which the original Greek celebrates but also embody return in their being themselves recollection. With their "gift" of recovery, they thus oppose "the sweet, sad . . . melancholy years" of the second quatrain and their implied irretrievable loss that "flung / A shadow" across the speaker's life. This shadow suddenly gives way in the sestet to the awareness of "a mystic Shape" which seems to echo and combine those visionary episodes of Eliphaz in Job (4:12–16), Jacob in Genesis (32:27–30), and Paul in Acts (9:3–5).[12] It violently draws the speaker "backward by the hair" and eventually reveals itself as Love. In so doing, it rejects her expectations of Death and, by proximity, so merges Love and Death that, coevally as one is led by "mystic" and the calculated incoherence into the realm of the sublime, one is returned to Theocritus and the associations there of love and death with Adonis and Venus and Persephone and Dis. Given Barrett Browning's Preface to *The Seraphim* (1838), one is led, in addition, to Christ's death as love and the Christ-like imagery that will surround the suitor of the sequence.[13]

Moreover, one has in the conflation of referents for the "mystic Shape" an example of the inability to grasp exactly and, therefore, the need to try several metaphors that the sublime occasions.[14] In their edition of *The Complete Works* (1900), Charlotte Porter and Helen Clarke identify the wording of the incident with Athena's action toward Achilles in Book 1 of the Iliad (1:197–98).[15] There is, however, in the Barrett Browning telling no anger, a reversal of gender and no prior acquaintance with the deity. Achilles recognizes the goddess immediately. The incident does seem to suggest what theologians call "catabatic mysticism" (i.e., divinity's approaching the human), and it is the suggestion of such an approach that the verses from Job, Genesis, and Acts make their claims. In *A Philosophical Enquiry into the Origin of Our Ideas of the Sublime and Beautiful* (1757, 1759), Edmund Burke calls the Job passage "amazingly sublime," and Job's passing from joy to loss to regained joy parallels the speaker's passage in the sequence from "childhood joy" to the loss of a brother to regained happiness. But here, too, differences exist. In Job, the mystic shape appears *before* not *behind* Eliphaz and draws him forward to the belief that one cannot comprehend and, therefore, should not presume to interpret God's measure. In the parallels from Genesis and Acts, the violence which the figure displays by drawing the speaker backward by the hair is echoed in Jacob's wrestling and Paul's unhorsing and their efforts to know the figure's name in the speaker's query and disclosure.[16] The failure of the sonnet's content, consequently, to fit formal demands is understandable, given the poem's sublime elements.

In the second sonnet, a different kind of confusion associated with sublimity occurs. The suitor is introduced, and the seemingly boundless realm which deity inhabits is imaged as terrifying audible darkness.[17] Deity's opposing Nay, which furnishes the speaker's first effort at dissuasion, is so absolute that even death could not make her feel more closed to the gentleman than she now feels. Expressed as visual exclusion, this sense speaks to the suitor's physical being and, building on the "only" and "all" of the sonnet's opening line, contrasts with the presumed limitlessness of God. Had God so ordained, the poem ventures, as terrifying and vast as the greatest efforts of man and nature are, they would not have been able to prevent the union.

> But only three in all God's universe
> Have heard this word thou hast said,—Himself beside
> Thee speaking, and me listening! and replied
> One of us . . *that* was God, . . and laid the curse
> So darkly on my eyelids, as to amerce
> My sight from seeing thee,—that if I had died,
> The deathweights, placed there, would have signified
> Less absolute exclusion. "Nay" is worse
> From God than from all others, O my friend!
> Men could not part us with their worldly jars,
> Nor the seas change us, nor the tempests bend;
> Our hands would touch for all the mountain-bars,—
> And, heaven being rolled between us at the end,
> We should but vow the faster for the stars.

In drawing the expanses of personal terror and shrinkage which accompany the sublime when it is associated with deity, the sonnet again displays confusion and incoherence. Phrase is piled upon phrase, and orderly progressions of thought are twice interrupted by qualifying parenthetical matter. First, in line 4, "one" is identified as "God," and then, in a further compounding of confusion, the "curse" of line 4 is identified as a punishment before its exclusionary nature is given. "Amerce," as scholars have pointed out, joins the speaker's fate verbally to those angels of *Paradise Lost* who for Satan's fault are "amerc't / Of Heav'n" (1:609–10). Presumably, her similar opposition to divine will by allowing the suit will deprive her of the gentleman's "Christlike" sight as these angels have been deprived of the sight of God. But one has almost to eliminate the interruption in order to understand the situation fully. These syntactical and sequential confusions lessen as the poem moves in the sestet to a sense of positive expansion associated with the natural sublime and recalls the impediments to "the marriage of true minds" that Shakespeare writes of in Sonnet 116. This move from confusion and incoherence is conveyed in lines which, despite their negations, honor rhyme and formal line end. They restore the worldly and literary senses of order on which the sequence opened and, hence, round off the sonnets from or bridge them to the remainder of the sequence. The sonnets are further separated from succeeding accounts by their being cast in the past tense.

Sincerity in these opening sonnets is not at issue, since the speaker's role in regard to determining significant action remains essentially passive. She does not choose the appearance of the "mystic Shape" or God's judgment against a courtship. One would suspect that, as the poems deal more with choice, "daily life," and a realm which the lovers inhabit, oppositions of form and content and confusion as signs of sublimity should diminish and more traditional and containable approaches to sincerity appear. This, however, is not the case. Syntax, for the most part, does grow less obscure, but there are in the remaining sonnets only seven—4, 8, 13, 16, 27, 35, and 43—which can be divided cleanly into octet and sestet. Despite the often balanced and dialectical nature of the subjects, there is, moreover, little or no attention paid to rhetorical balance or proportion. Sentences are constructed loosely as in conversation, and interruptions and paddings for the sake of rhyme persist. As in the opening sonnets, one draws from the informality, immediacy, italicized words, and many bracketed phrases the same sense of the speaker's catching suddenly at vastness with new and more animated expressions that Lowth associates with sublimity. But whereas the kind of conflation which occurs in the image of the "mystic Shape" of Sonnet 1 seems not to recur, there is in the treatment of subjects, as in Sonnet 25, an amplification or diffusion, "many circumstances being added, and a variety of imagery introduced for the purpose of illustration." Lowth associates this amplification with sublimity, and, as in verses of a song, the differing allusions and metaphors of the "varied robes" extend and ornament the subject, supporting an impression of poetic range and individual versatility.[18]

The changes to the image of the heart as a heavy weight on which Sonnet 25 begins exemplify the practice. As Hayter notes, the image appears to change as if the speaker were unaware "where [it was] leading her, as one [is] in conversation."[19] This "conversational" artlessness continues in the speaker's failures to limit her statements to either quatrain or octet. Line 4 is made to overflow by simile, and line 8, by withholding "my heavy heart" for emphasis, and one has none of the reflection or shifting viewpoint that is customary to the sonnet sestet.

> A heavy heart, Belovèd, have I borne
> From year to year until I saw thy face,
> And sorrow after sorrow took the place
> Of all those natural joys as lightly worn
> As the stringed pearls . . each lifted in its turn
> By a beating heart at dance-time. Hopes apace
> Were changed to long despairs, till God's own grace
> Could scarcely lift above the world forlorn
> My heavy heart. Then *thou* didst bid me bring
> And let it drop adown thy calmly great
> Deep being! Fast it sinketh, as a thing
> Which its own nature doth precipitate,
> While thine doth close above it, mediating
> Betwixt the stars and the unaccomplished fate.

The key to the poem, however, lies not, as Hayter proposes, in the contrasting "heavy heart" and "stringed pearls" of lines 1 and 5 but in the "dance-time" of line 6. The allusion is to Ecclesiastes 3:4 and its mention of "a time to mourn, and a time to dance" and corresponds to Barrett Browning's use of women "stringing pearls" amid "universal anguish" (2:207) in *Aurora Leigh* (1856). The "heavy heart" of the opening line is, thus, not only, as Hayter conjectures, "the heart as a heavy locket," but more than an item of jewelry: it is, once again, as in Sonnet 1, the heart in mourning, and perhaps even Job's "heart of stone" (41:24). As so often in the sequence, the poet appears to be moved coevally by the death of her brother and the sheltered existence to which women are relegated, and by being so complexly moved, she lends strong support to Angela Leighton's argument for the sequence's dual Muses and to recent feminist interpretations. In regard especially to the former, Leighton notes that "the harsh superimposition of love on grief in the *Sonnets* betrays the extent to which the role[s]" of the dead brother and live suitor are "the same." They are objects of the poet's "imaginative desire to write."[20]

Readers are thus to infer that before the suitor's arrival, the speaker's heavy heart had come to resemble that heart described by God just before Job's submission and the restoration of his good fortune. Sorrows have replaced what, in the brother's company, had been "natural joys," until, in a reference to Luke 24:2, "God's own grace / Could scarcely lift [it]." Here, in a recurrent but not continuous analogy of the suitor's impact to Christ's, the heart/stone becomes the stone of Christ's tomb, and, through the suggestion of redemption through Christ's death and resurrection, the speaker approaches a status similar to that grace which Job enjoys at his trial's end. Immediately, the next line returns to Ecclesiastes and "a time to cast away stones" (3:5). The statement is, as biblical interpreters note, "a metaphor implying the act of marital intercourse." Sinking beneath the surface of what appears to be well water, the heart/stone finds itself being closed over by the suitor. The action not only conveys a wifely Pauline submergence of self to replace the sheltered life of lines 4–6 but, as in a number of sonnets, mediates a middleground "Betwixt the stars and unaccomplished fate." In these differing appearances, the "heart" image offers neither the opening sonnet's conflation of allusions nor a unified binding image by which, as in Donne's sonnets, readers may infer a unified character and sincerity. Rather, it presents a series or cluster of images loosely associated about a belief in the determined seasons, life rhythms, contrasts, and accountings of Ecclesiastes.

Along with Sonnet 22, Sonnet 43, which Heilman attacks, locates the place of these seasons as existing, like the Theocritean text of Sonnet 1, somewhere between divine sublimity and the "daily life" of what Sonnet 22 calls "the unfit / Contrarious moods of men." The sonnets, thus, form part of a treatment of distance whose romantic development Stephenson touches on. Not only, as she argues, are the distances between the speaker and suitor indicative of stages in worldly desire, distances between the speaker and subsequently the lovers and God indicate stages of heavenly desire. In a kind of pre-Eliotic "mythic method," Barrett Browning shapes these distances to a belief that "the contemplation of excellence produces excellence, if not similar, yet parallel."[21] Again, as elsewhere in the sequence, this "excellence" includes literary models as well as poetic impulses, and again, Paul's depictions of worldly and divine love color the models on which the poems focus. In both sonnets, Barrett Browning endorses Paul's views on marriage's place, but unlike him, she advocates here not the male priority of Sonnet 25 but parity between the worldly participants. The advocacy reflects what critics describe as the poet's deep dissatisfaction with women's role in marriage. Barrett Browning knew that her mother's marriage had not been happy, and, as Hayter notes, "she had seen too many instances of mistakes and disillusions, treacheries and tyrannies, in other marriages."[22] Nonetheless, the poet appears to except from attack her own present circumstances, having insisted in Sonnet 14 that the suitor's love "be for nought" but "love's sake only," agreeing with Shakespeare's Sonnet 116 that "love is not love / Which alters when it alteration finds."

Having accepted the suit as part of God's will and restoration to grace, she imagines the worldly consequences of its acknowledgment and fulfillment:

> When our two souls stand up erect and strong,
> Face to face, silent, drawing nigh and nigher,
> Until the lengthening wings break into fire
> At either curvéd point,—what bitter wrong
> Can the earth do to us, that we should not long

> Be here contented? Think. In mounting higher,
> The angels would press on us, and aspire
> To drop some golden orb of perfect song
> Into our deep, dear silence. Let us stay
> Rather on earth. Belovèd,—where the unfit
> Contrarious moods of men recoil away
> And isolate pure spirits, and permit
> A place to stand and love in for a day,
> With darkness and the death-hour rounding it.

Again, as in Sonnet 25, neither the formalities of line, quatrain, or octet are adhered to. Lines 4 and 8 overflow once more into 5 and 9. The expression "face to face" appears in 1 Corinthians after Paul's description of love as the manner in which one will see when "the imperfect will pass away" (13:4–8, 10), and Exodus 25:18–20 and the ark of the covenant have been suggested as the origin of the souls as two angels standing face to face. Dante, Shelley, Milton, and Blake may have contributed, moreover, to the angels' "lengthening wings break[ing] into fire / At either curvéd point."[23] The angels' being "face to face" measures, in addition, the movement toward parity which has occurred since Sonnet 3 when, because of the pair's difference, their "ministering two angels" could only "look surprise / On one another, as they [struck] athwart / Their wings in passing." Determined to stay on earth where their "pure spirits" will be separated from the unfit moods of men, they accept the world's "darkness and the death-hour," knowing that, in the rightness of their love, whatever "bitter wrong" the earth can do them, their feelings will survive. This knowledge reinforces the closing "natural" sublime of Sonnet 2, where had they had God's approval, "Men could not part [them] with their worldly jars." No longer, it appears, is it deity but the world and her family who pose obstacles ("bitter wrongs") to which their spirits—so long as they do not presume on heaven—are more than a match.

Pauline echoes are again present in the opening lines of Sonnet 43. Involved here is Paul's prayer that the faithful, grounded in love "may be able to comprehend with all saints what is the breadth, and length, and depth, and height" of Christ's love (Ephesians 3:17–19).[24] When "feeling out of sight" of such ends, the speaker senses the suitor's less expansive love having metaphorically filled the void. On a different level, the sonnet complements the substitution of the suitor and life for the "visions" and books of Sonnet 26. The human measures of this love occupy lines 5–8, opposing the apostle's revealed Being and Grace in line 4 with man's imagined Right and Praise. Returning by way of contrast to Paul's statements on divine love in 1 Corinthians 13:11 and Ephesians 3:18, the speaker recounts in the sestet a history of her conversion from "old griefs" and "childhood's faith" to a love that seemed to restore her "lost saints" and, should God "choose," will grow better after death:

How do I love thee? Let me count the ways.
I love thee to the depth and breadth and height
My soul can reach, when feeling out of sight
For the ends of Being and ideal Grace.
I love thee to the level of everyday's
Most quiet need, by sun and candlelight.
I love thee freely, as men strive for Right;
I love thee purely, as they turn from Praise.
I love thee with the passion put to use
In my old griefs, and with my childhood's faith.
I love thee with a love I seemed to lose
With my lost saints,—I love thee with the breath,
Smiles, tears, of all my life!—and, if God choose,
I shall but love thee better after death.

The sonnet is one of those few that theoretically can be divided into qua-train, octet, and sestet, though internally the proportions of the seven ways in which the speaker loves and an eighth manner which she projects are anything but balanced. They run from three to one line in length and do, as Heilman charges, contain a lot of abstractions. Purists, in addition, may object to the near rhymes of "ways" and "Grace," "use" and "lose," and "faith" and "breath." Still, in light of the sonnet's careful demarcations of divine, human, and personal realms, Heilman's complaints of faulty verse technique, insin-cerity, and platform rhetoric appear excessive. William T. Going's response that "in context" the sonnet "is not 'embarrassing . . . platform rhetoric,' " while promising, raises new questions.[25] Foremost among them is how con-sistently is the sequence to be read. If, as critics charge, Barrett Browning is unable at times to carry an image through one sonnet, how valid is an approach that insists upon a selective consistency of "former phrases or images"? How much weight, for instance, can be given the poet's possible uses of Achilles in Sonnets 1 and 27 or her return to Theocritus in Sonnet 40? Thematically the problem of irreconcilable opposites (Polyphemus and Galatea) seems to have been resolved earlier, and although Lowth mentions Theocritus's elegance and knowledge of Solomon's Song of Songs, he cites neither Idyll 11 or 15.[26] True, Polyphemus's ability to use song to overcome his feelings for the unresponsive sea nymph contrasts with the suitor's unwa-vering fidelity, but is anything more specifically intended than a general bookishness from which the speaker claims disruption in Sonnet 26?

Readers have experienced, moreover, at least two methods of associative development in the sequence influencing their understanding—conflation and amplification. In Sonnet 43, one has, in addition, an unreconciled refine-ment of language usage similar to that separating thought and feeling in Eliot's "dissociation of sensibility" and echoing that division of literary and everyday language in Sonnet 1. There are in the poem's three divisions the mind "elevated to heaven" by its incorporation of Pauline allusion and religious language ("soul," "out-of-sight," "Being," and "ideal" rather than social "Grace"); human aspiration in references to "everyday," "need," "sun and candlelight," and associations of both "Right" and "Praise" with man; and personal history in the sestet's movement from "childhood's faith" and "lost saints" to an image of eternity. While recapturing thematically the sequence's associative "fields" of religion, daily life, and personal history, the divisions, by their exclusions of one another, result not in perhaps an intended echo of choral strophe, antistrophe, and epode but in what nineteenth-century psychologists call a "divided self."[27] Not so much the abstractions that Heilman cites but the failure of these "fields of consciousness" to unite into a credible literary voice produces the sonnet's impressions of insincerity and "embarrassing . . . platform rhetoric." Clearly, had Barrett Browning been able early to infuse her theological and learned bent into common speech, the absence of conviction which Heilman associates with an inability to find "images to realize, to prove her existence" might not have occurred.

Still, if the objections which Heilman raises in response to Sonnet 43 can be identified with the failure of the sequence's non-sublime poems to achieve what Louis L. Martz calls "the unity" of a "meditative style,"[28] the other readers' objections to the sequence's formal transgressions and "careless" verse technique remain unchallenged. Given that the divisions of the conventional sonnet are best suited in narratives whose lines are familiar and that, by impeding horizontal movement, they assist vertical self-definition, a narrative line which chooses to confuse gender roles and refuses to adhere to Victorian stereotypes or Renaissance conventions must be seen as novel. The novelty is increased, moreover, by the poet's belief in the language, if not the actual existence, of a worldly "divided self." For such a narrative, expository and lyrical strains cannot be expected to occur at pre-set and regular intervals, and for readers to expect that they should is perhaps a bit unrealistic.[29] Given the singularity that Barrett Browning assigns to the suit, it seems unrealistic as well to expect either adherence to conventionalizing measures and closes or exact correspondence in the work's biblical and literary allusions. The protagonist is not offered as a new ideal. Thus, much as imprecision and formal violations function in the sublime poems to suggest a release from religious preconceptions, imprecision and formal violations function in these sonnets of daily life to convey release from social expectations. The poet's success in both endeavors can be measured positively in the surprise which critics note in their readings of *Sonnets from the Portuguese* and negatively in the "embarrassment" and "Peeping Tom sensations" that they complain of.

Notes

1. Robert B. Heilman, "Elizabeth Barrett Browning's *Sonnets from the Portuguese* XLIII," *Explicator* 4 (1945): Item 3.

2. T. S. Eliot, "The Metaphysical Poets," *Selected Essays*. 3rd ed. enlarged (London: Faber, 1958) 288; William Wordsworth, "Preface to *Lyrical Ballads*," in *Critical Theory since Plato*, ed. Hazard Adams (New York: Harcourt, 1971) 435. Robert Lowth, *Lectures on the Sacred Poetry of the Jews*, trans. G. Gregory. 2 vols (London: Ogles, Duncan, and Cochran, 1816).

3. See in particular Samuel Holt Monk, *The Sublime* (New York: Modern Language Association, 1935); Ernest Lee Tuveson, *The Imagination as a Means of Grace* (1960; rpt. New York: Gordian, 1974); Albert O. Wlecke, *Wordsworth and the Sublime* (Berkeley: U of California P, 1973); Patrick Holland, "Wordsworth and the Sublime," *The Wordsworth Circle* 5 (1974):17–22; Thomas Weiskel, *The Romantic Sublime* (Baltimore: Johns Hopkins UP, 1976); and Jonathan Lamb, "Hartley and Wordsworth: Philosophical Language and Figures of the Sublime," *MLN* 97 (1982):1064–85. In this essay I have relied for my verse quotations on Miroslava Wein Dow's variorum edition of *Sonnets from the Portuguese* (Troy, NY: Whitston, 1980).

4. Elizabeth Barrett Browning, *Poetical Works* (London: Oxford UP, 1932) 1, 2, 29, 30, 79, 80, 103, 139, 140.

5. R. H. Horne, *A New Spirit of the Age* (London: Oxford UP, 1907) 338–39.

6. See, for example, Susan Zimmerman, "*Sonnets from the Portuguese:* A Negative and A Positive Context," *Mary Wollstonecraft Newsletter* 2/1 (1973):7–20; Glennis Stephenson, *Elizabeth Barrett Browning and the Poetry of Love* (Ann Arbor: UMI, 1989); and Daniel Karlin, *The Courtship of Robert Browning and Elizabeth Barrett* (Oxford: Clarendon P, 1985).

7. For a discussion of these issues, see my essay "Striking through the Mask: Donne and Herbert at Sonnets," in *Like Season'd Timber: New Essays on George Herbert*, ed. Edmund Miller and Robert DiYanni (New York: Lang, 1987) 241–53, and "Gaining Authority: John Milton at Sonnets," *Essays in Literature* 15 (1988):3–12.

8. Dow, xii: Alethea Hayter, *Mrs. Browning: A Poet's Work and Its Setting* (New York: Barnes, 1963) 105, 106, 107.

9. Dorothy Mermin, "The Female Poet and the Embarrassed Reader: Elizabeth Barrett Browning's *Sonnets from the Portuguese*," *ELH* 48 (1981):352. Stephenson, 75.

10. Lowth 1:317–18, 325, 326, 330, 352, 2:247. Coleridge as quoted in Wlecke 74.

11. Samuel Johnson, *Johnson on Shakespeare*, ed. Arthur Sherbo (New Haven: Yale UP, 1968) 1:62, 64. For passion or the pathetic's role in sublimity, especially among English writers, see Monk.

12. Grover Smith offers an additional parallel in the verses of Titus Petronius Arbiter, although he recognizes that it is unlikely that Barrett Browning knew that poet's work: see *Notes and Queries* 191 (1946):190. In her *"Sonnets from the Portuguese" and the Love Sonnet Tradition* (New York: Philosophical Library, 1985). Shaakeh S. Agajanian proposes that the sonnet is an "Annunciation" of sorts and compares its implied interior and, hence, bounded domestic space to "medieval and early Renaissance paintings of the event" (69–70).

13. Browning, *Poetical Works*, 78. See, in addition, her "Loved Once" and "A Supplication for Love" (282–83, 317). One might also wish to compare the abruptness of this "mystic Shape" to the orderliness of the "mystic dame" of "A Vision of Life and Death" (66–67).

14. Lowth 1:107–08; Weiskel 21–22, 35.

15. *The Complete Works of Elizabeth Barrett Browning*, ed. Charlotte Porter and Helen Clarke (1900; rpt. New York: AMS, 1973), as cited by Dow, Mermin, et al.

16. Edmund Burke, *A Philosophical Enquiry into the Origin of Our Ideas of the Sublime and Beautiful*, ed. J. T. Boulton (London: Routledge, 1958) 63. Again, readers must decide whether the "impression" of these differences facilitates or impedes understanding. For "catabatic mysticism," see *The Writings of St. Paul*, ed. Wayne A. Meeks (New York: Norton, 1972) 381.

17. I am not one of the critics who equates the "mystic Shape" of Sonnet 1 and the "thou" of Sonnet 2. See Agajanian 72. That Barrett Browning felt God stood as a barrier to their love is stated in a letter dated 16 September 1845: "But something worse than even a

sense of unworthiness, GOD, has put between us!"—*The Letters of Robert Browning and Elizabeth Barrett Barrett 1845–1846,* ed. Elvan Kintner (Cambridge: Harvard UP, 1969) 1:195.

18. Lowth, 1:351. It should be noted, perhaps, that Longinus distinguishes between amplification and sublimity in Part 12 of his treatise. See Adams 85.

19. Hayter 106.

20. Hayter 106. Angela Leighton, *Elizabeth Barrett Browning* (Sussex: Harvester, 1986) 107.

21. Barrett Browning, *Poetical Works,* 138. Stephenson 77–80.

22. Hayter 189. See also Wendell Stacy Johnson, *Sex and Marriage in Victorian Poetry* (Ithaca: Cornell UP, 1975) 54–57.

23. Robert M. Gay, "E. B. Browning's *Sonnets from the Portuguese,*" *Explicator* 1 (December 1942): Item 24. Barrett Browning's letters reveal that she was acquainted with the works of each of these writers prior to the publication of the *Sonnets* in 1850, albeit her knowledge of Dante was gained through Henry Francis Cary's translation. Gay also suggests that popular illustrations of angels may have influenced her description.

24. John S. Phillipson. " 'How Do I Love Thee?'—an Echo of St. Paul," *Victorian Newsletter* 22 (1962):22.

25. William T. Going, "E. B. Browning's *Sonnets from the Portuguese* XLIII," *Explicator* 11 (June 1953): Item 58.

26. Lowth 2:307–08. See Zimmerman for a view of the *Sonnets* relationship to Solomon's Song of Songs.

27. William James, *The Varieties of Religious Experience* (New Hyde Park: University Books, 1963) 166–88. This "divided self" resembles more that "presentation of self" which Erving Goffman writes of in *The Presentation of Self in Everyday Life* (New York: Anchor, 1959) than "the divided self" of R. D. Laing's *The Divided Self* (Baltimore: Penguin, 1965). Barrett Browning uses Greek choral odes elsewhere as in *Prometheus Bound* (1833) and *The Seraphim* (1838), and it would require no major adjustments to the sonnet form to interpret its traditional three divisions in such a manner.

28. Louis L. Martz, *The Poetry of Meditation* (New Haven: Yale UP, 1954) 323–24.

29. For a discussion of these matters, see S. T. Coleridge, *Biographia Literaria,* ed. J. Shawcross (Oxford: Oxford UP, 1907) 2:23–24, and my *Transformations in the Renaissance English Lyric* (Ithaca: Cornell UP, 1970) 144–45. For the dual strains of poetic autobiography, see my *The Figure of Dante* (Princeton: Princeton UP, 1981) 117–38.

Elizabeth Barrett Browning's Hebraic Conversions: Feminism and Christian Typology in *Aurora Leigh*

CYNTHIA SCHEINBERG

> then, surprised
> By a sudden sense of vision and of tune,
> You feel as conquerors though you did not fight,
> And you and Israel's other singing girls,
> Ay, Miriam with them, sing the song you choose.
> —*Aurora Leigh*

Miriam, called a prophetess, appears after the passage of the Red sea as heading the women of Israel in that responsive song in which the glorious deliverance was celebrated (Exodus xv. 20, 21). The next occasion in which she is mentioned presents a dark contrast to that earlier day of joy. Miriam, by whom the Lord had spoken, and whom he had sent before his people unites with Aaron in jealous murmuring against Moses. Her sin is immediately visited with frightful punishment. She is struck with leprosy; and Aaron as the priest has to look on his accomplice, and officially pronounce her unclean; and consequently for seven days, till healed and cleansed by the mercy of God, she is excluded from the camp (Numbers xii; Deut. xxiv. 9). It must have read an impressive lesson to Israel that God will by no means spare the guilty.
> —*The Treasury of Bible Knowledge,* 1870.

The moment in which Aurora claims Miriam as the mother of women's "song" in *Aurora Leigh* is a moment of great triumph, both in terms of the epic's narrative structure, as well as in terms of Aurora's personal development as poet/narrator. "Happy and unafraid of solitude" (3.169), Aurora has

Reprinted from *Victorian Literature and Culture* 22 (1994): 55–72. Used by permission of the publisher.

set herself up as an independent woman writer in London. When she likens herself and other women writers to Miriam and "Israel's other singing girls" (3.202), she invokes the Hebraic type for female, prophetic agency—and she invokes literary and theological authority for women writers.

But to invoke this particular image of Miriam is to tell only half of Miriam's story. As Ayre's *Treasury of Bible Knowledge* (1870) points out all too clearly, Miriam's moment of religious agency and leadership is short-lived. Indeed, God and the patriarchs of Israel condemned Miriam, striking her with leprosy and ejecting her from the Israelite community. The language of *The Treasury*, "plain, popular information . . . for general readers" (xiv), casts Miriam's demise as a moral lesson about the "guilty" who challenge patriarchal authority. Though she and Aaron share in the crime of false prophecy against Moses, it is Miriam who bears the immediate brunt of their punishment, a punishment that is enacted significantly upon her body and her rights as a member of the community. Miriam's fall is a far one: from divine poet to unclean woman, and her contradictory function in this interpretation of history becomes for us a paradigm for how women poets act, interact, and are acted upon in religious communities.

Although Miriam's biblical experiences serve as a central organizing narrative in *Aurora Leigh*, Barrett Browning does not make any mention of Miriam's ultimate fate in Jewish history. I do not think this is because she did not know the end of the story; indeed, her knowledge of the Hebrew scriptures was exhaustive, in part because she read them in Hebrew.[1] Barrett Browning's allusions to and transformation of Miriam's narrative throughout *Aurora Leigh* respond to a deep anxiety that Victorian Christian culture had towards not only Jews and Hebrew history but also towards vocal, intellectual, poetic women. While Barrett Browning's very complex idealization of the Hebrew woman is crucial to her development of an authoritative female poetic identity, the identification with the Hebraic also threatens the establishment of Christian transcendence at the end of the poem. Barrett Browning's goals of authorizing women's poetry and imagining new kinds of heterosexual and Christian relationships require a complicated narrative of conversions: Aurora must be "converted" to the transcendent state of Christian wife while still maintaining her poetic voice; Romney, as her male counterpart, must be converted from a dominant, patriarchal oppressor to a "true" Christian husband. Emphasizing the central role the Hebraic and conversion strategies play in Barrett Browning's epic enables feminist readers to understand that this poem both challenges and submits to dominant discourses of gender and religion.[2]

In *Victorian Types, Victorian Shadows,* George Landow has suggested that Barrett Browning "founds a theory of the arts upon typology" (6), and Landow uses *Aurora Leigh* as a paradigm for Victorian typological practice. While correctly noting the central role typology plays in the poem, Landow's study does not explore the relation between the poem's feminist and typological missions. By reading typologically through a feminist lens, a number of contradictions in these practices become evident, contradictions that are constantly at play throughout the poem. In *Aurora Leigh,* Christian typological practice and feminist poetics collide, leaving Barrett Browning a very complicated task of extricating Christian transcendence from a narrative that is overtly concerned with sexual difference. In this reading of *Aurora Leigh,* I argue that Barrett Browning elides the discourses of Christian typology and sexual difference in order to affirm women's experience while simultaneously maintaining that women can speak with universal Christian poetic authority.

In nineteenth-century women's poetry, the adoption of a Christian voice offered women a way to assert a "transcendent" poetic voice, a voice that did not call attention to gender difference but rather emphasized its ability to speak of the "universal" Christian experience.[3] Unlike women, it could be argued, Christians can speak for everyone, because Christian salvation is supposedly not dependent on conditions of gender and ethnicity. However, if a poet also wanted to find a way to speak her particular difference—whether as Jew or woman (or both)—then adopting the position of the Christian speaker posed a potential problem, since such a transcendent voice, in its conventional construction, erases sexual difference.[4] Barrett Browning, especially in her earlier poems like "A Drama of Exile" and "The Seraphim," positioned her voice as one with Christian authority; the goal she sets for herself in *Aurora Leigh* is to maintain that authority while also speaking as a woman, and it is Miriam who provides a legitimate Biblical precedent for a female poet. In this epic poem Barrett Browning tries to engage with the discourse of sexual difference as well as maintain a universal Christian stance; she images Aurora as the Hebraic Miriam in order to establish an authoritative figure of challenge to Christian patriarchy, but it is only by converting this Hebraic figure by the end of the epic that Barrett Browning can emerge with acceptable Christian closure.

Invocations of Miriam are made repeatedly in *Aurora Leigh,* signaling Barrett Browning's replacement of Eve as the paradigm for female experience in the Hebrew Scriptures.[5] Barrett Browning had attempted in her earlier books of poetry to find precedents for female poetic agency in the figures Eve and Mary. But her use of these female figures as models of poetic authority proved somewhat limited, in part because the weight of the culturally imbedded representations of these women: Eve as the primary example of women's intellectual and linguistic naivete, Mary as the silent suffering Pietà.[6] In many ways, Miriam solves the problem that Eve and Mary could not: Miriam's status as singer and prophet creates a legitimized model of female poetic authority. The use of Hebrew scriptural women corresponds with a renewed interest in typology in the Victorian era; just as male theologians and writers like Cardinal Newman, Henry Hart Milman, and Matthew Arnold made repeated references to "the Hebraic" and Hebrew Scripture, Jewish and

Christian women poets used Hebraic scriptural women in a number of different ways to legitimate their own literary authority.[7]

The most common form of Christian typology interprets the Hebrew scriptures from a Christian point of view; the Hebrew type gains its significance in its relation to or prefigurement of an antitype, namely events, people, or concepts from Christ's life and gospels. Of course, the talmudic tradition in Judaism had always concerned itself with the interpretation of Hebrew Scripture for the use of the present community, so it is important to see that the act of interpreting Hebrew scriptural event is not what distinguishes Christian typology as a practice. What is different in a specifically Christian practice is that the Hebraic event, figure, or idea is wrenched from its literary and historical context in Hebrew scripture and read within a completely different hermeneutic frame, that of Christian revelation. Imbedded within Christian typological practice, therefore, is the assumption that hermeneutic frames are changeable and transferrable across religious histories and doctrines. Likewise, Christian conversion also assumes that an individual can choose or change his/her religious hermeneutic, an idea made clearer by comparing Christian and Jewish doctrine on conversion. Whereas being Christian is not dependent on one's ethnic identity, in Judaism, one is a Jew through dual ethnic and religious heritage—birth, not conversion, generally determines whether one is a Jew. Even Jews who ostensibly convert to other religions remain Jews in Jewish law, and there is no re-conversion process that they must undergo to re-enter the Jewish covenant with God; being Jewish is a religious condition, but it is also an ethnic, familial condition.[8]

This idea that interpretative frames are mutable is at the heart of the difference between Jewish and Christian doctrine. As Rosemary Radford Ruether writes,

> Christianity confront[s] Judaism with a demand for a conversionist relation to its own past that abrogate[s] that past, in the sense that the past itself no longer provide[s] a covenant of salvation. Christianity [does] not ask Judaism merely to extend itself in continuity with its past, but to abrogate itself by substituting one covenantal principle from the past for another provided by Jesus. (80)

Ruether's emphasis on "abrogation" is crucial here, for the term makes explicit the rupture, break, and annulment of the Jewish covenant that Christian typology insists upon; though the notion of a Judeo-Christian tradition is based upon the idea that Christianity and Judaism are connected doctrinally, Ruether's description reminds us that Judaism and Christianity are based on completely different relationships to the Godhead, completely different notions of that covenant, and thus completely different hermeneutic codes. From a dominant Christian perspective, the hermeneutic of Christianity offers a "transcendent" interpretative frame in which to place Hebrew history. But of course Jews do not acknowledge that "transcendent frame," since Judaism does not recognize Jesus as the messiah. More importantly, it is not just that Christianity asserts the possibility of reading Jewish history from a Christian perspective; the typological impulse goes further in insisting that Hebrew history has no independent significance without the larger context of Christianity. Thus, typology sets up a relationship between Hebrew history and Christianity that might be termed "significance through relationship"; in such a relationship, the ongoing nature of Jewish history as well as the presence of actual Jews are erased.

This typological assumption of "significance through relationship" has an implicit connection to discourses surrounding gender in the nineteenth century, a discourse that Barrett Browning invokes throughout *Aurora Leigh*. The contemporary "moral sphere" arguments for women's influence claimed women had importance only through their effect on sons and husbands.[9] Likewise, until the Married Women's Property Acts (1870, 1882), women's property was "absorbed" into the estate of her husband; thus, both in terms of economic and moral agency, female identity was constructed as significant only through intercourse with men. The feminist challenge throughout *Aurora Leigh* works to recast this notion of female significance onto women themselves, going so far as to assert that Aurora can effect political and social change through her own poetic voice and through simultaneous attention to the domestic and public spheres of Victorian life.

The feminist impulse in *Aurora Leigh* insists that the experiences of women matter in themselves, and throughout this epic Barrett Browning foregrounds the domestic and physical realities of women's lives. For example, Marian's oppression by patriarchy is explicitly described in terms of the physical effects it has on her body; her rape is named as such, rather than alluded to in universalized terms of oppression. Likewise, Lady Waldemar's body is described in searing terms, emphasizing the corrupt nature of her social and sexual practice. Finally, Aurora herself works to learn the importance of the life of her body, and its sexual desire, in relation to the life of her intellect; even as she strives to enter the public world of literature and politics, she learns to remember her "private" life as well.[10]

But if one is interested in asserting a Christian vision while simultaneously exploring issues of sexual difference and woman's material experience—thus refuting the claim of "significance through relationship"—the assumptions underlying Christian typology become problematic. That is, the idealization of Hebrew scriptural women as independent heroic agents works in terms of the poem's feminist appeal, but it contradicts the assertion of Hebraic deficiency which is at the heart of Christian typology. What is fascinating about the poem is that it is remarkably self-conscious about its own typological practice; there is subtext running throughout the epic on what might be considered "correct" and "incorrect" typology, as Aurora tries to recast the role of women in Christian culture. Barrett Browning needs

Miriam as a figure of Biblically-sanctioned poetic authority for women and so uses typology to invoke her, but the contradictions typology poses for a Christian feminist, as outlined above, insist that she re-evaluate typology, or re-evaluate feminist practice, or both, as I argue. Likewise, her investment in the marriage plot that will unite Romney and Aurora in the perfect Christian union also makes problematic her feminist claims, as other critics have suggested.[11] By carefully charting Barrett Browning's typology and feminism in *Aurora Leigh,* we can see how contradictory this identification with Hebraic figures can be for a woman writer. Barrett Browning defuses this threat by "converting" the more dangerous elements of her feminism into acceptable Christian closure.

Casa Guidi Windows (1851), the book published prior to *Aurora Leigh,* offers Barrett Browning's first reference to Miriam as a symbol for female poetic identity, and this reference also suggests Barrett Browning's possible resistance to conventional Christian typology. In Part 1, the speaker suggests that moral (and poetic) progress relies on the cumulative work of successive men and generations, "[h]ow step by step was worn, / As each man gained on each securely" (300–01). She illustrates this idea as follows:

> Because old Jubal blew into delight
> The souls of men with clear-piped melodies,
> If youthful Asaph were content at most
> To draw from Jubal's grave, with listening eyes,
> Traditionary music's floating ghost
> Into the grass grown silence, were it wise?
> And was't not wiser, Jubal's breath being lost,
> That Miriam clashed her cymbals to surprise
> The sun between her white arms flung apart
> With new glad golden sounds? that David's strings
> O'erflowed his hand with music from his heart?
> So harmony grows full from many springs
> And happy accident turns holy art.
>
> (1. 307–19)[12]

This chronological recounting of Hebrew scriptural "singers" (and musicians) offers a new evolutionary vision of poetic history: Jubal and Asaph are both figures connected to musical instruments and song in the Hebrew scripture (Gen. 4:21 and 1 Chron. 6:39). Barrett Browning suggests that these individual "singers" become significant as each successive singer builds on the song of his/her predecessors. The fact that Judaism recognizes female prophets enables Barrett Browning's construction of male and female poetic heritage in this passage. And while issues of gender are implicit but not central concerns in *Casa Guidi Windows,* the inclusion of male and female singers in this list signals Barrett Browning's growing interest in finding authoritative scriptural precedents for poetic women.

Significantly, Barrett Browning resists the conventional Christian typological gesture that would situate these Hebraic figures in relation to the Christian narrative. Barrett Browning maintains Jubal, David, and Miriam's existence in Hebrew history; their significance is asserted in terms of their historical connection to each other and in terms of what such a cooperative notion of song can teach her readers about historical links in poetic practice. By resisting the typological interpretation from the "transcendent" assumptions of Christianity, Barrett Browning is able to make her point that poetic history is cumulative and evolutionary and that women have played a significant part in that history. If she had made the conventional move to connect these figures to Christian narrative, the radical nature of her gender claims would be erased, since there are no female counterparts for Miriam in Christianity.

When we turn to Barrett Browning's next allusion to Miriam, which occurs in Book 2 of *Aurora Leigh,* Barrett Browning's typological practice seems to have shifted. It is Romney who speaks of Miriam first in *Aurora Leigh;* through his initially misguided character, Barrett Browning initiates her self-conscious exploration of how typology might mean differently for men and women. Romney's patriarchal Christian view of Miriam is a vision significantly revised from that of Miriam in *Casa Guidi Windows* "clash[ing] her cymbals to surprise / The sun between her white arms flung apart / With new glad golden sounds. . . ." In *Aurora Leigh,* Romney denigrates both poetry and women, saying to Aurora:

> Who has time,
> An hour's time . . . think! . . . to sit upon a bank
> And hear the cymbal tinkle in white hands!
> When Egypt's slain, I say, let Miriam sing!—
> Before . . . where's Moses?
>
> (2. 168–72)

Romney minimizes Miriam's significance, transforming the cymbals' "clash" to a mere "tinkle," just as the forceful synecdoche of "white arms flung apart" is reduced to "white hands."[13] And this diminution symbolizes a larger typological point: in Romney's eyes, "Egypt" is a symbol for the "captive" state of Victorian culture. His typology suggests that the historical event of the defeat of Egypt exists only as analogue for the still "enslaved" condition of England; Romney thus erases the significance of the actual (scriptural) historical defeat of Egypt. Romney's point in this allusion is twofold, designed to claim that a woman cannot be a significant poet because she cannot speak to "universal" male experience and that likewise, for Romney, Jewish history has no significance outside of a Christian typological code.

This first conversation about Miriam and Moses (which is also ostensibly about the possibility of Aurora and Romney marrying) suggests that Romney and Aurora each have completely different interpretations of the Biblical narrative. Their argument begins the lengthy discussion of gender roles in both Hebrew history and contemporary Victorian society that makes up the first half of Book 2. Aurora goes on to extend Romney's initial allusion to Miriam and Moses, also questioning Romney's own aspirations to Moses' role. She transforms his question "Where's Moses?" from a repudiation of women poets into a comment on Moses' humble beginnings.

> Ah, exactly that,
> Where's Moses?—is a Moses to be found?
> You'll seek him vainly in the bulrushes,
> While I in vain touch cymbals. Yet concede,
> Such sounding brass has done some actual good.
>   (2. 172–76)

What Aurora does in this passage is to galvanize other aspects of the Mosaic narrative that include Miriam as a central figure. There is no Moses to be found in contemporary life; he remains hidden in the "bulrushes," and her reference to Moses' infancy reminds the listener/reader of the primary moment of his "saving" in Biblical tradition, which was enacted by women— indeed, probably by Miriam herself.[14] Aurora's image calls on the figure of Moses at his most vulnerable and compares it to an image of Miriam, singing at her most powerful moment; her figure insists that poetry and women have the ability to create significant social and moral good.

In citing the "vain" search in the bulrushes, Aurora also makes a pun about the motives behind typological comparison: Romney's male vanity, she implies, motivates his desire to model the contemporary savior on a Hebraic man. This notion of Romney's vanity—indeed his hubris in believing he can be the Moses for the century—suggests the potential moral danger in typological comparisons that do not recognize that in a Christian hermeneutic Moses must be a type for Christ, not for a mere human reformer like Romney. Aurora's response suggests that this initial argument between Romney and Aurora is about two issues: their potential marriage and "correct" typological comparison. For Romney, typology allows him to cast himself as a potential Moses (in his penchant for explicit social action) as he simultaneously casts Moses' sister as a minor figure. From Aurora's point of view, however, incorrect typology exposes Romney's vanity, while her feminist typological vision allows her to claim the significance of Miriam's role as poet. What is increasingly clear in this first interchange between the epic's two main characters is that they do not share an interpretative code which would allow consensus.

Besides his misguided attempt to serve as Moses' antitype, Romney's other main flaw is his misinterpretation of women, as signalled by his misreading of Miriam's song. For it turns out that Romney's argument for a marriage in which woman is "helpmeet" to man hinges on denying to women the ability to emulate or symbolize the Christian antitype. He tells Aurora:

> Women as you are,
> Mere women, personal and passionate,
> You give us doting mothers and chaste wives.
> Sublime Madonnas, and enduring saints!
> We get no Christ from you,—and verily
> We shall not get a poet, in my mind.
>
> (2. 220–25)

Romney's "We get no Christ from you" is Barrett Browning's clearest articulation of a male bias in standard typological interpretation. This statement makes it evident that, since the aim of most conventional typology centers on finding a correlation to Christ's life, women are inevitably excluded from this goal because of their sexual difference from Christ. But Romney once again exhibits his misunderstanding of typological significance; it is not the human individual who provides "a Christ"—indeed, this is almost blasphemy; rather, there can only be emulation of Christ's example. His statement implies that men can provide a "Christ," and so just as he "vainly" turned to Moses as the "type" for his own Christian action above, he also rejects the possibility that women's roles in society can be modelled on Christ, since the only available figures of women in Christian narrative, in his mind, are the Madonna, saints, mothers, and wives. There is an implicit contradiction in Romney's reasoning (and a pun from Barrett Browning) in the use of the term "get," since a "Madonna" did "get" a Christ according to Christian doctrine. But for Romney, "getting a Christ" refers to finding the man who will become the savior of England; his desire to be the next Christ limits his ability to see the mythic origins of Jesus in Mary's body.[15] Romney's words assert a link between Christian agency, gender, and poetry; just as "we get no Christ" from women, so will we "get no poets." Romney assumes that a poet must be able to transcend the "personal and passionate," which mark women's expression for him. What the poem must resolve, then, in terms of Barrett Browning's larger project of articulating a Christian, female poetic identity, is how to construct an authoritative female identity that has a distinct agency within Christianity without wrongly aspiring to be Christ. Romney's accusation is exactly what Aurora must challenge; her dilemma is how to find an authoritative voice as a Christian that is also as "personal and passionate" as a woman.

Romney's speech makes plain the patriarchal role delegated to women in Christian history, and they are exactly those roles which Aurora refuses to adopt throughout the poem. In revising the image of female identity, Aurora continues to use Miriam to force a radical departure from conventional Christian concepts of women. Aurora's affinity for Miriam clearly rejects the idea that she takes "sublime Madonnas," "doting mothers," and "chaste wives" as her models, since Miriam was neither mother, nor wife, nor, indeed, "sub-lime" in her eventual uprising against Moses.[16] Thus, by claiming Miriam specifically as her personal point of Hebraic reference, Aurora finds a biblical figure whose model includes an element of poetic agency and a degree of independence from male dominance. To make Miriam's importance clearer, Aurora refuses comparison to another, perhaps less autonomous, Hebraic female figure.

> Why sir, you are married long ago.
> You have a wife already whom you love,
> Your social theory. Bless you both, I say.
> For my part, I am scarcely meek enough
> To be the handmaid of a lawful spouse.
> Do I look a Hagar, think you?
> (2. 408–13)

In rejecting Romney's marriage proposal, Aurora also rejects typological comparison to Hagar, whose experiences could be interpreted as oppressive within Hebrew polygamy. Aurora's rhetorical question articulates her resistance to being cast in a role like Hagar's and, in so doing, allows her to refuse certain standard roles of martyrdom that have functioned as paradigms of women's roles in Christian culture. By claiming Miriam, not Hagar, for her self-identification, Aurora casts herself as prophetess as opposed to "handmaid" or "wife." Implicitly, she also points to Marian's role as a Hagar, a surrogate wife to Romney, and, later, a seeming "handmaid" to Aurora.

It is Romney who first introduced the figure of Miriam into the poem, and he does so, as we saw above, to voice denial of her significance in the Exodus narrative, as well as implicitly to suggest himself as a Mosaic successor. To him, Miriam is a mere "tinkler" on the cymbals. But in Book 3, Aurora reclaims the figure of Miriam at the exact moment in which she is most independent from Romney, recasting his derisive use of Miriam into her most triumphant image of the contemporary female poet. In discussing how urban life suits a poet's purposes, Aurora explains:

> No one sings,
> Descending Sinai: on Parnassus mount,
> You take a mule to climb, and not a muse,
> Except in fable and figure: forests chant
> Their anthems to themselves, and leave you dumb.
> But sit in London, at the day's decline,
> And view the city perish in the mist
> Like Pharaoh's armaments in the deep Red Sea,—
> The chariots, horsemen, footmen, all the host.
> Sucked down and choked to silence—then, surprised
> By a sudden sense of vision and of tune,

> You feel as conquerors though you did not fight,
> And you and Israel's other singing girls,
> Ay, Miriam with them, sing the song you choose.
>
> (3. 190–203)

This apocalyptic passage is at the heart of Barrett Browning's ideas about poetic production, and it represents the culmination of her inclusion of the Hebraic into her feminist poetics. Pointing to the two central traditions of literary and theological authority—Moses' transcription of God's word on Sinai and the classical source of poetic inspiration, Mt. Parnassus—Aurora suggests that they do not symbolize the sort of poetic inspiration she seeks. Or rather, Aurora debunks the myth of these moments of inspiration. When Moses "descends" Sinai, he has just conversed with God and thus is the prophet of divine word, but this interaction has not resulted in his own poetic production: rather, he carries the tablet "written by the finger of God"—not his own finger. Similarly, the female "muses" of classical poetry exist not in "fable and figure"; the truth of climbing Parnassus is that one needs a "mule" because it is hard work. Aurora also rejects the claim that nature can be a poetic source; for her, nature has its own language, which is not available for human use. Finally, having rejected the conventional models of poetic inspiration, Aurora locates true poetry within human culture. What is striking about her comparison to "Israel's singing girls" is that their "song" is born out of a moment of intense social and political conflict, which the simile compares to a vision of the city. Further, the moment of Miriam's song is a moment of worship and praise to God; this particular Biblical moment combines political triumph with divine praise, thus locating the poetic as simultaneously religious, denaturalized, and female. The poet is related to the position of women in the idea that s/he "did not fight"—poets and women, that is, even when outside direct physical action, are nevertheless of central importance to society through their acts of prophetic vision and inspiration to a community.[17]

Thus, in the middle of her autobiographical narrative, Aurora positions herself as a Hebrew woman, singing as a prophet and in full possession of creative agency. But this self-proclaimed "novel poem" has certain demands for narrative closure that impinge upon the figures that have been established at this point. The use of the two types, Miriam and Moses, will not really provide the figurative closure the poem seeks, since to carry Miriam's mythic narrative to conclusion would place her as Moses' antagonistic sister as well as an unclean woman expelled from the Hebrew camp. The poem must also bridge the differences in Romney's and Aurora's interpretations of the Bible, healing Romney's diseased vision of himself as a Mosaic successor, while simultaneously showing Aurora the potential joys of Christian marriage. Thus, as the poem moves toward closure in Books 8 and 9, Barrett Browning must revise Miriam's narrative in order to contain the threat that Miriam (and women poets) pose to Christian patriarchy. Likewise, she produces a revised Romney, who becomes the Christian husband who can accept the idea of a poetic wife. The three goals of this poem, authorizing female experience, asserting women's poetic authority, and imagining new Christian heterosexual relationships, come into conflict. Barrett Browning's strategy to resolve these contradictions hinges on the idea of conversion, in order that the threatening Hebraic woman can be refigured as a Christian. Likewise, Romney must also be converted from his incorrect relationships to the Hebraic and to women.

Miriam is explicitly invoked once more by Romney, in Book 8, to signal his changed opinion of Aurora and her work.

> Oh, deserved,
> Deserved! that I, who verily had not learnt
> God's lesson half, attaining as a dunce
> To obliterate good words with fractious thumbs
> And cheat myself of the context—I should push
> Aside, with male ferocious impudence,
> The world's Aurora who had conned her part
> On the other side the leaf! ignore her so,
> Because she was a woman and a queen,
> And had no beard to bristle through her song,—
> My teacher, who has taught me with a book,
> My Miriam, whose sweet mouth, when nearly drowned
> I still heard singing on the shore!
>
> (8. 323–35)

Romney understands not only Aurora's poetic contributions but also his own sexism in his previous refusal to grant her poetic authority. He attributes his previous "blindness" to "male ferocious impudence" and understands how he had imagined maleness—figured as a "beard"—as a prerequisite to song. But the most interesting moment of his figure comes at its conclusion, when Romney positions himself as "nearly drowned" while Aurora/Miriam is "singing on the shore." With the enjambment on "nearly drowned," Barrett Browning casts Romney as an Egyptian, an oppressor, hearing the victorious song of Miriam and the Israelites right before he drowns. The text thus makes an intrinsic connection between the position of the Jews in Egypt and the position of women and oppressed groups in England, since the Christian male and Egyptian soldiers are equated metaphorically in opposition to Miriam on the shore. The lines also provide another more radical possibility as Romney suggests that Miriam reached the shore before he, figured as Moses, did: she saved him with her singing, and so Miriam is figured as the true leader of the Jews at that moment. The invocation of the Miriam and Moses figures alludes to Aurora's and Romney's earlier discussion of gender roles in Book 2, while also typologically figuring women poets as analogues to the Biblical Jews. What has changed is that Romney now is able to see the significance of Miriam's contribution as female poet.

But if these figures of Romney as oppressor and Aurora as Miriam were maintained, there could be no "new" heterosexual Christian union at the end of the poem. In part, Barrett Browning deals with the problem of Romney's male oppression by literally blinding him, a deformation which mirrors his own understanding of his previous flaw. This blindness complicates Romney's complete identification with Moses, who, as the poem has reminded us, ends his life in a moment of vision of Pisgah.[18] But one element of Romney's speech resists his complete renunciation of his prior authority: he refers to Aurora as "my Miriam." Romney's possessive metaphor makes new claims on Aurora; as "his" Miriam, she is literally possessed and absorbed into male, Christian history. Typologically Romney's "my" lifts the Miriam narrative out of its position in Hebraic history, and so this moment in the poem also reclaims Christian typology: Romney has finally learned the correct way to possess Aurora and Hebrew history. Barrett Browning elides the discourses of sexual difference and typology in order to reposition Aurora in relation to her feminist claims.

Romney's final figuring of Aurora as "[his] Miriam" enables Barrett Browning to equate Jewish oppression and female oppression and also to position Jewish types within the larger appropriate context of Christian history. But Romney remains a strangely ambiguous figure at this moment in the poem, a possible lover, "brother," or oppressor in the system of typological metaphor Barrett Browning has established. As the poem moves toward closure, it works to resolve Romney's ambivalent position, as well as to contain the "Hebraic" context in which Aurora repeatedly has been invoked. The following passage, describing Romney in his converted state ("converted" in terms of his understanding of Miriam's Hebraic importance), works to link Romney with the Hebraic figuration that has marked Aurora's identity throughout the poem.

> And then calm, equal, smooth with weights of joy,
> His voice rose, as some chief musician's song
> Amid the old Jewish temple's Selah-pause,
> And bade me mark how we two met at last
> Upon this moon-bathed promontory of earth,
> To give up much on each side, then, take all.
>
> (9. 843–48)

Aurora's comparison of Romney's voice to that of the chief musician once again locates the source of song in Hebrew culture. This passage figuratively joins Romney to Aurora as they both do work that requires a religious, inspired "voice." The reference to the "Selah-pause" displays Barrett Browning's sophisticated knowledge of Hebrew terms, the "Selah-pause" being alternatively interpreted as the moment in the service when the voice is raised up in response to the instruments or as a moment when there is a pause in the voice that directs the instruments. But even more interestingly, the 1870

Treasury of Bible Knowledge suggests that the pause would occur "where very warm emotions would have been expressed," just as they have been in the text of the poem (Ayre 809). Finally, this reference also refers to the practice of actual "old Jew[s]," rather than abstracted biblical "Hebrews," and so implicitly points to the ongoing nature of Jewish practice.

This acknowledgment of actual Jewish practice, as well as the comparison of Romney to a cantor, however, could be a potentially dangerous admission for such a typologically charged text, since it is the continuing presence of unconverted Jews that is a standard sign in Christianity that God's kingdom is not yet achieved on earth. Thus, as Barrett Browning reconciles the lovers, she also transforms this union into a moment of Christian revelation, necessitating that Romney's Jewish voice of the cantor be converted as it gradually begins to speak Christian doctrine.

> "Beloved" it sang, "we must be here to work;
> And men who work, can only work for men,
> And, not to work in vain, must comprehend
> Humanity, and, so work humanely,
> And raise men's bodies still by raising souls,
> As God did, first."
>   "But stand upon the earth,"
> I said, "to raise them,—(this is human too;
> There's nothing high which has not first been low;
> My humbleness, said One, has made me great!)
> As God did, last."
>   "And work all silently,
> And simply," he returned, "as God does all;
> Distort our nature never, for our work,
> Nor count our right hands stronger for being hoofs.
> The man most man, with tenderest human hands,
> Works best for men,—as God in Nazareth."
>   (9. 849–63)

The "voice" is referred to in the abstract, as Aurora describes how "it sang" to her; this abstraction enacts the distance needed to erase the threatening image of Romney in "an old Jewish temple." More importantly, "the voice" makes frequent ambiguous reference to God, as one who "raise[d] men's bodies still by raising souls." Aurora's voice joins in this passage, uniting their two voices in prophecy of future Christian work. Romney then makes the final pointed allusion to "God in Nazareth," significantly refiguring God as Jesus. The possession of the Jews is completed in this passage, as the figure of the "Jewish" cantor is recast as a Christian, speaking with his Miriam who has also been appropriated into a Christian epistemology.

Finally, in line 950, Aurora cries "My Romney," enacting the final conversion of the poem. She claims him, accepts him possessively just as he had claimed her as "my Miriam." It is significant that she does not say "My Moses," avoiding the comparison between Romney and Moses that had been Romney's downfall. Her resistance to typological comparison here signals that, while she and Romney have come to a clear understanding, Aurora still operates in a different kind of typological hermeneutic. Her possession of Romney signals her own revision of gender roles in Christian heterosexuality, while also cementing the idea that Romney has been converted into an acceptance of Aurora. Indeed, Romney has just described the effect her book has had on him; reading her text has been a central factor in his conversion narrative. The figure of Miriam is central, then, not only for how it authorizes Aurora's poetic identity but also for how the figure finally teaches Romney a new covenantal relationship to Moses, Christianity, and woman. Woman is no longer mere "wifely hand maid" to Romney but rather the poet/prophet who will enable the communication of his Christian vision to those "at the bottom" of Pisgah.

Barrett Browning establishes conventional closure by rewriting Miriam's narrative so that it can be a source not only for women's poetry but also for refiguring heterosexual union. In the first part of the poem, standard typological practice is both invoked and criticized; in particular, Romney is presented as a misguided typologist (or Christian) and a sexist, while Aurora seeks to reeducate him in both areas by pointing to Miriam's example. But as the "novel-poem" seeks a traditional comic ending of marriage, the initial identifications with and idealizations of Hebraic figures are gradually converted into their Christian significance.[19] While her initial use of Miriam asserts a radical and feminist understanding of typology (as the Hebrew female prophets and singers legitimate the idea of woman poet), Barrett Browning eventually "converts" her own "Hebrew" characters in order to satisfy the demands of her larger Christian narrative. The generic demands of narrative closure, her feminist concern to claim woman's poetic identity, and her Christian affiliation all converge in the second half of *Aurora Leigh* and allow us to see how genre conventions, feminist poetics, and religious identity have inseparable influences on each other in this text.

By focusing on *Aurora Leigh*'s use of Hebrew history and Hebraic figures, we can understand Barrett Browning's creation of a female figure who is both radical and conservative, one who seeks to challenge the sexual politics of her moment while nevertheless reclaiming the Christian ideology that supported Victorian separate spheres.[20] What feminist critics have ignored in reading *Aurora Leigh* is the text's explicit concern with typology (just as typology-centered readings like Landow's have ignored the poem's feminist impulses). Assuming the poem to be conventional in its religious doctrine, critics overlook Barrett Browning's careful exploration of feminist practice within a particular religious hermeneutic. It is because the Hebrew scriptures provide figures of women that stand as agents, prophets, and speakers that Christian women writers like Barrett Browning could use these figures as sanctioned sources of female agency. Yet as Barrett Browning's conversionary maneuvers at the end of *Aurora Leigh* suggest, the Christian woman's identification with the Hebraic woman was fraught with contradiction, since any typological construction of Hebraic identity would necessarily construct the Hebraic woman as "lacking," even as the Christian woman tried to figure Hebraic women as "complete" in their achieved prophetic status. Indeed, the desire to find a complete Christian identity necessitated the rejection of even the possibility that Jewish/Hebraic identity could ever be complete in itself. Thus, the idealization of the Hebraic woman completely unravels the assumptions of Jewish/Hebraic lack upon which Christian typology is based. Barrett Browning solves this problem by imbedding her Hebraic female figure in a larger discourse of heterosexual marriage in which (in *Aurora Leigh*) *both* male and female characters must undergo a sort of conversion. Indeed, it is Barrett Browning's critique of the idea that woman is significant only in relation to a man that allows her to imagine this dual conversion process. For Barrett Browning, typology resolves the tensions of sexual difference and religious difference simultaneously, so that she can assert the possibility of a Christian, female heroic identity at the end of *Aurora Leigh*.

Notes

1. See Mermin on Barrett Browning's study of Hebrew (*Origins,* 19, 47).

2. This issue of whether the feminist politics of *Aurora Leigh* are radical or conservative is at the heart of the critical debate surrounding this text, though few critics include an extended discussion of religion in their feminist approach (with the exception of Dorothy Mermin and Helen Cooper). See Blake, Case, Cooper, David, Friedman, Gelpi, Kaplan, Mermin, Stone, and Zonana.

3. See Mermin, *Origins,* and Cooper on how Christianity provided a viable position from which women poets could speak. The "transcendent" voice of the Christian poet is also related to the issue of finding lyric universality, especially in a poetic tradition that assumes Christianity to be normative; for two discussions of lyric universality, see Adorno and Rorty.

4. In other chapters of this project, I explore these issues of poetic voice in relation to Christina Rossetti and the Anglo-Jewish women poets Grace Aguilar (1816–47) and Amy Levy (1861–89).

5. See Cooper's book for a discussion of the centrality of Eve figures in Barrett Browning's work.

6. See Smith, chap. 2, for an excellent discussion of Eve's relationship to language and public discourse.

7. Nor is the use of Hebraic women unusual for Christian women writers; the women of Hebrew Scripture fascinate women poets like Christina Rossetti, Felicia Hemans, and Alice Meynell, perhaps because these female characters are often agents of theological and political reform within Hebrew history. This examination of women writers' use of typology becomes even more interesting when we include women of differing religious backgrounds; Grace Aguilar, for example, writing as a Jewish woman, constructed very different notions of gender identity that are also based on female figures from Hebrew history. Aguilar's *Women of Israel* (1845) examines Hebrew scriptural women from a Jewish perspective.

8. For more on Christian typology from both Jewish and Christian perspectives see Charity, Cohen, Frei, Landow, Josipovici, Miner, and Ruether.

9. The influential "moral sphere" argument made popular by writers like Sarah Stickney Ellis (*The Women of England,* 1838) and Sarah Lewis (*Woman's Mission,* 1839) asserted that women had moral superiority to men, and that their role in Christian culture was to use this moral and spiritual superiority to guide and influence their husbands and sons; see also Davidoff and Hall, Taylor, and Levine.

10. I am in debt to Joyce Zonana for suggesting that in this way Aurora represents a "complete" poetic self.

11. See David, and Mermin, *Elizabeth Barrett Browning.*

12. This and all subsequent references to Barrett Browning's poetry are from *The Poetical Works of Elizabeth Barrett Browning* (New York: Macmillan, 1903).

13. The emphasis on "whiteness" here is a fascinating repression of Miriam's Semitic skin.

14. It is often surmised that it is Miriam, referred to only as "Moses' sister" in Exodus 2:4–8, who really enables his adoption by Pharaoh's daughter. See Plaut (388).

15. Barrett Browning explicitly explores this issue of Mary's agency in bearing Christ in her dramatic monologue "The Virgin Mary to the Child Jesus."

16. There is some scriptural evidence that Miriam married; however, she stands out from other Biblical female prophets in not being immediately identified as "wife of" in the first mention of her name.

17. Aurora's assertion that she and the other "girls . . . sing the song [they] choose" claims Miriam's authorial relation to her words, rather than suggesting they are a derivation of Moses' earlier song, the Shirah. Most English translations of Miriam's song are an exact replica of Moses' earlier words, and Hebrew scholarship offers two interpretations of the relationship between Miriam's and Moses' songs. In his commentary on the Torah, Plaut suggests some earlier authorial source for her song, making her a "performer" (many interpretations also stress her role as a "dancer") rather than an original poet (487). It is unclear whether Barrett Browning had access to such information, but her inclusion of Miriam singing the song she chooses asserts choice, agency, and creativity into the Miriam narrative.

18. In Book 5, Sir Blaise compares Romney to Moses "getting to the top of Pisgah hill"; he goes on to make the connection to his flawed vision by asserting that "Leigh . . . is scarce advanced to see as far as this" (5. 730, 734).

19. For an excellent discussion of how conversion works as a narrative figure, see Ragussis; for more on linguistic conversion see Gilman.

20. Not surprisingly, the evaluation of this poem as radical or conservative has been at the heart of current critical debate. Readers like Cora Kaplan assert that we can read the poem "as contributing to a feminist theory of art which argues that women's language, precisely because it has been suppressed by patriarchal societies, re-enters discourse with a shattering revolutionary force" (11). This reading makes implicit the identification of Aurora with Miriam, challenging the patriarchal control of language; Aurora's identification with Miriam suggests that women can make prophetic claims to authority and song in Hebrew history, an authority which Barrett Browning transfers metaphorically onto Aurora and into Victorian culture.

Other readings of the poem find this a text that finally "submits" to patriarchal ideology. For Deirdre David, the conflation of Aurora's sexual identity with her poetic creativity impinges upon the poem's more radical assertions about women's poetic authority, and so the poem is read as "a coherent expression of Barrett Browning's conservative political views, with which her sexual politics are consistently coherent" (98). David's reading acknowledges the anxiety about poetic, theological women that the second half of *Aurora Leigh* seeks to mediate through conversion strategies. I argue that *Aurora Leigh* both challenges and submits to dominant ideological positions for women through a figure of conversion.

Works Cited

Adorno, Theodor W. "Lyric Poetry and Society." *Telos* 20 (1974): 56–71.

Ayre, Reverend John. *The Treasury of Bible Knowledge.* London: Longman Green, 1870.

Blake Kathleen. "Elizabeth Barrett Browning and Wordsworth: The Romantic Poet as a Woman." *Victorian Poetry* 24 (1986): 387–98.

Browning, Elizabeth Barrett. *The Poetical Works of Elizabeth Barrett Browning.* New York: Macmillan, 1903.

Case, Alison. "Gender and Narration in *Aurora Leigh.*" *Victorian Poetry* 29 (1991): 17–32.

Charity, A. C. *Events and Their Afterlife: The Dialectic of Typology in the Bible and Dante.* Cambridge: Cambridge UP, 1966.

Cohen, Arthur. *The Myth of the Judeo-Christian Tradition.* New York: Harper and Row, 1970.

Cooper, Helen. *Elizabeth Barrett Browning, Woman & Artist.* Chapel Hill: U of North Carolina P, 1988.

David, Deirdre. *Intellectual Women and Victorian Patriarchy: Harriet Martineau, Elizabeth Barrett Browning, George Eliot.* Ithaca: Cornell UP, 1987.

Davidoff, Leonore, and Catherine Hall. *Family Fortunes: Men and Women of the English Middle Class, 1780–1850.* Chicago: U of Chicago P, 1987.

Frei, Hans W. *The Eclipse of Biblical Narrative.* New Haven: Yale UP, 1974.

Friedman, Susan Stanford. "Gender and Genre Anxiety: Elizabeth Barrett Browning and H. D. as Epic Poets." *Tulsa Studies in Women's Literature* 5 (1986): 203–28.

Gelpi, Barbara Charlesworth. "*Aurora Leigh:* The Vocation of the Woman Poet." *Victorian Poetry* 19 (1981): 35–48.

Gilman, Sander L. *Jewish Self-Hatred.* Baltimore: Johns Hopkins UP, 1986.

Josipovici, Gabriel. *The Book of God: A Response to the Bible.* New Haven: Yale UP, 1988.

Kaplan, Cora. Introduction. *Aurora Leigh and Other Poems.* London: The Women's P, 1978.

Landow, George. *Victorian Types, Victorian Shadows.* London: Routledge Kegan Paul, 1980.

Levine, Philippa. *Victorian Feminism: 1850–1900.* Tallahassee: Florida State UP, 1987.

Mermin, Dorothy. *Elizabeth Barrett Browning: The Origins of a New Poetry.* Chicago: U of Chicago Press, 1989.

———. "The Damsel, the Knight, and the Victorian Woman Poet." *Critical Inquiry* 13 (1986): 64–80.

Miner, Earl, ed. *Literary Uses of Typology.* Princeton: Princeton UP, 1977.

Plaut, W. Gunther, ed. *The Torah: A Modern Commentary.* New York: Union of American Hebrew Congregations, 1981.

Ragussis, Michael. "Representation, Conversion, and Literary Form: *Harrington* and the Novel of Jewish Identity." *Critical Inquiry* 16 (Autumn 1989): 113–43.

Rorty, Richard. "Chapter 2: The Contingency of Selfhood." *Contingency, Irony and Solidarity.* Cambridge: Cambridge UP, 1979. 23–43.

Ruether, Rosemary Radford. *Faith and Fratricide: The Theological Roots of Anti-Semitism.* New York: Seabury Press, 1974.

Smith, Sidonie. *A Poetics of Women's Autobiography.* Bloomington: Indiana UP, 1987.

Stone, Marjorie. "Genre Subversion and Gender Inversion: *The Princess* and *Aurora Leigh.*" *Victorian Poetry* 25 (1987): 101–27.

Taylor, Barbara. *Eve and the New Jerusalem: Socialism and Feminism in the Nineteenth Century.* New York: Pantheon, 1983.

Zonana, Joyce. "The Embodied Muse: Elizabeth Barrett Browning's *Aurora Leigh* and Feminist Poetics." *Tulsa Studies in Women's Literature* 8 (1989): 241–62.

Lady's Greek without the Accents:
Aurora Leigh and Authority

ALICE FALK

Recent critics of Barrett Browning have quite properly paid serious attention to her early studies and to what Dorothy Mermin calls her "unquenchable passion for Greek."[1] Yopie Prins and Mary Loeffelholz in papers delivered at this conference have offered compelling arguments for the importance of Barrett Browning's reading and translations. Elsewhere, I have argued that her second *Prometheus Bound* reveals the poet winning control over material that had threatened to hinder the development of her own voice.[2] In this paper I want to suggest that Barrett Browning's altered stance toward Greek and the classical legacy of the past also works significantly through her later works, particularly *Aurora Leigh,* a poem that recapitulates her efforts to build on male tradition while learning to speak with a woman's voice.

On the face of it, I undertake an uphill argument in maintaining that Greek is important as late as *Aurora Leigh.* Barrett Browning herself seems to be on the other side of the debate. For although she had written in her teens that "to be a good linguist is the height of my ambition & I do not believe that I can ever cease desiring to attain this!!"[3] it appears that her passionate desire was indeed quenched by her late thirties. Think of her letters: to Mary Russell Mitford she observed, "As for the ancient languages, or any acquirement in the particular department of languages, you cant think how little I care for it."[4] And in 1845, she wrote to Anne Thomson, whose anthology was to include several translations from her:

> Perhaps I do not (also) partake quite your "divine fury" for converting our sex into Greek scholarship—and I do not, I confess, think it as desirable as you do. Where there is a love for poetry and thirst for beauty strong enough to justify labour . . . let these impulses, which are noble, be obeyed; but in the case of the multitude, it is different; and the mere *fashion of scholarship* among women, w^d. be a disagreeable vain thing, and worse than vain.[5]

Reprinted from *Studies in Browning and His Circle* (Armstrong Browning Library, Baylor University, Waco, Tex.) 19 (1996): 84–92. Used by permission of the publisher. This paper and those of Prins and Loeffelholz mentioned herein were presented at a panel at the November 1993 conference on Elizabeth Barrett Browning at the Armstrong Browning Library of Baylor University.

Perhaps Barrett Browning exempted herself from the multitude, but by age fifty she was ready to declare of her own Greek studies: "For years I did nothing else. My belief is, that, though this was done in early youth, I lost time by it—and life. I *believe* that nothing helps the general faculties so little as the study of languages."[6] And there is discouraging evidence in her poetry as well: doesn't "The Dead Pan," placed emphatically at the end of her two-volume collection of 1844, mark her determination to leave behind what she calls in that poem "the vain false gods of Hellas" and outgrown "mythic fancies" (stanzas 31, 34)?

But we need to look at what Barrett Browning does as well as what she says. We should note that it is *after* writing "The Dead Pan" that she revisits the myth of Prometheus in a wholly new translation of Aeschylus. In fact, in her later writings she leaves behind neither the Greek myths nor the Greek language: she could not simply bid them farewell. And even as she turns to the present as the proper sphere of her poetry, she continues to draw on the authority gained by having both mastered this male tradition so important to the forefathers of nineteenth-century poetry and reshaped it to her own satisfaction. Her relationship with Greek is emblematic of her more general relation to poetic tradition and a patriarchal past. Furthermore, the Greek language has an important figurative role, especially in *Aurora Leigh*.

We might begin by glancing at the *Sonnets from the Portuguese,* poems crucial to Barrett Browning's development of her voice as a female subject. They contain a surprising number of classical references. The very first sonnet begins with the speaker thinking of "how Theocritus had sung" and ends with an allusion to Homer's *Iliad.*[7] Significantly, her musings over Theocritus's thought take place "in his ancient tongue," thereby establishing not only "her cultural credentials," as Mermin points out,[8] but also her authority to manipulate the culture, establishing her control of both myth and genre. That authority is linked to her earlier control over Greek. Thus she can cast herself as an Electra carrying a funeral urn that contains potentially dangerous live ashes, "red wild sparkles" threatening her "Beloved" with a passionate conflagration.[9] That hidden power enables her to script her own story despite the voice of Love speaking to her "in mastery."[10] Barrett Browning's strength as a writer depends on revising, not abandoning, her relationships with those masters.

This theme of productive connection, not rejection, can be seen very clearly in *Casa Guidi Windows,* where to imagine a better and viable future, it is necessary to engage with the past. This ambitious political poem reveals Barrett Browning's new confidence about her relationship to poetic tradition. Here the poet begins hopefully to claim Italy as what Sandra M. Gilbert has called a "matria," a land of female subjectivity liberated from male political machinations as well as from the Austrians, a land where the literary fathers are respected but not allowed to dominate.[11]

Rather than somehow transcending the past, Barrett Browning finds productive continuities.[12] Her attitude toward the greatness of the past, built on both respect and self-confidence, is particularly evident in part 1. From her vantage in Italy, "Where worthier poets stood and sang before," she pays homage while declaring her independence: "I kiss their footsteps yet their words gainsay" (50–51). She recognizes that the future is built on the past, and chides those who would reject their heritage outright: "We, who are the seed/ Of buried creatures, if we turned and spat/ Upon our antecedents, we were vile" (287–89). Not only vile, but self-defeating: "If we tried/ To sink the past beneath our feet, be sure/ The future would not stand" (417–19). As Helen Cooper suggests, Barrett Browning is grateful to her predecessors without being nostalgic.[13] Indeed, the narrator's strongest claim of freedom, the assertion that "We do not serve the dead—the past is past" (217), comes only after she suggests that former greatness is instrumental in promoting change; Italy's "memories undismayed" and "graves implore/ Her future to be strong and not afraid;/ Her very statues send their looks before" (213–16). The best of the living will themselves "be invoked/ By future generations, as their Dead" (248–49). Transformations, and even self-will, need not require severing all connections with older traditions. In the poem's terms, Barrett Browning is one of the "heirs in art" who avoids being "disinherited" (374, 441).[14]

In her 1842 essay on the history of English poets, Barrett Browning insists that ancient poetry could not simply be pigeonholed as "classic," dismissing the labels "Romanticism and Classicism" as "popular cant" because she "believe[s] the old Greek BEAUTY to be both new and old."[15] Similarly, she writes to Robert that the "antique moulds," which she rejects, are improperly called classical.[16] She wants to use the label "classical" more idiosyncratically and positively. In *Casa Guidi Windows,* she deftly claims the statues and graves as partners in refusing to "join those old thin voices" of antiquarians "with my new" (1.162). Her own relationship with the classics has been intensely personal and not antiquarian. Her method of rejecting "imitations & conventionalisms," her announced aim as early as 1837,[17] does not mean creation from nothing. Instead, she needs to fashion an alliance with her truly classic predecessors against "rhymers sonneteering in their sleep,/ And archaists mumbling dry bones up the land,/ And sketchers lauding ruined towns aheap" (CGW 1.148–50). Those inhibiting dead who "cling to us/ With rigid hands of desiccating praise,/ And drag us backward" (230–32) are quite different from the patriot dead of whom she writes, "These Dead be seeds of life" (2.663).

By learning to distinguish self-restrictive worship of the past from the positive act of building on it, the narrator of *Casa Guidi Windows* gains the hope of progress in poetry as well as politics.

> The poet shall look grander in the face
> Than even of old (when he of Greece began

To sing "that Achillean wrath which slew
   So many heroes")—seeing he shall treat
The deeds of souls heroic toward the true,
   The oracles of life[.]

(1.731–36)

The possibility of fulfilling her childhood dream to be "the feminine of Homer"—"a little taller than Homer if anything"[18]—thus begins to be realized in *Casa Guidi Windows*. But the emphasis has shifted to redefining "feminine," as she learns she need not pose in male styles to "look grander in the face" than the Greek poet. The (woman) poet celebrating thinkers will surpass the (male) poet immortalizing fighters. The fullest realization of her dream is clearly offered by *Aurora Leigh,* the poem in which Barrett Browning not only addresses most directly questions of language and of her evolution as a poet, but also redefines Homer's genre into a very different kind of epic.

The language of book 5 strongly suggests that its author saw *Aurora Leigh* as itself the "unscrupulously epic" work Aurora demands as a fit representative of her own age (5.214)—a poem Barrett Browning described as "intensely modern, crammed from the times (not the 'Times' newspaper) as far as my strength will allow."[19] And yet her heroine engages in a fierce struggle with the past, both literary and personal. The graves that await Aurora in Italy are literal, not—as in *Casa Guidi Windows*—belonging to poetic ancestors. Angela Leighton, tracing the poem's extraordinary preoccupation with death, identifies Aurora's obsession about the past with her and Barrett Browning's search for a lost father. She argues that only when both past and father are abandoned can the poet grow.[20] But as we have already seen, it is only by coming to terms with the past that the poet can find her power.

Aurora thus must confront not only graves but also her cousin Romney, who represents both her personal past and, more generally, patriarchal authority—the power to mock her gently for writing "lady's Greek/ Without the accents" (2.76–77), a phrase to which we will return. It is through the process of reclaiming him that she can finally "shine on" as the sun "Which rul'st for evermore both day and night!" (9.830–32).[21] The happy Aurora "flung closer to his breast,/ As sword that, after battle, flings to sheath" (9.833–34), in imagery, remarkable for its sexual charge and sexual reversal, that suggests the "large/ Man's doublet" of classical learning bestowed by her father (1.727–28) has not so much been abandoned as grown into.[22] This poet, for whom books are figured as a battlefield (1.750–75), is finally able to fight as an equal.[23]

That doublet of classical learning was, as Barbara Gelpi wittily observes, "a shirt of Nessus," carrying with it the poison of "male derogation of the feminine."[24] In devoting herself to the Greek and Latin patrimony, a woman risks identifying herself wholly with the educated men whom she emulates.

Thus, as "a printing woman," Aurora insists that she be addressed "man to man" (5.806, 811); similarly, Barrett Browning herself could not "help exulting in the compliment" when H. S. Boyd wrote of part of her essay on the English poets that "nobody can find the least sign of its being written 'by a female.' "[25] Thus a "reverent love for the grandfathers" such as Barrett Browning's could thwart the development of a woman poet, who risks what Judith Fetterley has labeled "immasculation."[26] Yet even while Barrett Browning admires women who possess a "manly soul," she declares she detests *"manly"* men.[27] Perhaps only a woman's soul can manage "manliness" without disastrous consequences: in the account of Aurora's education, we can find hints that Barrett Browning's alter ego will avoid being overwhelmed by the words of the fathers.

In a sly allusion to an ancient story of Aeschylus's death, Barrett Browning suggests that women can learn to wear their classical attainments without masquerading as men. In England, the books of Aurora's father are an escape from her aunt's demands that she attain ladylike accomplishments, including the needlework that she (and Elizabeth Barrett) loathed. Aurora recalls one less than happy effort, a pink-eyed shepherdess, "Her head uncrushed by that round weight of hat/ So strangely similar to the tortoise-shell/ Which slew the tragic poet" (1.453–55). Aurora herself seems to invite explication of her reluctant artwork, as immediately after this reminiscence she asserts that "The works of women are symbolical" (1.456). One possibility, suggested by Sandra Gilbert and Susan Gubar, is that the act of embroidering itself "slew the tragic poet," a reading to terrify any woman poet.[28] But Aurora's cross-stitching also ensures an *uncrushed* head, suggesting that women writers may be able to survive both the cultural pressures to "kill [themselves] into arts and crafts"[29] and the weight of male tradition that Aeschylus's tortoise represents.

A similarly double-edged image is used to relate Aurora's encounter with her father's books. On the one hand, her own importance dwindles as she creeps "in and out/ Among the giant fossils of my past,/ Like some small nimble mouse between the ribs/ Of a mastodon," nibbling as she goes (1.835–38). Yet at the same time the mouse manages to take away some substance from the extinct giant without becoming trapped within those dry bones. For a poet, such entrapment would mean singing songs as dead as "poems made on . . . chivalric bones," irremediably moribund—"And that's no wonder: death inherits death" (5.198–99). As we have seen in *Casa Guidi Windows,* the problem of how to use this past without joining the "archaists mumbling dry bones up the land" (1.149) was a major concern of Barrett Browning as well as of Aurora. Her father's books leave their mark on Aurora, but she ultimately controls them, and in fact leaves her mark on them. She saves a copy of Proclus not for the sake of its "dear quaint contracted Grecian types," but for the stain (for which her father reproved her) that came from "pressing in't my Florence iris-bell" (5.1229, 1235).

With the money raised by the sale of her father's books, Aurora travels to Italy, thereby providing as sharp a break with Greek as Barrett Browning herself seems to display. Should we then conclude that the "trick of Greek/ And Latin" taught by her father (1.714–15) was useless, a kind of marginalia to her development? That has been the dominant view. But perhaps, like Prometheus's "trick of loving men" (1850 trans.; 12), it is no trick at all. As we have already seen, Romney gently scoffs at Aurora's notes in "lady's Greek/ Without the accents" (2.76–77), suggesting that even her painstaking studies can never make her the equal of men in classical knowledge. Mermin uses the phrase as evidence of Barrett Browning's own feelings of linguistic inadequacy.[30] But let us not "misconceive the question like a man" (2.434). Romney's observation actually underscores not so much a difference in attainments as Aurora's freedom from formal education; the letters of Shelley, Peacock, and Robert Browning reveal that men were equally content to drop accents when quoting Greek out of school.[31] In fact, for a woman, learning Greek outside of male institutions could be an advantage; she "did not have the opportunity to be repelled by the classical curriculum," as Harry Levin dryly noted of Shelley's expulsion from Oxford.[32] And because she was in a sense marginalized, she was freer to appropriate and refashion the ancient language for herself. Aurora's accentless Greek, written "upon the margin" of her book (2.76), represents her different relationship to male tradition, a difference vital to her development and to working through her connection to the past.

Aurora's interest in Greek was driven in part by her desire to find an appropriate language of her own. Her return to England as an orphan forces her to set aside "sweet Tuscan words," the mother's tongue, which appears inadequate in any case. For while her mother's eyes licensed "the child's riot," her words enforced silence: "Hush, hush—here's too much noise" (1.19, 17). Yet Aurora also feels distanced from English, for she hears her "father's language first/ From alien lips" (1.387, 254–55). Even the gap between the living and the dead is seen in linguistic terms, death "mak[ing] us part as those at Babel did/ Through sudden ignorance of a common tongue" (5.554–55). In this poem, books are alive, and men can be read, dog-eared, and translated like books; indeed, the only use of "translate" in the poem is Romney's protestation to Aurora, "you translate me ill" (2.369). It is no wonder that she is pressed to linguistic extremes in her search for the language that will reveal truth and will do her work (in addition to Latin and Greek and her modern languages, Aurora casts herself as a Chaldean [2.818, 835], and claims that her heart is "writ in Sanskrit" [8.477]). Italy, as a land that for her "would not mix its tenses" (7.1158), puts language to the test. But there, accompanied by Marian Erle—now "nothing more/ But just a mother" (6.823–24)—and drawing on the authority gained through her long apprenticeship as a poet and through her recent successful volume, Aurora is at last able to speak with a woman's voice. In large part, she has succeeded in wresting her father's tongue away from the fathers. Barrett Browning has merged the feminine stereotype with the authority of male literary tradition to create a vision of woman's writing that recuperates "femininity" as strength.

For Aurora, as for Barrett Browning, the process of engaging with Greek had effects lasting far beyond the actual engagement. As a child wishing "to be considered an authoress," Barrett Browning abandoned novels, studying instead poetry and essays and feeling "the most ardent desire to understand the learned languages"; her early difficulties with Greek led to "a secret vow . . . manfully to wade thro the waves of learning."[33] In the middle of her career, her sonnets about George Sand expressed her fear that a woman who wrote "manfully" must suffer in agony because of her "woman-heart" until God would finally "unsex [her] on the heavenly shore/ Where unincarnate spirits purely aspire!"[34] But she came to believe more confidently in a mix of "womanly" and "manly" that made possible startling power in the name of "femininity": thus she could believe that, in the famous claim of "A Curse for a Nation" (1860), "A curse from the depths of womanhood/ Is very salt, and bitter, and good." For Barrett Browning, immersing herself in and confronting the male tradition was crucial to becoming able to write a triumphant woman's epic.

Notes

1.　Dorothy Mermin, *Elizabeth Barrett Browning: The Origins of a New Poetry* (Chicago: U of Chicago P, 1989) 18.

2.　See "Elizabeth Barrett Browning and Her Prometheuses: Self-Will and a Woman Poet," *Tulsa Studies in Women's Literature* 7 (1988): 69–85.

3.　Philip Kelley, Ronald Hudson, and Scott Lewis, eds., *The Brownings' Correspondence*, vol. 1 (Winfield, KS: Wedgestone Press, 1984–) 355. Future references to this edition of the letters will be designated *BC*.

4.　*BC* 5: 225.

5.　*BC* 10: 222.

6.　Edward McAleer, ed., "New Letters from Mrs. Browning to Isa Blagden," *PMLA* 66 (1951): 601.

7.　See the notes for this poem in Charlotte Porter and Helen A. Clarke, eds., *The Complete Works of Elizabeth Barrett Browning*, vol. 3 (New York: Crowell, 1900) 392–93. Grover Smith, in "Petronius Arbiter and Elizabeth Barrett" (*Notes and Queries* 191 [1946]: 190) argues instead that the imagery of the end of the poem is closer to Latin verses of Petronius Arbiter (no. 26) than to Homer. For other classical allusions, see sonnets 18, 19, 27, 37, and 40 and their annotations in Porter and Clarke.

8.　Mermin 138.

9.　*Sonnets from the Portuguese* 5.

10.　*Sonnets from the Portuguese* 1.

11.　Sandra M. Gilbert, "From *Patria* to *Matria:* Elizabeth Barrett Browning's Risorgimento," *PMLA* (1984): 194–211. "Matria" is Gilbert's coinage, but see also Helen Cooper, *Elizabeth Barrett Browning, Woman and Artist* (Chapel Hill: U of North Carolina P, 1988) 124–44.

12.   Barrett Browning is able to thus envision a better future for Italy because she incorporated contemporary Florence into her own past: she wrote, "I love [Florence], and with somewhat of the kind of blind, stupid, respectable, obstinate love which people feel when they talk of 'beloved native lands.' I feel this for Italy, by mistake for England" (Frederic G. Kenyon, ed., *The Letters of Elizabeth Barrett Browning,* vol. 2 [New York: Macmillan, 1897] 285). On her relationship to the past, see also George Eliot's journal entry of 19 Feb. 1862: "I have lately read again with great delight Mrs. Browning's *Casa Guidi Windows.* It contains amongst other admirable things a very noble expression of what I believe to be the true relation of the religious mind to the Past" (Gordon S. Haight, ed., *The George Eliot Letters,* vol. 4 [New Haven: Yale UP, 1978] 15).

13.   Cooper 130.

14.   Clearly, I am here disagreeing with Angela Leighton's thesis that *acceptance* of her disinherited state is necessary for Barrett Browning's poetic growth. See Angela Leighton, *Elizabeth Barrett Browning* (Bloomington: Indiana UP, 1986) esp. 52, 116, 132, 134; cf. Mermin's claim that "the artistic heirs have a reciprocal obligation to honor the memory of their precursors" (171).

15.   "The Book of the Poets," Porter and Clarke 6: 272.

16.   *BC* 10: 135.

17.   *BC* 3: 279.

18.   *BC* 1: 361.

19.   Kenyon 2: 112. On *Aurora Leigh* as a fulfillment of Barrett Browning's childhood epic ambitions, see Mermin 217; more generally on the feminization of epic conventions, see Susan Stanford Friedman, "Gender and Genre Anxiety: Elizabeth Barrett Browning and H.D. as Epic Poets," *Tulsa Studies in Women's Literature* 5 (1986): 203–28.

20.   According to Leighton, the abandonment of that search makes possible the more productive quest for a sister (114–40, esp. 118).

21.   On the sun as a patriarchal image, see Virginia Steinmetz, "Beyond the Sun: Patriarchal Images in *Aurora Leigh,*" *Studies in Browning and His Circle* 9.2 (1981): 18–41, esp. 28–41.

22.   Though it is clear that on her, the clothing looks different. Compare the terms in which a contemporary review of *Aurora Leigh* faults Barrett Browning: "She assumes as it were the gait and garb of a man, but the stride and strut betray her" (Rev. of *Aurora Leigh, Dublin University Magazine* 49 [1857]: 470).

23.   Robert Browning uses similar imagery, though without allowing the woman an active role, in a poem published the year before *Aurora Leigh,* "The Statue and the Bust" (1855): when the Duke first sees the lady, "lo, a blade for a knight's emprise/Filled the fine empty sheath of a man" (*Robert Browning: The Poems,* ed. John Pettigrew, supplemented and completed by Thomas J. Collins, vol. 1 [New Haven: Yale UP, 1981] 596).

24.   Barbara Charlesworth Gelpi, "*Aurora Leigh:* The Vocation of the Woman Poet," *Victorian Poetry* 19 (1981): 42.

25.   *BC* 6: 31.

26.   Judith Fetterley, *The Resisting Reader: A Feminist Approach to American Fiction* (Bloomington: Indiana UP, 1981). The term refers to the process by which women learn to think as men (Fetterley xiii–xxvi). So Aurora harshly judges herself: "It seems as if I had a man in me,/ Despising such a woman" (7.213–14). For Barrett Browning's love of the grandfathers, see Kenyon 1: 232.

27.   Kenyon 2: 128, 134.

28.   Sandra M. Gilbert and Susan Gubar, *The Madwoman in the Attic: The Woman Writer and the Nineteenth-Century Literary Imagination* (New Haven: Yale UP, 1979) 560.

29.   Tricia A. Lootens, "Elizabeth Barrett Browning: The Poet as Heroine of Literary History," diss., Indiana U, 1988, 28.

There is a highly suggestive juxtaposition in a letter to Robert. Immediately before Barrett declares her "chief *intention* to write a sort of novel-poem ... rushing into draw-ingrooms & the like 'where angels fear to tread' "—a passage cited by innumerable critics—she writes that she is contemplating "a monologue on Aeschylus as he sate a blind exile on the flats of Sicily and recounted the past to his own soul, just before the eagle cracked his great massy skull" (*BC* 10: 102–3). The death of Aeschylus, which she describes here with some relish, seems if anything to sustain her own ambitions.

30. Mermin 20.

31. Barrett Browning herself was quite conscious of accents, writing to Boyd early in their acquaintance: "I observe that all your MS & printed Greek is without accents,—& am rather curious to know whether you omit them upon Sir Uvedale Price's view—with regard to their *application*,—or upon Dr. Gally's,—with regard to their *authenticity*" (*BC* 2: 101).

32. Harry Levin, *The Broken Column: A Study in Romantic Hellenism* (Cambridge: Harvard UP, 1931) 52.

33. *BC* 1: 350, 355.

34. "To George Sand, A Recognition" (1844).

The Discourse of Power in
Elizabeth Barrett Browning's Criticism

Daniel Karlin

Elizabeth Barrett Browning wrote little formal criticism. Most of her critical writing is in her letters, and most of the rest is in her poetry. Letters and poems plunge the activity of criticism into other genres and modes: discursive, narrative, rhapsodic, dramatic. Writing about books, art, politics, religion to a close friend or a lover mixes things up, to say the least. It does not allow for abstraction, for objectivity, for singlemindedness; it is subject to interruptions and digressions; personal feeling leaks into aesthetics, and vice versa. It is exciting to read, too, and I feel perversely dull and orthodox in drawing attention to one of the few occasions on which Barrett Browning resorted to what Aurora Leigh calls "the use / Of the editorial we in a review." But the "editorial we" also has another name, and that is the focus of my interest here.

The review was the *Athenaeum,* where, in 1842, Barrett Browning published three anonymous articles or review-essays: one on "The Greek Christian Poets," one on a contemporary anthology called "The Book of the Poets," and one on the most recent volume of Wordsworth's poems. Both the article on "The Greek Christian Poets" and the review of "The Book of the Poets" were published in instalments; the Wordsworth review was much shorter and was published complete. Subsequently, Barrett Browning incorporated the Wordsworth piece into "The Book of the Poets," or rather simply added it on at the end; in fact the join is very awkward and would probably not have been left in its present form had she lived to publish it herself. As it is the review-essay now known as "The Book of the Poets" was published in America with Browning's permission in 1863, along with "The Greek Christian Poets," and both have been reprinted in comprehensive collected editions such as Kenyon's in 1897 and Porter and Clarke's in 1900.

I am going to start with a quotation from "The Greek Christian Poets"—with its last sentence:

Reprinted from *Studies in Browning and His Circle* (Armstrong Browning Library, Baylor University, Waco, Tex.) 20 (1997): 30–38. Used by permission of the publisher. This paper was presented at a panel at the November 1993 conference on Elizabeth Barrett Browning at the Armstrong Browning Library of Baylor University.

And the Genius of English Poetry, she who only of all the earth is worthy (Goethe's spirit may hear us say so, and smile), stooping, with a royal gesture, to kiss the dead lips of the Genius of Greece, stands up her successor in the universe, by virtue of that chrism, and in right of her own crown.

This sentence, to my mind, symbolically inaugurates Barrett Browning's survey of English poetry, which is what her ostensible "review" of "The Book of the Poets" actually turns out to be. The line of succession is female, one queen taking her authority from another in a characteristically ambivalent gesture of homage and appropriation, where *stooping* may represent humility or condescenscion, and where the kiss is both given and stolen. The coronation of Queen Victoria in 1837 had stimulated interest in such matters, not just from female poets of course; Browning placed two of the poems of *Dramatic Lyrics,* published in the same year as Barrett Browning's essay, under the collective title of "Queen-Worship." But although the "Genius of English Poetry" may be female, English poets themselves are not. Barrett Browning's essay mentions only a few, and then in a context of violent hostility, which I will come to later. We are on similar ground here to "A Vision of Poets," published two years later, in which a female spirit crowns an all-male gallery, with the single exception of Sappho. In many respects "A Vision of Poets" acts out in its mode the plot of "The Book of the Poets": in both the images of royalty, of power, of mastery, of dominion, recur throughout, and in the essay at least, and arguably in the poem as well, these images constitute the defining terms and the basis of its analytical and expressive method. To this royal plot, however, there is also a subversive twist.

The essay itself begins with a power-play—the dismissal, by means of an unkind grammatical cut, of the anthology under review as a feeble and unworthy compilation:

[. . .] this book, which is not Campbell's Selection from the British Poets, nor Southey's, nor different from either by being better, resembles many others of the nobly named, whether princes or hereditary legislators, in bearing a name too noble for its desert. This book, consisting of short extracts from the books of the poets, beginning with Chaucer, ending with Beattie, and missing sundry by the way,—we call it indefinitely "A book of the poets," and leave it thankful.

Barrett Browning's satirical allusion to the monarchy and the House of Lords is in keeping with the middle-class radicalism which she shared with numerous other intellectuals at this period. The "hereditary legislators" are evidently not Shelley's "unacknowledged legislators" (the Defence of Poetry had been first published two years before); but Barrett Browning almost immediately refigures the notion of inheritance and succession in her description of Chaucer:

Up rose the sunne, and uprose Emilie, and uprose her poet, the first of a line of kings, conscious of futurity in his smile. He is a king and inherits the earth, and expands his great soul smilingly to embrace his great heritage.

This sets the tone for the essay: Gower, for example, is compared to Chaucer in these terms:

> Side by side with Chaucer comes Gower, who is ungratefully disregarded too often, because side by side with Chaucer. He who rides in the king's chariot will miss the people's "hic est." Could Gower be considered apart, there might be found signs in him of an independent royalty, however his fate might seem to lie in waiting for ever in his brother's antechamber, like Napoleon's tame kings.

Gower's stories, we are told,

> are indeed told gracefully and pleasantly enough [. . .] Chaucer himself having done more honour to their worth as stories than we can do in our praise, by adopting and crowning several of their number for king's sons within his own palaces.

So it goes on: the Earl of Dorset "stands too low for admeasurement with Spenser: and we must look back [. . .] to some one of a loftier and more kingly stature." The effect is quite complex here: Spenser, who was all his life dependent on the patronage of the nobility, ranks higher than Dorset, his social superior; yet rank itself is being used as a metaphor for his superiority. An even odder and more disturbing instance comes with Barrett Browning's qualified praise for Beaumont and Fletcher:

> Their conceptions all tremble on a peradventure—"peradventure they shall do well": there is no royal absolute will that they should do well: the poets are less kings than workmen. And being workmen they are weak—the moulds fall from their hands—are clutched with a spasm or fall with a faintness.

The highest kind of poet, then, is an absolute monarch, not a "workman," a thought which would surprise Carlyle on the one hand, and a Chartist on the other. It is passages like these (not just in Barrett Browning of course) which make you realize what Whitman felt he was up against. Barrett Browning can be as plain about it as in this comment on Milton's *Paradise Lost:*

> The circumstances of the production of his great work are worthy in majesty of the poem itself; and the writer is the ideal to us of the majestic personality of a poet.

On reflection this is not so plain; the majesty of the republican Milton forms part of that twist in the royal plot which I spoke of. But before I get to that, let me emphasise that all this imagery of kingship is materially linked with that of strength, of power, in which the physical attribute has the same metaphorical function as the social attribute in conveying intellectual supremacy. For example, if you expand the quotation about Beaumont and Fletcher which I gave just now you get the following:

> From the rest [of the Elizabethan dramatists] they stand out contrastingly, as the Apollo of the later Greek sculpture-school,—too graceful for divinity and too vivacious for marble,—placed in a company of the antiquer statues with their grand blind look of the almightiness of repose. [. . .] They had an excellent genius, but not a strong enough invention to include judgment; judgment being the consistency of invention, and consistency always, whether in morals or literature, depending on strength. [. . .] Their conceptions all tremble on a peradventure—"peradventure they shall do well": there is no royal absolute will that they should do well: the poets are less kings than workmen. And being workmen they are weak—the moulds fall from their hands—are clutched with a spasm or fall with a faintness.

These spasmodic or fainting workmen connect to the decadence of late Greek sculpture (an art-historical commonplace at the time); throughout the essay a very Carlylean polemic is waged against weakness, gracefulness, slightness, elegance, terms which are all associated with femininity. The Earl of Surrey, for example, is damned with Cordelia's praise:

> [. . .] he did not belong to that order of master-minds with whom transitions originate, although qualified, by the quickness of a yielding grace, to assist effectually a transitional movement. [. . .] His poetry makes the ear lean to it, it is so sweet and low [. . .] the poems of his friend, Sir Thomas Wyatt, have [. . .] more of the attributes of masterdom [. . .]

These "attributes of masterdom" are not the same everywhere in the essay. There are images of brute physical strength, as in the description of Skelton:

> The man is very strong; he triumphs, foams, is rabid, in the sense of strength; he mesmerises our souls with the sense of strength—it is as easy to despise a wild beast in a forest, as John Skelton, poet laureate. He is as like a wild beast as a poet laureate can be. In his wonderful dominion over language, he tears it, as with teeth and paws, ravenously, savagely: devastating rather than creating, dominant rather for liberty than for dignity.

But there are also images of internal struggle, in which the "attributes of masterdom" belong to self-knowledge and the self-conscious will. At one point in the essay Barrett Browning pauses to consider the question of why most great poetry is tragic in conception:

> The philosophy is, perhaps, that the poetic temperament, half-way between

the light of the ideal and the darkness of the real, and rendered by each more sensitive to the other, and unable, without a struggle, to pass out clear and calm into either, bears the impress of the necessary conflict in dust and blood. The philosophy may be, that only the stronger spirits do accomplish this victory, having lordship over their own genius [. . .]

It is not only individual poets who display strength of one kind or another; Barrett Browning extends the term to account for the imperial reach given to English literature as a whole by the drama of Shakespeare and his Elizabethan contemporaries:

[. . .] high in the miraculous climax, come the dramatists—from whose sinews was knit the overcoming strength of our literature over all the nations of the world.

The tone of militant patriotism is certainly disturbing; it seems to confirm John Kenyon's accusation that Barrett Browning had "an immoral sympathy with power," a phrase which she herself repeated in several letters with a kind of shamefaced relish. It is a version of the charge made against Shakespeare, indeed against all artists, by Hazlitt in his essay on *Coriolanus*. The question now arises as to whether the essay on "The Book of the Poets" resolves itself into a royalist hymn.

The figure of Milton is crucial here, as he had been for Blake, for Shelley, for Wollstonecraft, and for other Romantic readers. As well as praising his "majestic personality," Barrett Browning also says of him:

He stood in the midst of those whom we are forced to consider the corrupt versificators of his day, an iconoclast of their idol rhyme, and protesting practically against the sequestration of pauses.

Here Milton is like the Abdiel in *Paradise Lost,* the only one of the rebel angels to stand up to Satan: "Among the faithless faithful only he." He *stands* in the midst of the "corrupt versificators" because he is refusing to *bow down,* to worship the "idol rhyme." In Barrett Browning's reading of literary history, something happens in the time of Dryden, something which she represents as follows:

The accession to the throne of the poets, of the *wits* in the new current sense of the term [. . .] was accompanied by the substitution of elegant thoughts for poetic conceptions, [. . .] of adroit illustrations for beautiful images, of ingenuity for genius.

Of Dryden himself she remarks:

He established finally the reign of the literati for the reign of the poets—and the critics clapped their hands. He established finally the despotism of the final emphasis [. . .]

The bright images of royalty and the succession of poet-kings have a dark side, that of usurpation and despotism. Dryden possesses the "royal absolute will" which Beaumont and Fletcher lack, but Dryden is a despot to be resisted and overthrown. So Milton's republicanism is called in aid: Barrett Browning recalls his attack on rhyme in the preface to *Paradise Lost* and links it with his politics; the "sequestration of pauses" to which she refers, that is the shift of the final emphasis from the middle of the iambic line to the last syllable in the heroic couplet, is like some unjust tax or law enacted by a tyrannical regime. Barrett Browning was as capable of revolutionary as of royalist fervour; and she characterizes what she sees as the *ancien regime* of Augustan verse, of Dryden, Pope, and their followers, with radical indignation. It is here, distressingly for feminists, that the only mention of women comes:

[. . .] oh, how sick to faintness grew the poetry of England! Anna Seward "by'r lady," was the muse of those days, and Mr. Hayley "the bard," and Hannah More wrote our dramas, and Helen Williams our odes, and Rosa Matilda our elegiacs,—and Blacklock, blind from birth, our descriptive poems, and Mr. Whalley our "domestic epics," and Darwin our poetical philosophy, and Lady Millar encouraged literature at Bath, with red taffeta and "the vase."

This picture is repeated in the opening of the essay on Wordsworth:

When Mr. Wordsworth gave his first poems to the public, it was not well with poetry in England. The "system" riveted upon the motions of poetry by Dryden and his dynasty had gradually added to the restraint of slavery its weakness and emasculation. [. . .] And oh! to see who sat then in England in the seats of the elders!

Women are associated with weakness and with weak men; again the images of tyranny and usurpation. This passage prefigures Aurora Leigh's self-contempt at the very success of her first works in attracting the mooningly sentimental admiration of young ladies and college students. "I worked with patience," Aurora says of herself—that pre-eminently female virtue—"which means almost power" (iii 204). Almost is not enough, in fact may be worse than nothing; this realization is a turning point for Aurora, who tears up her writing and starts again; always belated, yet always, as her name implies, striving for earliness and originative power, to sit by right "in the seats of the elders."

What of Barrett Browning herself in "The Book of the Poets"? Evidently she sees her own poetry as part of a revolutionary movement which begins with Cowper, in whom "the new era was alive," with Burns and with Percy's Reliques:

> It was the revival of poetry, the opening of the fifth era, the putting down of the Dryden dynasty, the breaking of the serf bondage, the wrenching of the iron from the soul. And Nature and Poetry did embrace one another! and all men who were lovers of either and of our beloved England were enabled to resume the pride of their consciousness, and looking round the world say gently, yet gladly, "Our Poets."

The original series in the *Athenaeum* ended with this rhetorical flourish, which combines Jacobin and abolitionist language in its utopian triumph. In the essay on Wordsworth, which was added later, the same point is made, but in a quite different way. The imagery is not that of political rebellion but of seasonal return and renewal. And these images are marked as female; in fact, the female returns in "The Book of the Poets" as mother Nature, who nurtures Wordsworth's child-like genius:

> Nature, the long-banished, re-dawned like the morning: Nature, the true mother, cried afar off to her children, "Children, I am here! come to me!" . . . As the chief of the movement, the Xenophon of the return, we are bound to acknowledge this great Wordsworth, and to admire how, in a bravery bravest of all because born of love, in a passionate unreservedness sprung of genius, and to the actual scandal of the world which stared at the filial familiarity, he threw himself not at the feet of Nature, but straightway and right tenderly upon her bosom.

Wordsworth does not pay homage to Nature, whether feudal or erotic, but suckles her (indecorously, in public). So the true dynasty is restored, this time with Nature as its guarantor of legitimacy: indeed, Barrett Browning is keen to stress that Wordsworth's "natural" style and interest in common life do not disqualify him from the throne. He may, she concedes, be at times "over-rustic," but this is "not through incapacity to be right royal":

> [. . .] of all poets, indeed, who have been kings in England, not one has swept the purple with more majesty than this poet, when it hath pleased him to be majestic. *Vivat rex,*—and here is a new volume of his reign.

But the plot of "The Book of the Poets," which seems directed towards the advent of Wordsworth as the true heir, has one further development. For Wordsworth's "reign" has not been entirely a matter for rejoicing. The "new volume" contains the sonnets on capital punishment, which Barrett Browning finds repugnant, and his early drama *The Borderers,* which she struggles to admire. More important than this local symptom of decline, however, is the condition of modern poetry generally, which Wordsworth was supposed to have rescued and rejuvenated. But Barrett Browning's concluding paragraphs are anxious and embattled. Wordsworth's popularity, at which she rejoices, has done little for the status of poetry itself.

"Art," it was said long ago, "requires the whole man," and "Nobody," it was said later, "can be a poet who is anything else"; but the present idea of Art requires the segment of a man, and everybody who is anything is a poet in a parenthesis. And our shelves groan with little books over which their readers groan less metaphorically; there is a plague of poems in the land apart from poetry; and many poets who live and are true do not live by their truth, but hold back their full strength from Art because they do not *reverence* it fully; and all booksellers cry aloud and do not spare, that poetry will not sell; and certain critics utter melancholy frenzies, that poetry is worn out for ever—as if the morning-star was worn out from heaven, or the "yellow primrose" from the grass. [. . .] In the meantime the hopeful and believing will hope,—trust on; and, better still, the Tennysons and the Brownings, and other high-gifted spirits, will work, wait on, until, as Mr. Horne has said—

> Strong deeds awake
> And, clamouring, throng the portals of the hour.

It is well for them and all to count the cost of this life of a master in poetry, and learn from it what a true poet's crown is worth [. . .]

The essay began with the image of Chaucer as a morning-star, and with Barrett Browning's praise of his nature poetry; Chaucer and Wordsworth join hands across time, each representing a new beginning; but whereas Chaucer stands at the head of a line of kings, Wordsworth's dynasty is personal and singular, and his example is as painful to contemplate as it is inspiring. Wordsworth's power has only ambiguously and uncertainly empowered *her;* it seems that despite "this life of a master in poetry" it is all to do again, at least as far as the public face of poetry is concerned. Contemporary poetry is feeble because it lacks the concentration and intensity which Barrett Browning found in, for example, the prose of Balzac and George Sand. What is needed to renew these diffused and exhausted energies is a revolutionary awakening: the "strong deeds" that "clamour" and "throng the portals" are like a mob, a crowd bursting into a palace. The image of returning spring may not, after all, be adequate to the need of poetry for a transforming power.

But the example of Wordsworth's life has another aspect, not that of public authority but private vocation. And it is to this inward and self-enclosed power that Barrett Browning finally turns. Up to this point she has used the "editorial we," the voice of an impersonal and institutional authority; the editorial we is also, I suggest, the royal we, and Barrett Browning's own claim to the poetic throne has been a tacit assumption (or presumption) that governs and directs the essay from the start. But right at the end she renounces the claim: she borrows another's voice in order to express an extreme abnegation of public power in favour of a private and self-authorising creativity. In the lines from Samuel Daniel's *Musophilus,* especially the last four, which she emphasises with capital letters and italics, she states an argument for poetry not as lordship but as vocation, not as royalty but as inner light, requiring no other justification than itself:

> And for my part, if only one allow
>   The care my labouring spirits take in this,
> He is to me a theatre large enow,
>   And his applause only sufficient is
> All my respect is bent but to his brow:
>   That is my all, and all I am is his:
> And if some worthy spirits be pleased too,
>   It shall more comfort breed, but not more will.
> BUT WHAT IF NONE? *It cannot yet undo*
>   *The love I bear unto this holy skill:*
> *This is the thing that I was born to do,*
>   *This is my scene, this part I must fulfil*

Barrett Browning prefaces this passage by calling it "the very code of chivalry for poets." Chivalry means service, not rule; it is a question of obligation: "this part I *must* fulfil." Daniel's imagery is not chivalric but theatrical: the poet is like an actor compelled to perform, even to an empty house. Yet the part he plays is truly himself, "the thing that I was born to do." It doesn't matter that the poet is not a king; it doesn't matter that the play is a flop with the public. In an eerie anticipation of Browning's Childe Roland, Barrett Browning's selfdramatising chivalric poet simply declares herself to be present. And that, perhaps, is the most powerful gesture of all.

Index

◆

The Volume Editor

◆

Sandra Donaldson is professor of English at the University of North Dakota, where she also directs the Women Studies Program. Her book *Elizabeth Barrett Browning: An Annotated Bibliography of the Commentary and Criticism, 1826–1990* was published by G. K. Hall in 1993. Donaldson is associate editor of *Victorian Literature and Culture* and writes the annual annotated bibliography of works on the Brownings for *VLC*. She has published essays on Virginia Woolf, Elizabeth Siddall Rossetti, and Margaret Atwood, as well as on Barrett Browning. Work as a Mellon Fellow at the University of Texas at Austin, as a library fellow at the Armstrong Browning Library at Baylor University, and at the Widener Library of Harvard University under a fellowship from the Bibliographical Society of America has contributed to her long-term goal of producing a new edition of Barrett Browning's collected works.

The General Editor

♦

Zack Bowen is professor of English at the University of Miami. He holds degrees from the University of Pennsylvania (B.A.), Temple University (M.A.), and the State University of New York at Buffalo (Ph.D.). In addition to being general editor of this G. K. Hall series, he is editor of the James Joyce series for the University of Florida Press and the *James Joyce Literary Supplement*. He is author and editor of numerous books on modern British, Irish, and American literature. He has also published more than one hundred monographs, essays, scholarly reviews, and recordings related to literature. He is past president of the James Joyce Society (1977–1986), former chair of the Modern Language Association Lowell Prize Committee, and current president of the International James Joyce Foundation.